JIM BUTCHER'S

the DRESDEN® FILES

GHOUL GOBLIN

GHOUL GOBLIN

It has been several months since Chicago's only wizard for hire, Harry Blackstone Copperfield Dresden, barely survived a case involving several packs of werewolves. And while he ultimately was able to prevent the Windy City from being completely engulfed in a bloodbath, it was no triumphant victory. The case began with the murder of his protege, saw Detective Ron Carmichael torn apart before his eyes, and ended with Harry estranged from Lt. Karrin Murphy, his best friend.

But Harry has no time to lick his wounds. There are still things going bump in the night, and millions of innocents who are unknowingly threatened by denizens of the Nevernever. It's his job to protect them, no matter how alone he sometimes feels.

And now, he's about to be drawn away from his home turf....

written by **JIM BUTCHER** & **MARK POWERS**

pencils by **JOSEPH COOPER**

colors by **MOHAN**

letters by **BILL TORTOLINI**

cover by **ARDIAN SYAF**

consulting editor: RICH YOUNG

thematic consultants: PRISCILLA SPENCER, MICHAEL ASHLEIGH FINN & FRED HICKS

Nick Barrucci, CEO / Publisher
Juan Collado, President / COO
Rich Young, Director Business Development
Keith Davidsen, Marketing Manager

Joe Rybandt, Senior Editor
Sarah Litt, Digital Editor
Josh Green, Traffic Coordinator
Molly Mahan, Assistant Editor

Josh Johnson, Art Director
Jason Ullmeyer, Senior Graphic Designer
Katie Hidalgo, Graphic Designer

ISBN-10: 1-60690-438-8
ISBN-13: 978-1-60690-438-1
First Printing
10 9 8 7 6 5 4 3 2 1

Visit us online at **www.DYNAMITE.com**
Follow us on Twitter **@dynamitecomics**
Like us on Facebook **/Dynamitecomics**
 Watch us on YouTube **/Dynamitecomics**

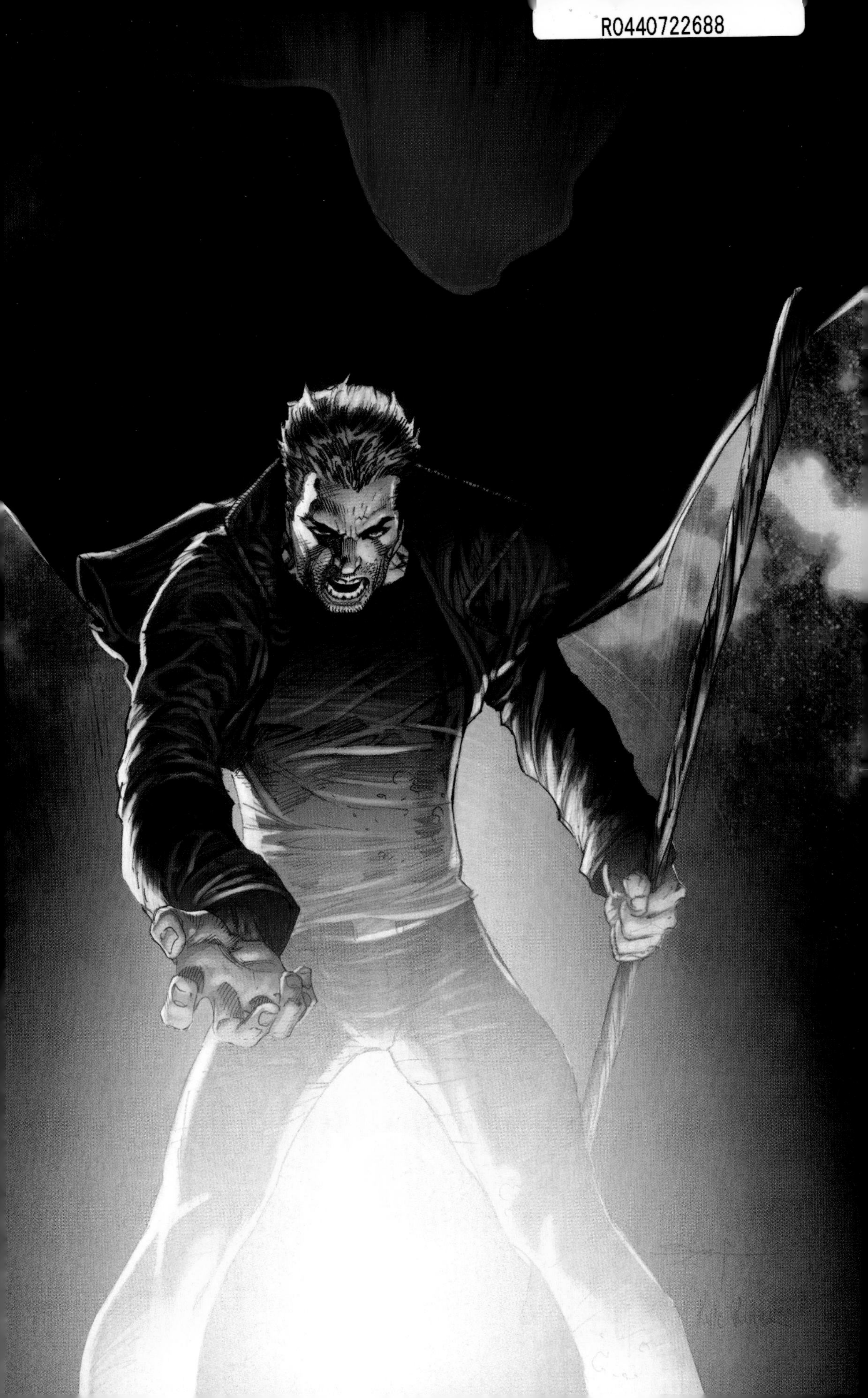

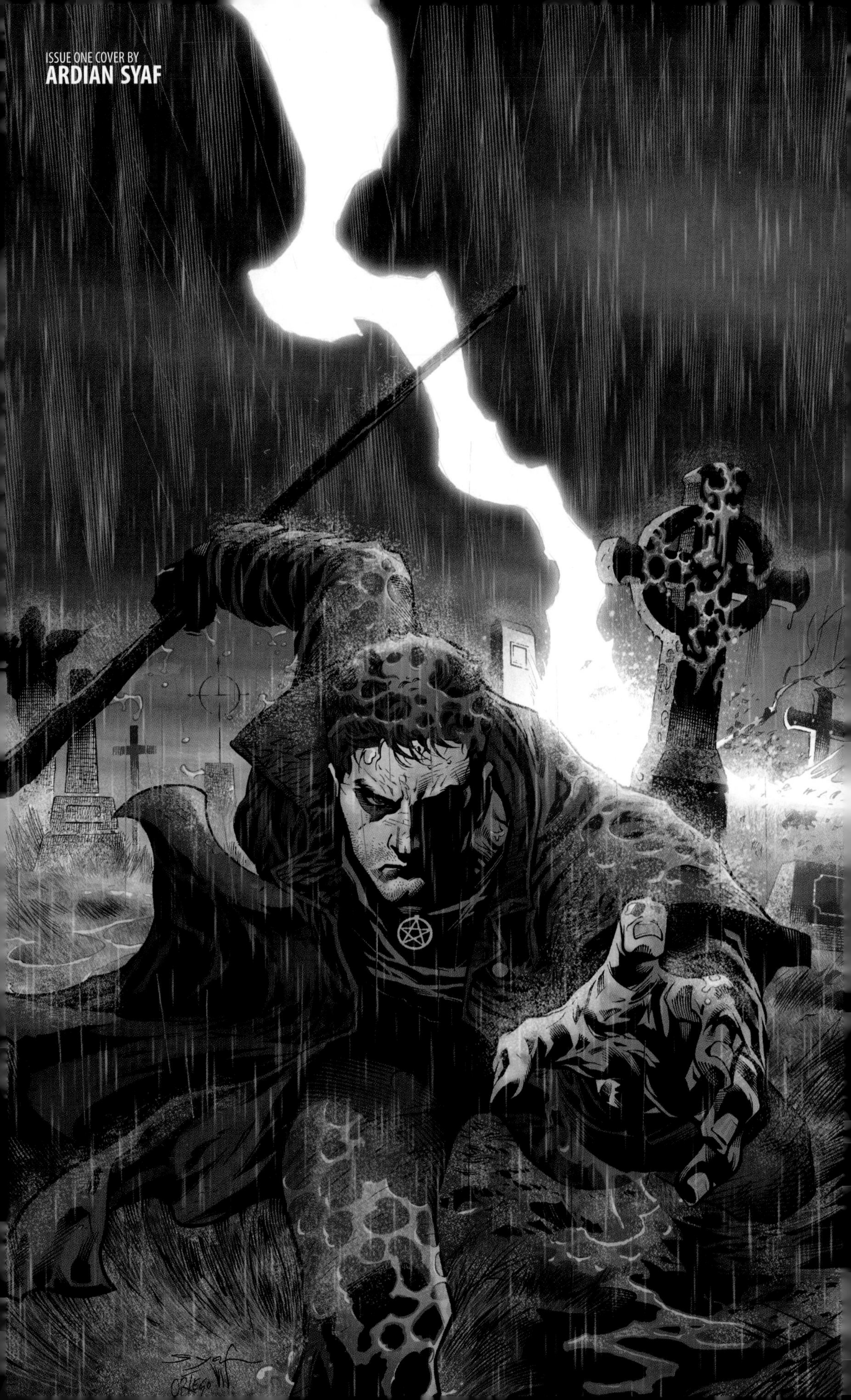

ISSUE ONE COVER BY
ARDIAN SYAF

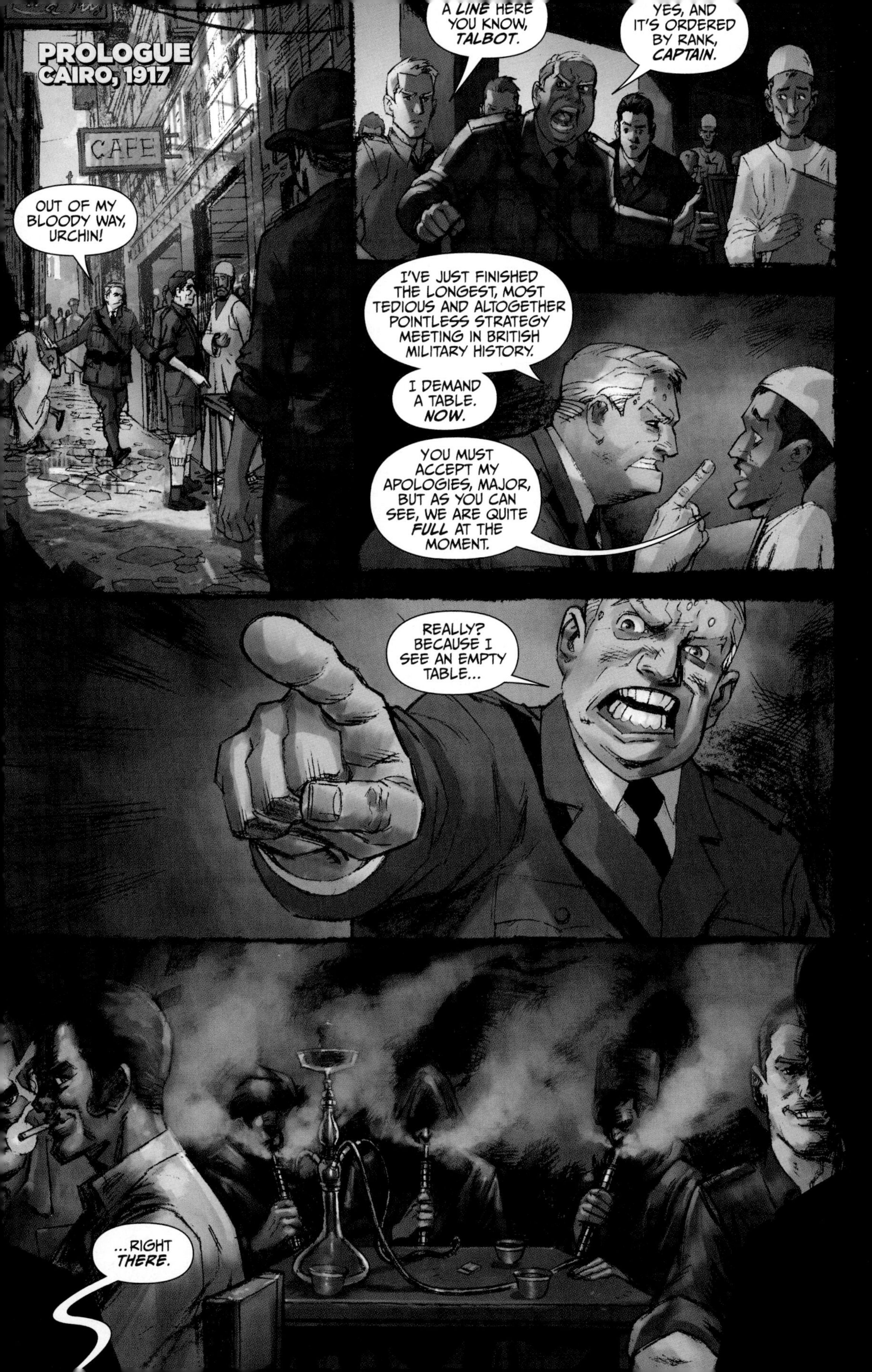
PROLOGUE
CAIRO, 1917
CAFE
OUT OF MY BLOODY WAY, URCHIN!
A LINE HERE YOU KNOW, TALBOT.
YES, AND IT'S ORDERED BY RANK, CAPTAIN.
I'VE JUST FINISHED THE LONGEST, MOST TEDIOUS AND ALTOGETHER POINTLESS STRATEGY MEETING IN BRITISH MILITARY HISTORY.
I DEMAND A TABLE. NOW.
YOU MUST ACCEPT MY APOLOGIES, MAJOR, BUT AS YOU CAN SEE, WE ARE QUITE FULL AT THE MOMENT.
REALLY? BECAUSE I SEE AN EMPTY TABLE...
...RIGHT THERE.

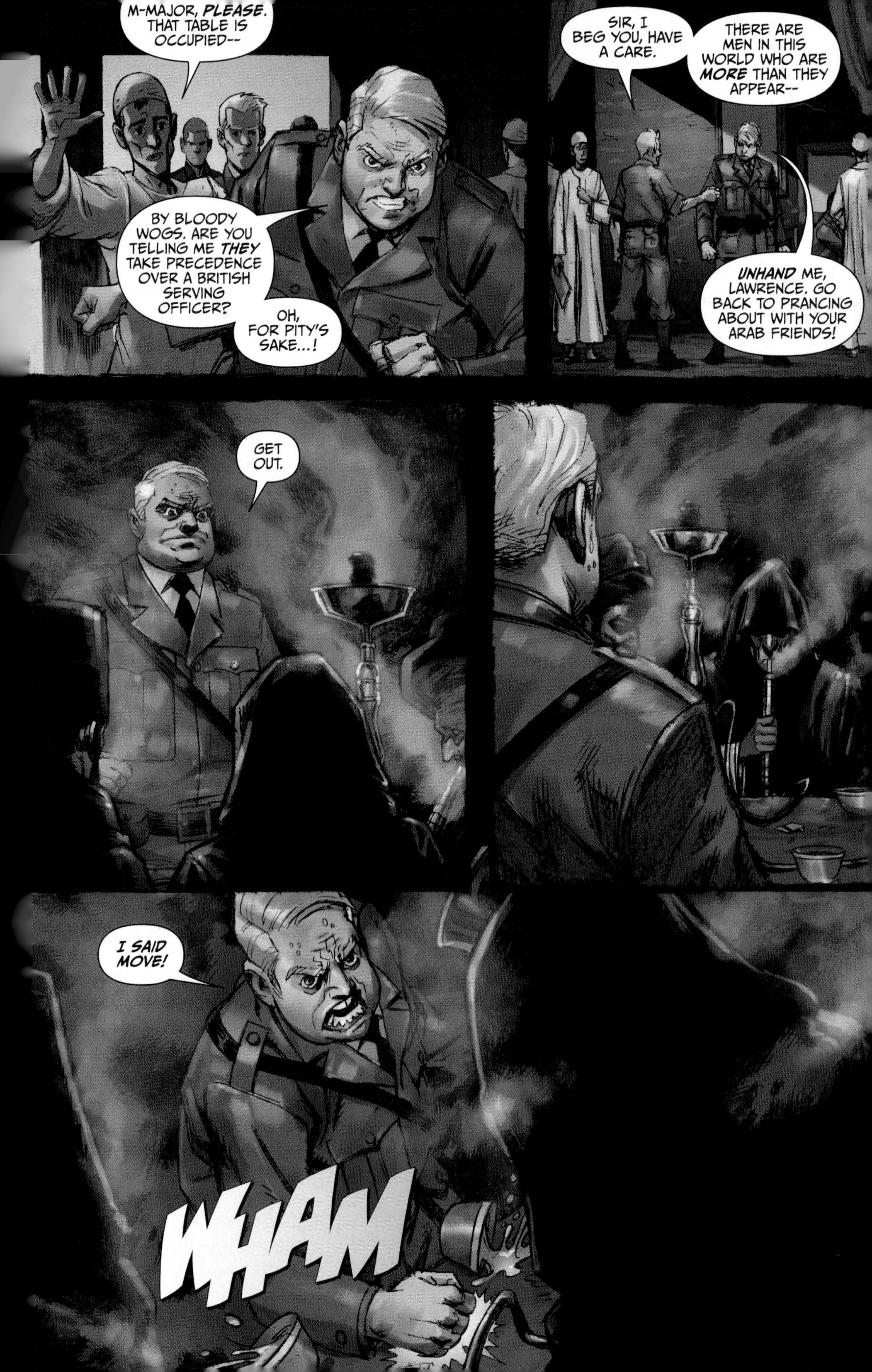

M-MAJOR, PLEASE. THAT TABLE IS OCCUPIED--
BY BLOODY WOGS. ARE YOU TELLING ME THEY TAKE PRECEDENCE OVER A BRITISH SERVING OFFICER?
OH, FOR PITY'S SAKE...!
SIR, I BEG YOU, HAVE A CARE.
THERE ARE MEN IN THIS WORLD WHO ARE MORE THAN THEY APPEAR--
UNHAND ME, LAWRENCE. GO BACK TO PRANCING ABOUT WITH YOUR ARAB FRIENDS!
GET OUT.
I SAID MOVE!
WHAM

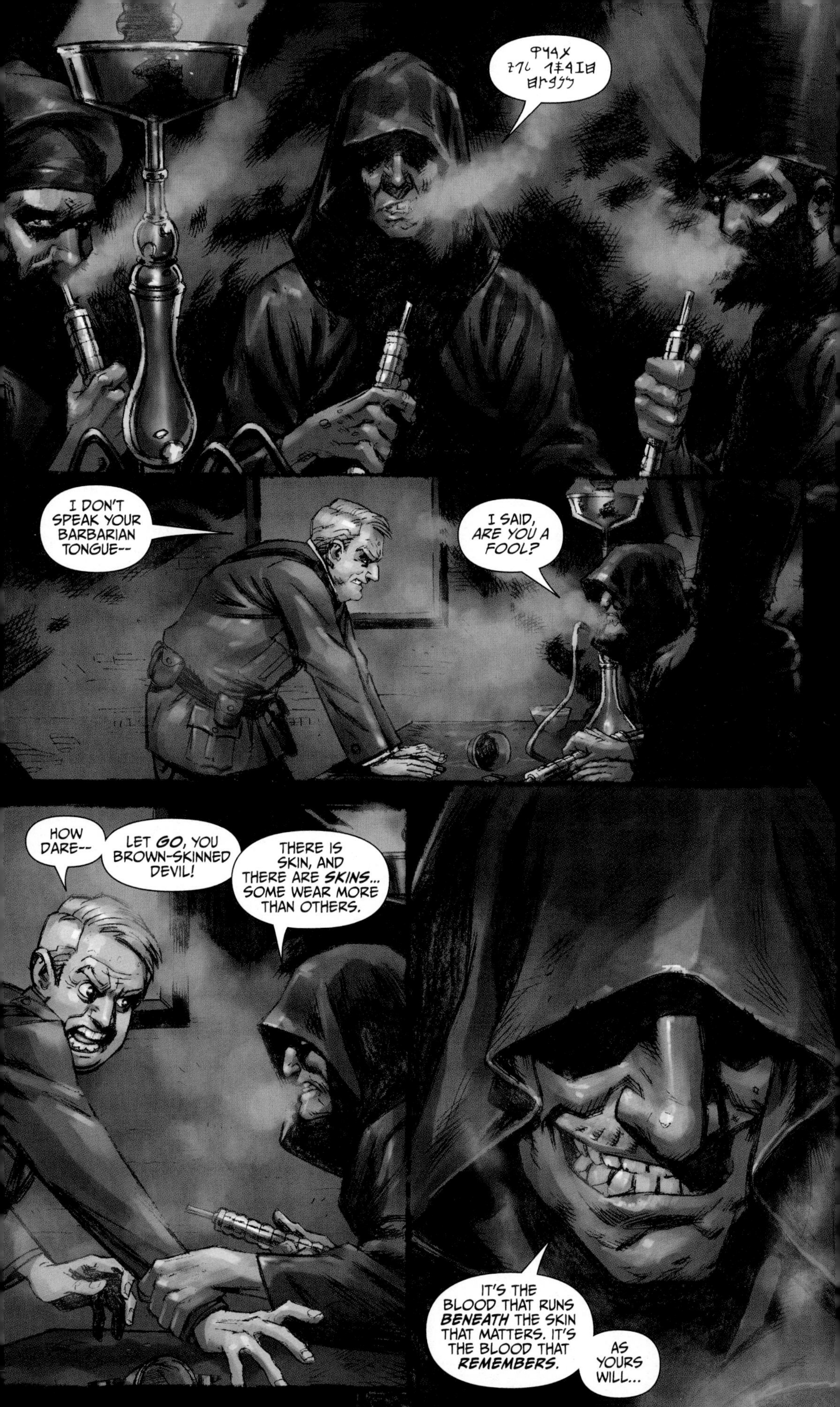
I DON'T SPEAK YOUR BARBARIAN TONGUE--
I SAID, *ARE YOU A FOOL?*
HOW DARE--
LET **GO**, YOU BROWN-SKINNED DEVIL!
THERE IS SKIN, AND THERE ARE **SKINS**... SOME WEAR MORE THAN OTHERS.
IT'S THE BLOOD THAT RUNS **BENEATH** THE SKIN THAT MATTERS. IT'S THE BLOOD THAT **REMEMBERS**.
AS YOURS WILL...

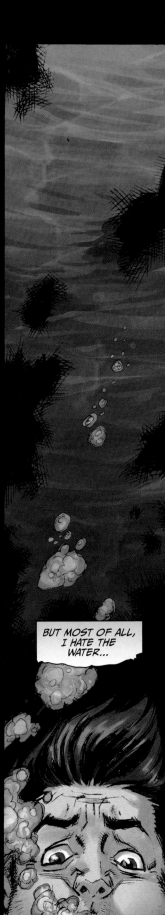

CHICAGO
TODAY

WAS NEVER A
BEACH PERSON.

I HATE SAND, AND
THE SUN HATES
MY LILY-WHITE
COMPLEXION.

BUT MOST OF ALL,
I HATE THE
WATER...

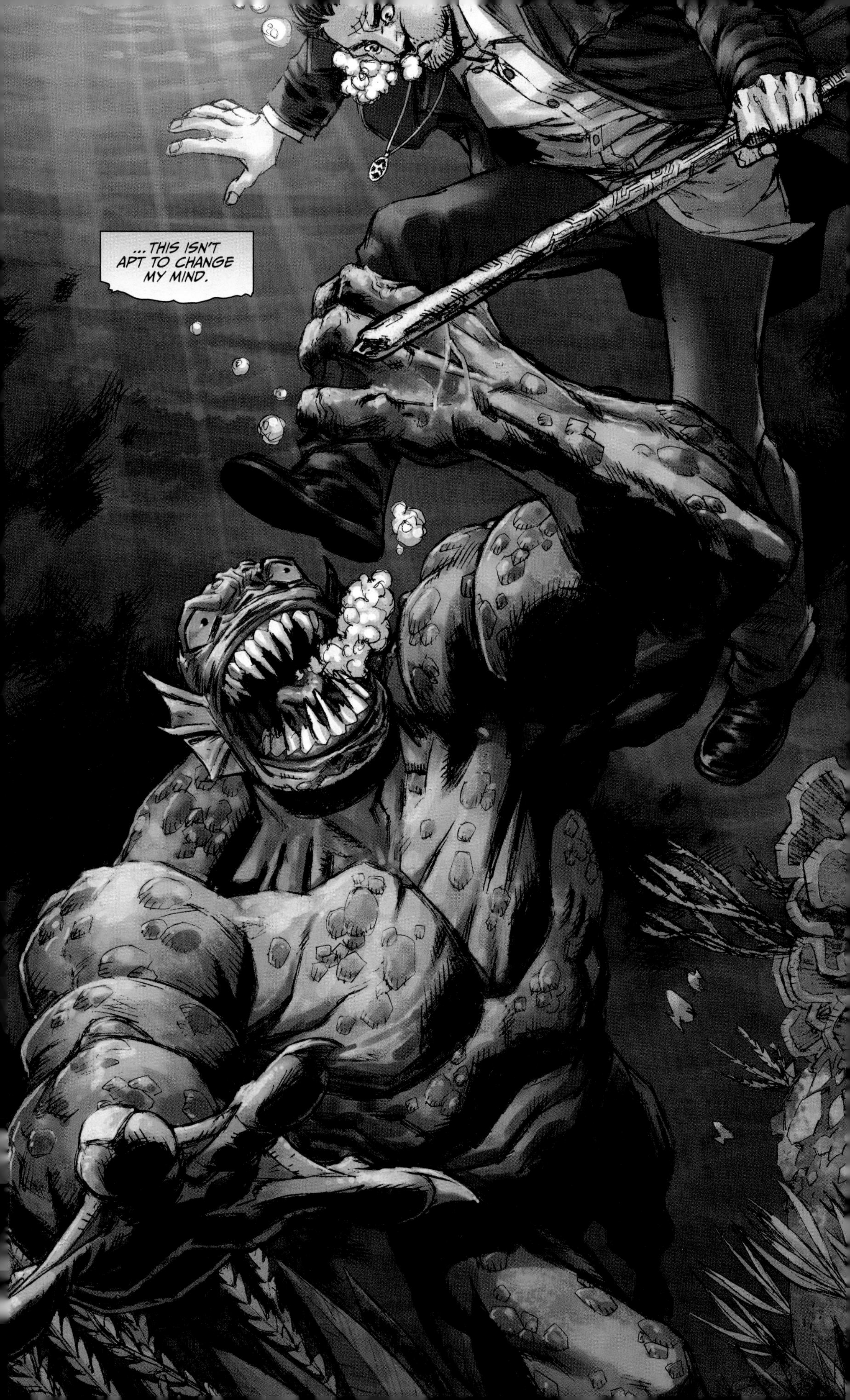
...THIS ISN'T APT TO CHANGE MY MIND.

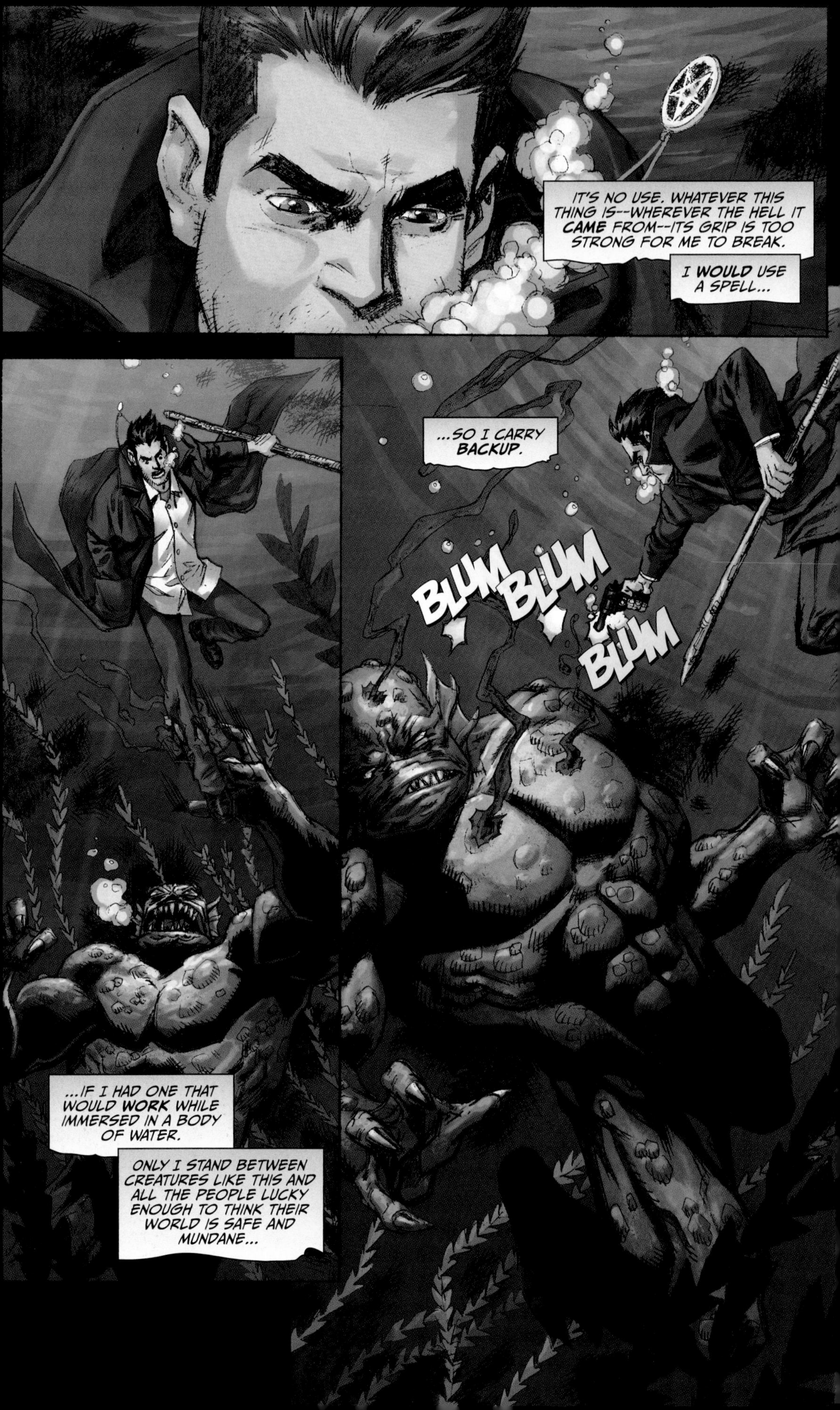
IT'S NO USE. WHATEVER THIS THING IS--WHEREVER THE HELL IT CAME FROM--ITS GRIP IS TOO STRONG FOR ME TO BREAK.
I WOULD USE A SPELL...
...IF I HAD ONE THAT WOULD WORK WHILE IMMERSED IN A BODY OF WATER.
ONLY I STAND BETWEEN CREATURES LIKE THIS AND ALL THE PEOPLE LUCKY ENOUGH TO THINK THEIR WORLD IS SAFE AND MUNDANE...
...SO I CARRY BACKUP.
BLUM BLUM BLUM

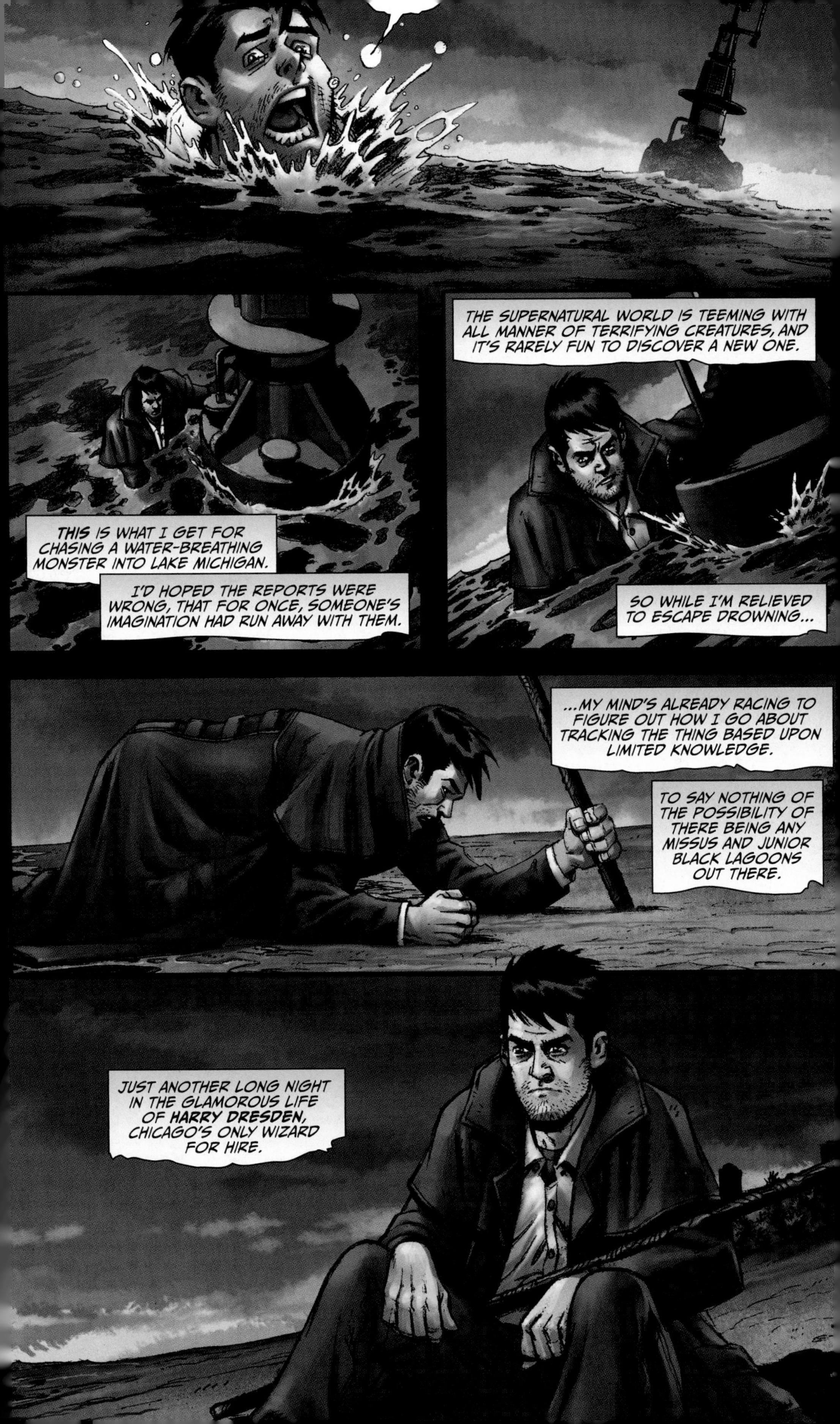
THIS IS WHAT I GET FOR CHASING A WATER-BREATHING MONSTER INTO LAKE MICHIGAN.
I'D HOPED THE REPORTS WERE WRONG, THAT FOR ONCE, SOMEONE'S IMAGINATION HAD RUN AWAY WITH THEM.
THE SUPERNATURAL WORLD IS TEEMING WITH ALL MANNER OF TERRIFYING CREATURES, AND IT'S RARELY FUN TO DISCOVER A NEW ONE.
SO WHILE I'M RELIEVED TO ESCAPE DROWNING...
...MY MIND'S ALREADY RACING TO FIGURE OUT HOW I GO ABOUT TRACKING THE THING BASED UPON LIMITED KNOWLEDGE.
TO SAY NOTHING OF THE POSSIBILITY OF THERE BEING ANY MISSUS AND JUNIOR BLACK LAGOONS OUT THERE.
JUST ANOTHER LONG NIGHT IN THE GLAMOROUS LIFE OF HARRY DRESDEN, CHICAGO'S ONLY WIZARD FOR HIRE.

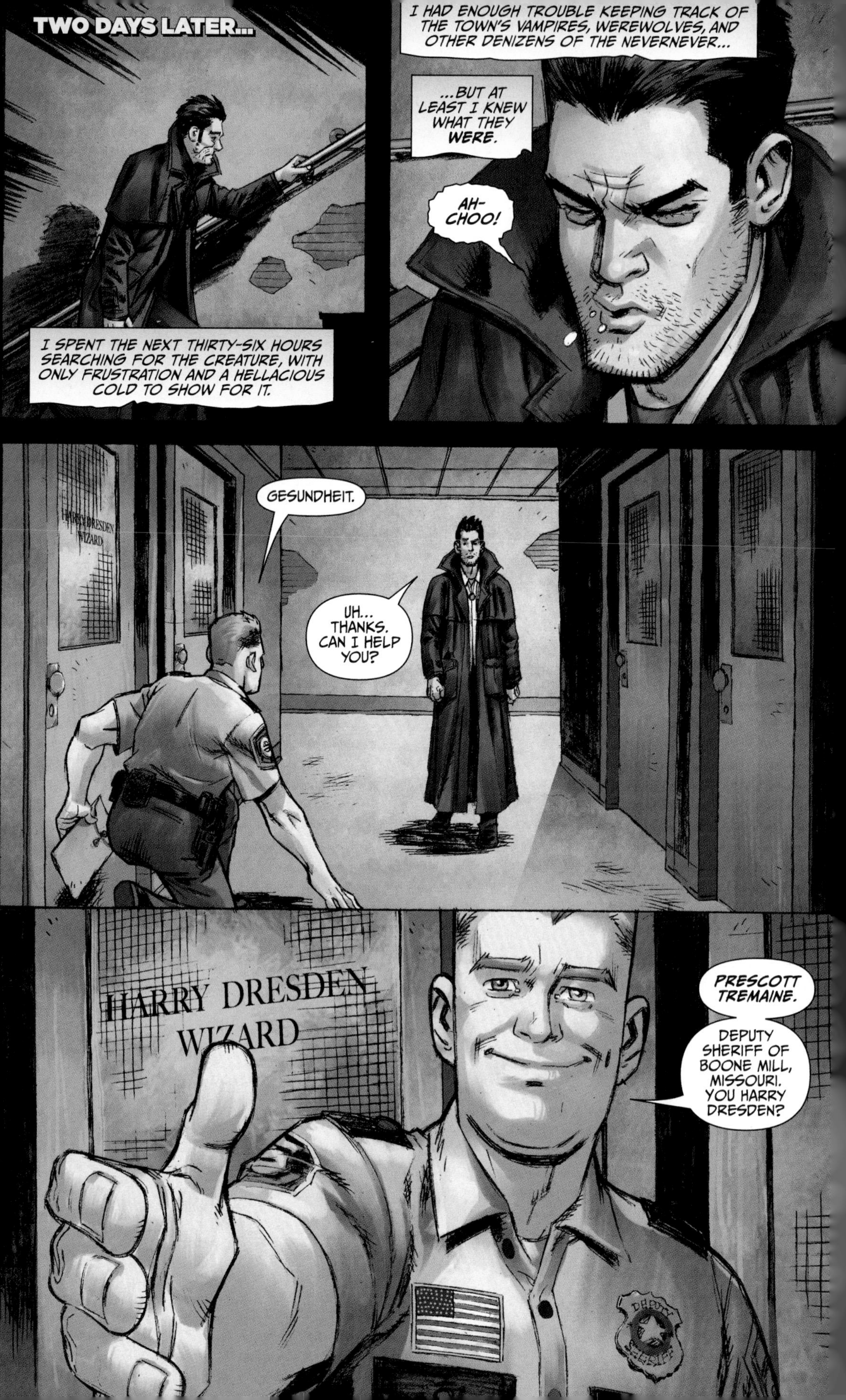
TWO DAYS LATER...
I SPENT THE NEXT THIRTY-SIX HOURS SEARCHING FOR THE CREATURE, WITH ONLY FRUSTRATION AND A HELLACIOUS COLD TO SHOW FOR IT.
I HAD ENOUGH TROUBLE KEEPING TRACK OF THE TOWN'S VAMPIRES, WEREWOLVES, AND OTHER DENIZENS OF THE NEVERNEVER...
...BUT AT LEAST I KNEW WHAT THEY WERE.
AH-CHOO!
HARRY DRESDEN WIZARD
GESUNDHEIT.
UH... THANKS. CAN I HELP YOU?
HARRY DRESDEN WIZARD
PRESCOTT TREMAINE.
DEPUTY SHERIFF OF BOONE MILL, MISSOURI. YOU HARRY DRESDEN?

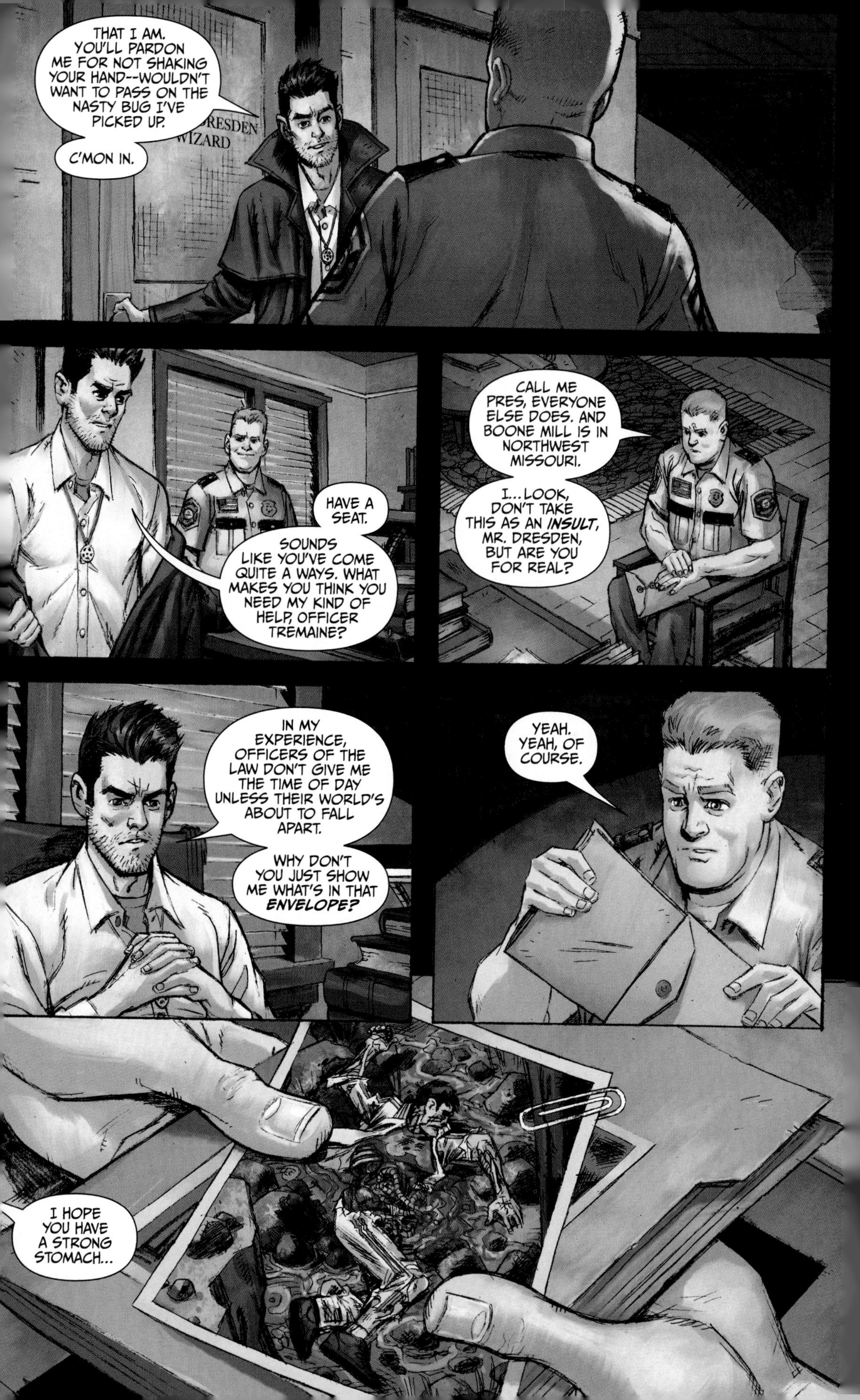
THAT I AM. YOU'LL PARDON ME FOR NOT SHAKING YOUR HAND--WOULDN'T WANT TO PASS ON THE NASTY BUG I'VE PICKED UP.
C'MON IN.
HAVE A SEAT.
SOUNDS LIKE YOU'VE COME QUITE A WAYS. WHAT MAKES YOU THINK YOU NEED MY KIND OF HELP, OFFICER TREMAINE?
CALL ME PRES, EVERYONE ELSE DOES. AND BOONE MILL IS IN NORTHWEST MISSOURI.
I...LOOK, DON'T TAKE THIS AS AN INSULT, MR. DRESDEN, BUT ARE YOU FOR REAL?
IN MY EXPERIENCE, OFFICERS OF THE LAW DON'T GIVE ME THE TIME OF DAY UNLESS THEIR WORLD'S ABOUT TO FALL APART.
WHY DON'T YOU JUST SHOW ME WHAT'S IN THAT ENVELOPE?
YEAH. YEAH, OF COURSE.
I HOPE YOU HAVE A STRONG STOMACH...

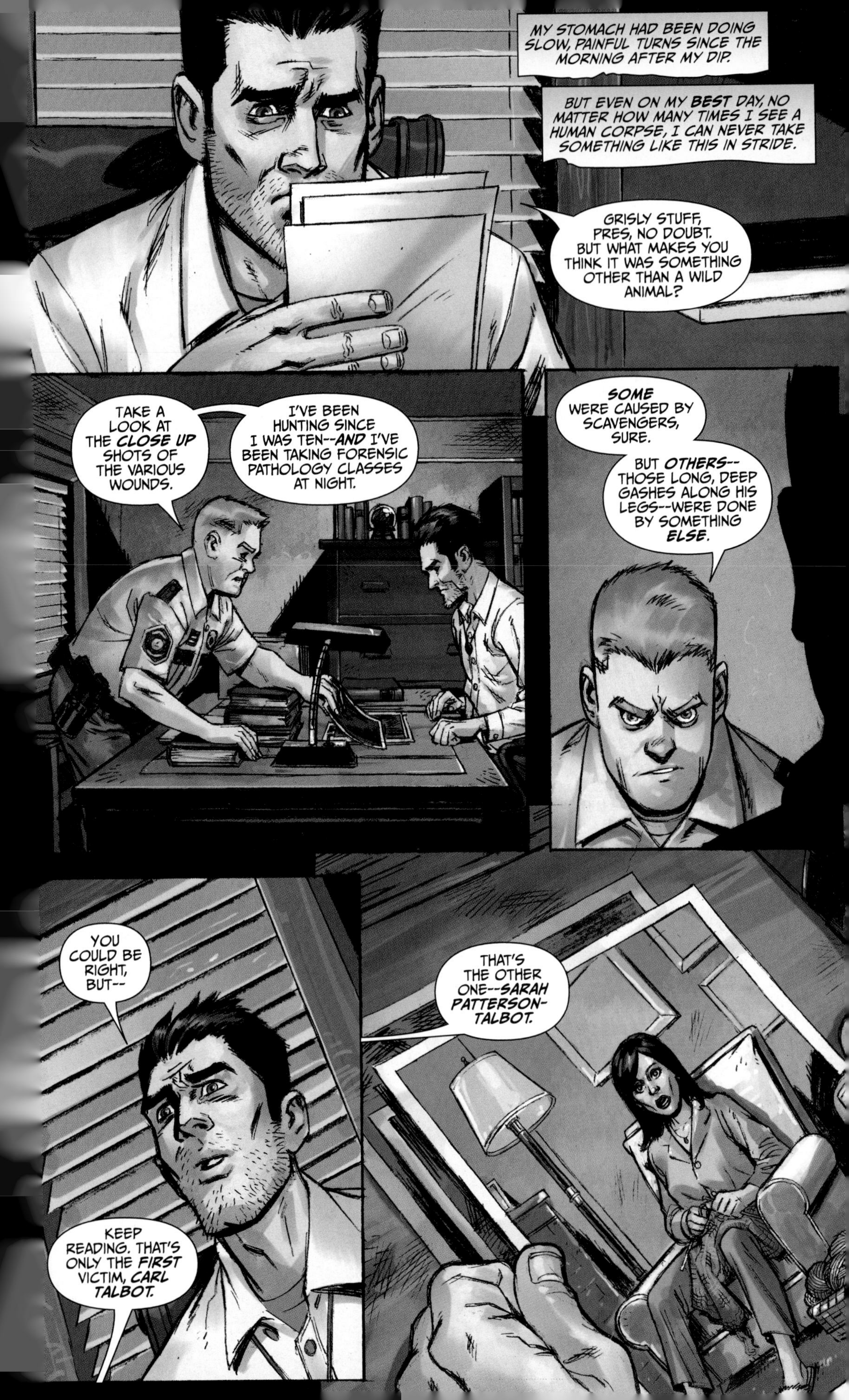
MY STOMACH HAD BEEN DOING SLOW, PAINFUL TURNS SINCE THE MORNING AFTER MY DIP.
BUT EVEN ON MY **BEST** DAY, NO MATTER HOW MANY TIMES I SEE A HUMAN CORPSE, I CAN NEVER TAKE SOMETHING LIKE THIS IN STRIDE.
GRISLY STUFF, PRES, NO DOUBT. BUT WHAT MAKES YOU THINK IT WAS SOMETHING OTHER THAN A WILD ANIMAL?
TAKE A LOOK AT THE **CLOSE UP** SHOTS OF THE VARIOUS WOUNDS.
I'VE BEEN HUNTING SINCE I WAS TEN--**AND** I'VE BEEN TAKING FORENSIC PATHOLOGY CLASSES AT NIGHT.
SOME WERE CAUSED BY SCAVENGERS, SURE.
BUT **OTHERS**--THOSE LONG, DEEP GASHES ALONG HIS LEGS--WERE DONE BY SOMETHING **ELSE**.
YOU COULD BE RIGHT, BUT--
KEEP READING. THAT'S ONLY THE **FIRST** VICTIM, **CARL TALBOT.**
THAT'S THE OTHER ONE--**SARAH PATTERSON-TALBOT.**

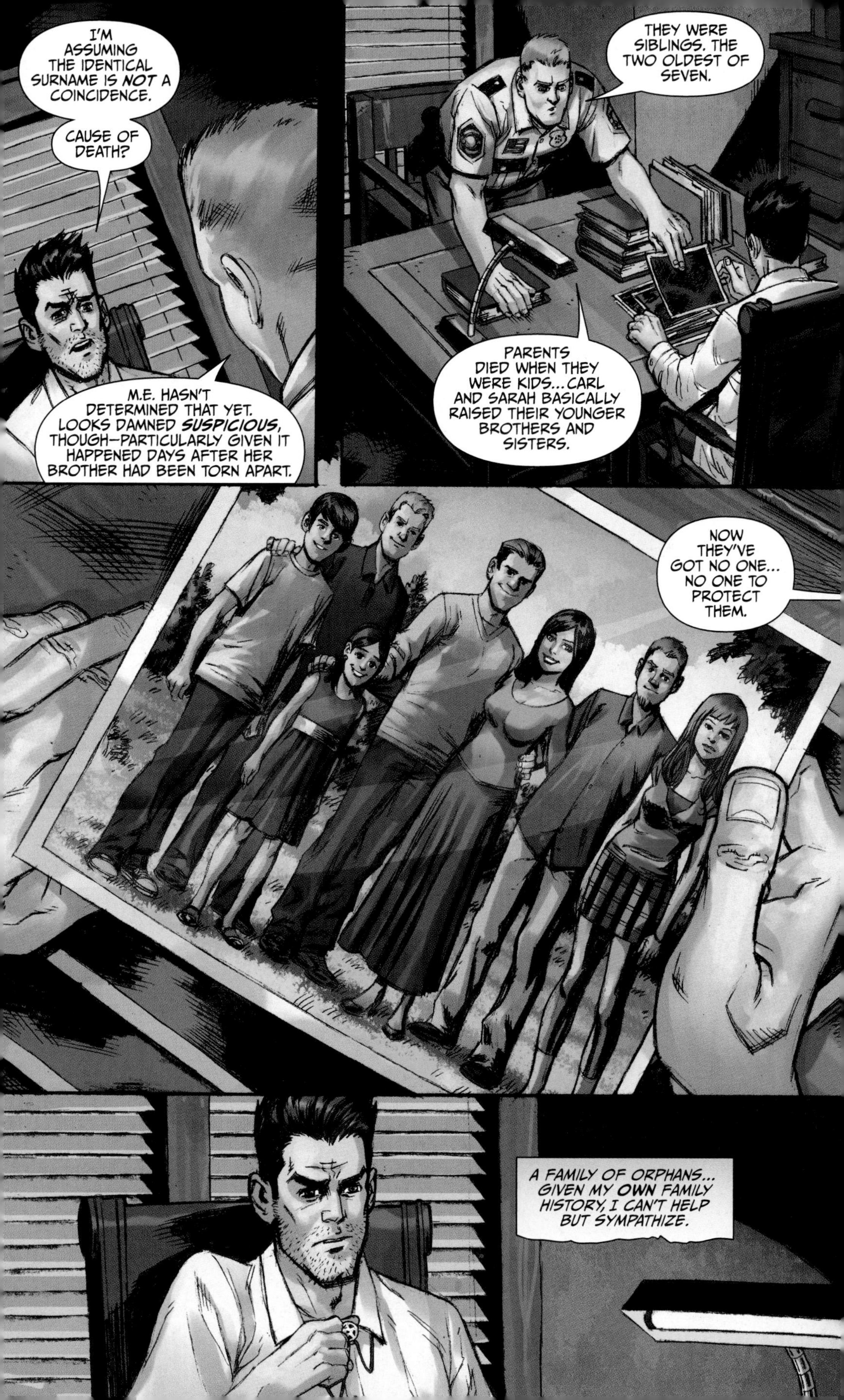
I'M ASSUMING THE IDENTICAL SURNAME IS *NOT* A COINCIDENCE.
CAUSE OF DEATH?
M.E. HASN'T DETERMINED THAT YET. LOOKS DAMNED *SUSPICIOUS*, THOUGH—PARTICULARLY GIVEN IT HAPPENED DAYS AFTER HER BROTHER HAD BEEN TORN APART.
THEY WERE SIBLINGS. THE TWO OLDEST OF SEVEN.
PARENTS DIED WHEN THEY WERE KIDS...CARL AND SARAH BASICALLY RAISED THEIR YOUNGER BROTHERS AND SISTERS.
NOW THEY'VE GOT NO ONE... NO ONE TO PROTECT THEM.
A FAMILY OF ORPHANS... GIVEN MY **OWN** FAMILY HISTORY, I CAN'T HELP BUT SYMPATHIZE.

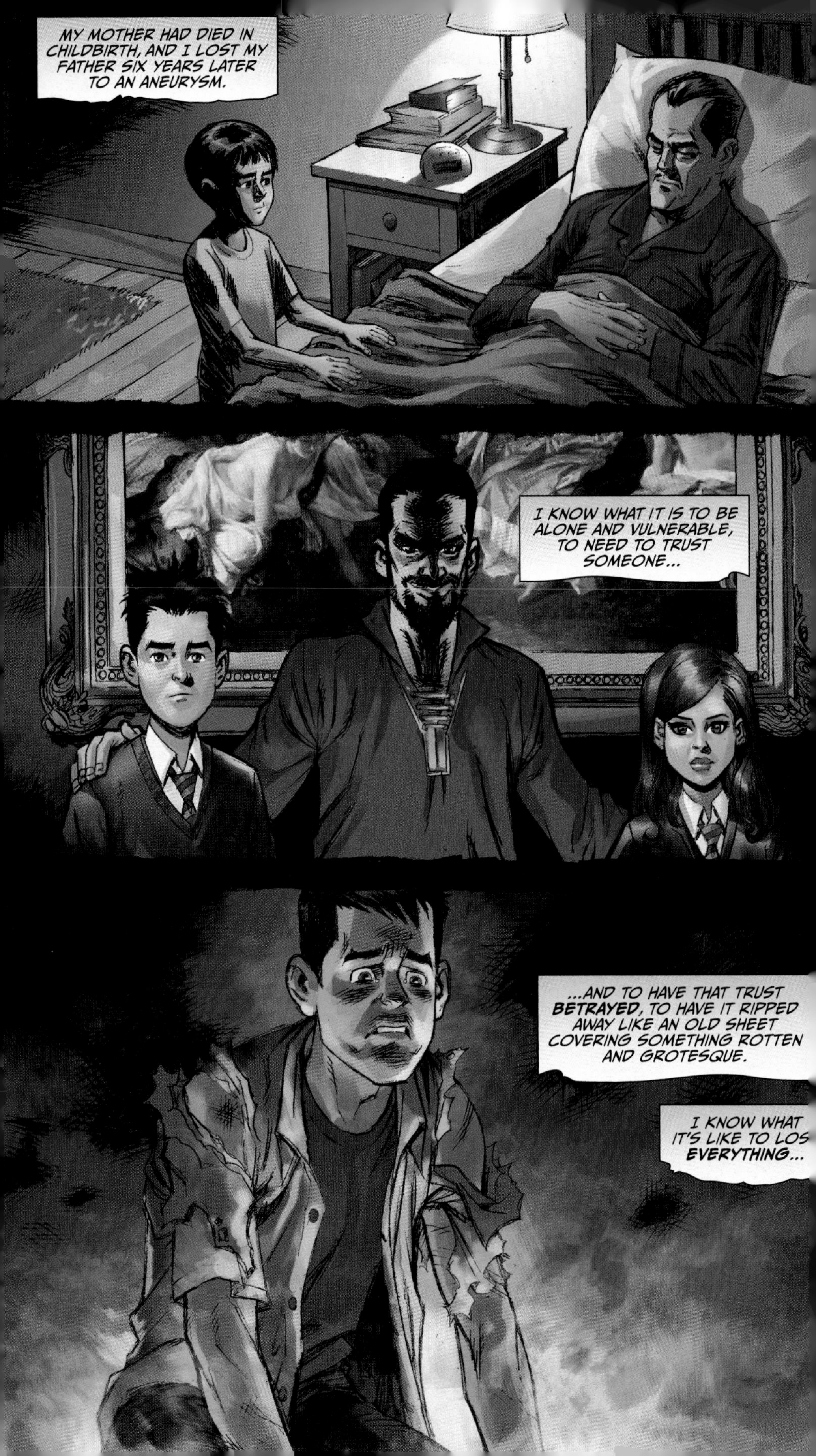
MY MOTHER HAD DIED IN CHILDBIRTH, AND I LOST MY FATHER SIX YEARS LATER TO AN ANEURYSM.
I KNOW WHAT IT IS TO BE ALONE AND VULNERABLE, TO NEED TO TRUST SOMEONE...
...AND TO HAVE THAT TRUST **BETRAYED**, TO HAVE IT RIPPED AWAY LIKE AN OLD SHEET COVERING SOMETHING ROTTEN AND GROTESQUE.
I KNOW WHAT IT'S LIKE TO LOS **EVERYTHING**...

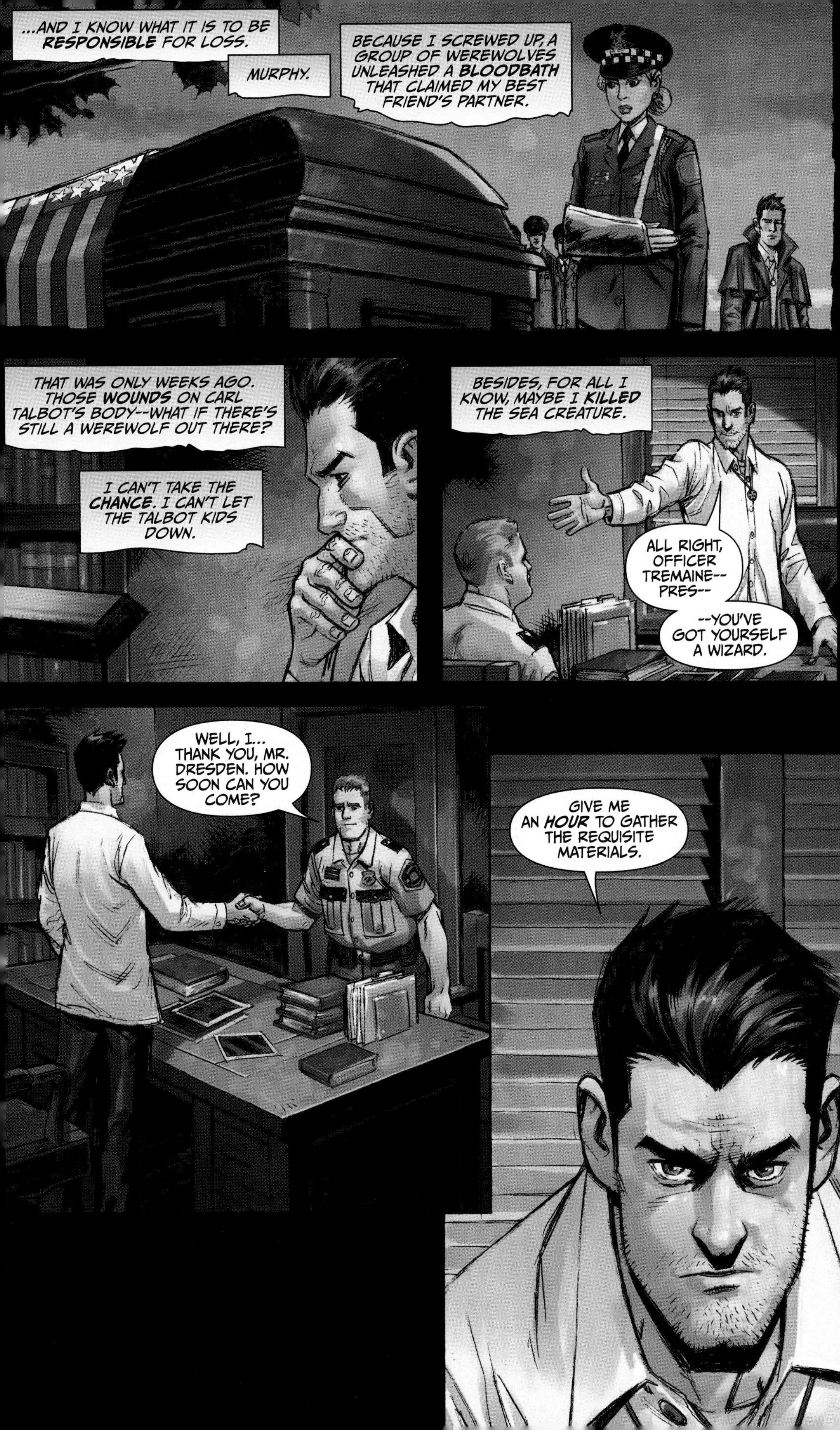

...AND I KNOW WHAT IT IS TO BE RESPONSIBLE FOR LOSS.
MURPHY.
BECAUSE I SCREWED UP, A GROUP OF WEREWOLVES UNLEASHED A BLOODBATH THAT CLAIMED MY BEST FRIEND'S PARTNER.
THAT WAS ONLY WEEKS AGO. THOSE WOUNDS ON CARL TALBOT'S BODY--WHAT IF THERE'S STILL A WEREWOLF OUT THERE?
I CAN'T TAKE THE CHANCE. I CAN'T LET THE TALBOT KIDS DOWN.
BESIDES, FOR ALL I KNOW, MAYBE I KILLED THE SEA CREATURE.
ALL RIGHT, OFFICER TREMAINE--PRES--
--YOU'VE GOT YOURSELF A WIZARD.
WELL, I... THANK YOU, MR. DRESDEN. HOW SOON CAN YOU COME?
GIVE ME AN HOUR TO GATHER THE REQUISITE MATERIALS.

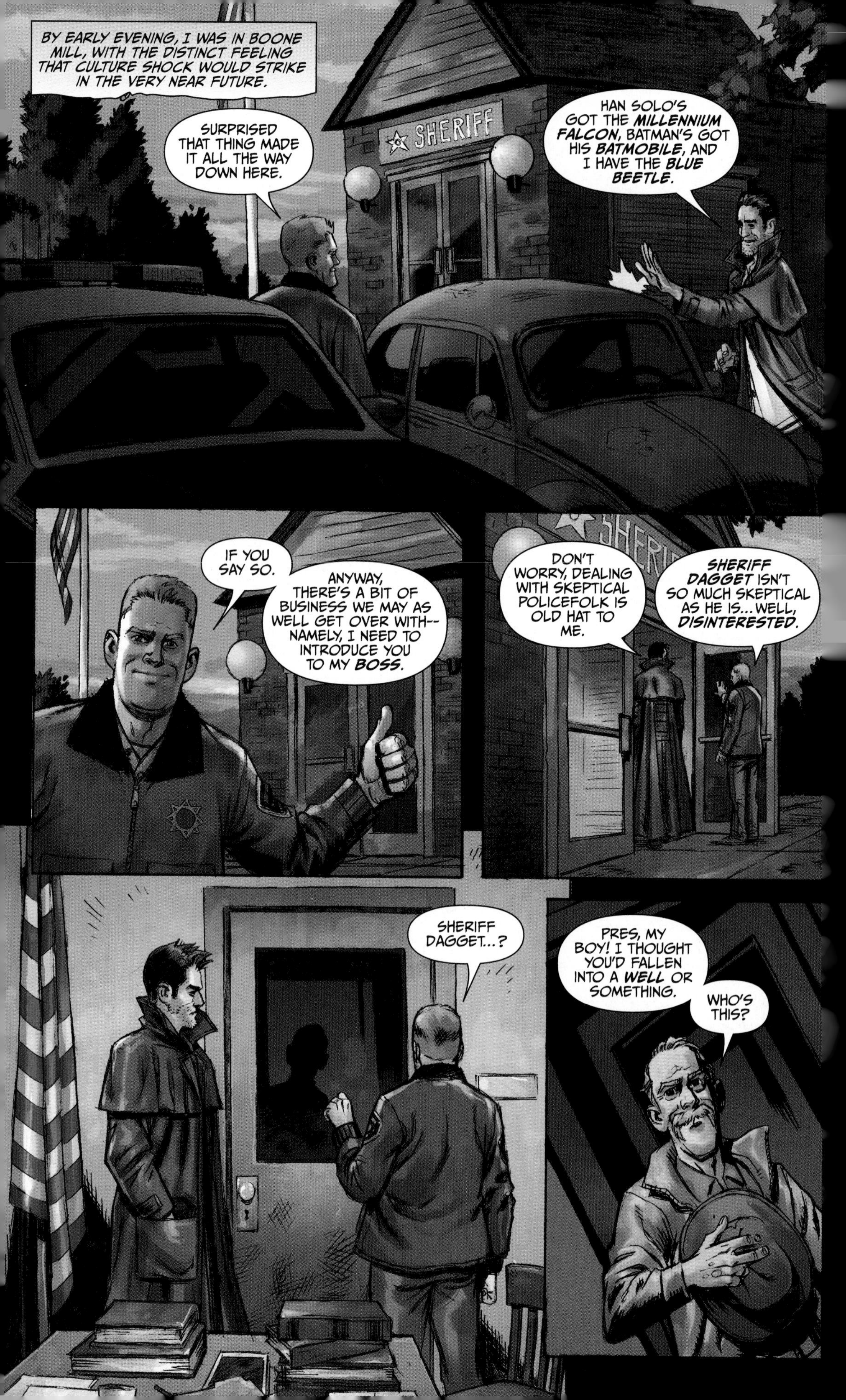
BY EARLY EVENING, I WAS IN BOONE MILL, WITH THE DISTINCT FEELING THAT CULTURE SHOCK WOULD STRIKE IN THE VERY NEAR FUTURE.
SHERIFF
SURPRISED THAT THING MADE IT ALL THE WAY DOWN HERE.
HAN SOLO'S GOT THE *MILLENNIUM FALCON*, BATMAN'S GOT HIS *BATMOBILE*, AND I HAVE THE *BLUE BEETLE*.
IF YOU SAY SO.
ANYWAY, THERE'S A BIT OF BUSINESS WE MAY AS WELL GET OVER WITH-- NAMELY, I NEED TO INTRODUCE YOU TO MY *BOSS*.
DON'T WORRY, DEALING WITH SKEPTICAL POLICEFOLK IS OLD HAT TO ME.
SHERIFF DAGGET ISN'T SO MUCH SKEPTICAL AS HE IS...WELL, *DISINTERESTED*.
SHERIFF DAGGET...?
PRES, MY BOY! I THOUGHT YOU'D FALLEN INTO A *WELL* OR SOMETHING.
WHO'S THIS?

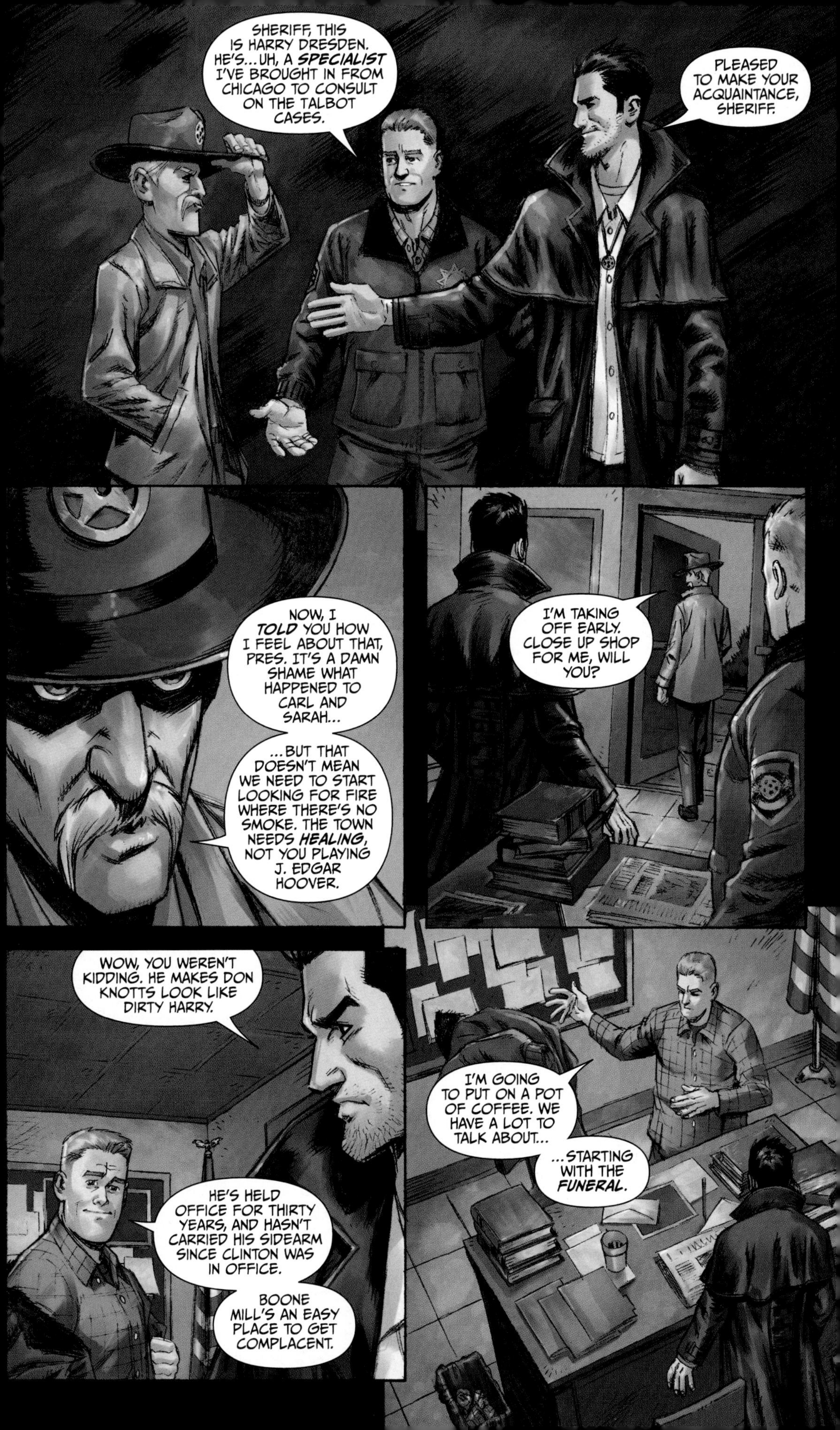
SHERIFF, THIS IS HARRY DRESDEN. HE'S...UH, A *SPECIALIST* I'VE BROUGHT IN FROM CHICAGO TO CONSULT ON THE TALBOT CASES.
PLEASED TO MAKE YOUR ACQUAINTANCE, SHERIFF.
NOW, I *TOLD* YOU HOW I FEEL ABOUT THAT, PRES. IT'S A DAMN SHAME WHAT HAPPENED TO CARL AND SARAH...
...BUT THAT DOESN'T MEAN WE NEED TO START LOOKING FOR FIRE WHERE THERE'S NO SMOKE. THE TOWN NEEDS *HEALING*, NOT YOU PLAYING J. EDGAR HOOVER.
I'M TAKING OFF EARLY. CLOSE UP SHOP FOR ME, WILL YOU?
WOW, YOU WEREN'T KIDDING. HE MAKES DON KNOTTS LOOK LIKE DIRTY HARRY.
HE'S HELD OFFICE FOR THIRTY YEARS, AND HASN'T CARRIED HIS SIDEARM SINCE CLINTON WAS IN OFFICE.
BOONE MILL'S AN EASY PLACE TO GET COMPLACENT.
I'M GOING TO PUT ON A POT OF COFFEE. WE HAVE A LOT TO TALK ABOUT...
...STARTING WITH THE *FUNERAL*.

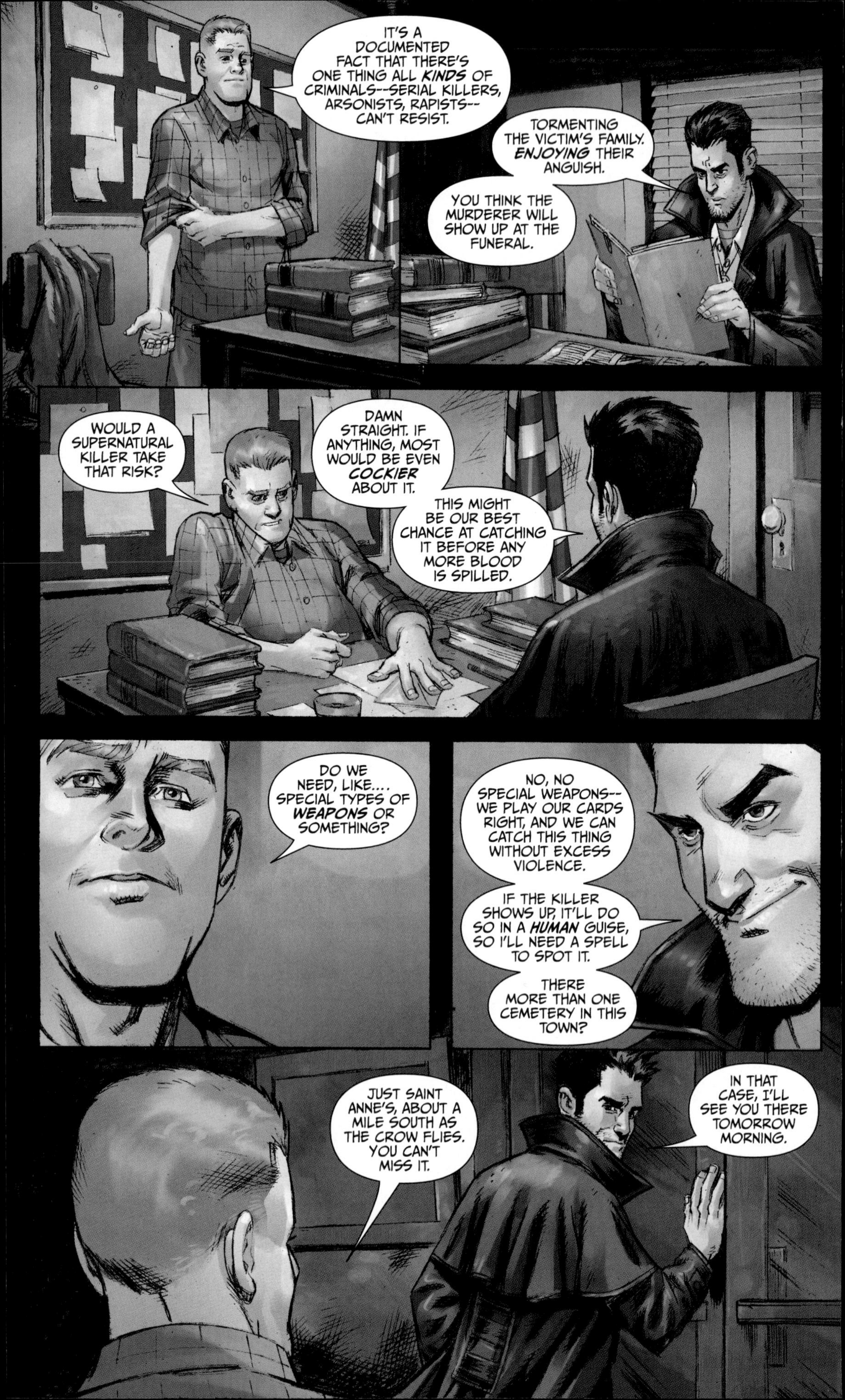

IT'S A DOCUMENTED FACT THAT THERE'S ONE THING ALL KINDS OF CRIMINALS--SERIAL KILLERS, ARSONISTS, RAPISTS--CAN'T RESIST.
TORMENTING THE VICTIM'S FAMILY. ENJOYING THEIR ANGUISH.
YOU THINK THE MURDERER WILL SHOW UP AT THE FUNERAL.
WOULD A SUPERNATURAL KILLER TAKE THAT RISK?
DAMN STRAIGHT. IF ANYTHING, MOST WOULD BE EVEN COCKIER ABOUT IT.
THIS MIGHT BE OUR BEST CHANCE AT CATCHING IT BEFORE ANY MORE BLOOD IS SPILLED.
DO WE NEED, LIKE.... SPECIAL TYPES OF WEAPONS OR SOMETHING?
NO, NO SPECIAL WEAPONS--WE PLAY OUR CARDS RIGHT, AND WE CAN CATCH THIS THING WITHOUT EXCESS VIOLENCE.
IF THE KILLER SHOWS UP, IT'LL DO SO IN A HUMAN GUISE, SO I'LL NEED A SPELL TO SPOT IT.
THERE MORE THAN ONE CEMETERY IN THIS TOWN?
JUST SAINT ANNE'S, ABOUT A MILE SOUTH AS THE CROW FLIES. YOU CAN'T MISS IT.
IN THAT CASE, I'LL SEE YOU THERE TOMORROW MORNING.

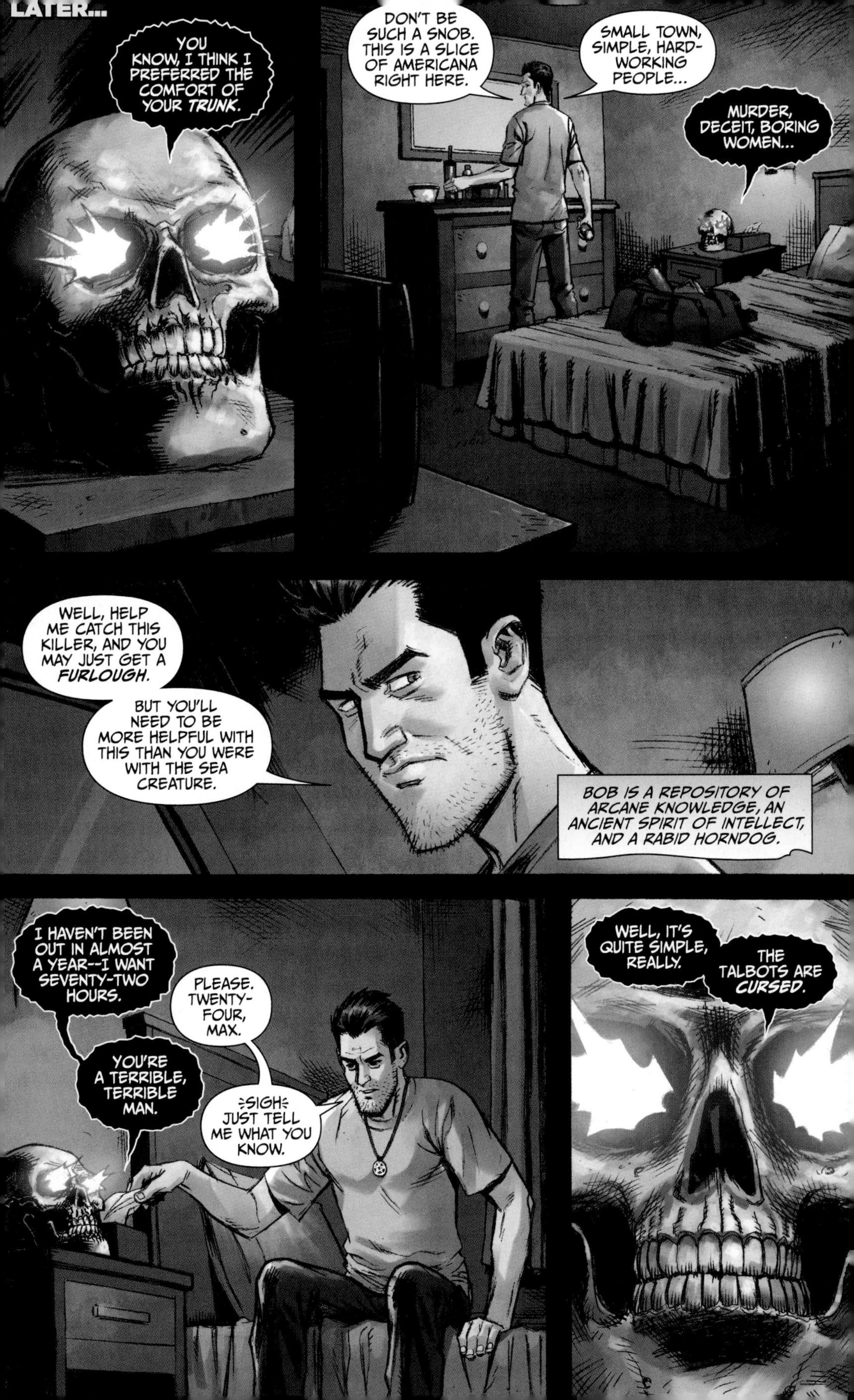
LATER...
YOU KNOW, I THINK I PREFERRED THE COMFORT OF YOUR *TRUNK*.
DON'T BE SUCH A SNOB. THIS IS A SLICE OF AMERICANA RIGHT HERE.
SMALL TOWN, SIMPLE, HARD-WORKING PEOPLE...
MURDER, DECEIT, BORING WOMEN...
WELL, HELP ME CATCH THIS KILLER, AND YOU MAY JUST GET A *FURLOUGH*.
BUT YOU'LL NEED TO BE MORE HELPFUL WITH THIS THAN YOU WERE WITH THE SEA CREATURE.
BOB IS A REPOSITORY OF ARCANE KNOWLEDGE, AN ANCIENT SPIRIT OF INTELLECT, AND A RABID HORNDOG.
I HAVEN'T BEEN OUT IN ALMOST A YEAR--I WANT SEVENTY-TWO HOURS.
PLEASE. TWENTY-FOUR, MAX.
YOU'RE A TERRIBLE, TERRIBLE MAN.
SIGH JUST TELL ME WHAT YOU KNOW.
WELL, IT'S QUITE SIMPLE, REALLY.
THE TALBOTS ARE *CURSED*.

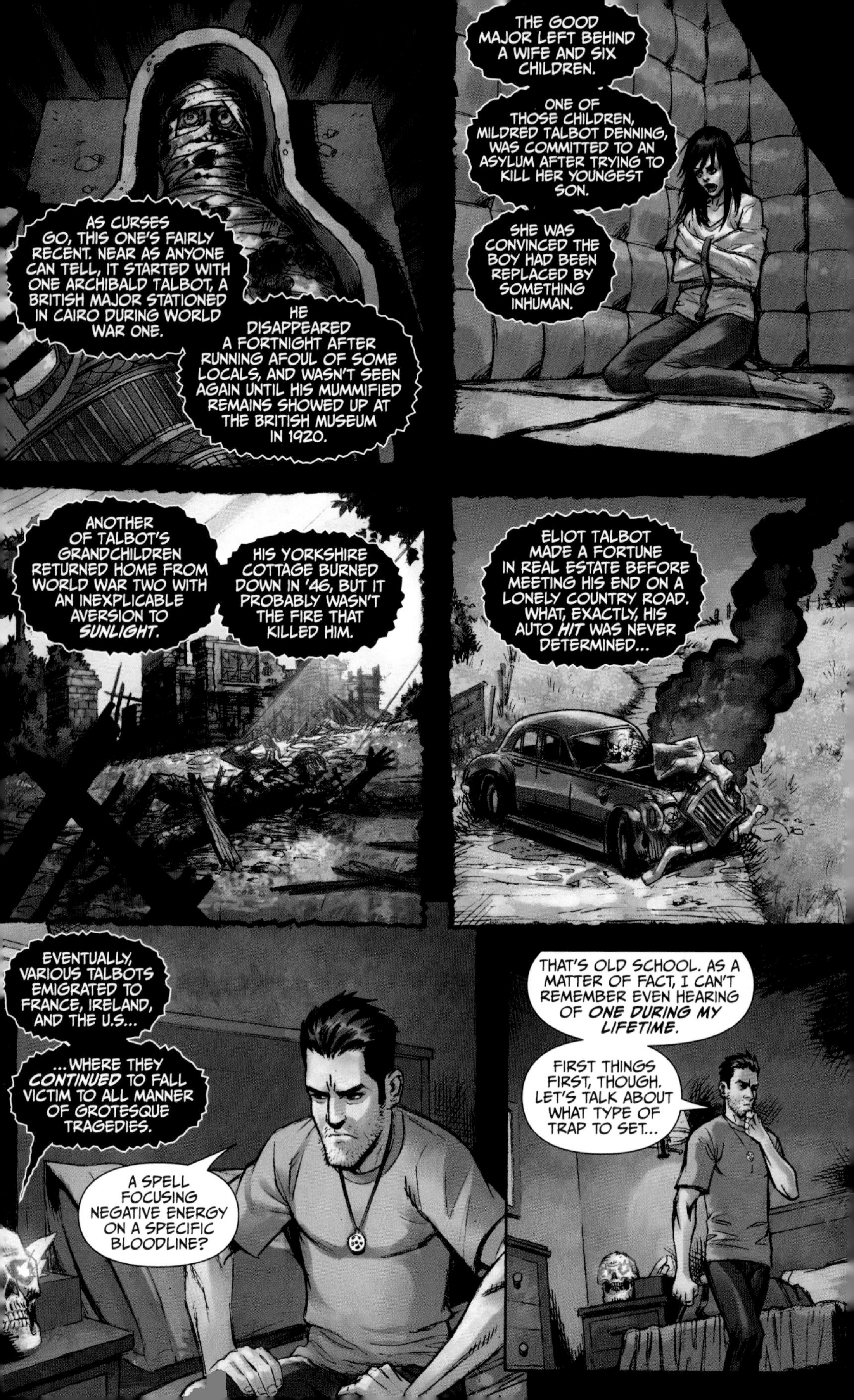
AS CURSES GO, THIS ONE'S FAIRLY RECENT. NEAR AS ANYONE CAN TELL, IT STARTED WITH ONE ARCHIBALD TALBOT, A BRITISH MAJOR STATIONED IN CAIRO DURING WORLD WAR ONE.
HE DISAPPEARED A FORTNIGHT AFTER RUNNING AFOUL OF SOME LOCALS, AND WASN'T SEEN AGAIN UNTIL HIS MUMMIFIED REMAINS SHOWED UP AT THE BRITISH MUSEUM IN 1920.
THE GOOD MAJOR LEFT BEHIND A WIFE AND SIX CHILDREN.
ONE OF THOSE CHILDREN, MILDRED TALBOT DENNING, WAS COMMITTED TO AN ASYLUM AFTER TRYING TO KILL HER YOUNGEST SON.
SHE WAS CONVINCED THE BOY HAD BEEN REPLACED BY SOMETHING INHUMAN.
ANOTHER OF TALBOT'S GRANDCHILDREN RETURNED HOME FROM WORLD WAR TWO WITH AN INEXPLICABLE AVERSION TO *SUNLIGHT*.
HIS YORKSHIRE COTTAGE BURNED DOWN IN '46, BUT IT PROBABLY WASN'T THE FIRE THAT KILLED HIM.
ELIOT TALBOT MADE A FORTUNE IN REAL ESTATE BEFORE MEETING HIS END ON A LONELY COUNTRY ROAD. WHAT, EXACTLY, HIS AUTO *HIT* WAS NEVER DETERMINED...
EVENTUALLY, VARIOUS TALBOTS EMIGRATED TO FRANCE, IRELAND, AND THE U.S...
...WHERE THEY *CONTINUED* TO FALL VICTIM TO ALL MANNER OF GROTESQUE TRAGEDIES.
A SPELL FOCUSING NEGATIVE ENERGY ON A SPECIFIC BLOODLINE?
THAT'S OLD SCHOOL. AS A MATTER OF FACT, I CAN'T REMEMBER EVEN HEARING OF *ONE DURING MY LIFETIME*.
FIRST THINGS FIRST, THOUGH. LET'S TALK ABOUT WHAT TYPE OF TRAP TO SET...

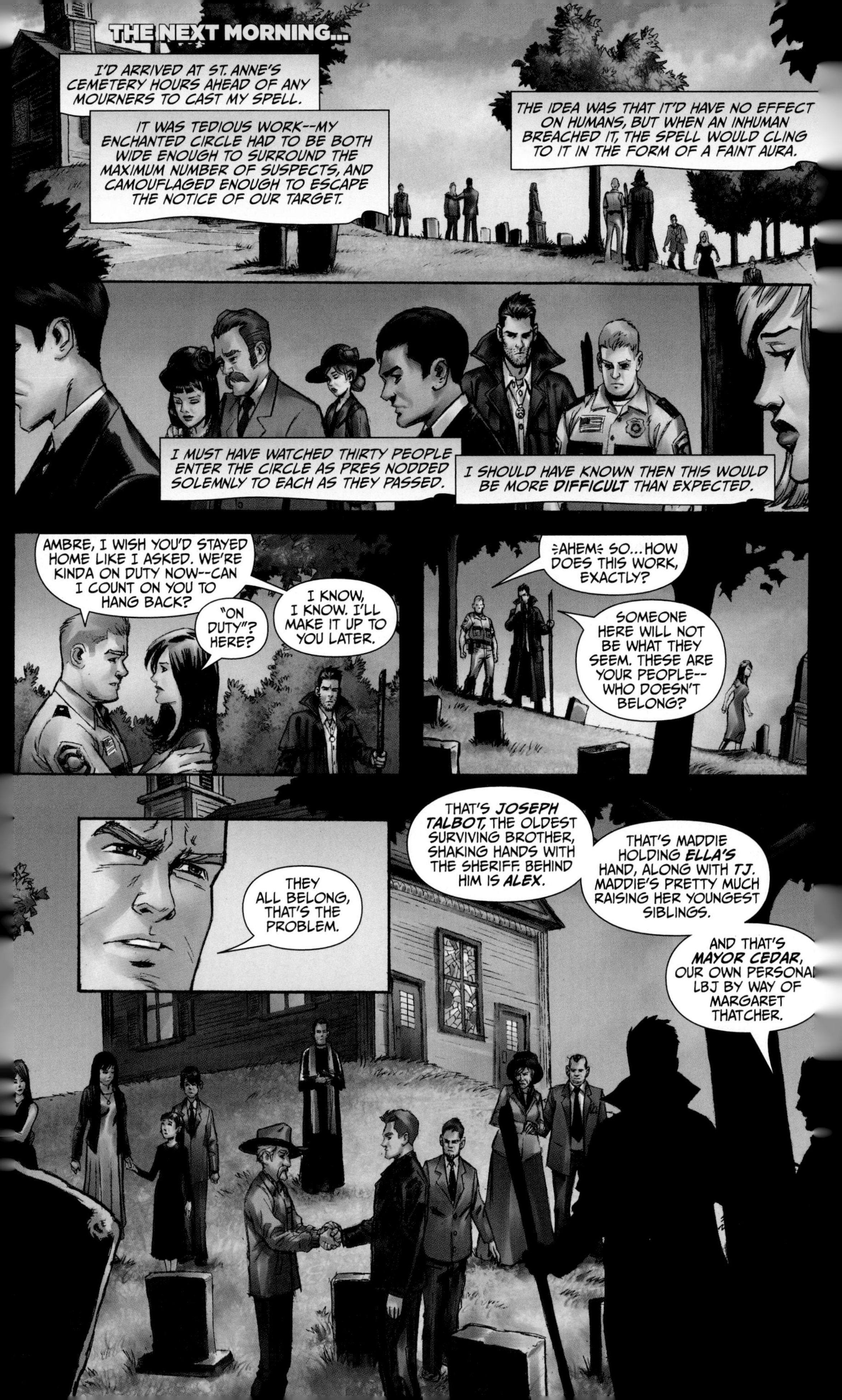
THE NEXT MORNING...
I'D ARRIVED AT ST. ANNE'S CEMETERY HOURS AHEAD OF ANY MOURNERS TO CAST MY SPELL.
IT WAS TEDIOUS WORK--MY ENCHANTED CIRCLE HAD TO BE BOTH WIDE ENOUGH TO SURROUND THE MAXIMUM NUMBER OF SUSPECTS, AND CAMOUFLAGED ENOUGH TO ESCAPE THE NOTICE OF OUR TARGET.
THE IDEA WAS THAT IT'D HAVE NO EFFECT ON HUMANS, BUT WHEN AN INHUMAN BREACHED IT, THE SPELL WOULD CLING TO IT IN THE FORM OF A FAINT AURA.
I MUST HAVE WATCHED THIRTY PEOPLE ENTER THE CIRCLE AS PRES NODDED SOLEMNLY TO EACH AS THEY PASSED.
I SHOULD HAVE KNOWN THEN THIS WOULD BE MORE DIFFICULT THAN EXPECTED.
AMBRE, I WISH YOU'D STAYED HOME LIKE I ASKED. WE'RE KINDA ON DUTY NOW--CAN I COUNT ON YOU TO HANG BACK?
"ON DUTY"? HERE?
I KNOW, I KNOW. I'LL MAKE IT UP TO YOU LATER.
AHEM SO...HOW DOES THIS WORK, EXACTLY?
SOMEONE HERE WILL NOT BE WHAT THEY SEEM. THESE ARE YOUR PEOPLE-- WHO DOESN'T BELONG?
THEY ALL BELONG, THAT'S THE PROBLEM.
THAT'S JOSEPH TALBOT, THE OLDEST SURVIVING BROTHER, SHAKING HANDS WITH THE SHERIFF. BEHIND HIM IS ALEX.
THAT'S MADDIE HOLDING ELLA'S HAND, ALONG WITH TJ. MADDIE'S PRETTY MUCH RAISING HER YOUNGEST SIBLINGS.
AND THAT'S MAYOR CEDAR, OUR OWN PERSONAL LBJ BY WAY OF MARGARET THATCHER.

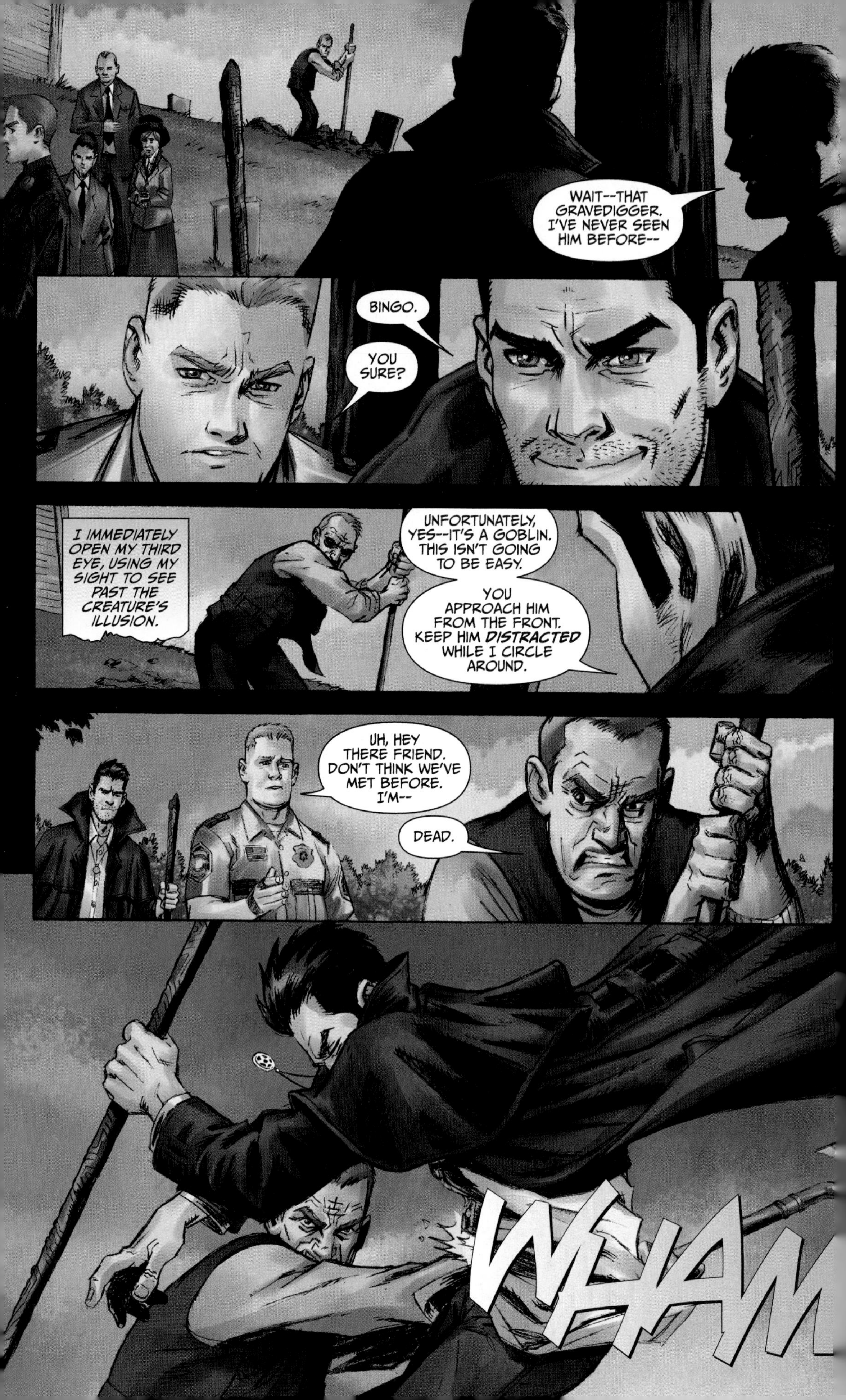
WAIT--THAT GRAVEDIGGER. I'VE NEVER SEEN HIM BEFORE--
BINGO.
YOU SURE?
I IMMEDIATELY OPEN MY THIRD EYE, USING MY SIGHT TO SEE PAST THE CREATURE'S ILLUSION.
UNFORTUNATELY, YES--IT'S A GOBLIN. THIS ISN'T GOING TO BE EASY.
YOU APPROACH HIM FROM THE FRONT. KEEP HIM DISTRACTED WHILE I CIRCLE AROUND.
UH, HEY THERE FRIEND. DON'T THINK WE'VE MET BEFORE. I'M--
DEAD.
WHAM

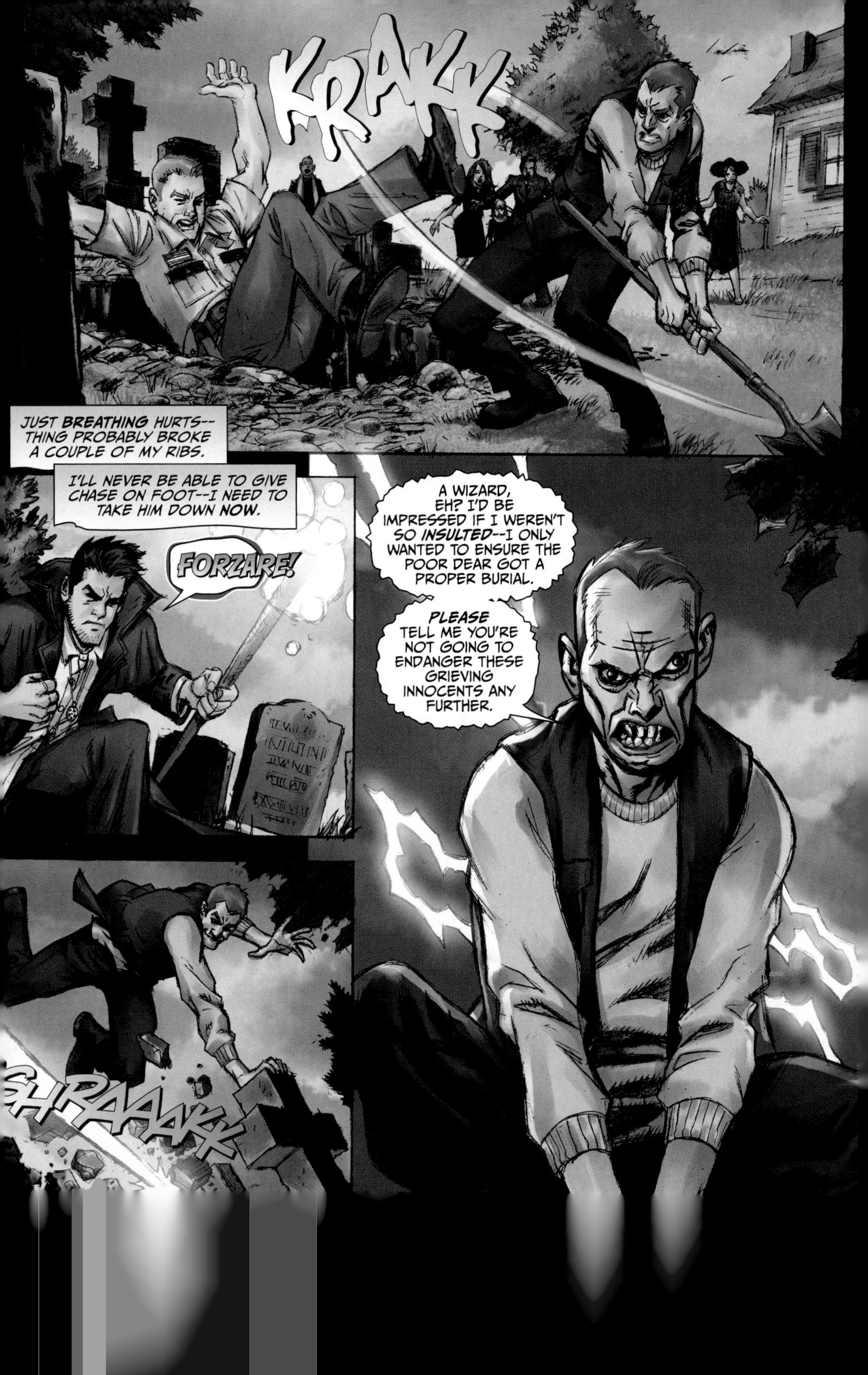
KRAKK
JUST BREATHING HURTS-- THING PROBABLY BROKE A COUPLE OF MY RIBS.
I'LL NEVER BE ABLE TO GIVE CHASE ON FOOT--I NEED TO TAKE HIM DOWN NOW.
FORZARE!
A WIZARD, EH? I'D BE IMPRESSED IF I WEREN'T SO INSULTED--I ONLY WANTED TO ENSURE THE POOR DEAR GOT A PROPER BURIAL.
PLEASE TELL ME YOU'RE NOT GOING TO ENDANGER THESE GRIEVING INNOCENTS ANY FURTHER.
SHRAAAKK

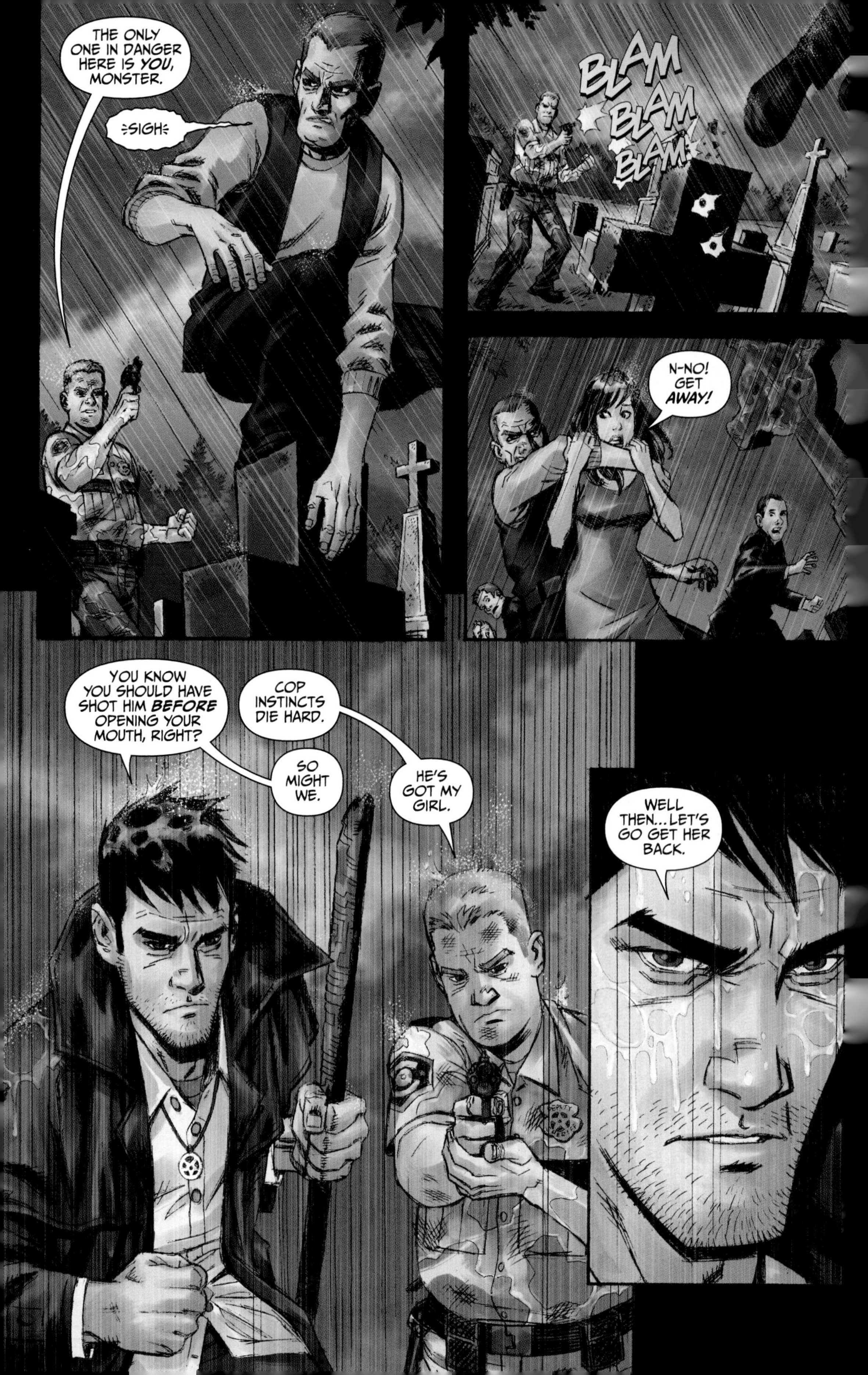
THE ONLY ONE IN DANGER HERE IS YOU, MONSTER.
SIGH
BLAM BLAM BLAM
N-NO! GET AWAY!
YOU KNOW YOU SHOULD HAVE SHOT HIM BEFORE OPENING YOUR MOUTH, RIGHT?
COP INSTINCTS DIE HARD.
SO MIGHT WE.
HE'S GOT MY GIRL.
WELL THEN...LET'S GO GET HER BACK.

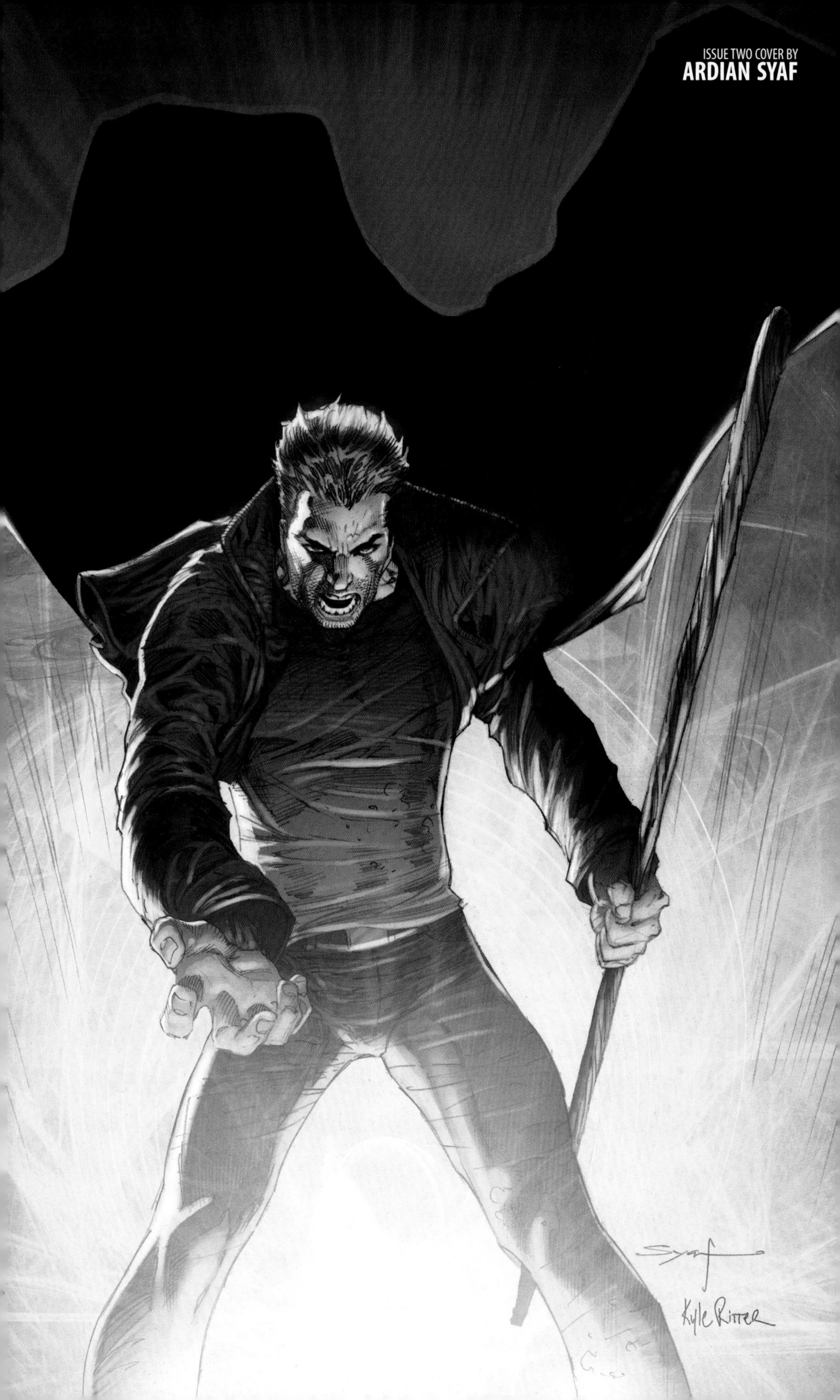
Kyle Ritter
ISSUE TWO COVER BY
ARDIAN SYAF

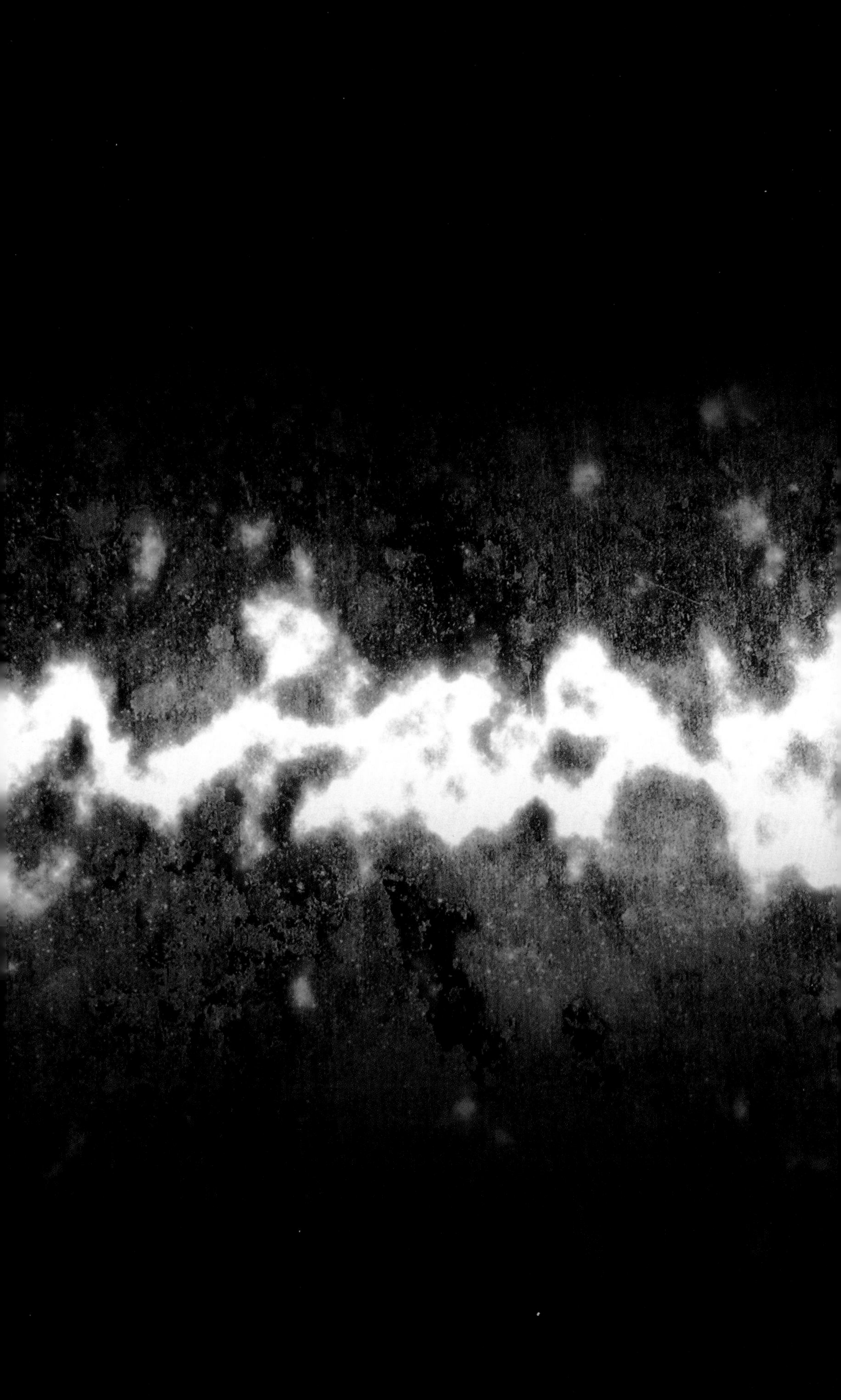

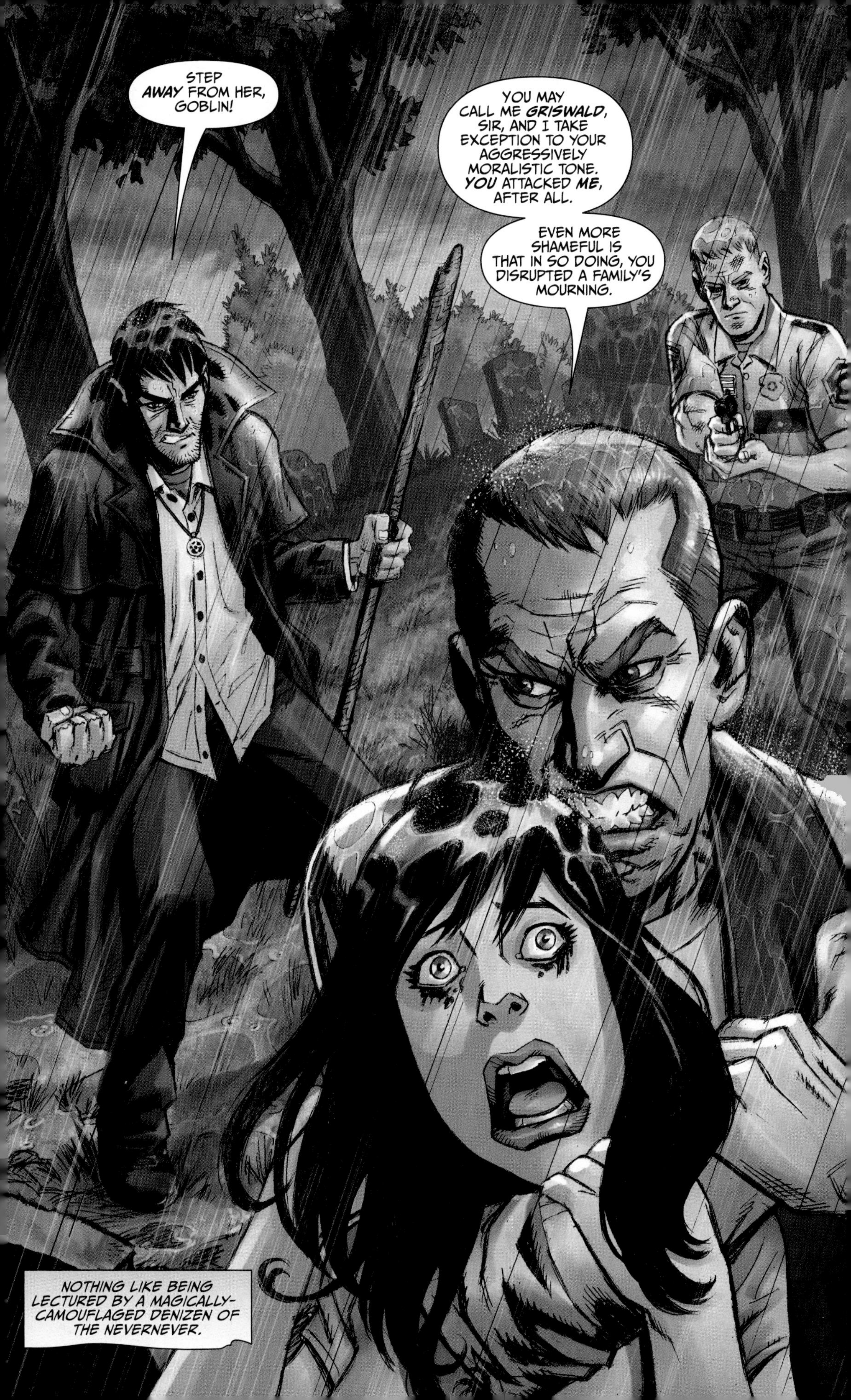
STEP AWAY FROM HER, GOBLIN!
YOU MAY CALL ME GRISWALD, SIR, AND I TAKE EXCEPTION TO YOUR AGGRESSIVELY MORALISTIC TONE. YOU ATTACKED ME, AFTER ALL.
EVEN MORE SHAMEFUL IS THAT IN SO DOING, YOU DISRUPTED A FAMILY'S MOURNING.
NOTHING LIKE BEING LECTURED BY A MAGICALLY-CAMOUFLAGED DENIZEN OF THE NEVERNEVER.

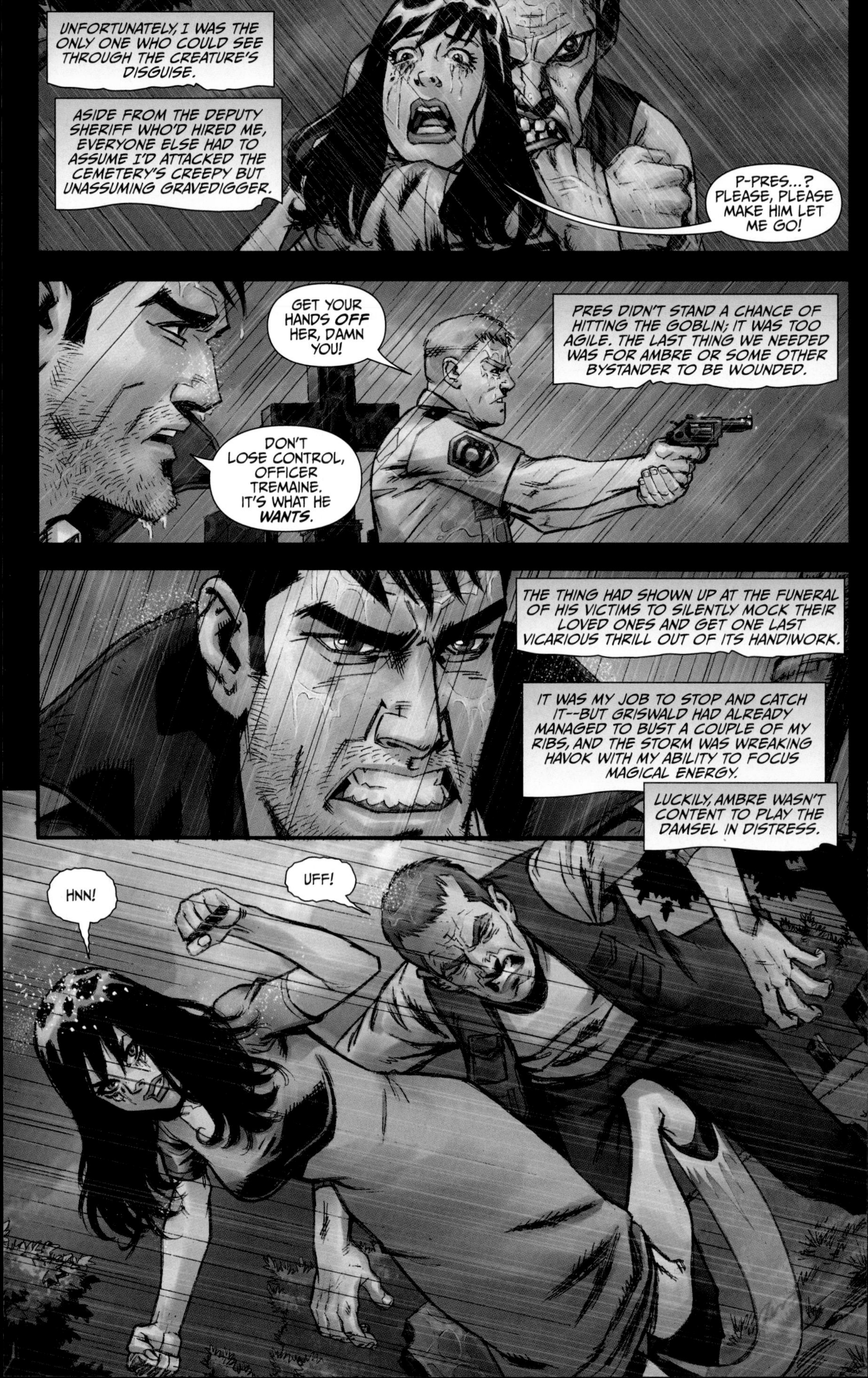
UNFORTUNATELY, I WAS THE ONLY ONE WHO COULD SEE THROUGH THE CREATURE'S DISGUISE.
ASIDE FROM THE DEPUTY SHERIFF WHO'D HIRED ME, EVERYONE ELSE HAD TO ASSUME I'D ATTACKED THE CEMETERY'S CREEPY BUT UNASSUMING GRAVEDIGGER.
P-PRES...? PLEASE, PLEASE MAKE HIM LET ME GO!
GET YOUR HANDS OFF HER, DAMN YOU!
PRES DIDN'T STAND A CHANCE OF HITTING THE GOBLIN; IT WAS TOO AGILE. THE LAST THING WE NEEDED WAS FOR AMBRE OR SOME OTHER BYSTANDER TO BE WOUNDED.
DON'T LOSE CONTROL, OFFICER TREMAINE. IT'S WHAT HE WANTS.
THE THING HAD SHOWN UP AT THE FUNERAL OF HIS VICTIMS TO SILENTLY MOCK THEIR LOVED ONES AND GET ONE LAST VICARIOUS THRILL OUT OF ITS HANDIWORK.
IT WAS MY JOB TO STOP AND CATCH IT--BUT GRISWALD HAD ALREADY MANAGED TO BUST A COUPLE OF MY RIBS, AND THE STORM WAS WREAKING HAVOK WITH MY ABILITY TO FOCUS MAGICAL ENERGY.
LUCKILY, AMBRE WASN'T CONTENT TO PLAY THE DAMSEL IN DISTRESS.
HNN!
UFF!

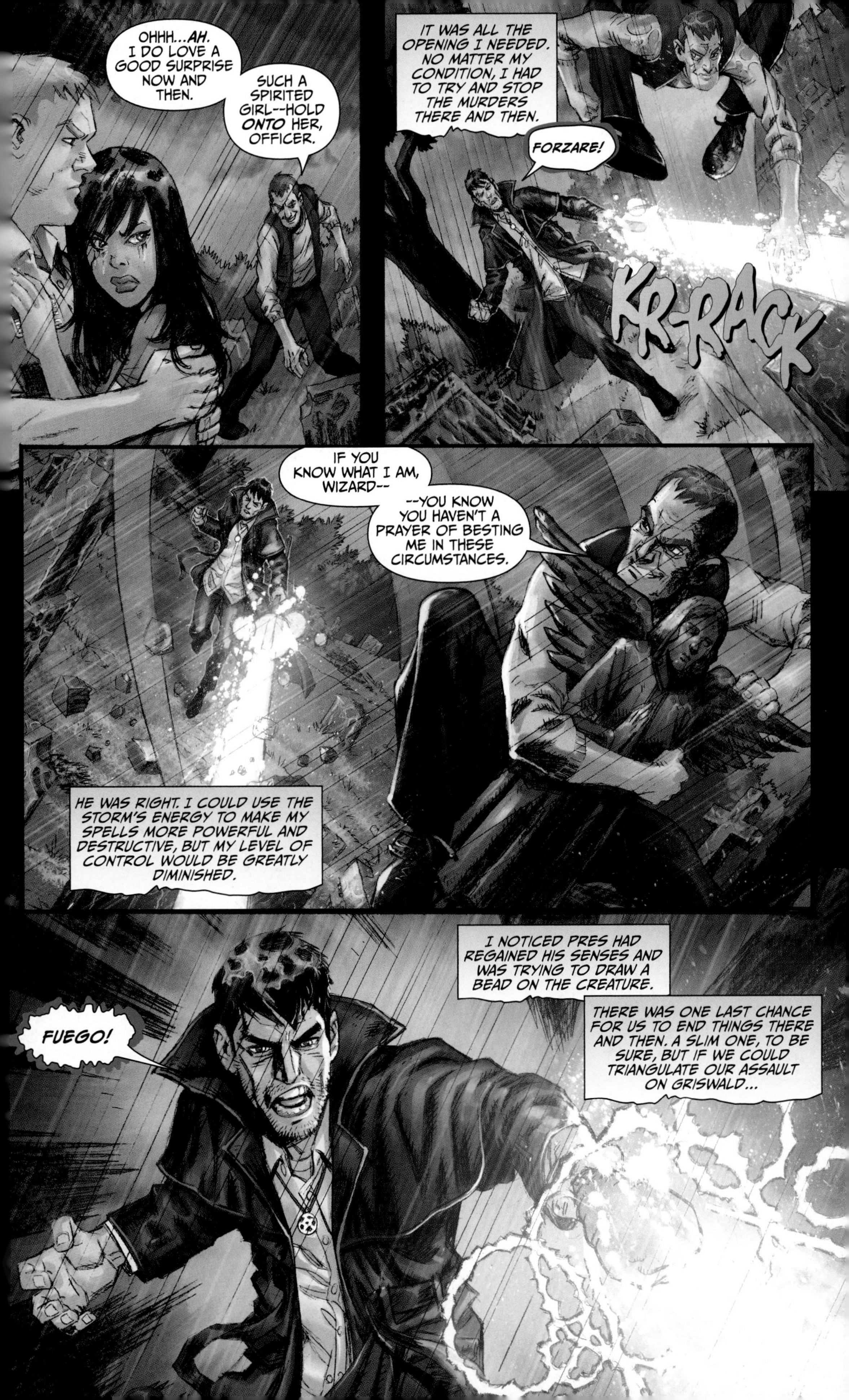
OHHH...AH. I DO LOVE A GOOD SURPRISE NOW AND THEN.
SUCH A SPIRITED GIRL--HOLD ONTO HER, OFFICER.
IT WAS ALL THE OPENING I NEEDED. NO MATTER MY CONDITION, I HAD TO TRY AND STOP THE MURDERS THERE AND THEN.
FORZARE!
KR-RACK
IF YOU KNOW WHAT I AM, WIZARD--
--YOU KNOW YOU HAVEN'T A PRAYER OF BESTING ME IN THESE CIRCUMSTANCES.
HE WAS RIGHT. I COULD USE THE STORM'S ENERGY TO MAKE MY SPELLS MORE POWERFUL AND DESTRUCTIVE, BUT MY LEVEL OF CONTROL WOULD BE GREATLY DIMINISHED.
I NOTICED PRES HAD REGAINED HIS SENSES AND WAS TRYING TO DRAW A BEAD ON THE CREATURE.
FUEGO!
THERE WAS ONE LAST CHANCE FOR US TO END THINGS THERE AND THEN. A SLIM ONE, TO BE SURE, BUT IF WE COULD TRIANGULATE OUR ASSAULT ON GRISWALD...

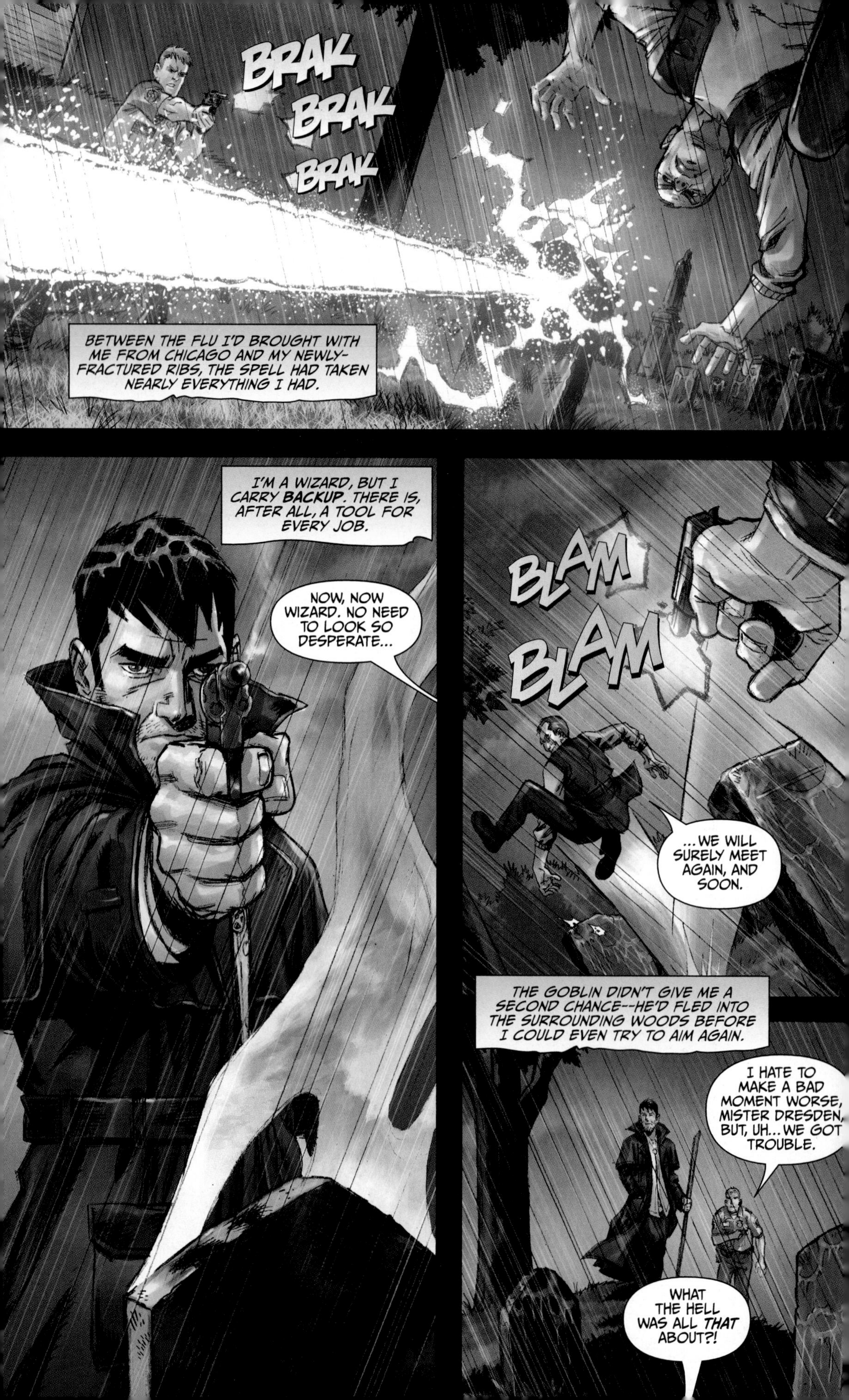
BRAK
BRAK
BRAK
BETWEEN THE FLU I'D BROUGHT WITH ME FROM CHICAGO AND MY NEWLY-FRACTURED RIBS, THE SPELL HAD TAKEN NEARLY EVERYTHING I HAD.
I'M A WIZARD, BUT I CARRY BACKUP. THERE IS, AFTER ALL, A TOOL FOR EVERY JOB.
NOW, NOW WIZARD. NO NEED TO LOOK SO DESPERATE...
BLAM
BLAM
...WE WILL SURELY MEET AGAIN, AND SOON.
THE GOBLIN DIDN'T GIVE ME A SECOND CHANCE--HE'D FLED INTO THE SURROUNDING WOODS BEFORE I COULD EVEN TRY TO AIM AGAIN.
I HATE TO MAKE A BAD MOMENT WORSE, MISTER DRESDEN, BUT, UH... WE GOT TROUBLE.
WHAT THE HELL WAS ALL THAT ABOUT?!

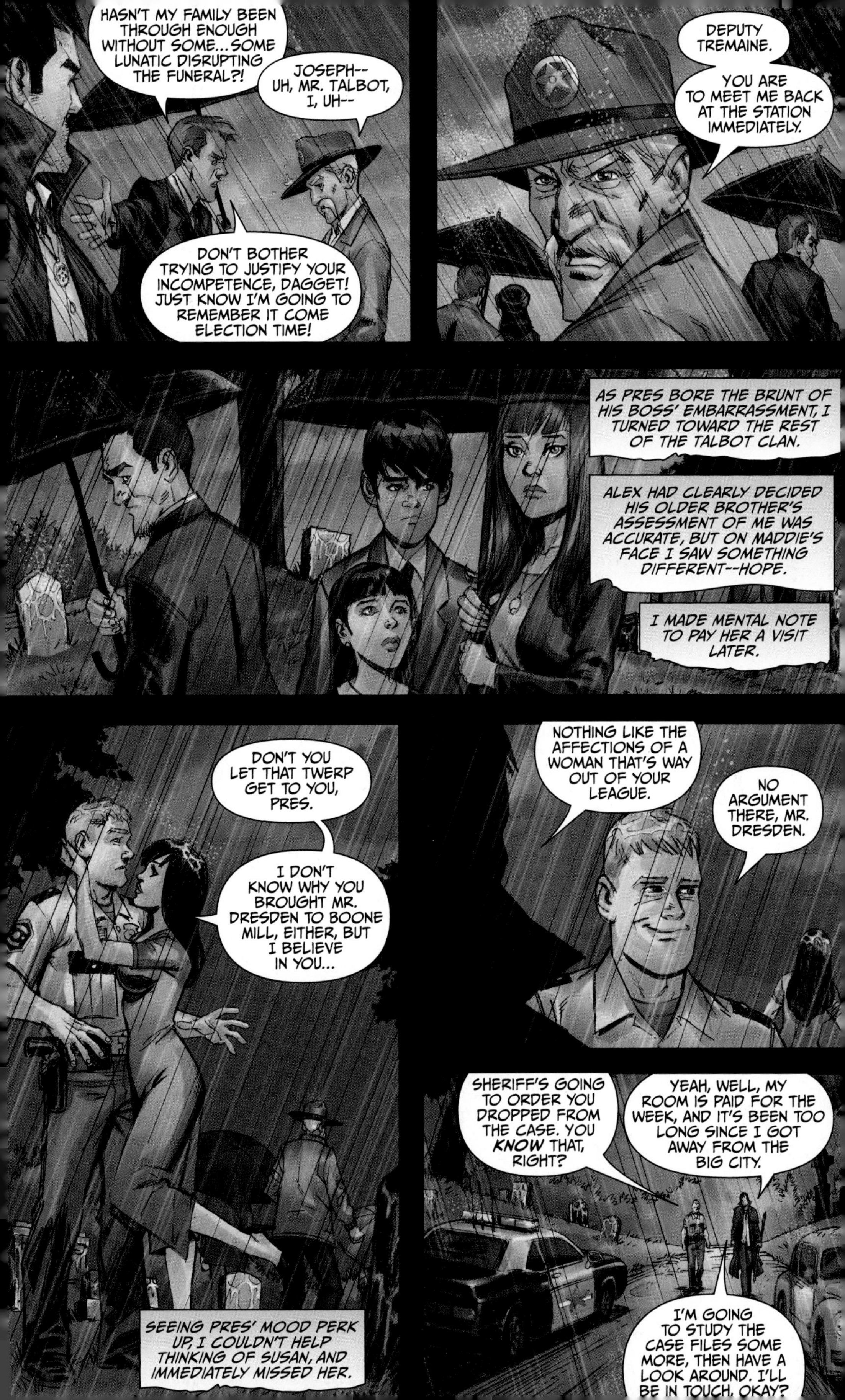

HASN'T MY FAMILY BEEN THROUGH ENOUGH WITHOUT SOME... SOME LUNATIC DISRUPTING THE FUNERAL?!
JOSEPH-- UH, MR. TALBOT, I, UH--
DON'T BOTHER TRYING TO JUSTIFY YOUR INCOMPETENCE, DAGGET! JUST KNOW I'M GOING TO REMEMBER IT COME ELECTION TIME!
DEPUTY TREMAINE.
YOU ARE TO MEET ME BACK AT THE STATION IMMEDIATELY.
AS PRES BORE THE BRUNT OF HIS BOSS' EMBARRASSMENT, I TURNED TOWARD THE REST OF THE TALBOT CLAN.
ALEX HAD CLEARLY DECIDED HIS OLDER BROTHER'S ASSESSMENT OF ME WAS ACCURATE, BUT ON MADDIE'S FACE I SAW SOMETHING DIFFERENT--HOPE.
I MADE MENTAL NOTE TO PAY HER A VISIT LATER.
DON'T YOU LET THAT TWERP GET TO YOU, PRES.
I DON'T KNOW WHY YOU BROUGHT MR. DRESDEN TO BOONE MILL, EITHER, BUT I BELIEVE IN YOU...
SEEING PRES' MOOD PERK UP, I COULDN'T HELP THINKING OF SUSAN, AND IMMEDIATELY MISSED HER.
NOTHING LIKE THE AFFECTIONS OF A WOMAN THAT'S WAY OUT OF YOUR LEAGUE.
NO ARGUMENT THERE, MR. DRESDEN.
SHERIFF'S GOING TO ORDER YOU DROPPED FROM THE CASE. YOU **KNOW** THAT, RIGHT?
YEAH, WELL, MY ROOM IS PAID FOR THE WEEK, AND IT'S BEEN TOO LONG SINCE I GOT AWAY FROM THE BIG CITY.
I'M GOING TO STUDY THE CASE FILES SOME MORE, THEN HAVE A LOOK AROUND. I'LL BE IN TOUCH, OKAY?

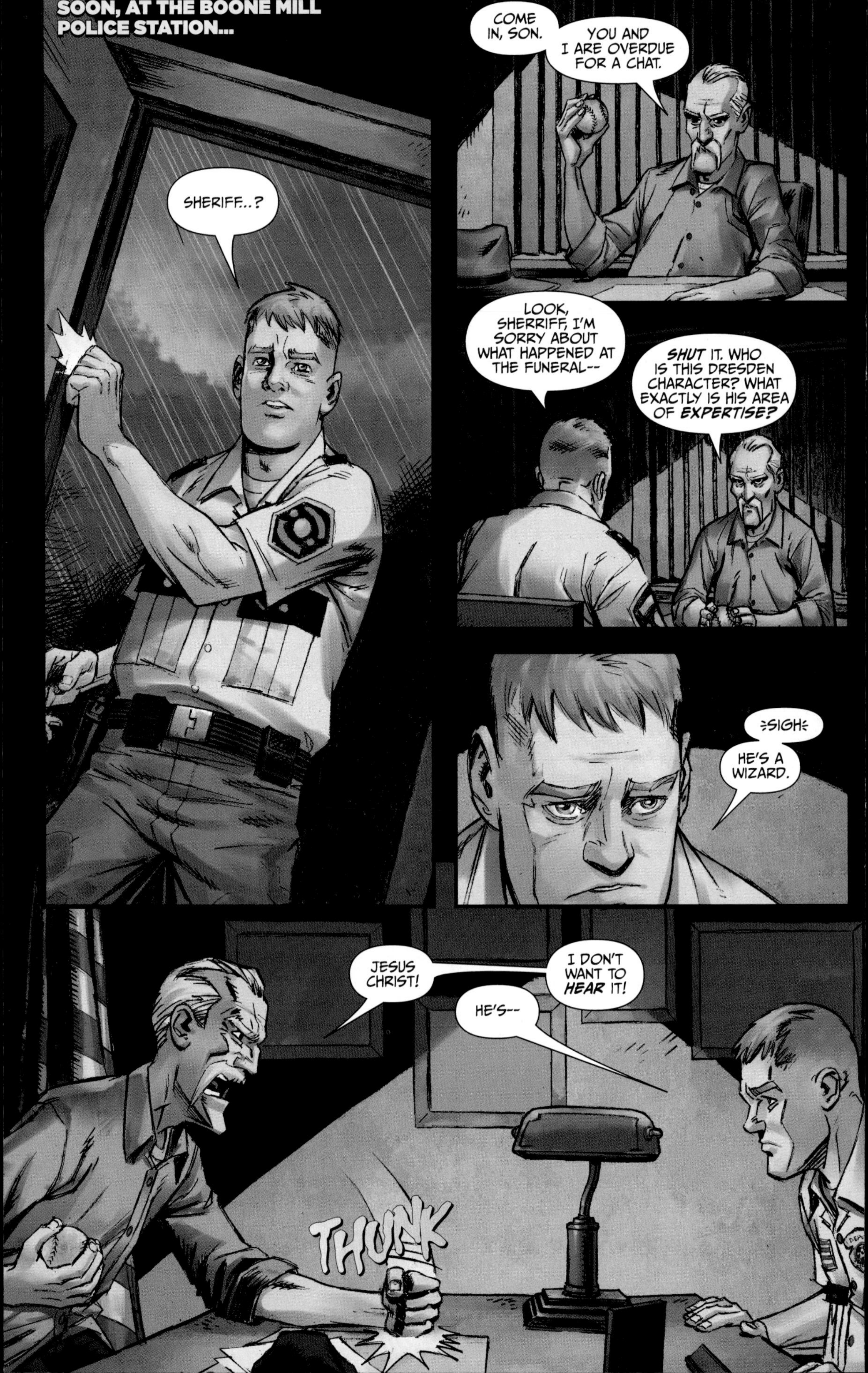
SOON, AT THE BOONE MILL POLICE STATION...
SHERIFF...?
COME IN, SON.
YOU AND I ARE OVERDUE FOR A CHAT.
LOOK, SHERRIFF, I'M SORRY ABOUT WHAT HAPPENED AT THE FUNERAL--
SHUT IT. WHO IS THIS DRESDEN CHARACTER? WHAT EXACTLY IS HIS AREA OF EXPERTISE?
≈SIGH≈
HE'S A WIZARD.
HE'S--
JESUS CHRIST!
I DON'T WANT TO HEAR IT!
THUNK

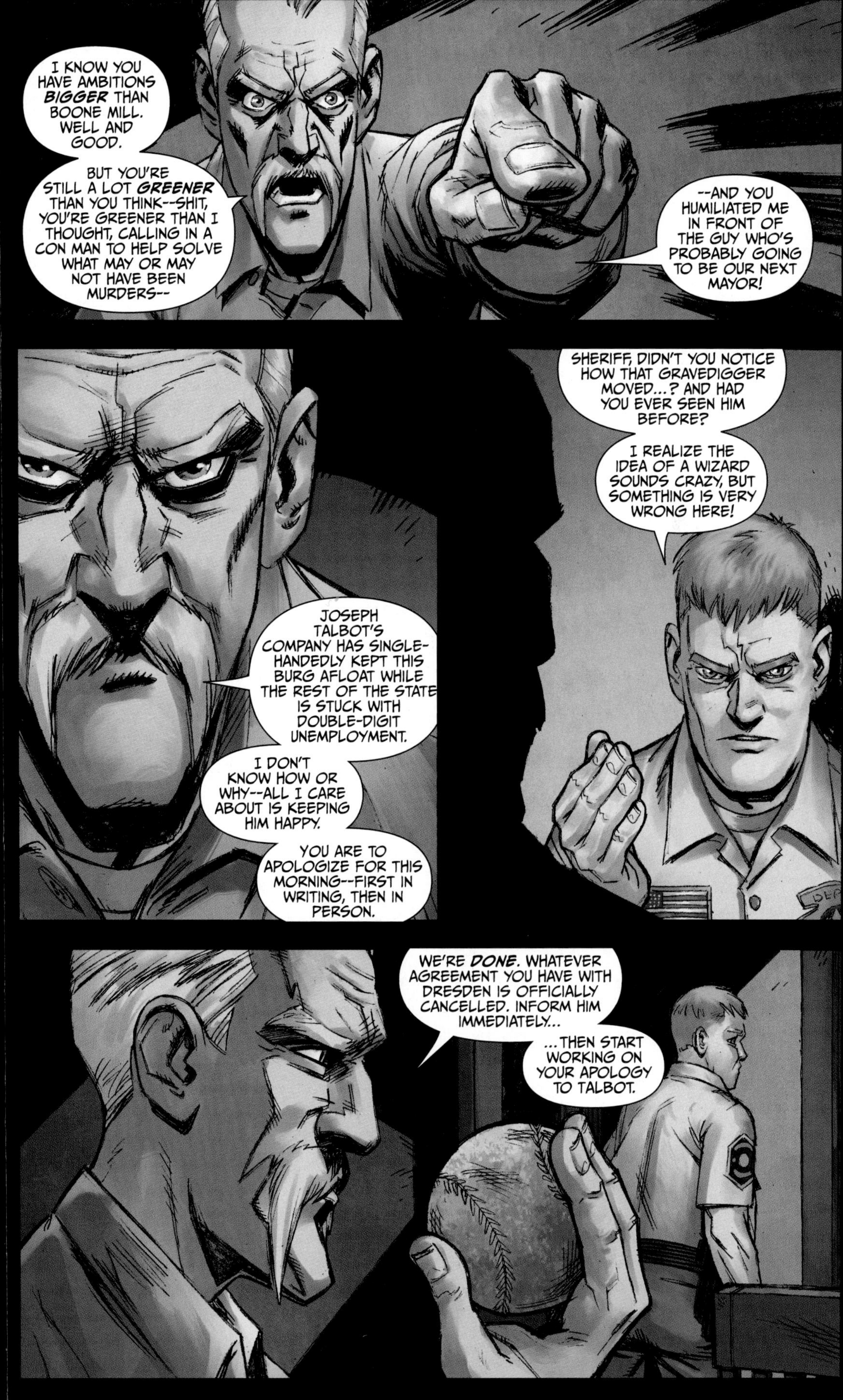
I KNOW YOU HAVE AMBITIONS *BIGGER* THAN BOONE MILL. WELL AND GOOD.
BUT YOU'RE STILL A LOT *GREENER* THAN YOU THINK--SHIT, YOU'RE GREENER THAN I THOUGHT, CALLING IN A CON MAN TO HELP SOLVE WHAT MAY OR MAY NOT HAVE BEEN MURDERS--
--AND YOU HUMILIATED ME IN FRONT OF THE GUY WHO'S PROBABLY GOING TO BE OUR NEXT MAYOR!
SHERIFF, DIDN'T YOU NOTICE HOW THAT GRAVEDIGGER MOVED...? AND HAD YOU EVER SEEN HIM BEFORE?
I REALIZE THE IDEA OF A WIZARD SOUNDS CRAZY, BUT SOMETHING IS VERY WRONG HERE!
JOSEPH TALBOT'S COMPANY HAS SINGLE-HANDEDLY KEPT THIS BURG AFLOAT WHILE THE REST OF THE STATE IS STUCK WITH DOUBLE-DIGIT UNEMPLOYMENT.
I DON'T KNOW HOW OR WHY--ALL I CARE ABOUT IS KEEPING HIM HAPPY.
YOU ARE TO APOLOGIZE FOR THIS MORNING--FIRST IN WRITING, THEN IN PERSON.
WE'RE *DONE*. WHATEVER AGREEMENT YOU HAVE WITH DRESDEN IS OFFICIALLY CANCELLED. INFORM HIM IMMEDIATELY...
...THEN START WORKING ON YOUR APOLOGY TO TALBOT.

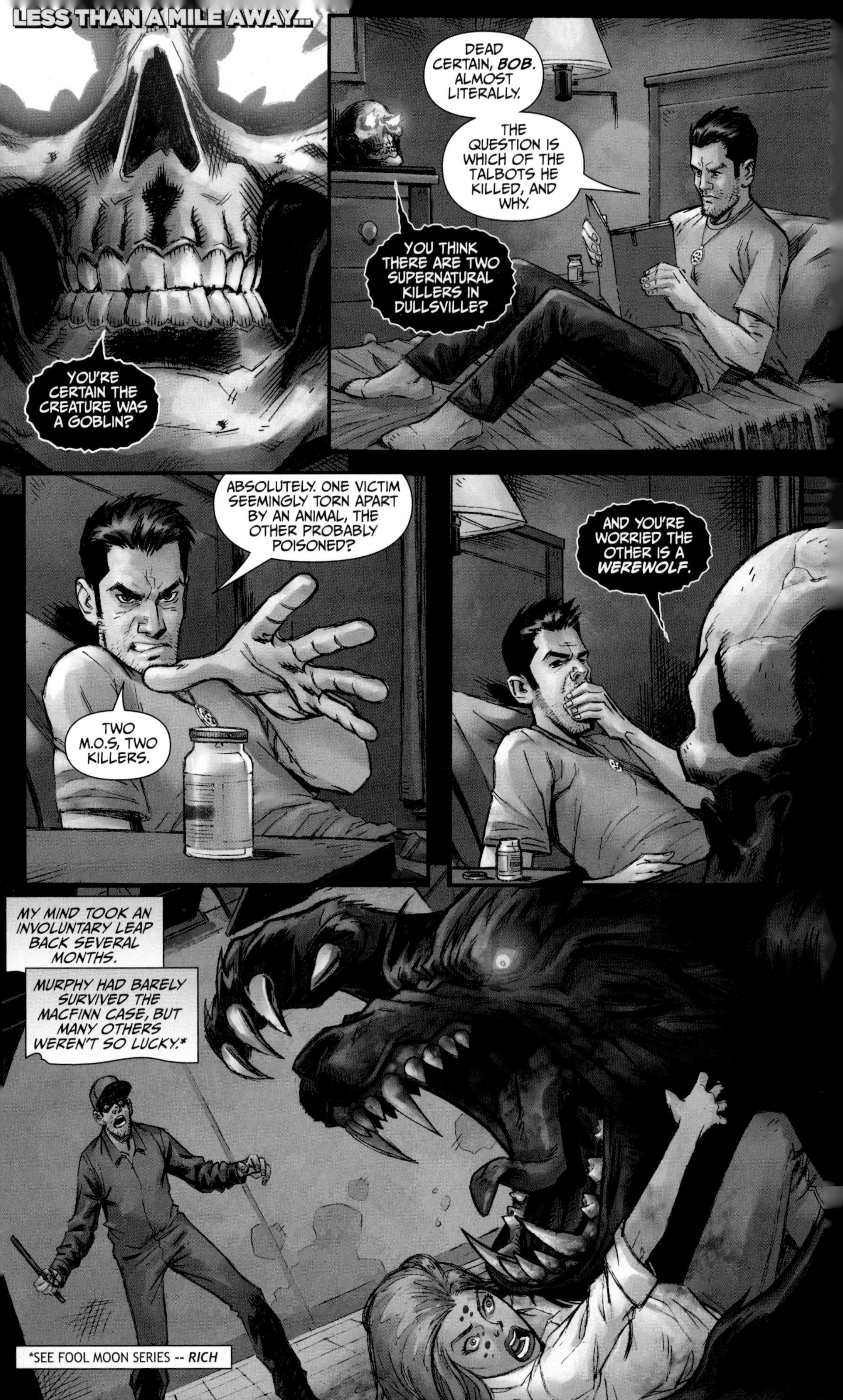
LESS THAN A MILE AWAY...
YOU'RE CERTAIN THE CREATURE WAS A GOBLIN?
DEAD CERTAIN, BOB. ALMOST LITERALLY.
THE QUESTION IS WHICH OF THE TALBOTS HE KILLED, AND WHY.
YOU THINK THERE ARE TWO SUPERNATURAL KILLERS IN DULLSVILLE?
ABSOLUTELY. ONE VICTIM SEEMINGLY TORN APART BY AN ANIMAL, THE OTHER PROBABLY POISONED?
TWO M.O.S, TWO KILLERS.
AND YOU'RE WORRIED THE OTHER IS A WEREWOLF.
MY MIND TOOK AN INVOLUNTARY LEAP BACK SEVERAL MONTHS.
MURPHY HAD BARELY SURVIVED THE MACFINN CASE, BUT MANY OTHERS WEREN'T SO LUCKY.*
*SEE FOOL MOON SERIES -- RICH

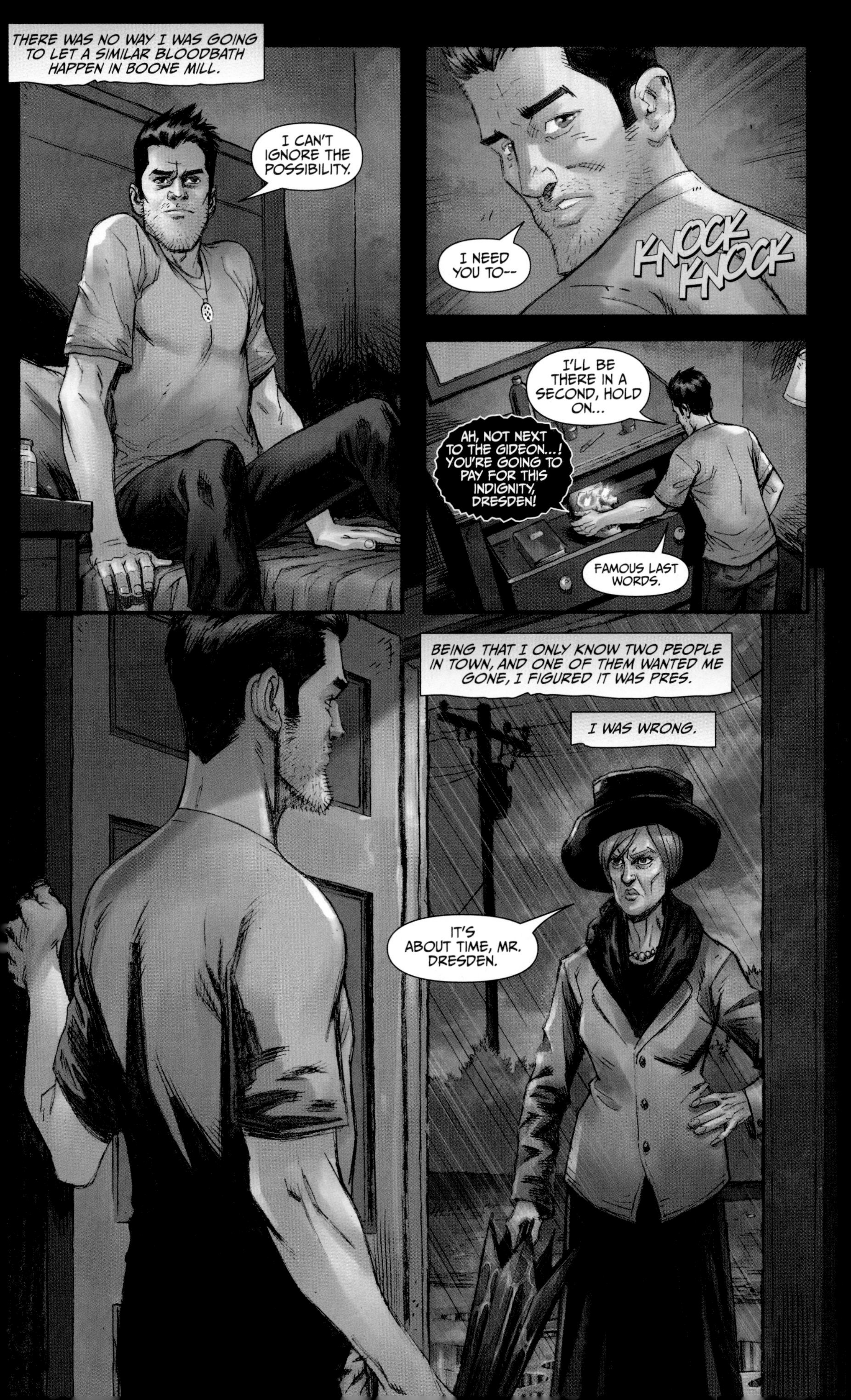

THERE WAS NO WAY I WAS GOING TO LET A SIMILAR BLOODBATH HAPPEN IN BOONE MILL.
I CAN'T IGNORE THE POSSIBILITY.
I NEED YOU TO--
KNOCK KNOCK
I'LL BE THERE IN A SECOND, HOLD ON...
AH, NOT NEXT TO THE GIDEON...! YOU'RE GOING TO PAY FOR THIS INDIGNITY, DRESDEN!
FAMOUS LAST WORDS.
BEING THAT I ONLY KNOW TWO PEOPLE IN TOWN, AND ONE OF THEM WANTED ME GONE, I FIGURED IT WAS PRES.
I WAS WRONG.
IT'S ABOUT TIME, MR. DRESDEN.

CLOSE THE DOOR, PLEASE. I'D RATHER NOBODY *SEE* ME HERE.

NEVER ACTUALLY BEEN *IN* ONE OF THESE ROOMS. NO WONDER WE GET SO FEW VISITORS.

HOW CAN I HELP YOU...?

SHE DIDN'T BOTHER WAITING FOR AN INVITATION--CLEARLY, THIS WAS A WOMAN ACCUSTOMED TO DEFERENCE.

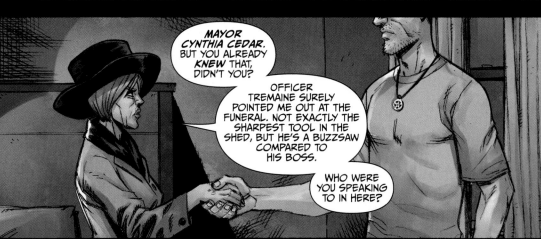

MAYOR CYNTHIA CEDAR. BUT YOU ALREADY *KNEW* THAT, DIDN'T YOU?

OFFICER TREMAINE SURELY POINTED ME OUT AT THE FUNERAL. NOT EXACTLY THE SHARPEST TOOL IN THE SHED, BUT HE'S A BUZZSAW COMPARED TO HIS BOSS.

WHO WERE YOU SPEAKING TO IN HERE?

UH, JUST TALKING TO MY ASSISTANT BACK IN CHICAGO--

NEVERMIND. I'M HERE TO DELIVER A VERY SIMPLE MESSAGE...

NO MATTER WHAT THAT BUFFOON OF A SHERIFF SAYS, *I* WANT YOU STICKING AROUND.

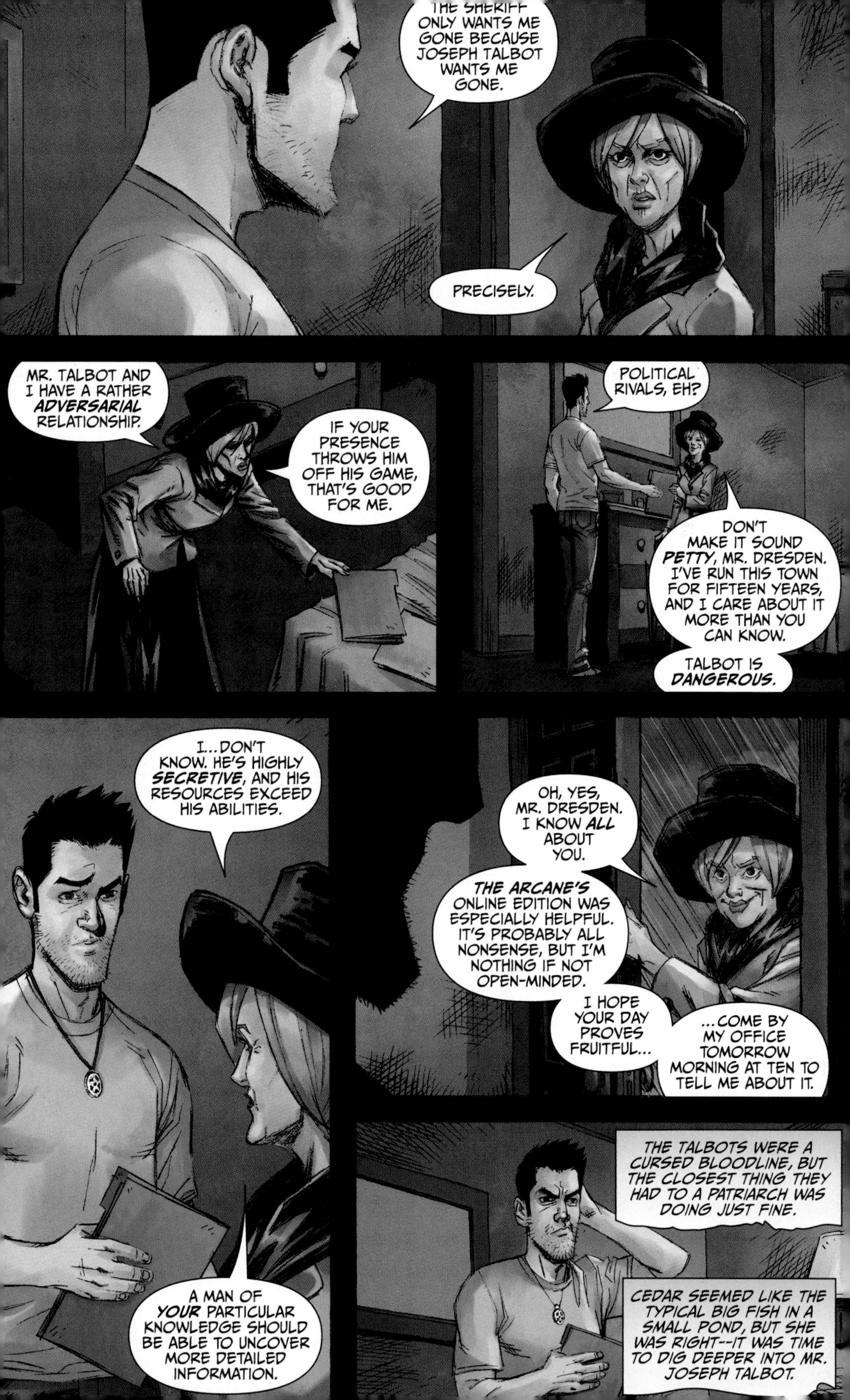

THE SHERIFF ONLY WANTS ME GONE BECAUSE JOSEPH TALBOT WANTS ME GONE.
PRECISELY.
MR. TALBOT AND I HAVE A RATHER *ADVERSARIAL* RELATIONSHIP.
IF YOUR PRESENCE THROWS HIM OFF HIS GAME, THAT'S GOOD FOR ME.
POLITICAL RIVALS, EH?
DON'T MAKE IT SOUND *PETTY*, MR. DRESDEN. I'VE RUN THIS TOWN FOR FIFTEEN YEARS, AND I CARE ABOUT IT MORE THAN YOU CAN KNOW.
TALBOT IS *DANGEROUS.*
I...DON'T KNOW. HE'S HIGHLY *SECRETIVE*, AND HIS RESOURCES EXCEED HIS ABILITIES.
A MAN OF *YOUR* PARTICULAR KNOWLEDGE SHOULD BE ABLE TO UNCOVER MORE DETAILED INFORMATION.
OH, YES, MR. DRESDEN. I KNOW *ALL* ABOUT YOU.
THE ARCANE'S ONLINE EDITION WAS ESPECIALLY HELPFUL. IT'S PROBABLY ALL NONSENSE, BUT I'M NOTHING IF NOT OPEN-MINDED.
I HOPE YOUR DAY PROVES FRUITFUL...
...COME BY MY OFFICE TOMORROW MORNING AT TEN TO TELL ME ABOUT IT.
THE TALBOTS WERE A CURSED BLOODLINE, BUT THE CLOSEST THING THEY HAD TO A PATRIARCH WAS DOING JUST FINE.
CEDAR SEEMED LIKE THE TYPICAL BIG FISH IN A SMALL POND, BUT SHE WAS RIGHT--IT WAS TIME TO DIG DEEPER INTO MR. JOSEPH TALBOT.

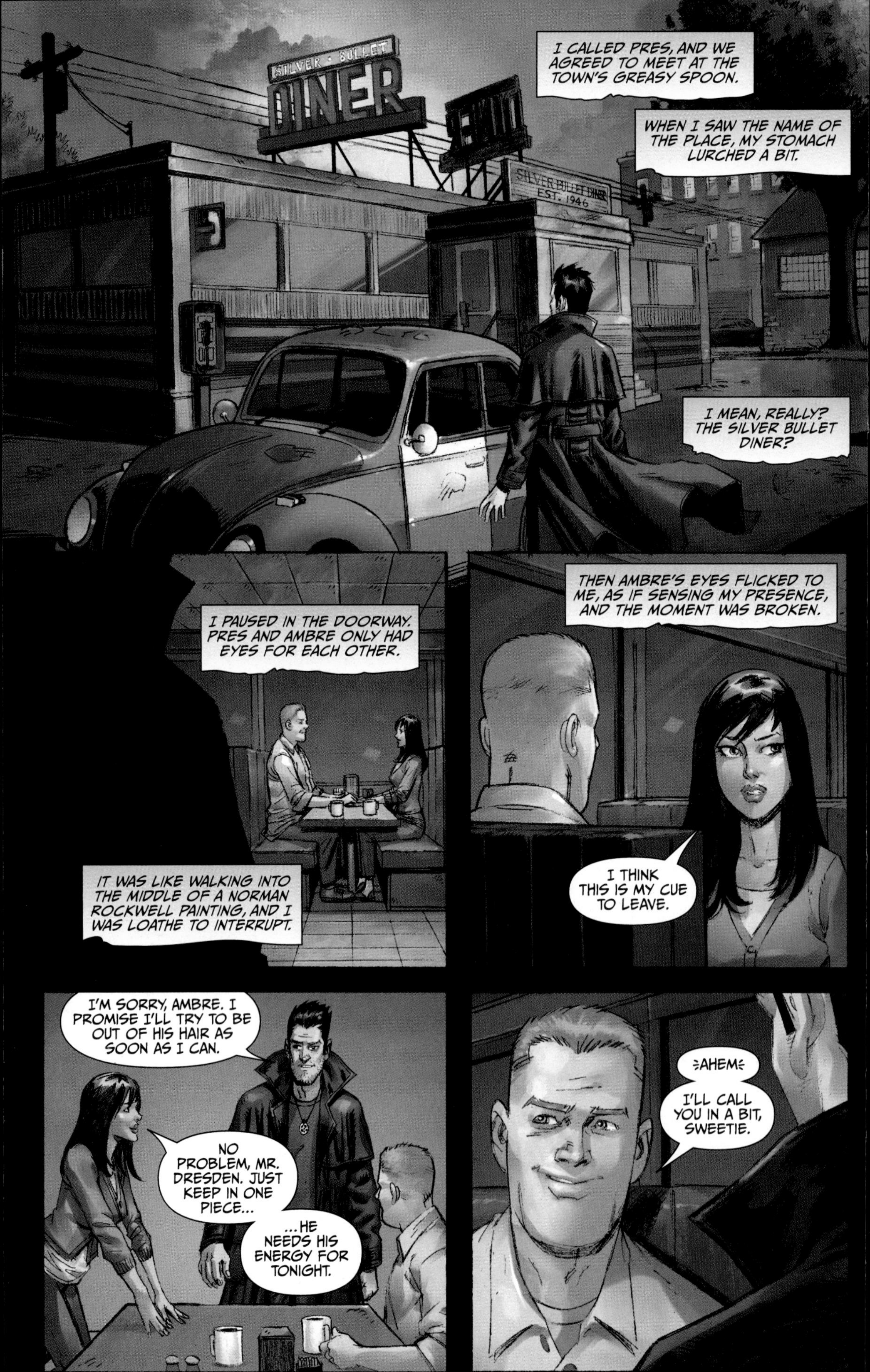
SILVER • BULLET
DINER
SILVER BULLET DINER EST. 1946
I CALLED PRES, AND WE AGREED TO MEET AT THE TOWN'S GREASY SPOON.
WHEN I SAW THE NAME OF THE PLACE, MY STOMACH LURCHED A BIT.
I MEAN, REALLY? THE SILVER BULLET DINER?
I PAUSED IN THE DOORWAY. PRES AND AMBRE ONLY HAD EYES FOR EACH OTHER.
IT WAS LIKE WALKING INTO THE MIDDLE OF A NORMAN ROCKWELL PAINTING, AND I WAS LOATHE TO INTERRUPT.
THEN AMBRE'S EYES FLICKED TO ME, AS IF SENSING MY PRESENCE, AND THE MOMENT WAS BROKEN.
I THINK THIS IS MY CUE TO LEAVE.
I'M SORRY, AMBRE. I PROMISE I'LL TRY TO BE OUT OF HIS HAIR AS SOON AS I CAN.
NO PROBLEM, MR. DRESDEN. JUST KEEP IN ONE PIECE...
...HE NEEDS HIS ENERGY FOR TONIGHT.
AHEM
I'LL CALL YOU IN A BIT, SWEETIE.

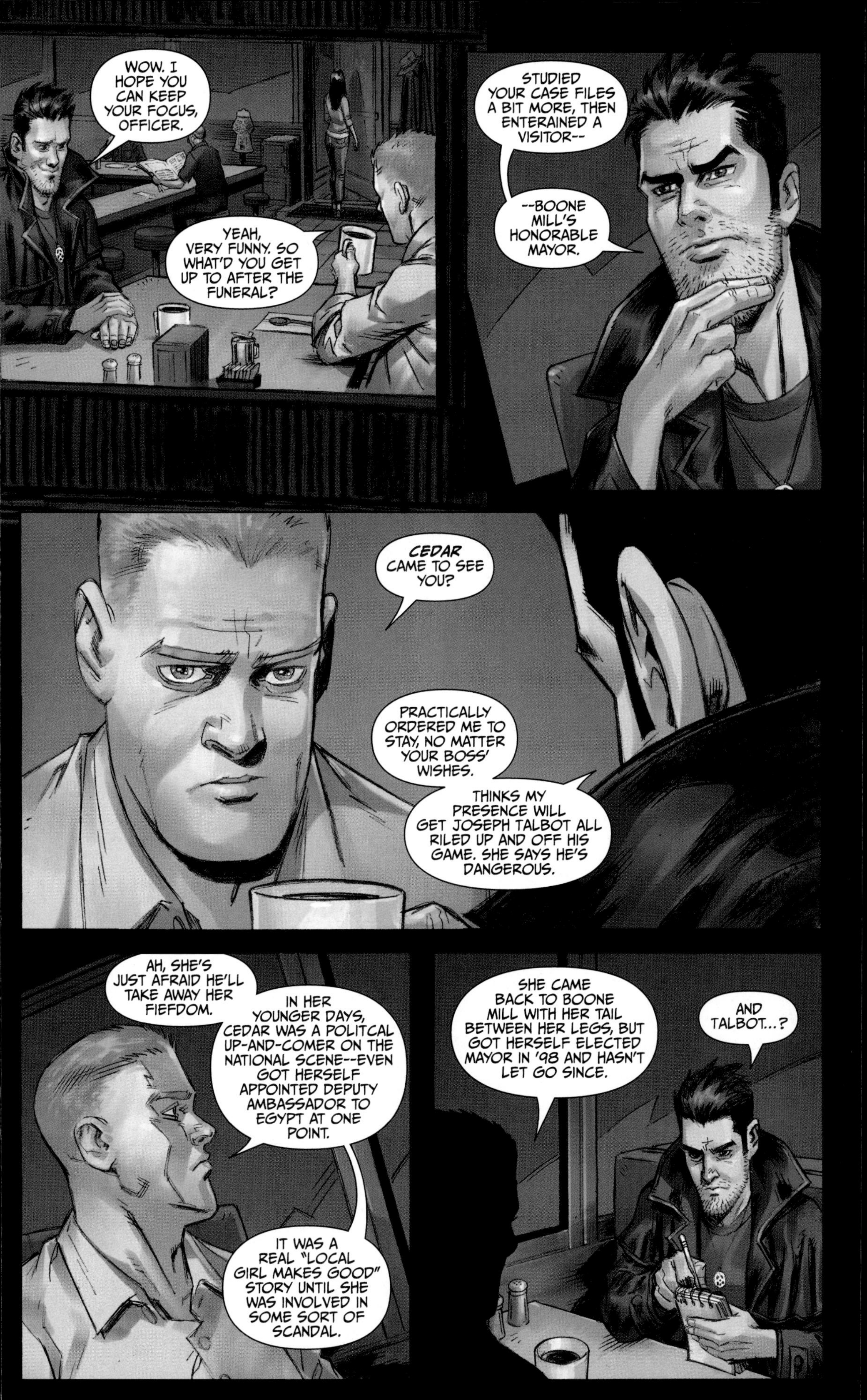
WOW. I HOPE YOU CAN KEEP YOUR FOCUS, OFFICER.
YEAH, VERY FUNNY. SO WHAT'D YOU GET UP TO AFTER THE FUNERAL?
STUDIED YOUR CASE FILES A BIT MORE, THEN ENTERAINED A VISITOR--
--BOONE MILL'S HONORABLE MAYOR.
CEDAR CAME TO SEE YOU?
PRACTICALLY ORDERED ME TO STAY, NO MATTER YOUR BOSS' WISHES.
THINKS MY PRESENCE WILL GET JOSEPH TALBOT ALL RILED UP AND OFF HIS GAME. SHE SAYS HE'S DANGEROUS.
AH, SHE'S JUST AFRAID HE'LL TAKE AWAY HER FIEFDOM.
IN HER YOUNGER DAYS, CEDAR WAS A POLITCAL UP-AND-COMER ON THE NATIONAL SCENE--EVEN GOT HERSELF APPOINTED DEPUTY AMBASSADOR TO EGYPT AT ONE POINT.
IT WAS A REAL "LOCAL GIRL MAKES GOOD" STORY UNTIL SHE WAS INVOLVED IN SOME SORT OF SCANDAL.
SHE CAME BACK TO BOONE MILL WITH HER TAIL BETWEEN HER LEGS, BUT GOT HERSELF ELECTED MAYOR IN '98 AND HASN'T LET GO SINCE.
AND TALBOT...?

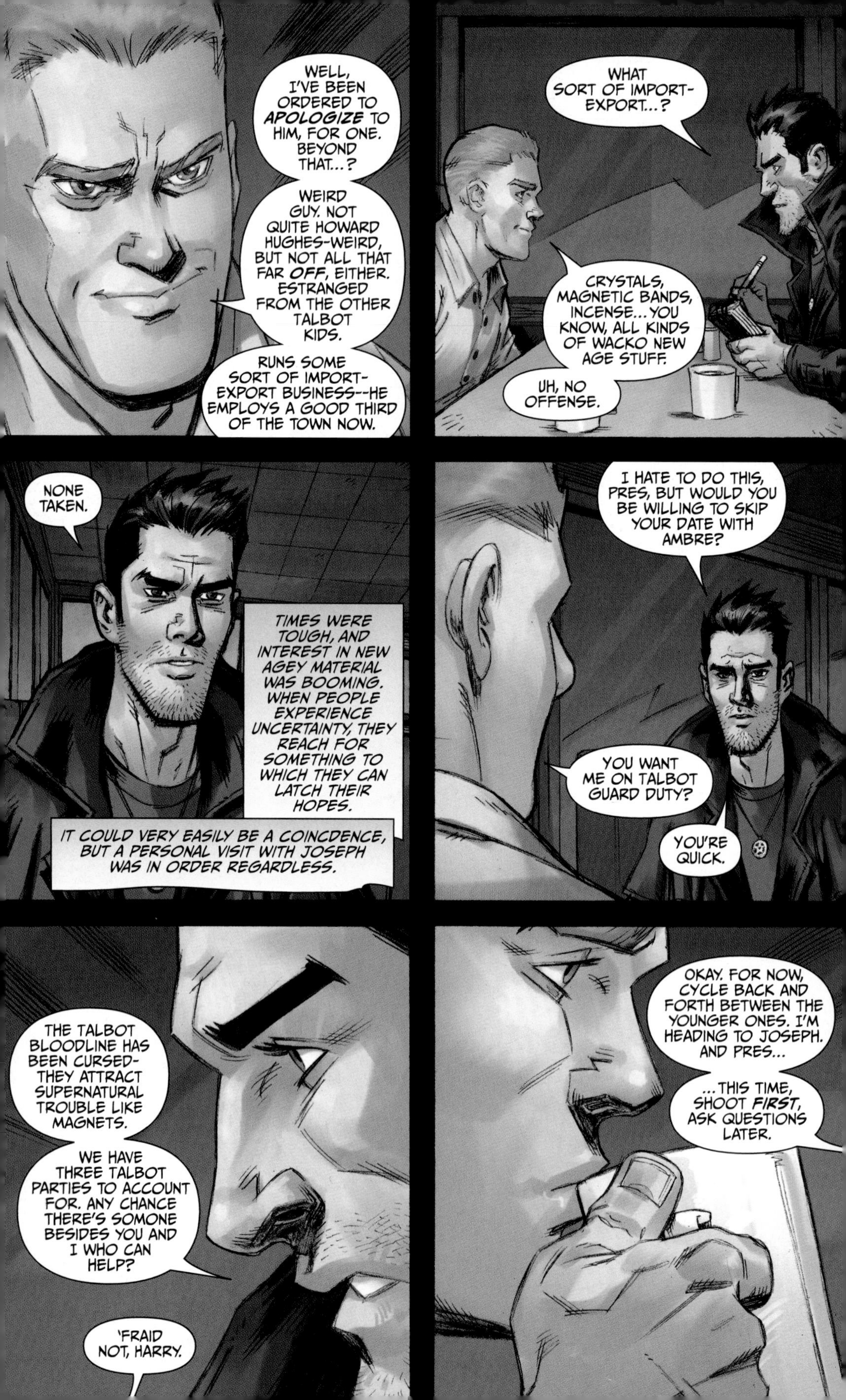
WELL, I'VE BEEN ORDERED TO APOLOGIZE TO HIM, FOR ONE. BEYOND THAT...?
WEIRD GUY. NOT QUITE HOWARD HUGHES-WEIRD, BUT NOT ALL THAT FAR OFF, EITHER. ESTRANGED FROM THE OTHER TALBOT KIDS.
RUNS SOME SORT OF IMPORT-EXPORT BUSINESS--HE EMPLOYS A GOOD THIRD OF THE TOWN NOW.
WHAT SORT OF IMPORT-EXPORT...?
CRYSTALS, MAGNETIC BANDS, INCENSE... YOU KNOW, ALL KINDS OF WACKO NEW AGE STUFF.
UH, NO OFFENSE.
NONE TAKEN.
TIMES WERE TOUGH, AND INTEREST IN NEW AGEY MATERIAL WAS BOOMING. WHEN PEOPLE EXPERIENCE UNCERTAINTY, THEY REACH FOR SOMETHING TO WHICH THEY CAN LATCH THEIR HOPES.
IT COULD VERY EASILY BE A COINCDENCE, BUT A PERSONAL VISIT WITH JOSEPH WAS IN ORDER REGARDLESS.
I HATE TO DO THIS, PRES, BUT WOULD YOU BE WILLING TO SKIP YOUR DATE WITH AMBRE?
YOU WANT ME ON TALBOT GUARD DUTY?
YOU'RE QUICK.
THE TALBOT BLOODLINE HAS BEEN CURSED-THEY ATTRACT SUPERNATURAL TROUBLE LIKE MAGNETS.
WE HAVE THREE TALBOT PARTIES TO ACCOUNT FOR. ANY CHANCE THERE'S SOMONE BESIDES YOU AND I WHO CAN HELP?
'FRAID NOT, HARRY.
OKAY. FOR NOW, CYCLE BACK AND FORTH BETWEEN THE YOUNGER ONES. I'M HEADING TO JOSEPH. AND PRES...
...THIS TIME, SHOOT FIRST, ASK QUESTIONS LATER.

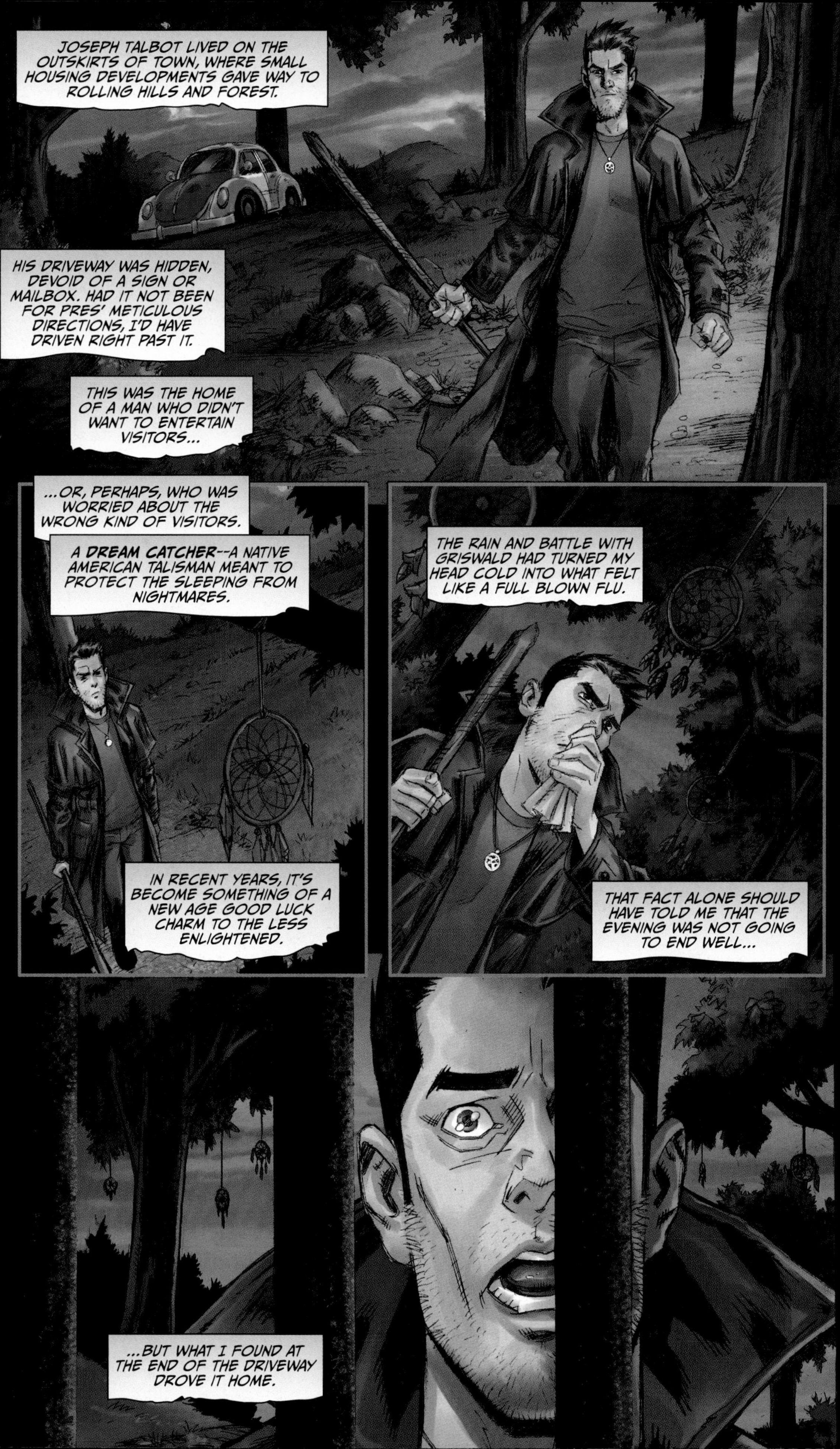
JOSEPH TALBOT LIVED ON THE OUTSKIRTS OF TOWN, WHERE SMALL HOUSING DEVELOPMENTS GAVE WAY TO ROLLING HILLS AND FOREST.
HIS DRIVEWAY WAS HIDDEN, DEVOID OF A SIGN OR MAILBOX. HAD IT NOT BEEN FOR PRES' METICULOUS DIRECTIONS, I'D HAVE DRIVEN RIGHT PAST IT.
THIS WAS THE HOME OF A MAN WHO DIDN'T WANT TO ENTERTAIN VISITORS...
...OR, PERHAPS, WHO WAS WORRIED ABOUT THE WRONG KIND OF VISITORS.
A DREAM CATCHER--A NATIVE AMERICAN TALISMAN MEANT TO PROTECT THE SLEEPING FROM NIGHTMARES.
IN RECENT YEARS, IT'S BECOME SOMETHING OF A NEW AGE GOOD LUCK CHARM TO THE LESS ENLIGHTENED.
THE RAIN AND BATTLE WITH GRISWALD HAD TURNED MY HEAD COLD INTO WHAT FELT LIKE A FULL BLOWN FLU.
THAT FACT ALONE SHOULD HAVE TOLD ME THAT THE EVENING WAS NOT GOING TO END WELL...
...BUT WHAT I FOUND AT THE END OF THE DRIVEWAY DROVE IT HOME.

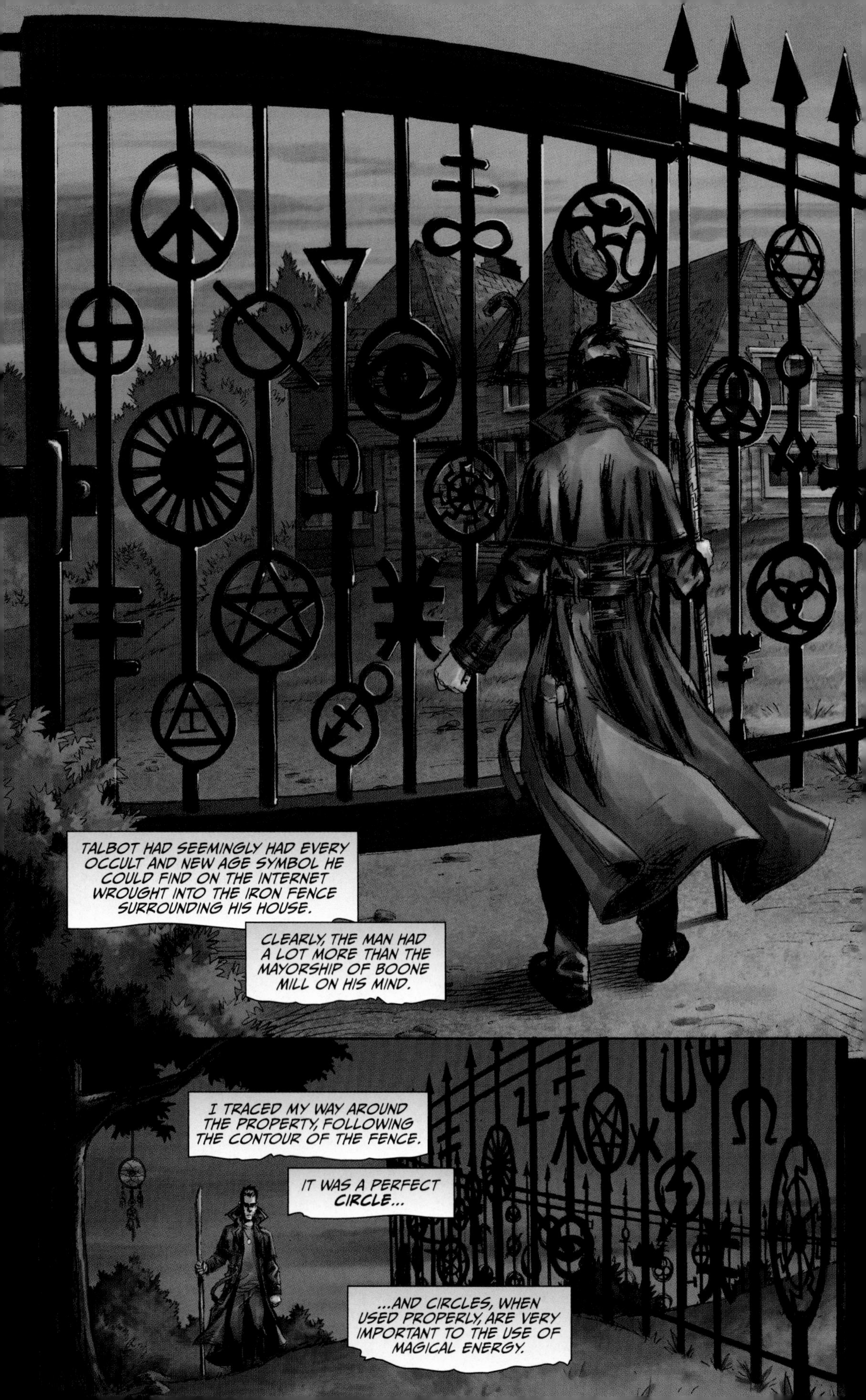
TALBOT HAD SEEMINGLY HAD EVERY OCCULT AND NEW AGE SYMBOL HE COULD FIND ON THE INTERNET WROUGHT INTO THE IRON FENCE SURROUNDING HIS HOUSE.
CLEARLY, THE MAN HAD A LOT MORE THAN THE MAYORSHIP OF BOONE MILL ON HIS MIND.
I TRACED MY WAY AROUND THE PROPERTY, FOLLOWING THE CONTOUR OF THE FENCE.
IT WAS A PERFECT **CIRCLE**...
...AND CIRCLES, WHEN USED PROPERLY, ARE VERY IMPORTANT TO THE USE OF MAGICAL ENERGY.

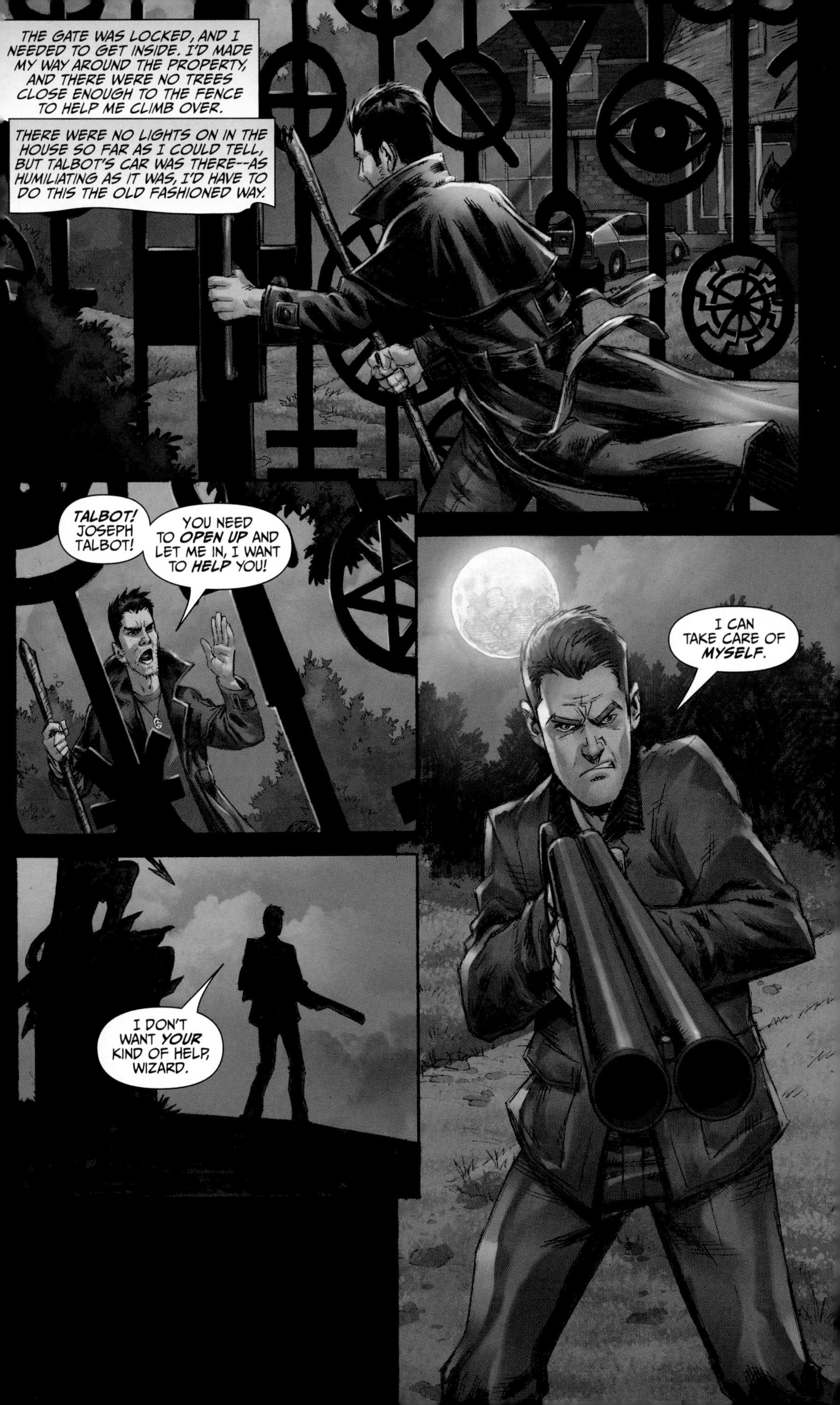
THE GATE WAS LOCKED, AND I NEEDED TO GET INSIDE. I'D MADE MY WAY AROUND THE PROPERTY, AND THERE WERE NO TREES CLOSE ENOUGH TO THE FENCE TO HELP ME CLIMB OVER.
THERE WERE NO LIGHTS ON IN THE HOUSE SO FAR AS I COULD TELL, BUT TALBOT'S CAR WAS THERE--AS HUMILIATING AS IT WAS, I'D HAVE TO DO THIS THE OLD FASHIONED WAY.
TALBOT! JOSEPH TALBOT!
YOU NEED TO OPEN UP AND LET ME IN, I WANT TO HELP YOU!
I CAN TAKE CARE OF MYSELF.
I DON'T WANT YOUR KIND OF HELP, WIZARD.

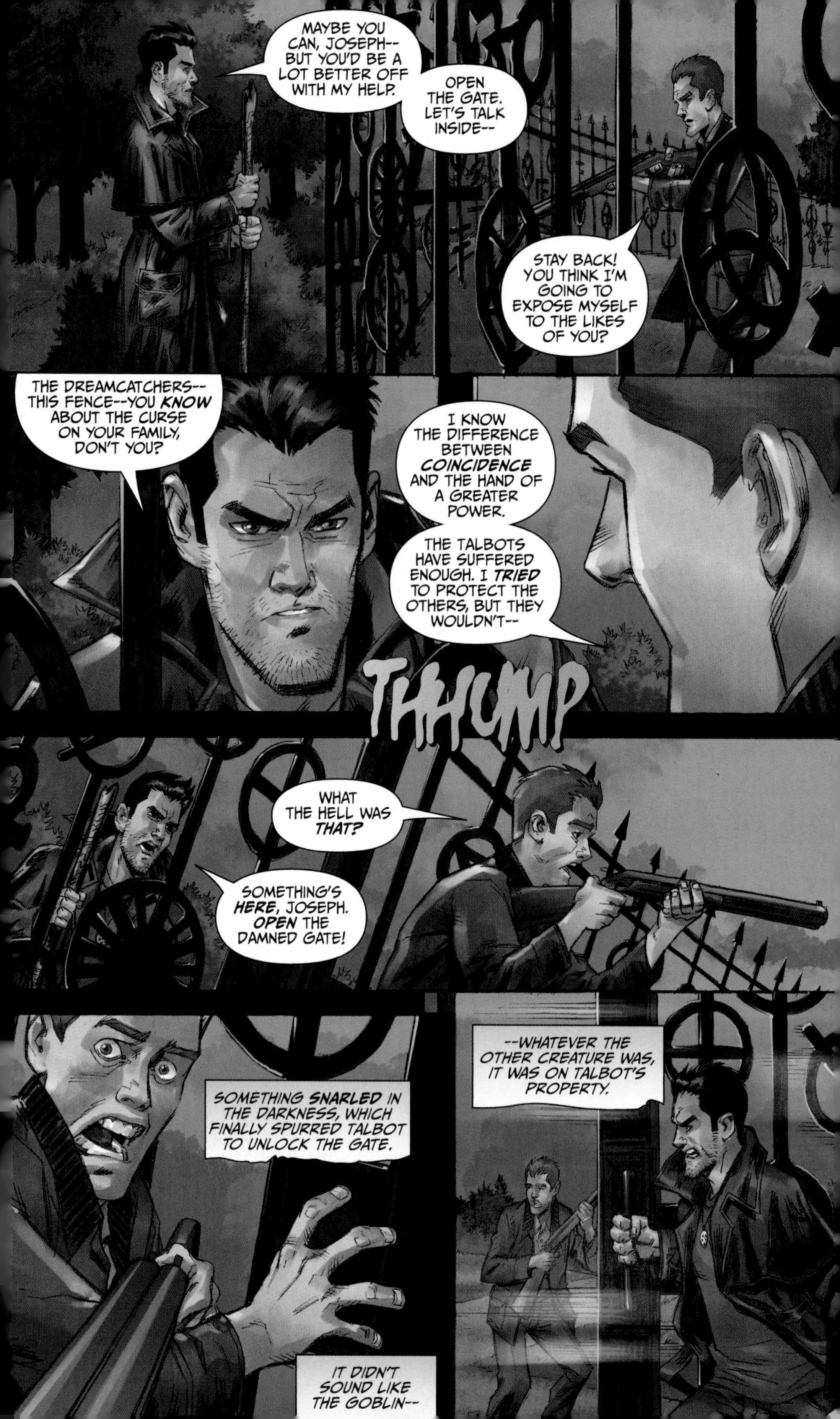
MAYBE YOU CAN, JOSEPH-- BUT YOU'D BE A LOT BETTER OFF WITH MY HELP.
OPEN THE GATE. LET'S TALK INSIDE--
STAY BACK! YOU THINK I'M GOING TO EXPOSE MYSELF TO THE LIKES OF YOU?
THE DREAMCATCHERS-- THIS FENCE--YOU KNOW ABOUT THE CURSE ON YOUR FAMILY, DON'T YOU?
I KNOW THE DIFFERENCE BETWEEN COINCIDENCE AND THE HAND OF A GREATER POWER.
THE TALBOTS HAVE SUFFERED ENOUGH. I TRIED TO PROTECT THE OTHERS, BUT THEY WOULDN'T--
THHUMP
WHAT THE HELL WAS THAT?
SOMETHING'S HERE, JOSEPH. OPEN THE DAMNED GATE!
SOMETHING SNARLED IN THE DARKNESS, WHICH FINALLY SPURRED TALBOT TO UNLOCK THE GATE.
IT DIDN'T SOUND LIKE THE GOBLIN--
--WHATEVER THE OTHER CREATURE WAS, IT WAS ON TALBOT'S PROPERTY.

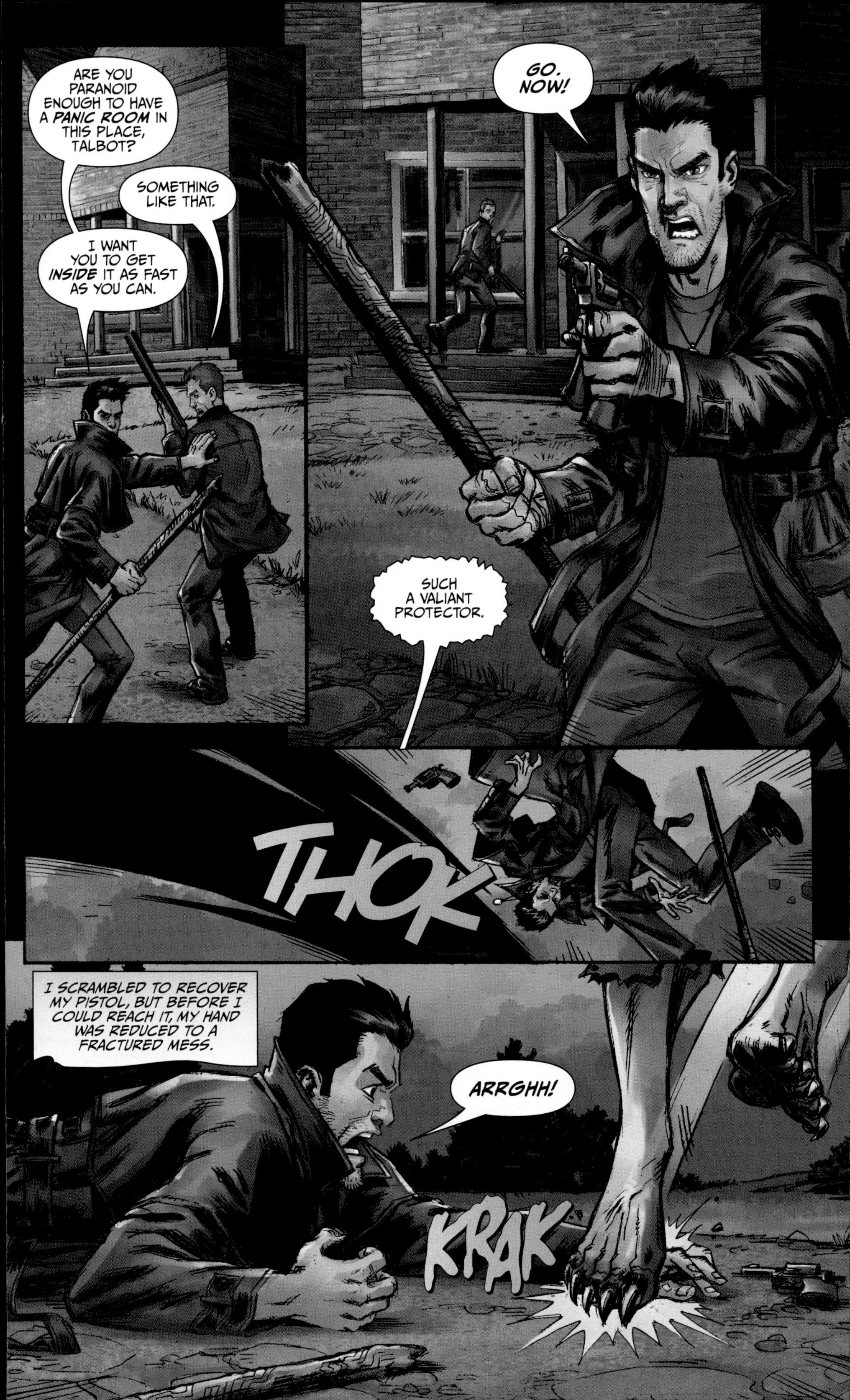
ARE YOU PARANOID ENOUGH TO HAVE A **PANIC ROOM** IN THIS PLACE, TALBOT?
SOMETHING LIKE THAT.
I WANT YOU TO GET **INSIDE** IT AS FAST AS YOU CAN.
GO. NOW!
SUCH A VALIANT PROTECTOR.
THOK
I SCRAMBLED TO RECOVER MY PISTOL, BUT BEFORE I COULD REACH IT, MY HAND WAS REDUCED TO A FRACTURED MESS.
ARRGHH!
KRAK

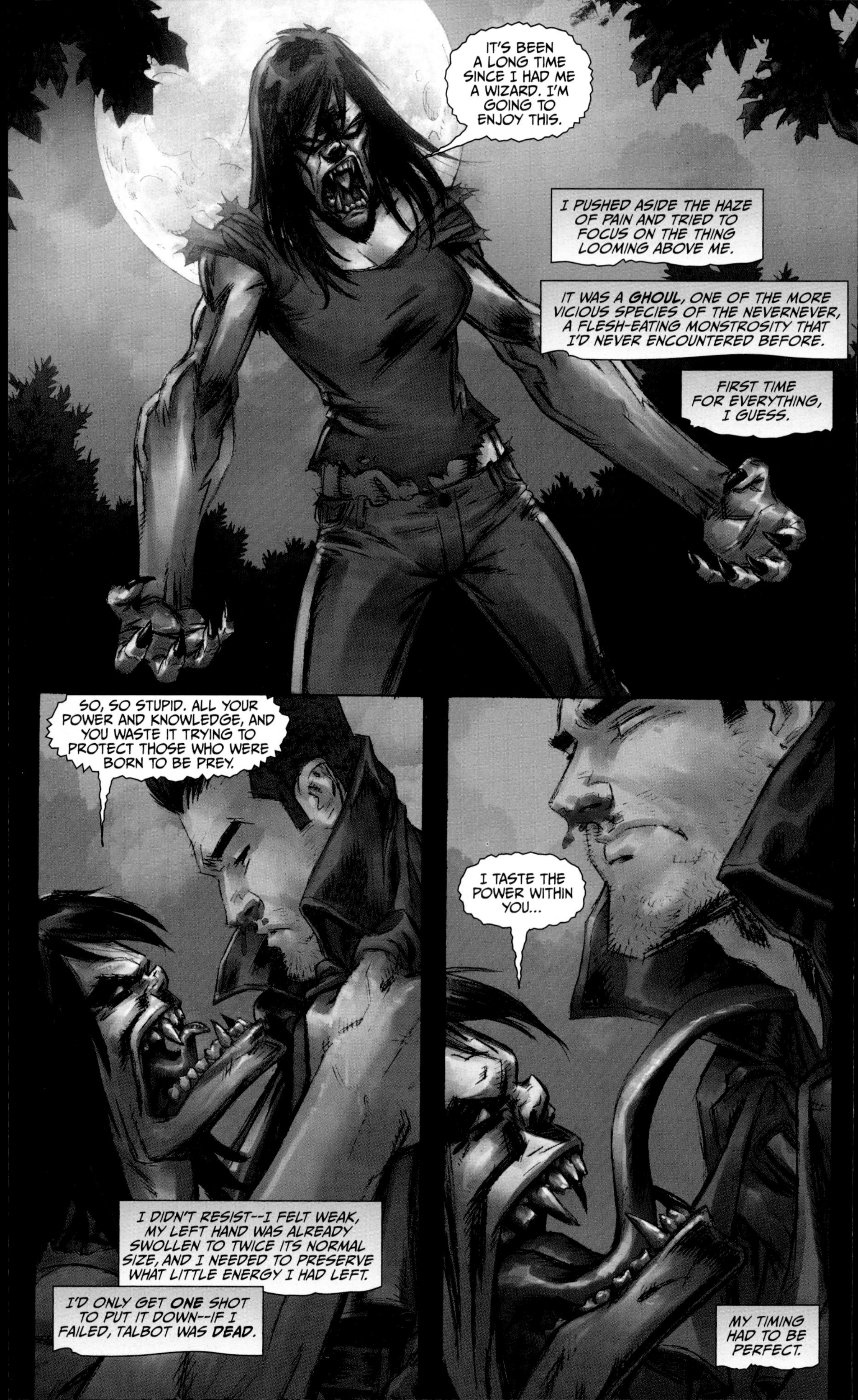
IT'S BEEN A LONG TIME SINCE I HAD ME A WIZARD. I'M GOING TO ENJOY THIS.
I PUSHED ASIDE THE HAZE OF PAIN AND TRIED TO FOCUS ON THE THING LOOMING ABOVE ME.
IT WAS A GHOUL, ONE OF THE MORE VICIOUS SPECIES OF THE NEVERNEVER, A FLESH-EATING MONSTROSITY THAT I'D NEVER ENCOUNTERED BEFORE.
FIRST TIME FOR EVERYTHING, I GUESS.
SO, SO STUPID. ALL YOUR POWER AND KNOWLEDGE, AND YOU WASTE IT TRYING TO PROTECT THOSE WHO WERE BORN TO BE PREY.
I DIDN'T RESIST--I FELT WEAK, MY LEFT HAND WAS ALREADY SWOLLEN TO TWICE ITS NORMAL SIZE, AND I NEEDED TO PRESERVE WHAT LITTLE ENERGY I HAD LEFT.
I'D ONLY GET ONE SHOT TO PUT IT DOWN--IF I FAILED, TALBOT WAS DEAD.
I TASTE THE POWER WITHIN YOU...
MY TIMING HAD TO BE PERFECT.

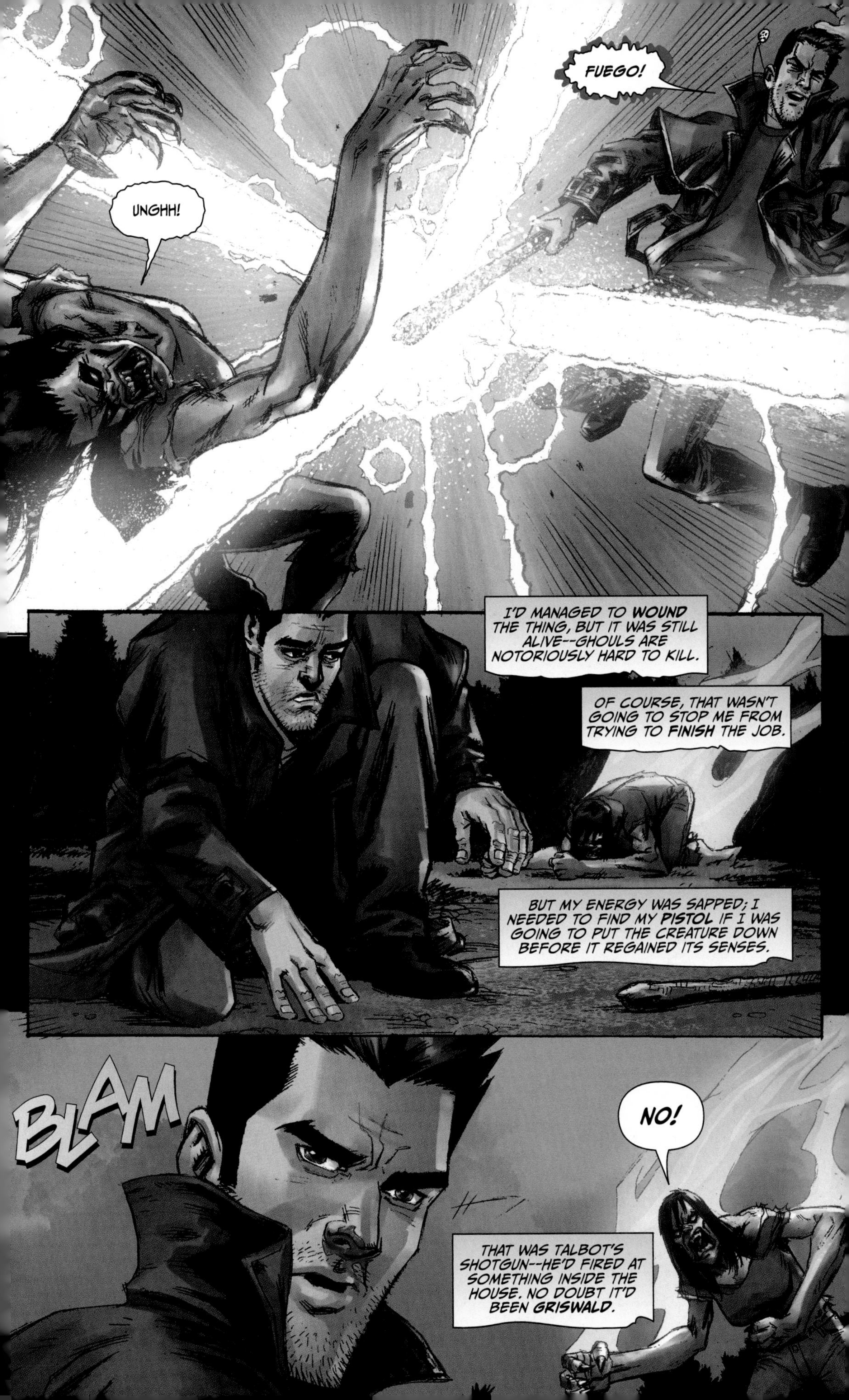
FUEGO!
UNGHH!
I'D MANAGED TO WOUND THE THING, BUT IT WAS STILL ALIVE--GHOULS ARE NOTORIOUSLY HARD TO KILL.
OF COURSE, THAT WASN'T GOING TO STOP ME FROM TRYING TO FINISH THE JOB.
BUT MY ENERGY WAS SAPPED; I NEEDED TO FIND MY PISTOL IF I WAS GOING TO PUT THE CREATURE DOWN BEFORE IT REGAINED ITS SENSES.
BLAM
NO!
THAT WAS TALBOT'S SHOTGUN--HE'D FIRED AT SOMETHING INSIDE THE HOUSE. NO DOUBT IT'D BEEN GRISWALD.

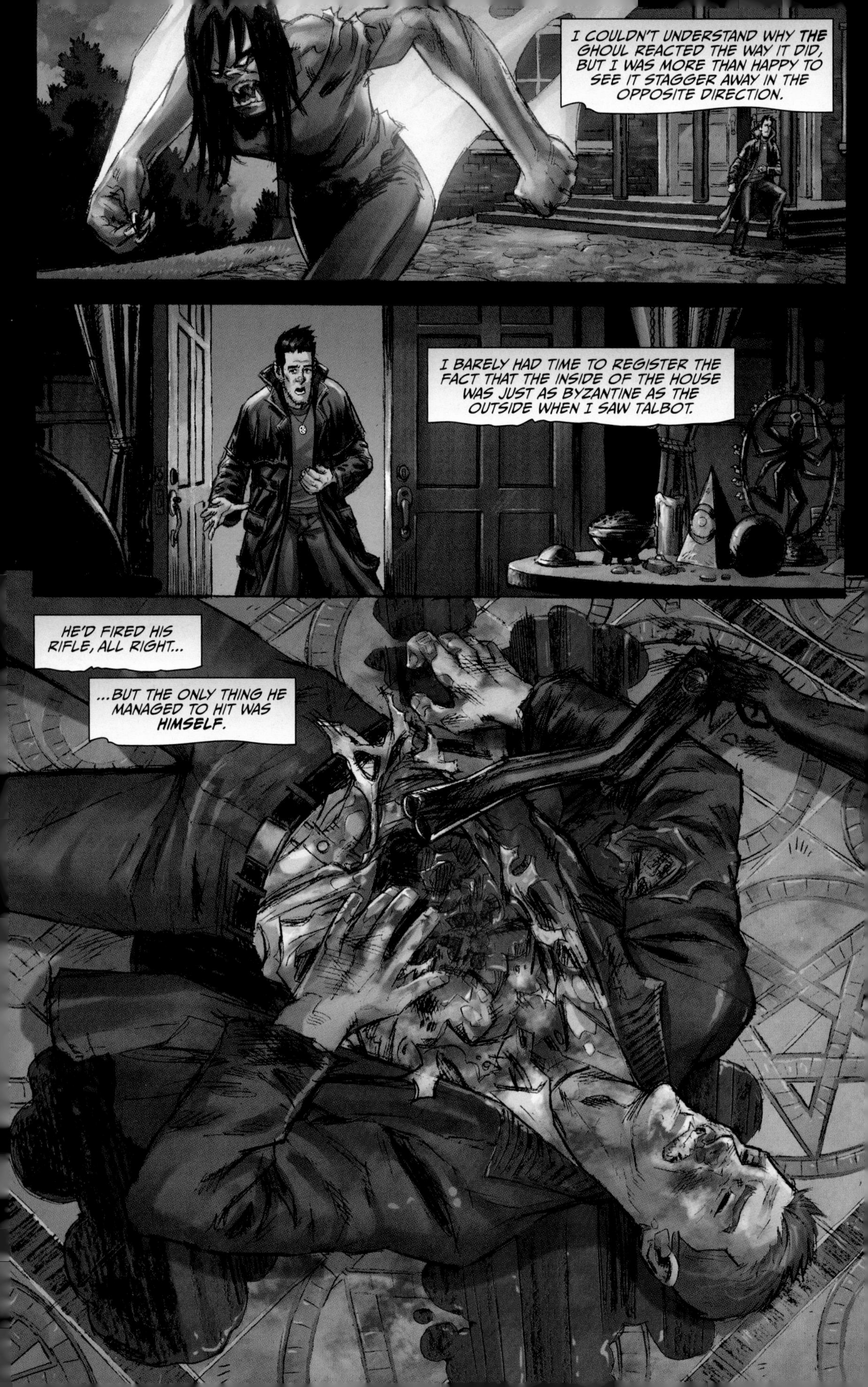
I COULDN'T UNDERSTAND WHY THE GHOUL REACTED THE WAY IT DID, BUT I WAS MORE THAN HAPPY TO SEE IT STAGGER AWAY IN THE OPPOSITE DIRECTION.
I BARELY HAD TIME TO REGISTER THE FACT THAT THE INSIDE OF THE HOUSE WAS JUST AS BYZANTINE AS THE OUTSIDE WHEN I SAW TALBOT.
HE'D FIRED HIS RIFLE, ALL RIGHT...
...BUT THE ONLY THING HE MANAGED TO HIT WAS **HIMSELF**.

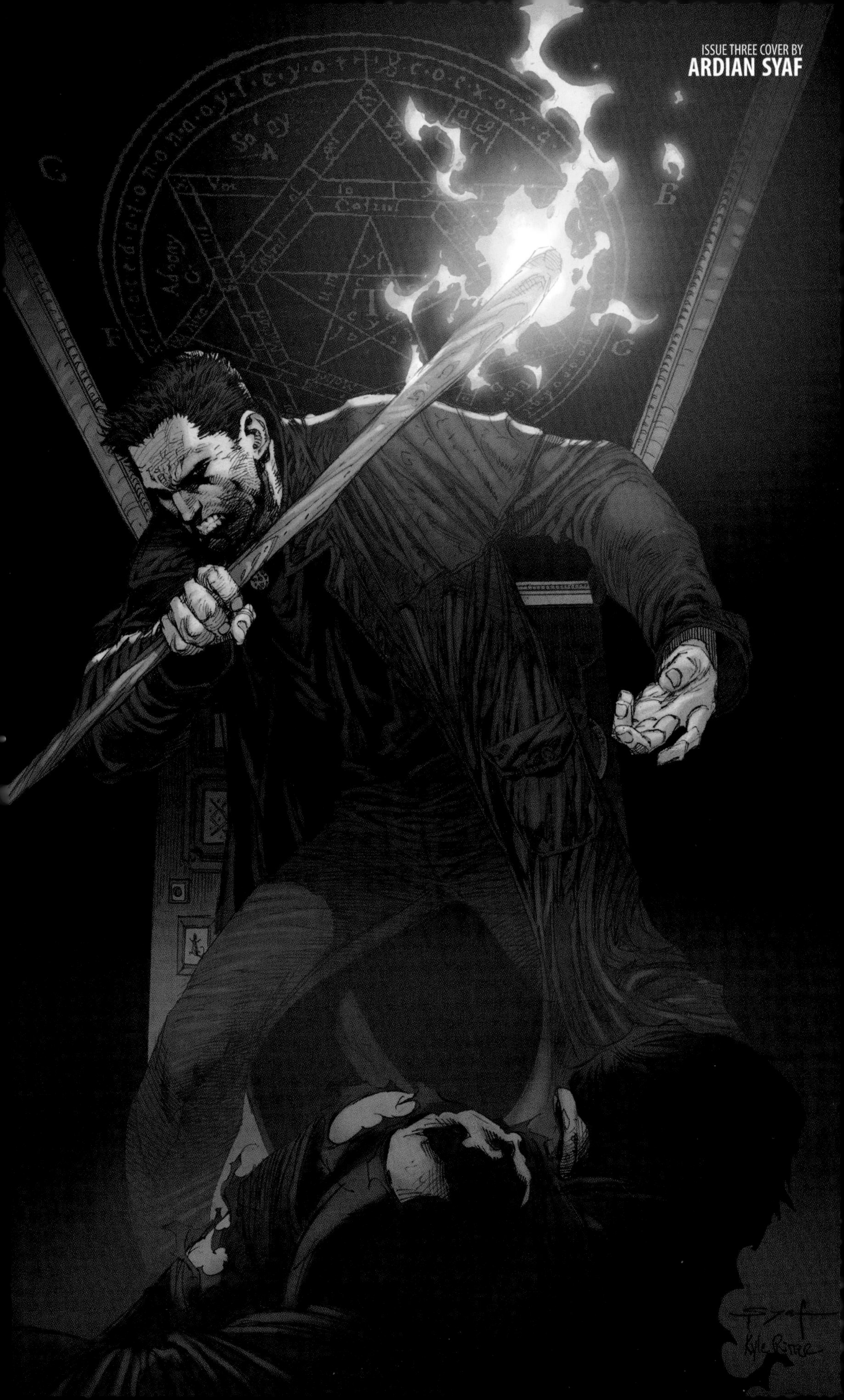

ISSUE THREE COVER BY
ARDIAN SYAF

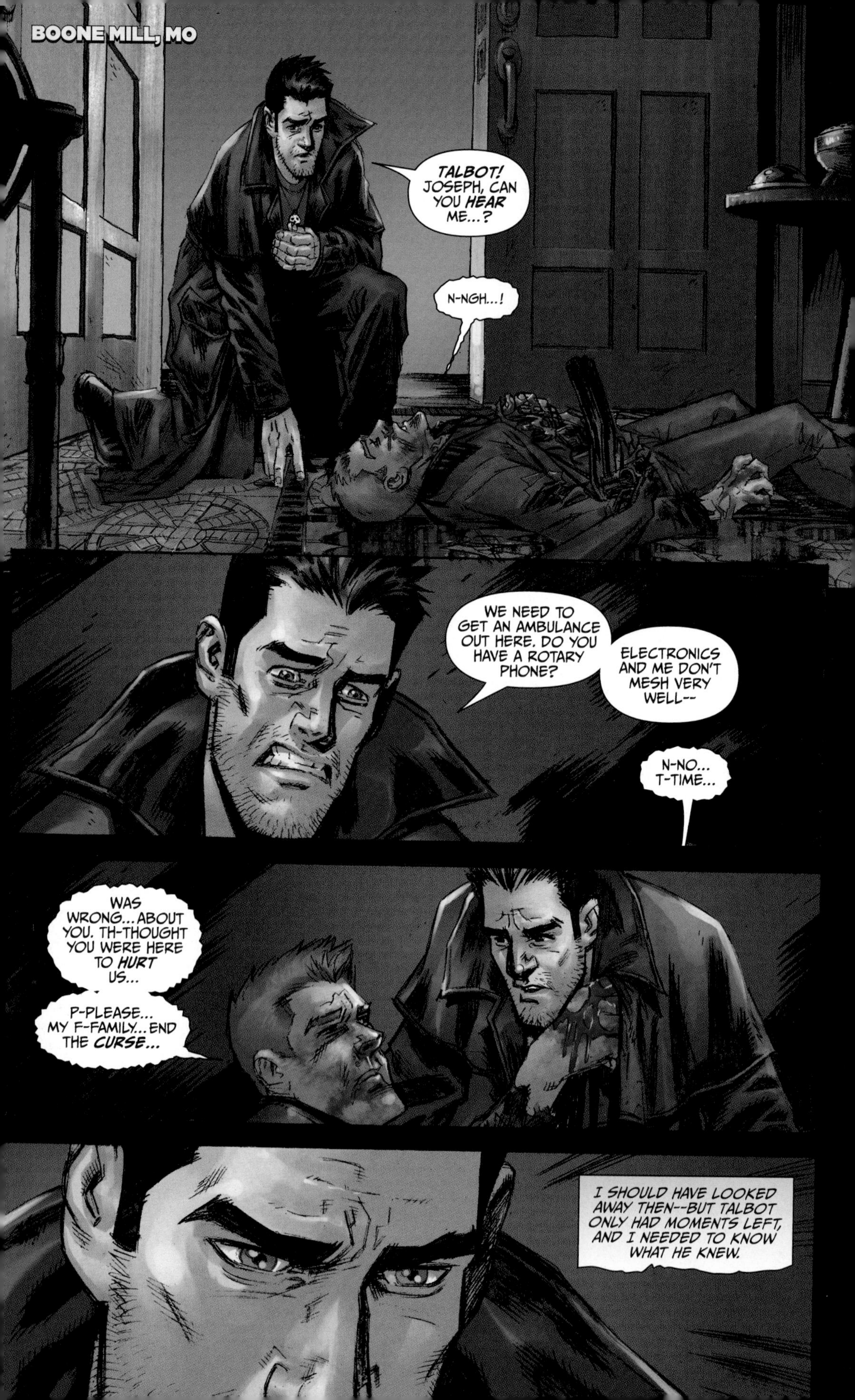
BOONE MILL, MO
TALBOT! JOSEPH, CAN YOU HEAR ME...?
N-NGH...!
WE NEED TO GET AN AMBULANCE OUT HERE. DO YOU HAVE A ROTARY PHONE?
ELECTRONICS AND ME DON'T MESH VERY WELL--
N-NO... T-TIME...
WAS WRONG...ABOUT YOU. TH-THOUGHT YOU WERE HERE TO HURT US...
P-PLEASE... MY F-FAMILY...END THE CURSE...
I SHOULD HAVE LOOKED AWAY THEN--BUT TALBOT ONLY HAD MOMENTS LEFT, AND I NEEDED TO KNOW WHAT HE KNEW.

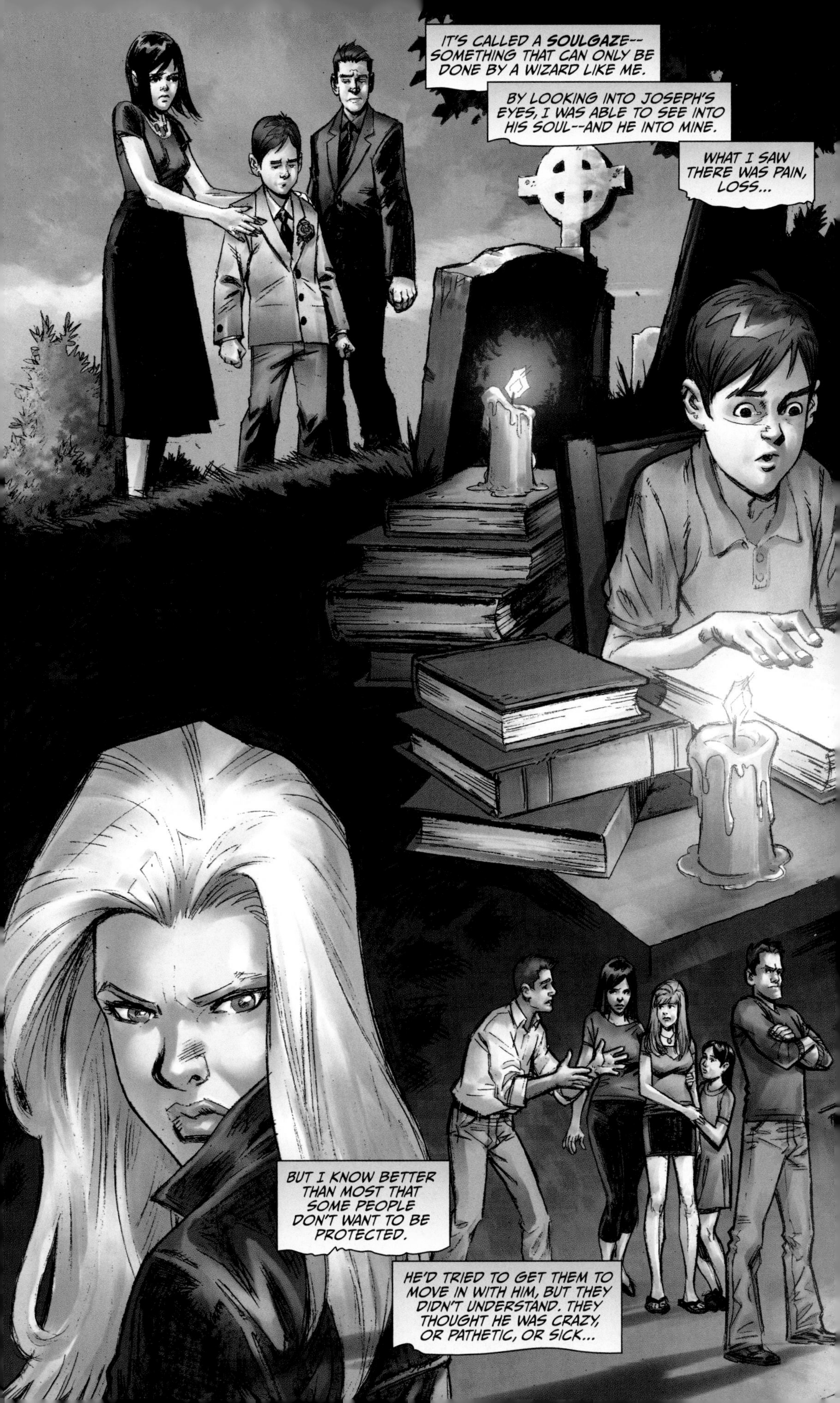
IT'S CALLED A SOULGAZE--SOMETHING THAT CAN ONLY BE DONE BY A WIZARD LIKE ME.
BY LOOKING INTO JOSEPH'S EYES, I WAS ABLE TO SEE INTO HIS SOUL--AND HE INTO MINE.
WHAT I SAW THERE WAS PAIN, LOSS...
BUT I KNOW BETTER THAN MOST THAT SOME PEOPLE DON'T WANT TO BE PROTECTED.
HE'D TRIED TO GET THEM TO MOVE IN WITH HIM, BUT THEY DIDN'T UNDERSTAND. THEY THOUGHT HE WAS CRAZY, OR PATHETIC, OR SICK...

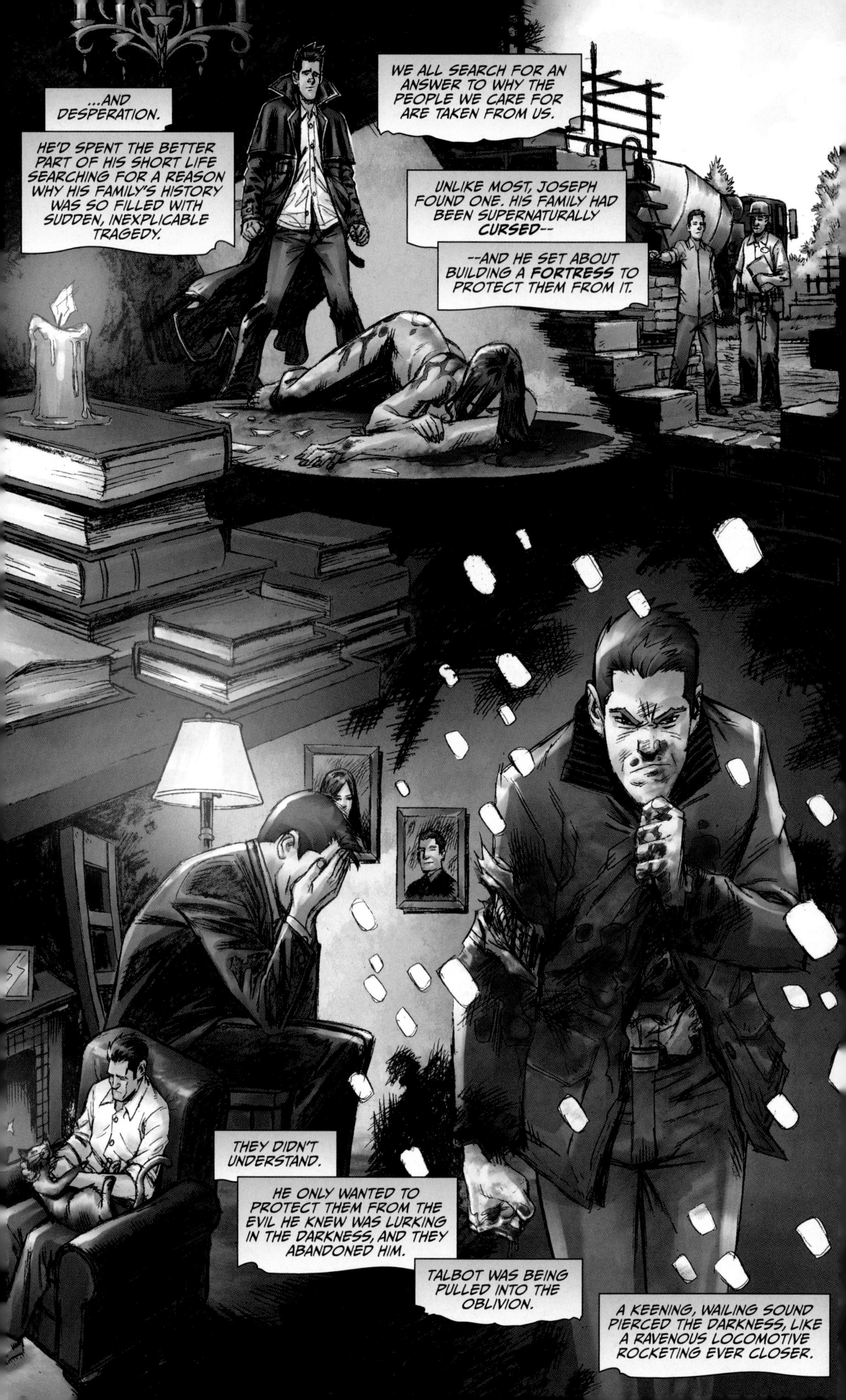
...AND DESPERATION.
HE'D SPENT THE BETTER PART OF HIS SHORT LIFE SEARCHING FOR A REASON WHY HIS FAMILY'S HISTORY WAS SO FILLED WITH SUDDEN, INEXPLICABLE TRAGEDY.
WE ALL SEARCH FOR AN ANSWER TO WHY THE PEOPLE WE CARE FOR ARE TAKEN FROM US.
UNLIKE MOST, JOSEPH FOUND ONE. HIS FAMILY HAD BEEN SUPERNATURALLY CURSED--
--AND HE SET ABOUT BUILDING A FORTRESS TO PROTECT THEM FROM IT.
THEY DIDN'T UNDERSTAND.
HE ONLY WANTED TO PROTECT THEM FROM THE EVIL HE KNEW WAS LURKING IN THE DARKNESS, AND THEY ABANDONED HIM.
TALBOT WAS BEING PULLED INTO THE OBLIVION.
A KEENING, WAILING SOUND PIERCED THE DARKNESS, LIKE A RAVENOUS LOCOMOTIVE ROCKETING EVER CLOSER.

I FELT MYSELF BEING DRAWN INTO THE HELLISH UNDERTOW, TOO...BUT IT WAS TALBOT WHO HELD ME BACK.

NO, MISTER DRESDEN. YOU NEED TO STAY. *YOU'RE* THE ONLY ONE WHO CAN SAVE THEM...

...YOU'RE THE ONLY ONE WHO CAN FREE THEM FROM THE CURSE.

AND LIKE THAT, HE WAS GONE.

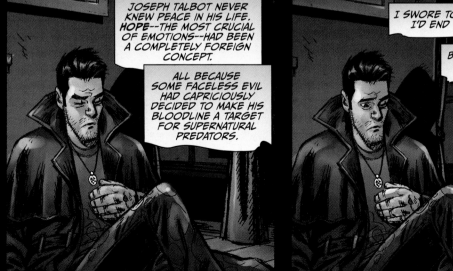

JOSEPH TALBOT NEVER KNEW PEACE IN HIS LIFE. *HOPE*--THE MOST CRUCIAL OF EMOTIONS--HAD BEEN A COMPLETELY FOREIGN CONCEPT.

ALL BECAUSE SOME FACELESS EVIL HAD CAPRICIOUSLY DECIDED TO MAKE HIS BLOODLINE A TARGET FOR SUPERNATURAL PREDATORS.

I SWORE TO MYSELF THAT I'D END THE CURSE.

BUT I WAS GOING TO NEED SOME HELP.

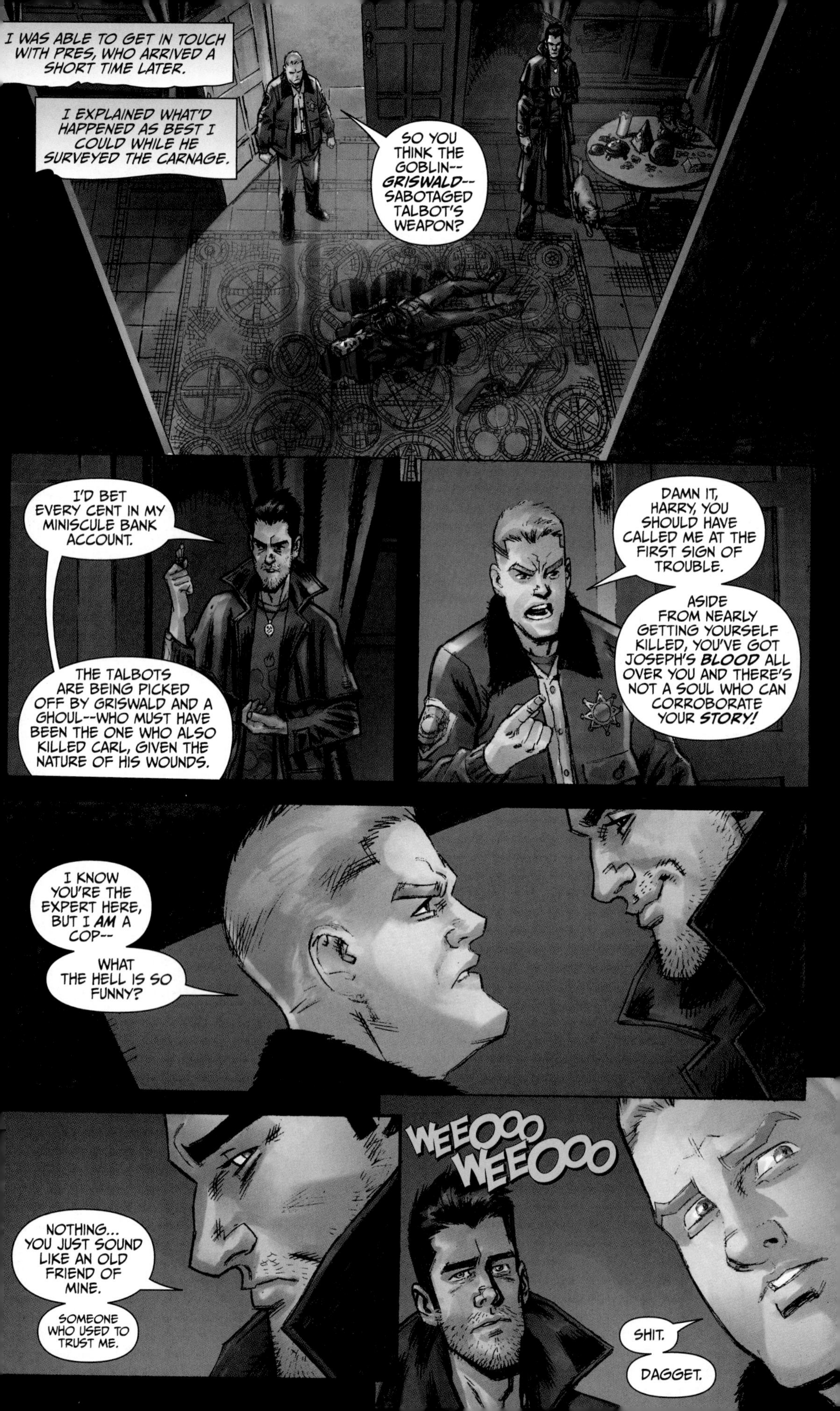
I WAS ABLE TO GET IN TOUCH WITH PRES, WHO ARRIVED A SHORT TIME LATER.
I EXPLAINED WHAT'D HAPPENED AS BEST I COULD WHILE HE SURVEYED THE CARNAGE.
SO YOU THINK THE GOBLIN-- GRISWALD-- SABOTAGED TALBOT'S WEAPON?
I'D BET EVERY CENT IN MY MINISCULE BANK ACCOUNT.
THE TALBOTS ARE BEING PICKED OFF BY GRISWALD AND A GHOUL--WHO MUST HAVE BEEN THE ONE WHO ALSO KILLED CARL, GIVEN THE NATURE OF HIS WOUNDS.
DAMN IT, HARRY, YOU SHOULD HAVE CALLED ME AT THE FIRST SIGN OF TROUBLE.
ASIDE FROM NEARLY GETTING YOURSELF KILLED, YOU'VE GOT JOSEPH'S BLOOD ALL OVER YOU AND THERE'S NOT A SOUL WHO CAN CORROBORATE YOUR STORY!
I KNOW YOU'RE THE EXPERT HERE, BUT I AM A COP--
WHAT THE HELL IS SO FUNNY?
NOTHING... YOU JUST SOUND LIKE AN OLD FRIEND OF MINE.
SOMEONE WHO USED TO TRUST ME.
WEEOOO WEEOOO
SHIT.
DAGGET.

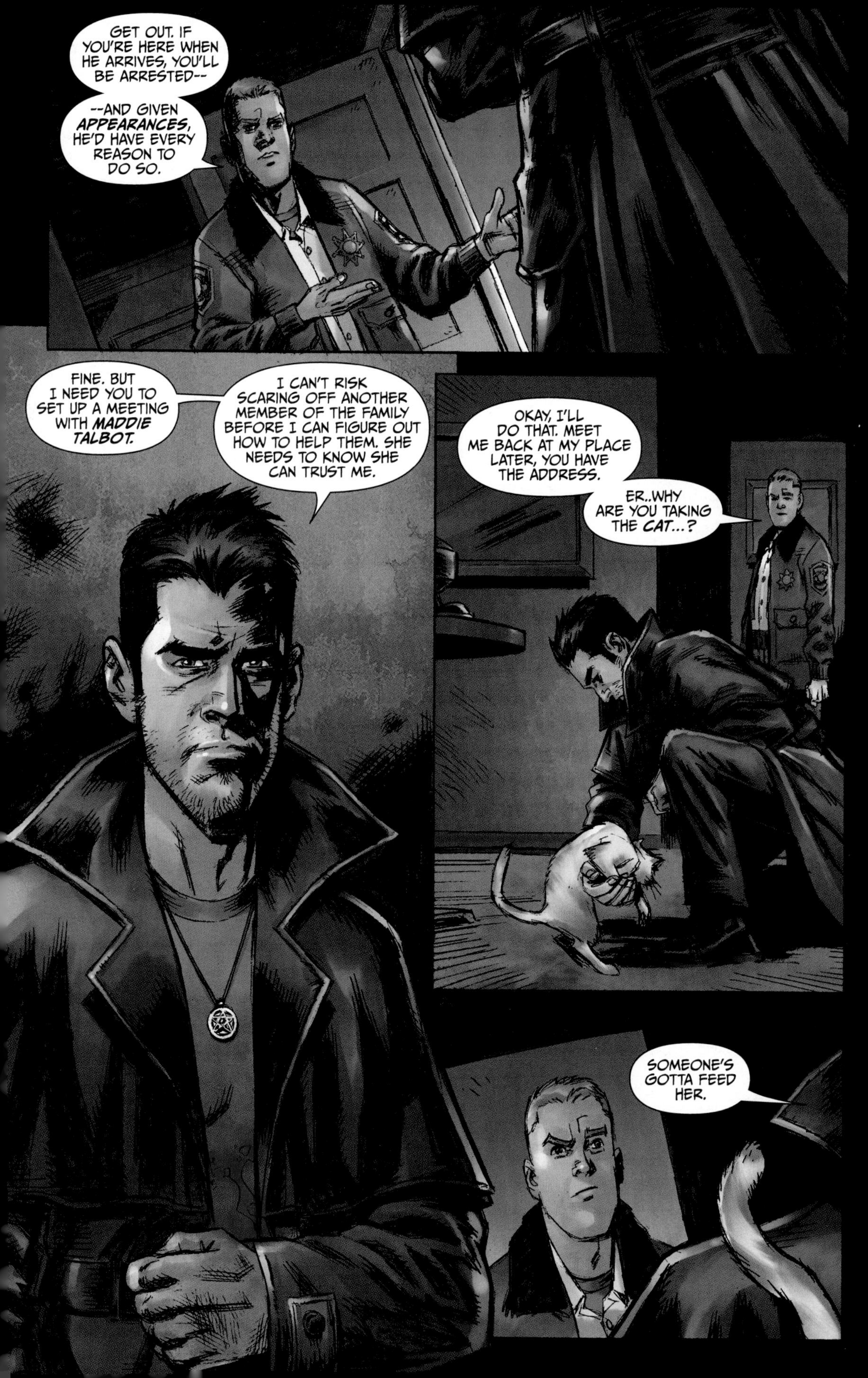
GET OUT. IF YOU'RE HERE WHEN HE ARRIVES, YOU'LL BE ARRESTED--
--AND GIVEN *APPEARANCES*, HE'D HAVE EVERY REASON TO DO SO.
FINE. BUT I NEED YOU TO SET UP A MEETING WITH *MADDIE TALBOT.*
I CAN'T RISK SCARING OFF ANOTHER MEMBER OF THE FAMILY BEFORE I CAN FIGURE OUT HOW TO HELP THEM. SHE NEEDS TO KNOW SHE CAN TRUST ME.
OKAY, I'LL DO THAT. MEET ME BACK AT MY PLACE LATER, YOU HAVE THE ADDRESS.
ER..WHY ARE YOU TAKING THE *CAT*...?
SOMEONE'S GOTTA FEED HER.

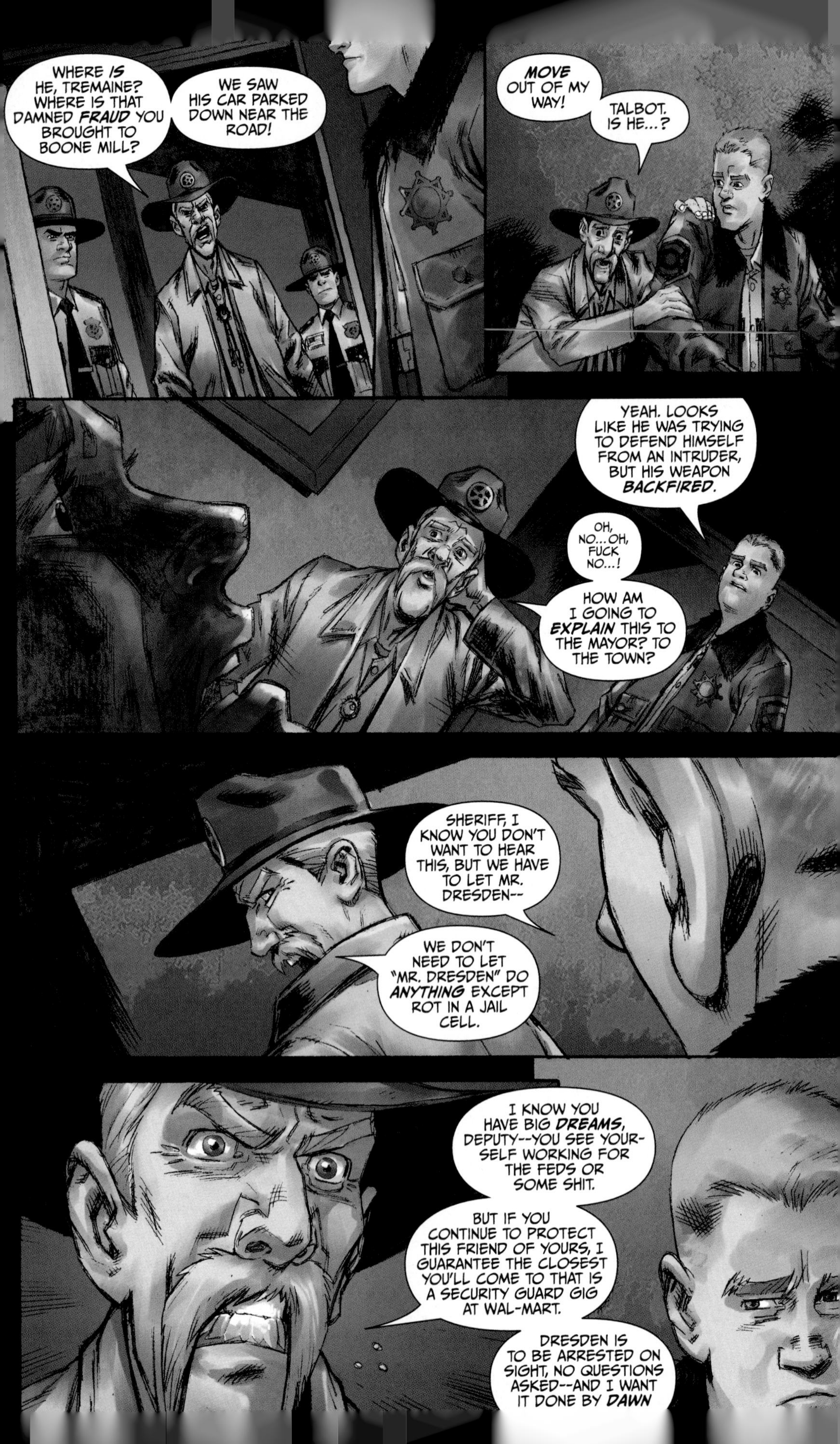
WHERE *IS* HE, TREMAINE? WHERE IS THAT DAMNED *FRAUD* YOU BROUGHT TO BOONE MILL?
WE SAW HIS CAR PARKED DOWN NEAR THE ROAD!
MOVE OUT OF MY WAY!
TALBOT. IS HE...?
YEAH. LOOKS LIKE HE WAS TRYING TO DEFEND HIMSELF FROM AN INTRUDER, BUT HIS WEAPON *BACKFIRED*.
OH, NO...OH, FUCK NO...!
HOW AM I GOING TO *EXPLAIN* THIS TO THE MAYOR? TO THE TOWN?
SHERIFF, I KNOW YOU DON'T WANT TO HEAR THIS, BUT WE HAVE TO LET MR. DRESDEN--
WE DON'T NEED TO LET "MR. DRESDEN" DO *ANYTHING* EXCEPT ROT IN A JAIL CELL.
I KNOW YOU HAVE BIG *DREAMS*, DEPUTY--YOU SEE YOURSELF WORKING FOR THE FEDS OR SOME SHIT.
BUT IF YOU CONTINUE TO PROTECT THIS FRIEND OF YOURS, I GUARANTEE THE CLOSEST YOU'LL COME TO THAT IS A SECURITY GUARD GIG AT WAL-MART.
DRESDEN IS TO BE ARRESTED ON SIGHT, NO QUESTIONS ASKED--AND I WANT IT DONE BY *DAWN*

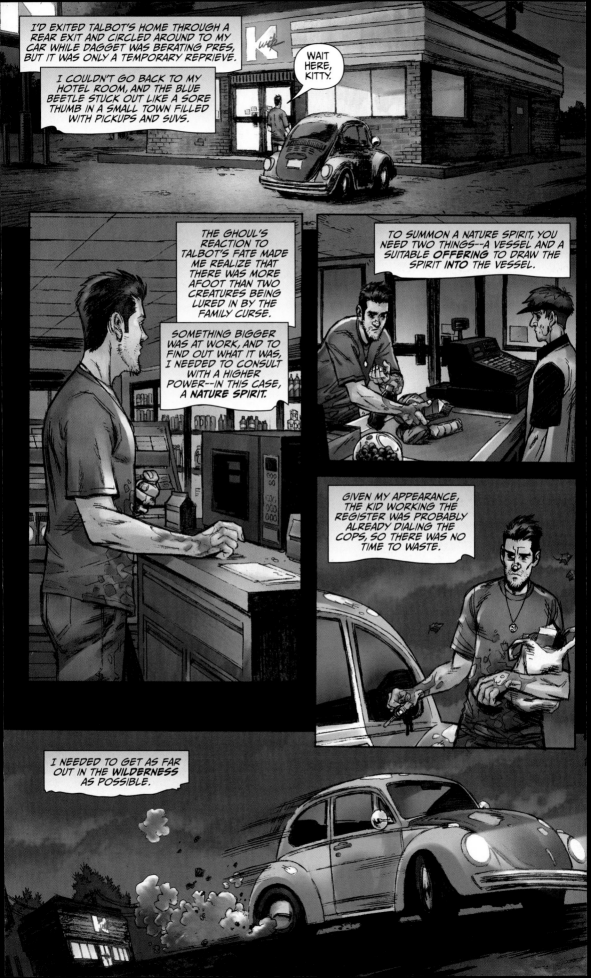

I'D EXITED TALBOT'S HOME THROUGH A REAR EXIT AND CIRCLED AROUND TO MY CAR WHILE DAGGET WAS BERATING PRES, BUT IT WAS ONLY A TEMPORARY REPRIEVE.

I COULDN'T GO BACK TO MY HOTEL ROOM, AND THE BLUE BEETLE STUCK OUT LIKE A SORE THUMB IN A SMALL TOWN FILLED WITH PICKUPS AND SUVS.

WAIT HERE, KITTY.

THE GHOUL'S REACTION TO TALBOT'S FATE MADE ME REALIZE THAT THERE WAS MORE AFOOT THAN TWO CREATURES BEING LURED IN BY THE FAMILY CURSE.

SOMETHING BIGGER WAS AT WORK, AND TO FIND OUT WHAT IT WAS, I NEEDED TO CONSULT WITH A HIGHER POWER--IN THIS CASE, A NATURE SPIRIT.

TO SUMMON A NATURE SPIRIT, YOU NEED TWO THINGS--A VESSEL AND A SUITABLE OFFERING TO DRAW THE SPIRIT INTO THE VESSEL.

GIVEN MY APPEARANCE, THE KID WORKING THE REGISTER WAS PROBABLY ALREADY DIALING THE COPS, SO THERE WAS NO TIME TO WASTE.

I NEEDED TO GET AS FAR OUT IN THE WILDERNESS AS POSSIBLE.

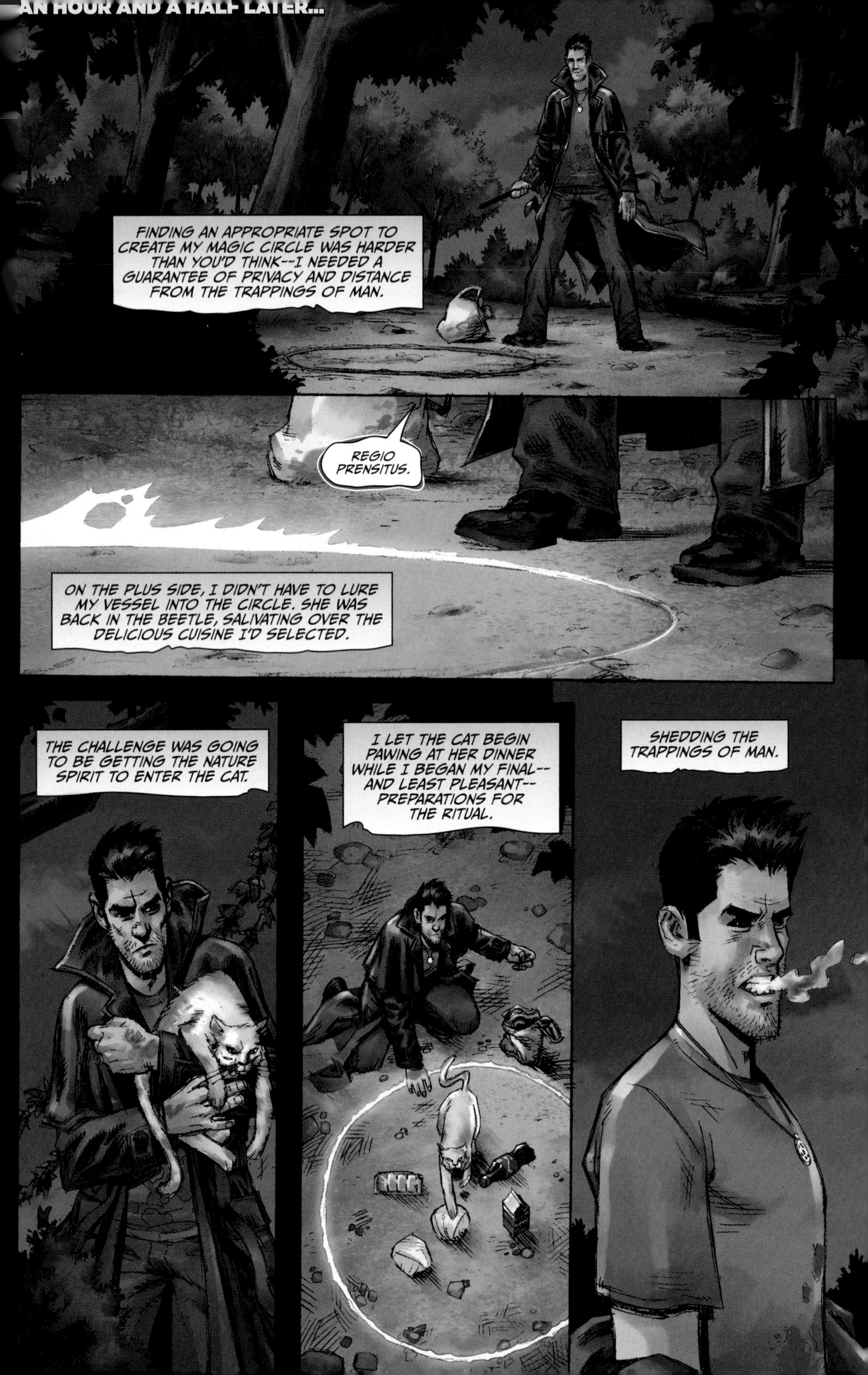
AN HOUR AND A HALF LATER...
FINDING AN APPROPRIATE SPOT TO CREATE MY MAGIC CIRCLE WAS HARDER THAN YOU'D THINK--I NEEDED A GUARANTEE OF PRIVACY AND DISTANCE FROM THE TRAPPINGS OF MAN.
REGIO PRENSITUS.
ON THE PLUS SIDE, I DIDN'T HAVE TO LURE MY VESSEL INTO THE CIRCLE. SHE WAS BACK IN THE BEETLE, SALIVATING OVER THE DELICIOUS CUISINE I'D SELECTED.
THE CHALLENGE WAS GOING TO BE GETTING THE NATURE SPIRIT TO ENTER THE CAT.
I LET THE CAT BEGIN PAWING AT HER DINNER WHILE I BEGAN MY FINAL--AND LEAST PLEASANT--PREPARATIONS FOR THE RITUAL.
SHEDDING THE TRAPPINGS OF MAN.

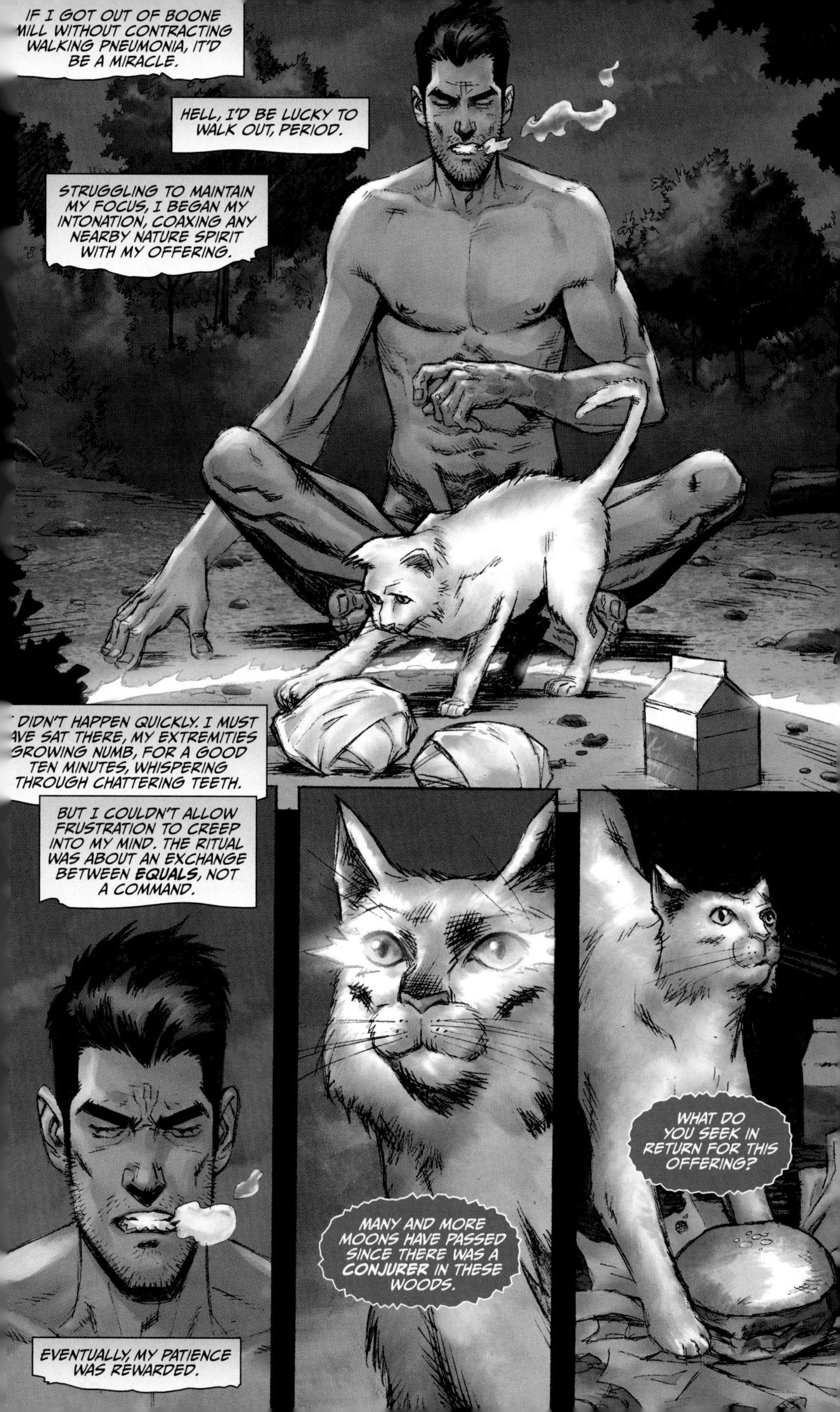
IF I GOT OUT OF BOONE MILL WITHOUT CONTRACTING WALKING PNEUMONIA, IT'D BE A MIRACLE.
HELL, I'D BE LUCKY TO WALK OUT, PERIOD.
STRUGGLING TO MAINTAIN MY FOCUS, I BEGAN MY INTONATION, COAXING ANY NEARBY NATURE SPIRIT WITH MY OFFERING.
DIDN'T HAPPEN QUICKLY. I MUST AVE SAT THERE, MY EXTREMITIES GROWING NUMB, FOR A GOOD TEN MINUTES, WHISPERING THROUGH CHATTERING TEETH.
BUT I COULDN'T ALLOW FRUSTRATION TO CREEP INTO MY MIND. THE RITUAL WAS ABOUT AN EXCHANGE BETWEEN **EQUALS**, NOT A COMMAND.
EVENTUALLY, MY PATIENCE WAS REWARDED.
MANY AND MORE MOONS HAVE PASSED SINCE THERE WAS A **CONJURER** IN THESE WOODS.
WHAT DO YOU SEEK IN RETURN FOR THIS OFFERING?

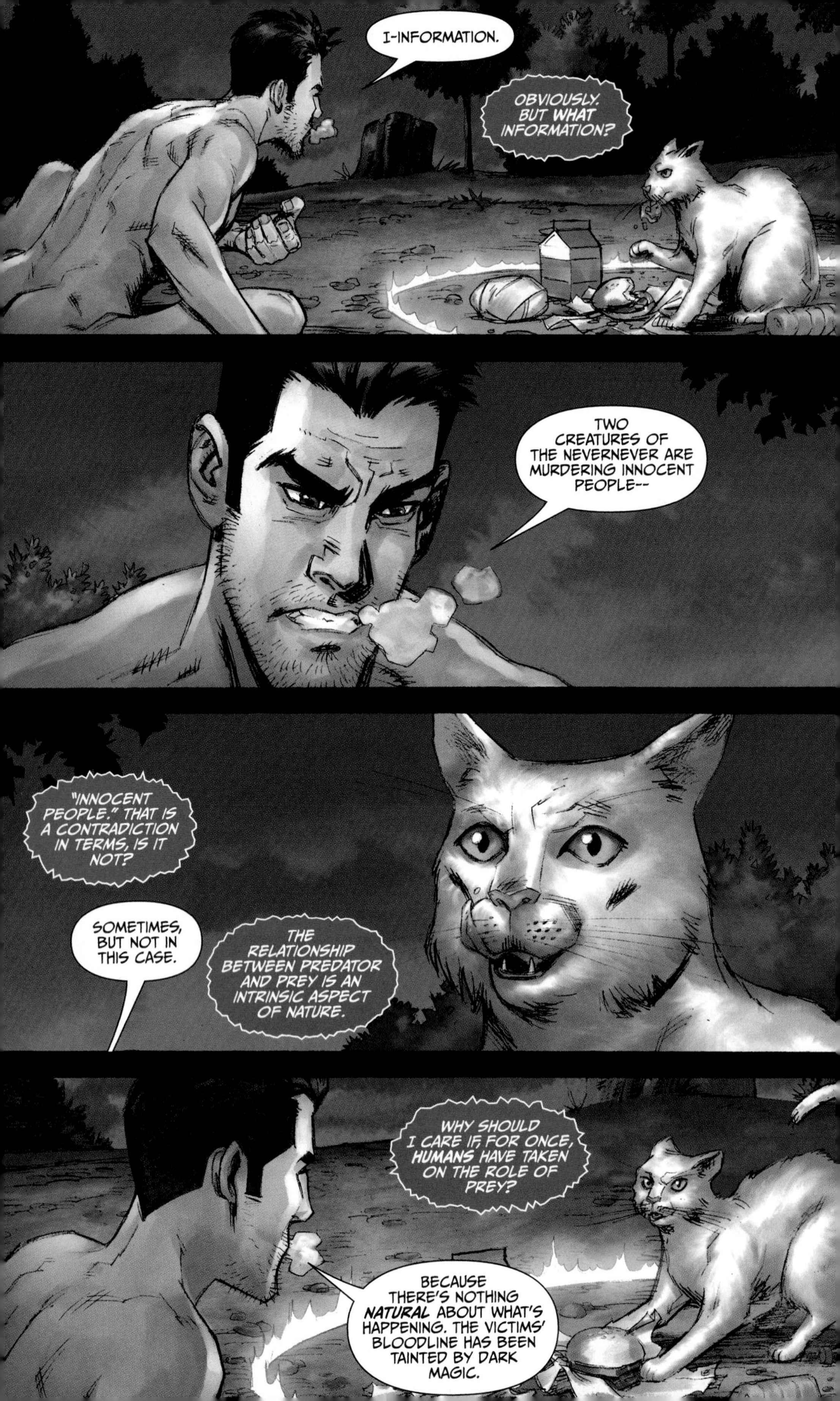

I-INFORMATION.
OBVIOUSLY. BUT WHAT INFORMATION?
TWO CREATURES OF THE NEVERNEVER ARE MURDERING INNOCENT PEOPLE--
"INNOCENT PEOPLE." THAT IS A CONTRADICTION IN TERMS, IS IT NOT?
SOMETIMES, BUT NOT IN THIS CASE.
THE RELATIONSHIP BETWEEN PREDATOR AND PREY IS AN INTRINSIC ASPECT OF NATURE.
WHY SHOULD I CARE IF, FOR ONCE, HUMANS HAVE TAKEN ON THE ROLE OF PREY?
BECAUSE THERE'S NOTHING NATURAL ABOUT WHAT'S HAPPENING. THE VICTIMS' BLOODLINE HAS BEEN TAINTED BY DARK MAGIC.

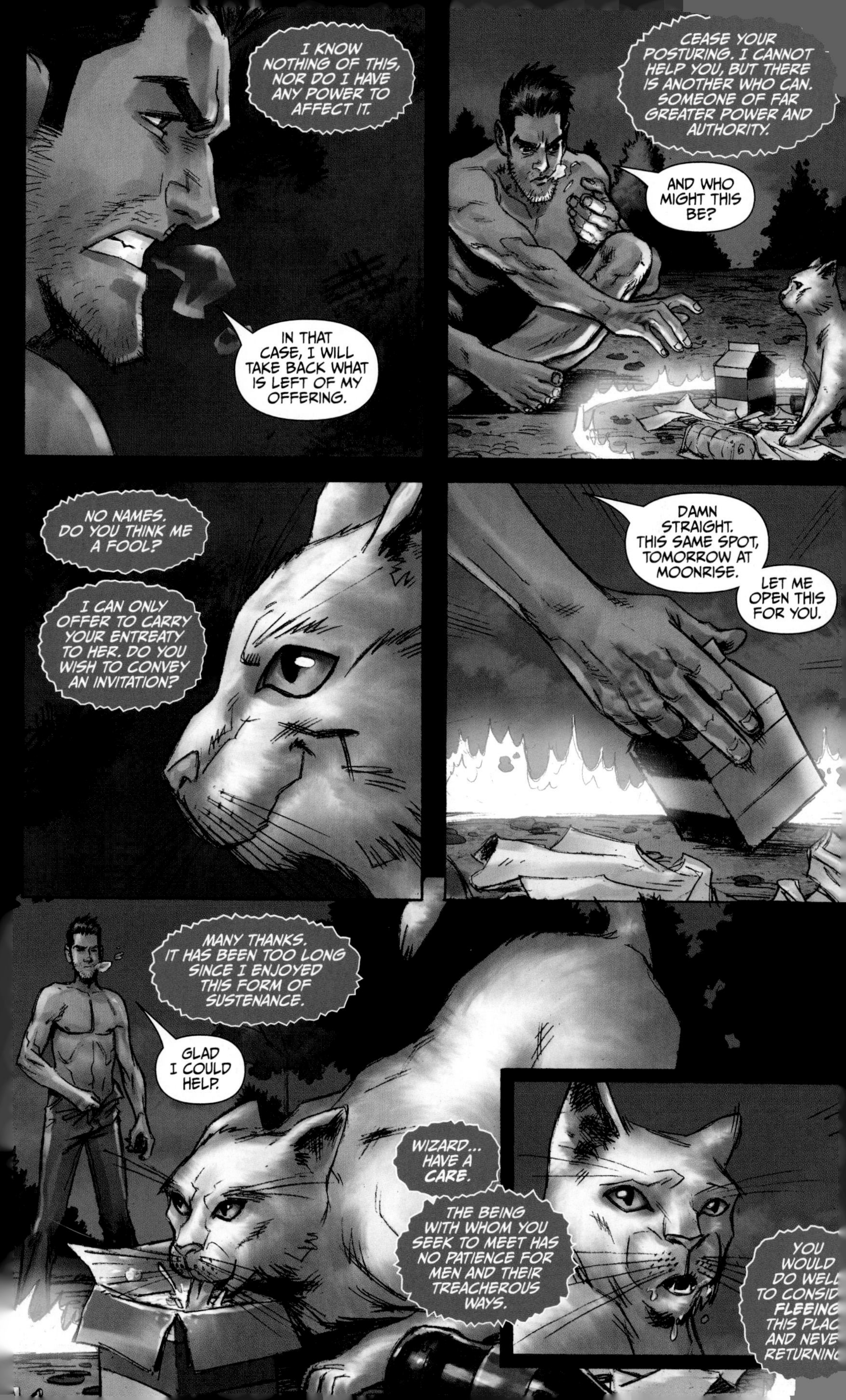
I KNOW NOTHING OF THIS, NOR DO I HAVE ANY POWER TO AFFECT IT.
IN THAT CASE, I WILL TAKE BACK WHAT IS LEFT OF MY OFFERING.
CEASE YOUR POSTURING. I CANNOT HELP YOU, BUT THERE IS ANOTHER WHO CAN. SOMEONE OF FAR GREATER POWER AND AUTHORITY.
AND WHO MIGHT THIS BE?
NO NAMES. DO YOU THINK ME A FOOL?
I CAN ONLY OFFER TO CARRY YOUR ENTREATY TO HER. DO YOU WISH TO CONVEY AN INVITATION?
DAMN STRAIGHT. THIS SAME SPOT, TOMORROW AT MOONRISE.
LET ME OPEN THIS FOR YOU.
MANY THANKS. IT HAS BEEN TOO LONG SINCE I ENJOYED THIS FORM OF SUSTENANCE.
GLAD I COULD HELP.
WIZARD... HAVE A CARE.
THE BEING WITH WHOM YOU SEEK TO MEET HAS NO PATIENCE FOR MEN AND THEIR TREACHEROUS WAYS.

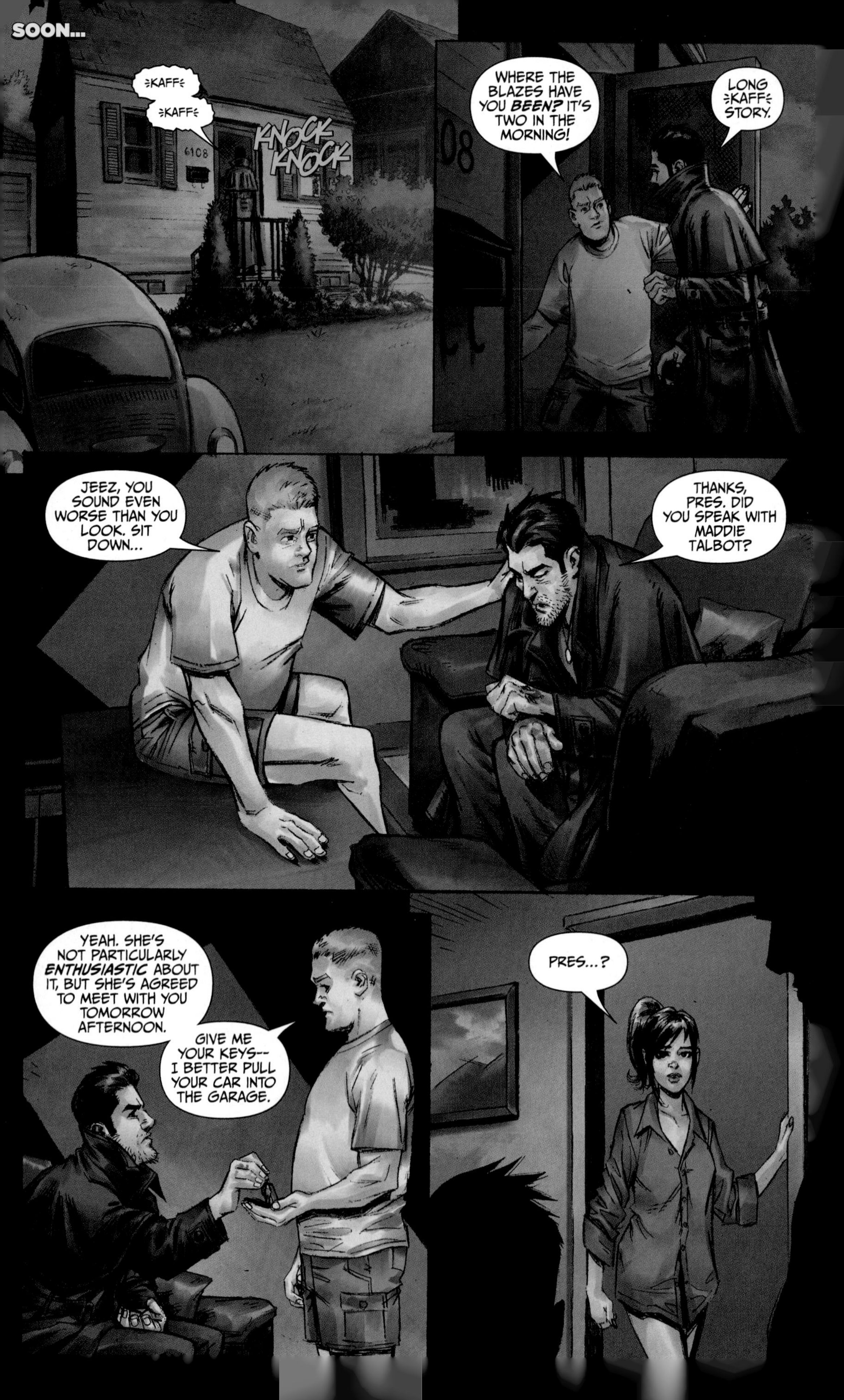
SOON...
⚟KAFF⚞
⚟KAFF⚞
6108
KNOCK KNOCK
WHERE THE BLAZES HAVE YOU *BEEN?* IT'S TWO IN THE MORNING!
LONG ⚟KAFF⚞ STORY.
JEEZ, YOU SOUND EVEN WORSE THAN YOU LOOK. SIT DOWN...
THANKS, PRES. DID YOU SPEAK WITH MADDIE TALBOT?
YEAH. SHE'S NOT PARTICULARLY *ENTHUSIASTIC* ABOUT IT, BUT SHE'S AGREED TO MEET WITH YOU TOMORROW AFTERNOON.
GIVE ME YOUR KEYS-- I BETTER PULL YOUR CAR INTO THE GARAGE.
PRES...?

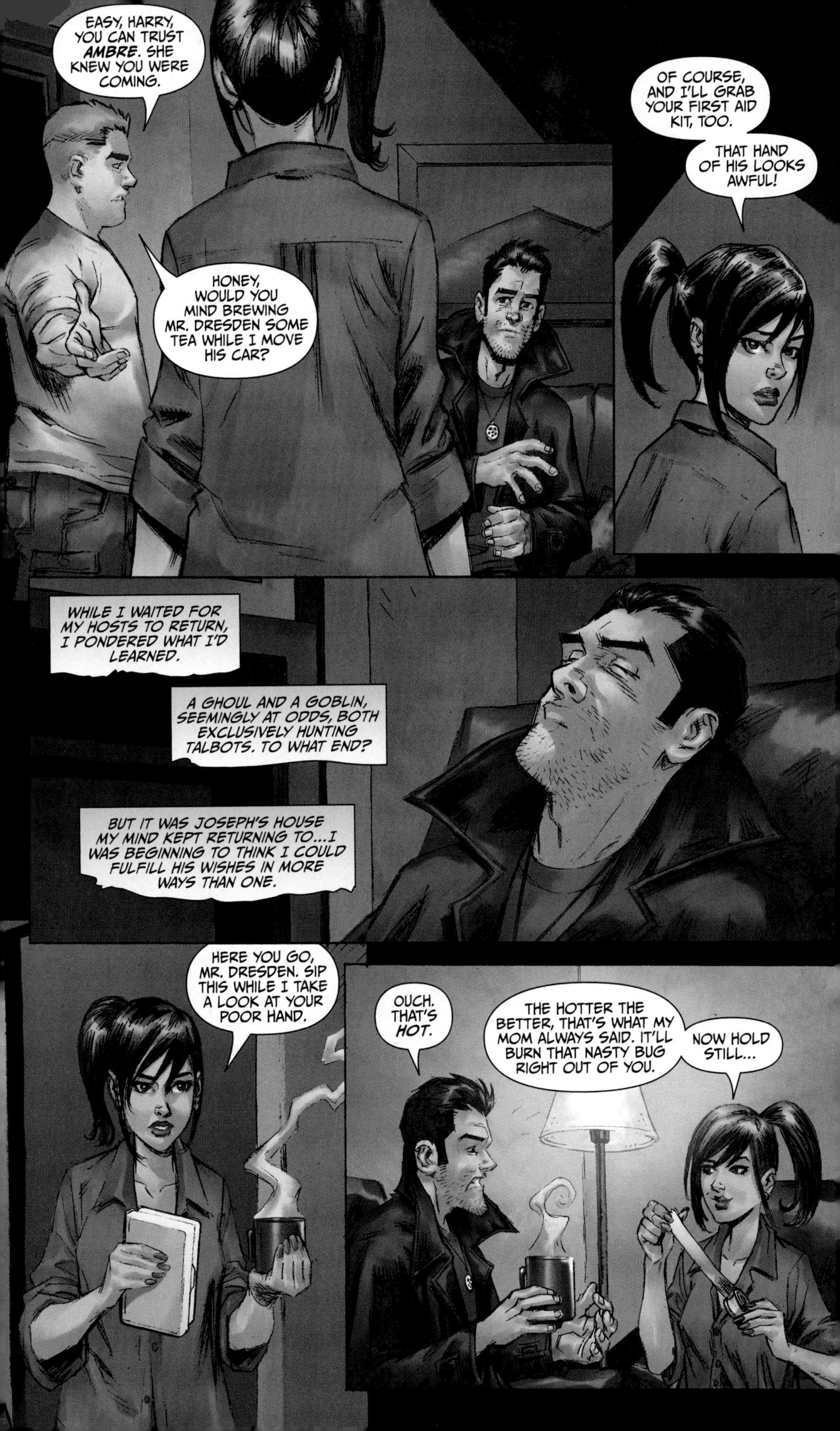
EASY, HARRY, YOU CAN TRUST AMBRE. SHE KNEW YOU WERE COMING.
HONEY, WOULD YOU MIND BREWING MR. DRESDEN SOME TEA WHILE I MOVE HIS CAR?
OF COURSE, AND I'LL GRAB YOUR FIRST AID KIT, TOO.
THAT HAND OF HIS LOOKS AWFUL!
WHILE I WAITED FOR MY HOSTS TO RETURN, I PONDERED WHAT I'D LEARNED.
A GHOUL AND A GOBLIN, SEEMINGLY AT ODDS, BOTH EXCLUSIVELY HUNTING TALBOTS. TO WHAT END?
BUT IT WAS JOSEPH'S HOUSE MY MIND KEPT RETURNING TO...I WAS BEGINNING TO THINK I COULD FULFILL HIS WISHES IN MORE WAYS THAN ONE.
HERE YOU GO, MR. DRESDEN. SIP THIS WHILE I TAKE A LOOK AT YOUR POOR HAND.
OUCH. THAT'S HOT.
THE HOTTER THE BETTER, THAT'S WHAT MY MOM ALWAYS SAID. IT'LL BURN THAT NASTY BUG RIGHT OUT OF YOU.
NOW HOLD STILL...

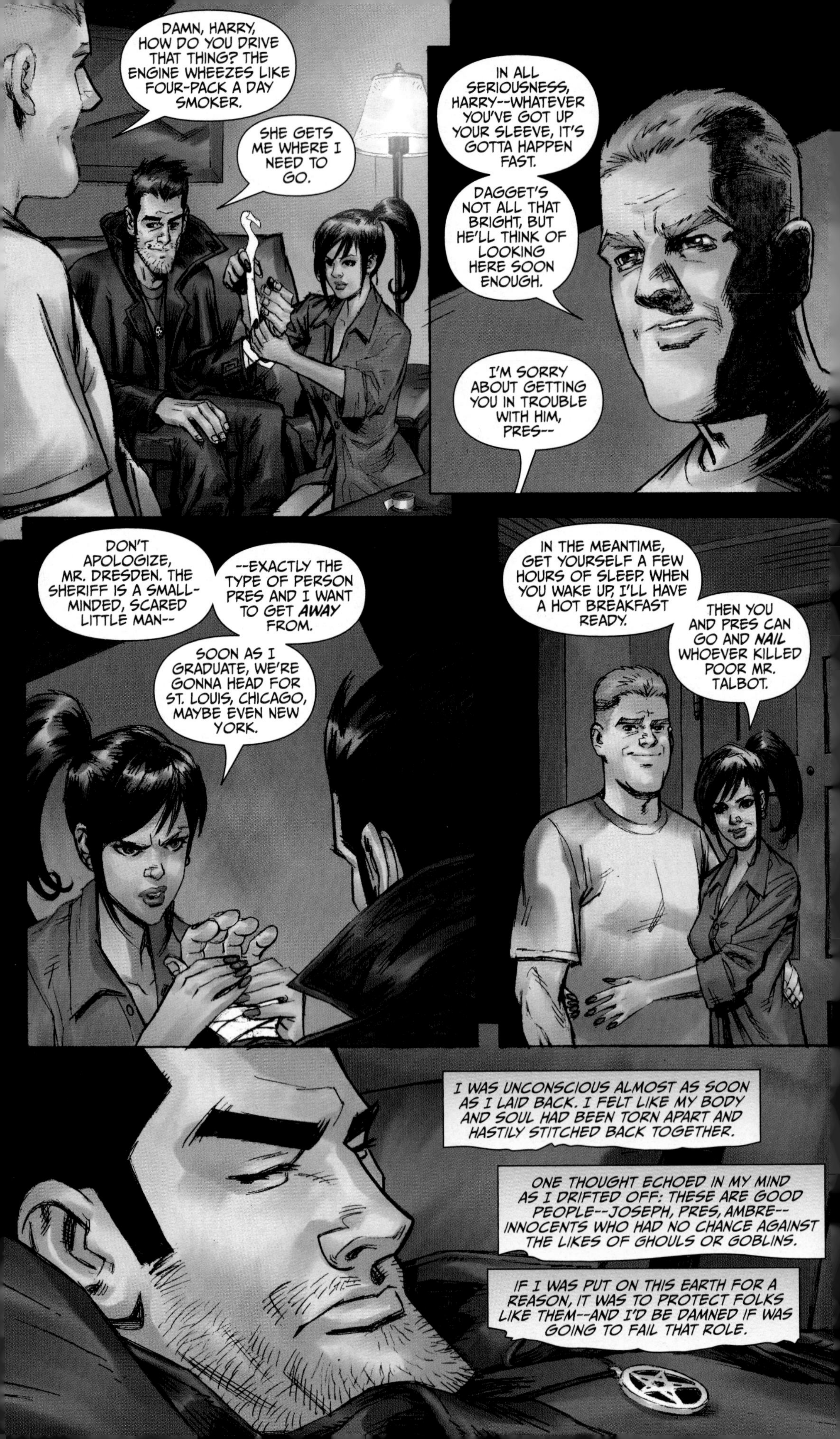
DAMN, HARRY, HOW DO YOU DRIVE THAT THING? THE ENGINE WHEEZES LIKE FOUR-PACK A DAY SMOKER.
SHE GETS ME WHERE I NEED TO GO.
IN ALL SERIOUSNESS, HARRY--WHATEVER YOU'VE GOT UP YOUR SLEEVE, IT'S GOTTA HAPPEN FAST.
DAGGET'S NOT ALL THAT BRIGHT, BUT HE'LL THINK OF LOOKING HERE SOON ENOUGH.
I'M SORRY ABOUT GETTING YOU IN TROUBLE WITH HIM, PRES--
DON'T APOLOGIZE, MR. DRESDEN. THE SHERIFF IS A SMALL-MINDED, SCARED LITTLE MAN--
--EXACTLY THE TYPE OF PERSON PRES AND I WANT TO GET *AWAY* FROM.
SOON AS I GRADUATE, WE'RE GONNA HEAD FOR ST. LOUIS, CHICAGO, MAYBE EVEN NEW YORK.
IN THE MEANTIME, GET YOURSELF A FEW HOURS OF SLEEP. WHEN YOU WAKE UP, I'LL HAVE A HOT BREAKFAST READY.
THEN YOU AND PRES CAN GO AND *NAIL* WHOEVER KILLED POOR MR. TALBOT.
I WAS UNCONSCIOUS ALMOST AS SOON AS I LAID BACK. I FELT LIKE MY BODY AND SOUL HAD BEEN TORN APART AND HASTILY STITCHED BACK TOGETHER.
ONE THOUGHT ECHOED IN MY MIND AS I DRIFTED OFF: THESE ARE GOOD PEOPLE--JOSEPH, PRES, AMBRE--INNOCENTS WHO HAD NO CHANCE AGAINST THE LIKES OF GHOULS OR GOBLINS.
IF I WAS PUT ON THIS EARTH FOR A REASON, IT WAS TO PROTECT FOLKS LIKE THEM--AND I'D BE DAMNED IF WAS GOING TO FAIL THAT ROLE.

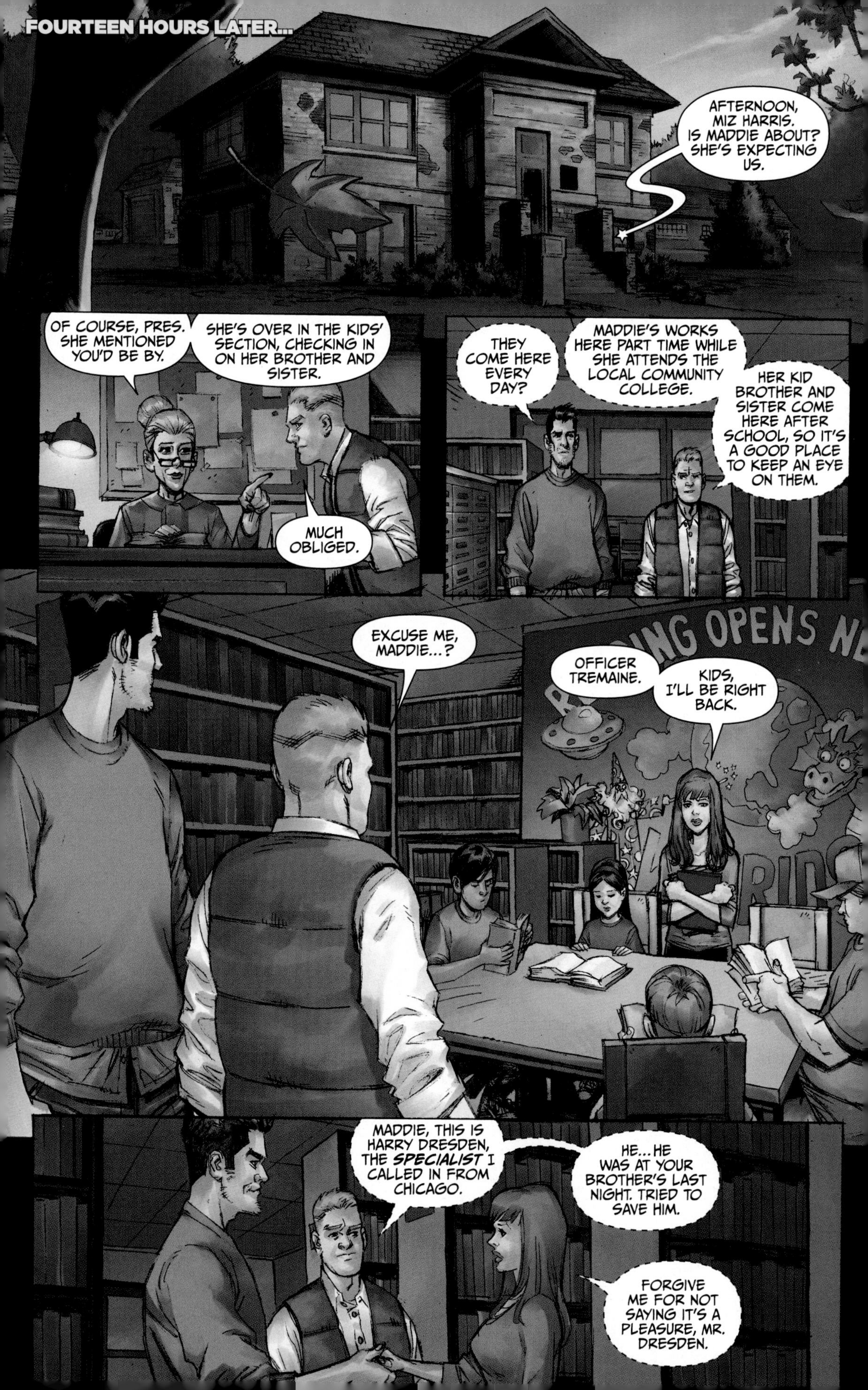
FOURTEEN HOURS LATER...
AFTERNOON, MIZ HARRIS. IS MADDIE ABOUT? SHE'S EXPECTING US.
OF COURSE, PRES. SHE MENTIONED YOU'D BE BY.
SHE'S OVER IN THE KIDS' SECTION, CHECKING IN ON HER BROTHER AND SISTER.
MUCH OBLIGED.
THEY COME HERE EVERY DAY?
MADDIE'S WORKS HERE PART TIME WHILE SHE ATTENDS THE LOCAL COMMUNITY COLLEGE.
HER KID BROTHER AND SISTER COME HERE AFTER SCHOOL, SO IT'S A GOOD PLACE TO KEEP AN EYE ON THEM.
EXCUSE ME, MADDIE...?
OFFICER TREMAINE.
KIDS, I'LL BE RIGHT BACK.
MADDIE, THIS IS HARRY DRESDEN, THE *SPECIALIST* I CALLED IN FROM CHICAGO.
HE... HE WAS AT YOUR BROTHER'S LAST NIGHT. TRIED TO SAVE HIM.
FORGIVE ME FOR NOT SAYING IT'S A PLEASURE, MR. DRESDEN.

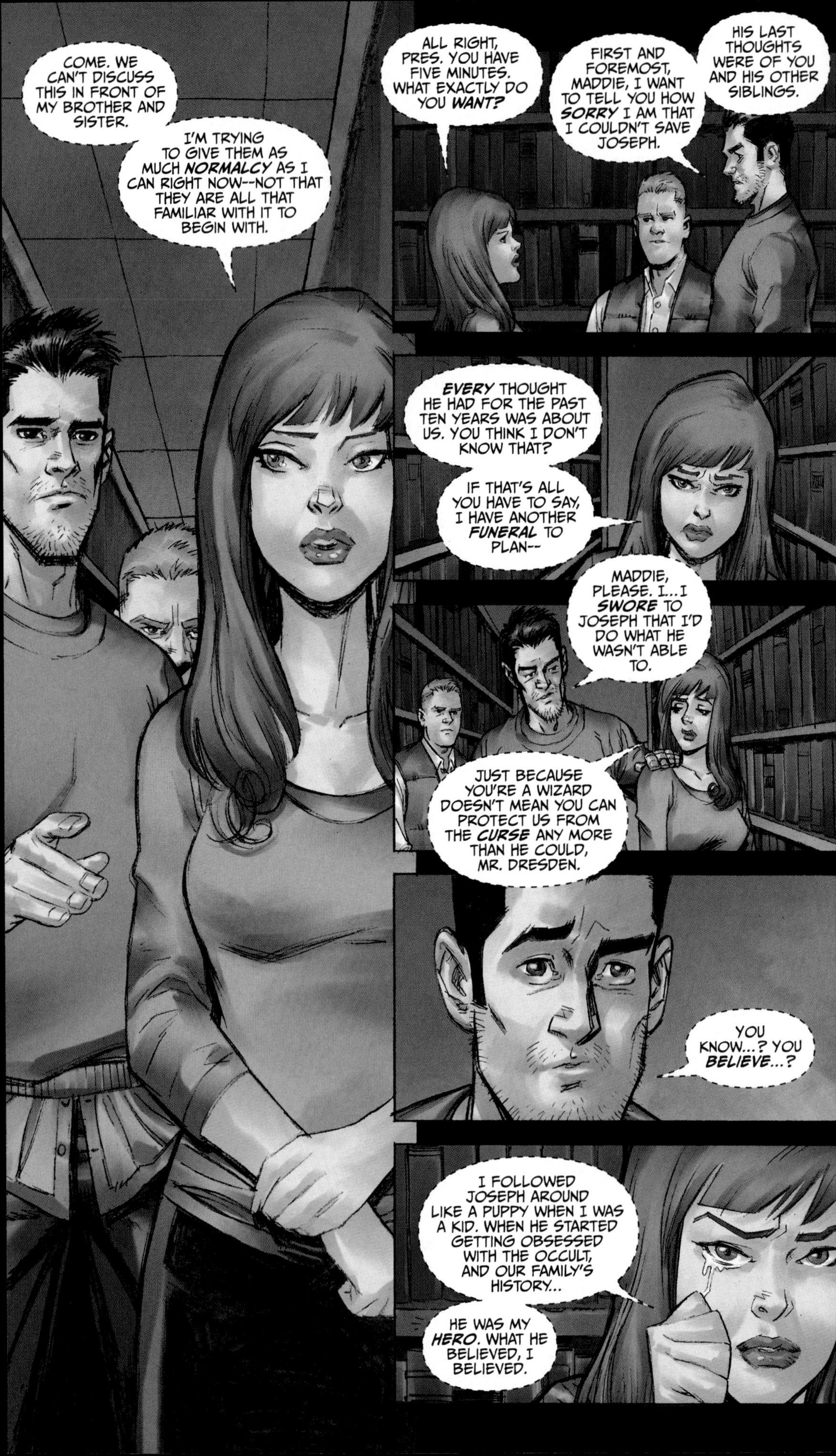
COME. WE CAN'T DISCUSS THIS IN FRONT OF MY BROTHER AND SISTER.
I'M TRYING TO GIVE THEM AS MUCH NORMALCY AS I CAN RIGHT NOW--NOT THAT THEY ARE ALL THAT FAMILIAR WITH IT TO BEGIN WITH.
ALL RIGHT, PRES. YOU HAVE FIVE MINUTES. WHAT EXACTLY DO YOU WANT?
FIRST AND FOREMOST, MADDIE, I WANT TO TELL YOU HOW SORRY I AM THAT I COULDN'T SAVE JOSEPH.
HIS LAST THOUGHTS WERE OF YOU AND HIS OTHER SIBLINGS.
EVERY THOUGHT HE HAD FOR THE PAST TEN YEARS WAS ABOUT US. YOU THINK I DON'T KNOW THAT?
IF THAT'S ALL YOU HAVE TO SAY, I HAVE ANOTHER FUNERAL TO PLAN--
MADDIE, PLEASE. I...I SWORE TO JOSEPH THAT I'D DO WHAT HE WASN'T ABLE TO.
JUST BECAUSE YOU'RE A WIZARD DOESN'T MEAN YOU CAN PROTECT US FROM THE CURSE ANY MORE THAN HE COULD, MR. DRESDEN.
YOU KNOW...? YOU BELIEVE...?
I FOLLOWED JOSEPH AROUND LIKE A PUPPY WHEN I WAS A KID. WHEN HE STARTED GETTING OBSESSED WITH THE OCCULT, AND OUR FAMILY'S HISTORY...
HE WAS MY HERO. WHAT HE BELIEVED, I BELIEVED.

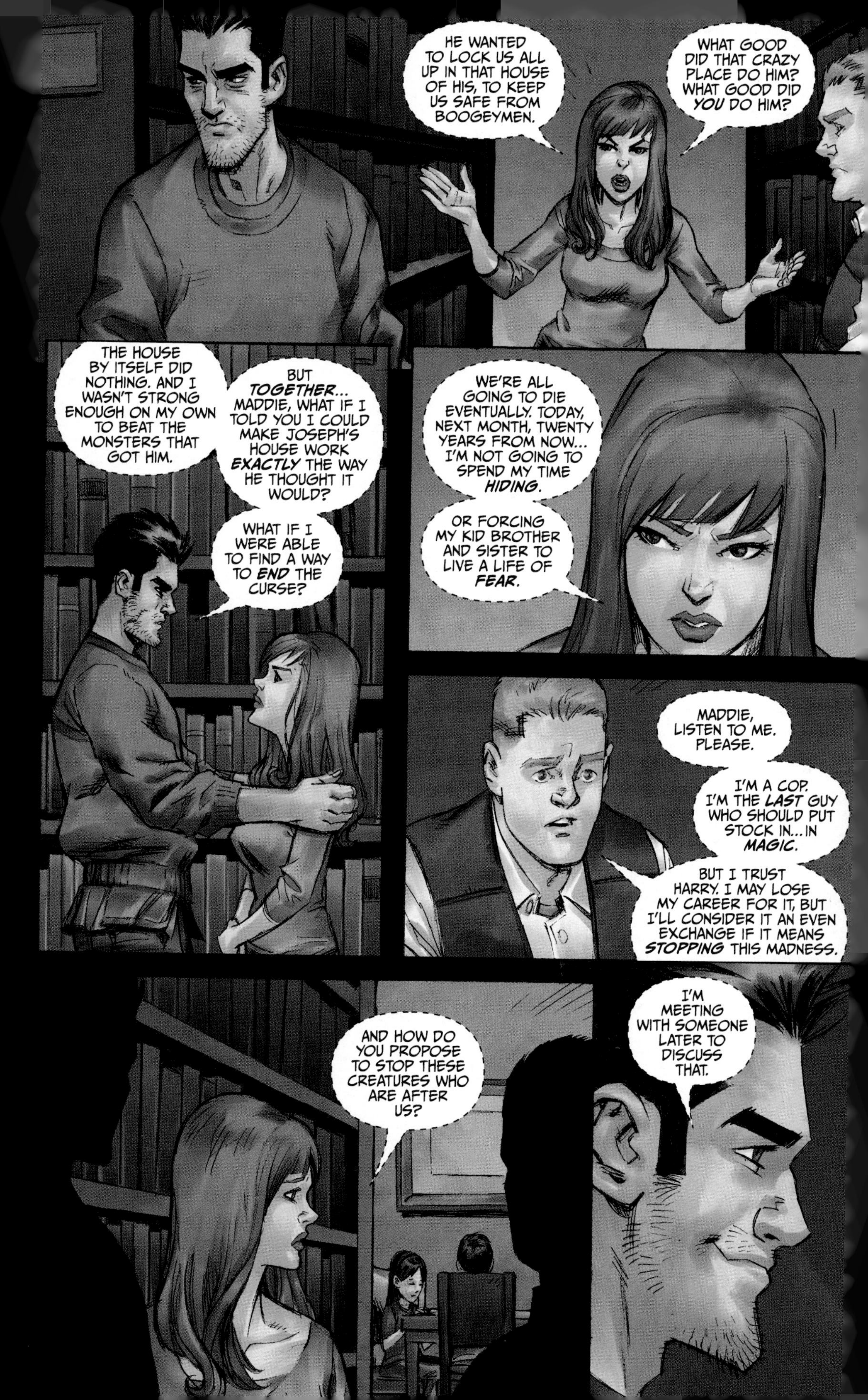
HE WANTED TO LOCK US ALL UP IN THAT HOUSE OF HIS, TO KEEP US SAFE FROM BOOGEYMEN.
WHAT GOOD DID THAT CRAZY PLACE DO HIM? WHAT GOOD DID *YOU* DO HIM?
THE HOUSE BY ITSELF DID NOTHING. AND I WASN'T STRONG ENOUGH ON MY OWN TO BEAT THE MONSTERS THAT GOT HIM.
BUT *TOGETHER*... MADDIE, WHAT IF I TOLD YOU I COULD MAKE JOSEPH'S HOUSE WORK *EXACTLY* THE WAY HE THOUGHT IT WOULD?
WHAT IF I WERE ABLE TO FIND A WAY TO *END* THE CURSE?
WE'RE ALL GOING TO DIE EVENTUALLY. TODAY, NEXT MONTH, TWENTY YEARS FROM NOW... I'M NOT GOING TO SPEND MY TIME *HIDING*.
OR FORCING MY KID BROTHER AND SISTER TO LIVE A LIFE OF *FEAR*.
MADDIE, LISTEN TO ME. PLEASE.
I'M A COP. I'M THE *LAST* GUY WHO SHOULD PUT STOCK IN... IN *MAGIC*.
BUT I TRUST HARRY. I MAY LOSE MY CAREER FOR IT, BUT I'LL CONSIDER IT AN EVEN EXCHANGE IF IT MEANS *STOPPING* THIS MADNESS.
AND HOW DO YOU PROPOSE TO STOP THESE CREATURES WHO ARE AFTER US?
I'M MEETING WITH SOMEONE LATER TO DISCUSS THAT.

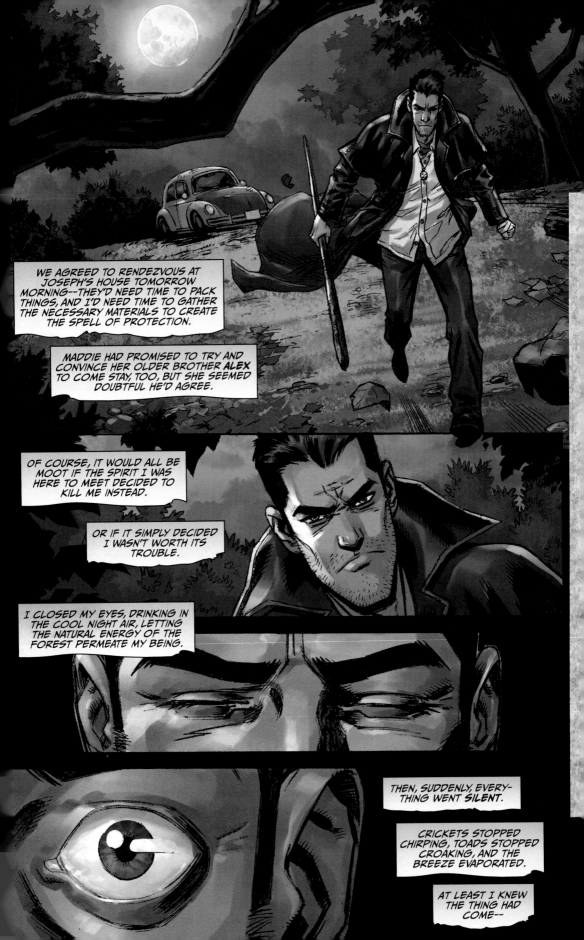

WE AGREED TO RENDEZVOUS AT JOSEPH'S HOUSE TOMORROW MORNING--THEY'D NEED TIME TO PACK THINGS, AND I'D NEED TIME TO GATHER THE NECESSARY MATERIALS TO CREATE THE SPELL OF PROTECTION.

MADDIE HAD PROMISED TO TRY AND CONVINCE HER OLDER BROTHER ALEX TO COME STAY, TOO, BUT SHE SEEMED DOUBTFUL HE'D AGREE.

OF COURSE, IT WOULD ALL BE MOOT IF THE SPIRIT I WAS HERE TO MEET DECIDED TO KILL ME INSTEAD.

OR IF IT SIMPLY DECIDED I WASN'T WORTH ITS TROUBLE.

I CLOSED MY EYES, DRINKING IN THE COOL NIGHT AIR, LETTING THE NATURAL ENERGY OF THE FOREST PERMEATE MY BEING.

THEN, SUDDENLY, EVERY-THING WENT SILENT.

CRICKETS STOPPED CHIRPING, TOADS STOPPED CROAKING, AND THE BREEZE EVAPORATED.

AT LEAST I KNEW THE THING HAD COME--

--WHETHER I'D SURVIVE THE ENCOUNTER WAS ANOTHER MATTER ENTIRELY.
WWWHISSSH
WHAT DO YOU SEEK HERE, MORTAL?
INFORMATION. TO PROTECT THE INNOCENT--
INFORMATION IS ADVANTAGE--
--AND THAT I CANNOT PROVIDE!
NGH

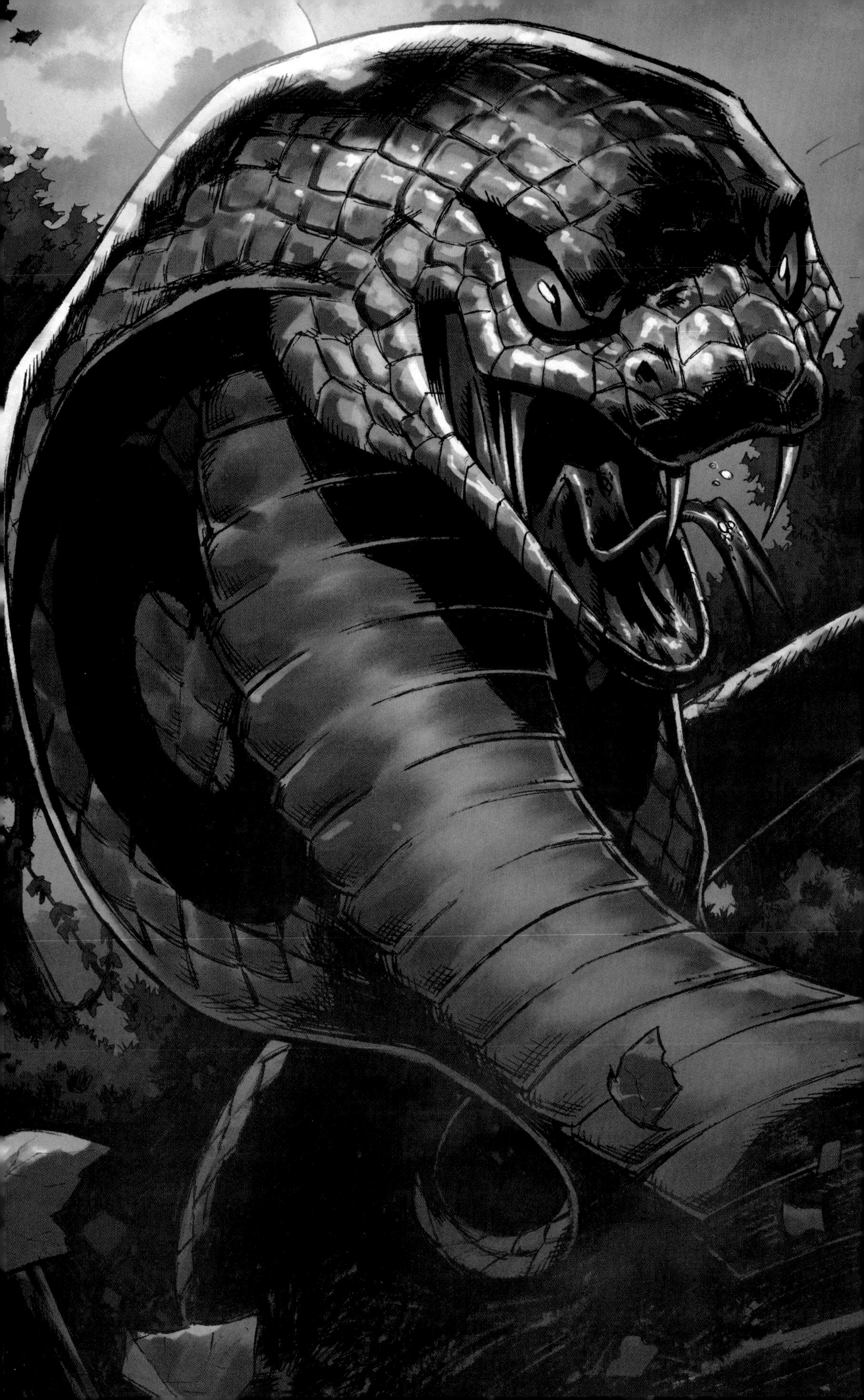

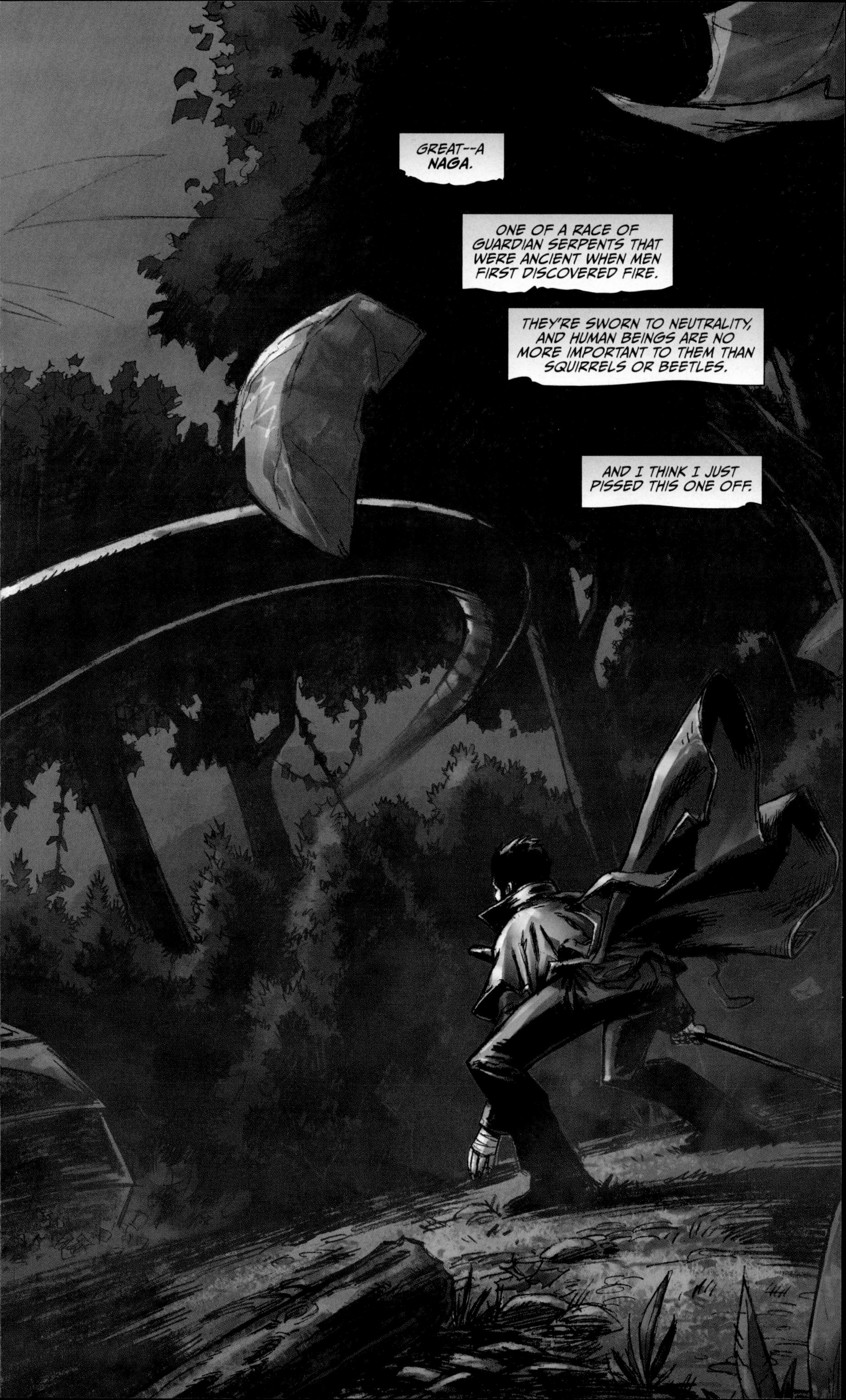
GREAT--A NAGA.
ONE OF A RACE OF GUARDIAN SERPENTS THAT WERE ANCIENT WHEN MEN FIRST DISCOVERED FIRE.
THEY'RE SWORN TO NEUTRALITY, AND HUMAN BEINGS ARE NO MORE IMPORTANT TO THEM THAN SQUIRRELS OR BEETLES.
AND I THINK I JUST PISSED THIS ONE OFF.

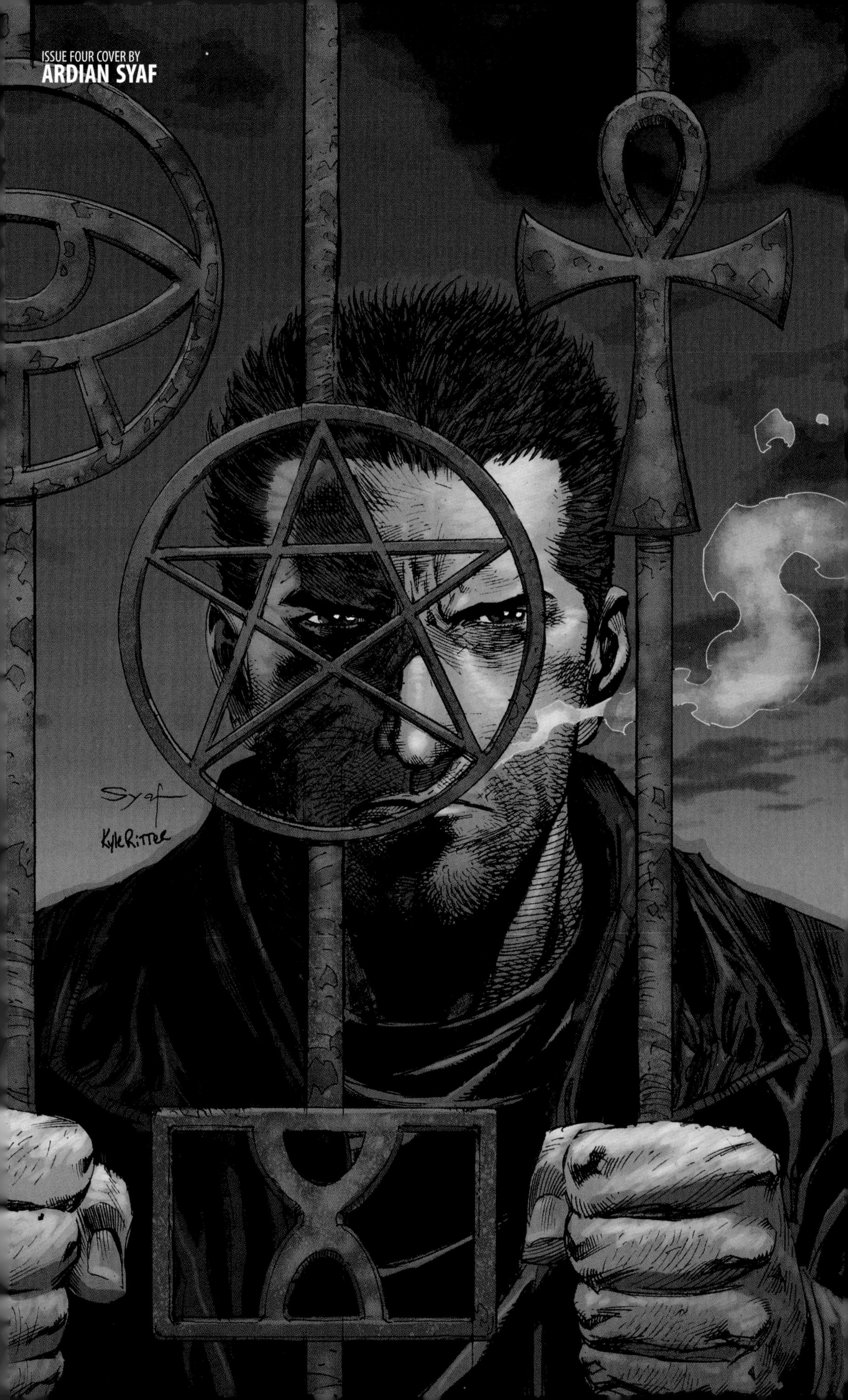
Syaf
Kyle Ritter

ISSUE FOUR COVER BY
ARDIAN SYAF

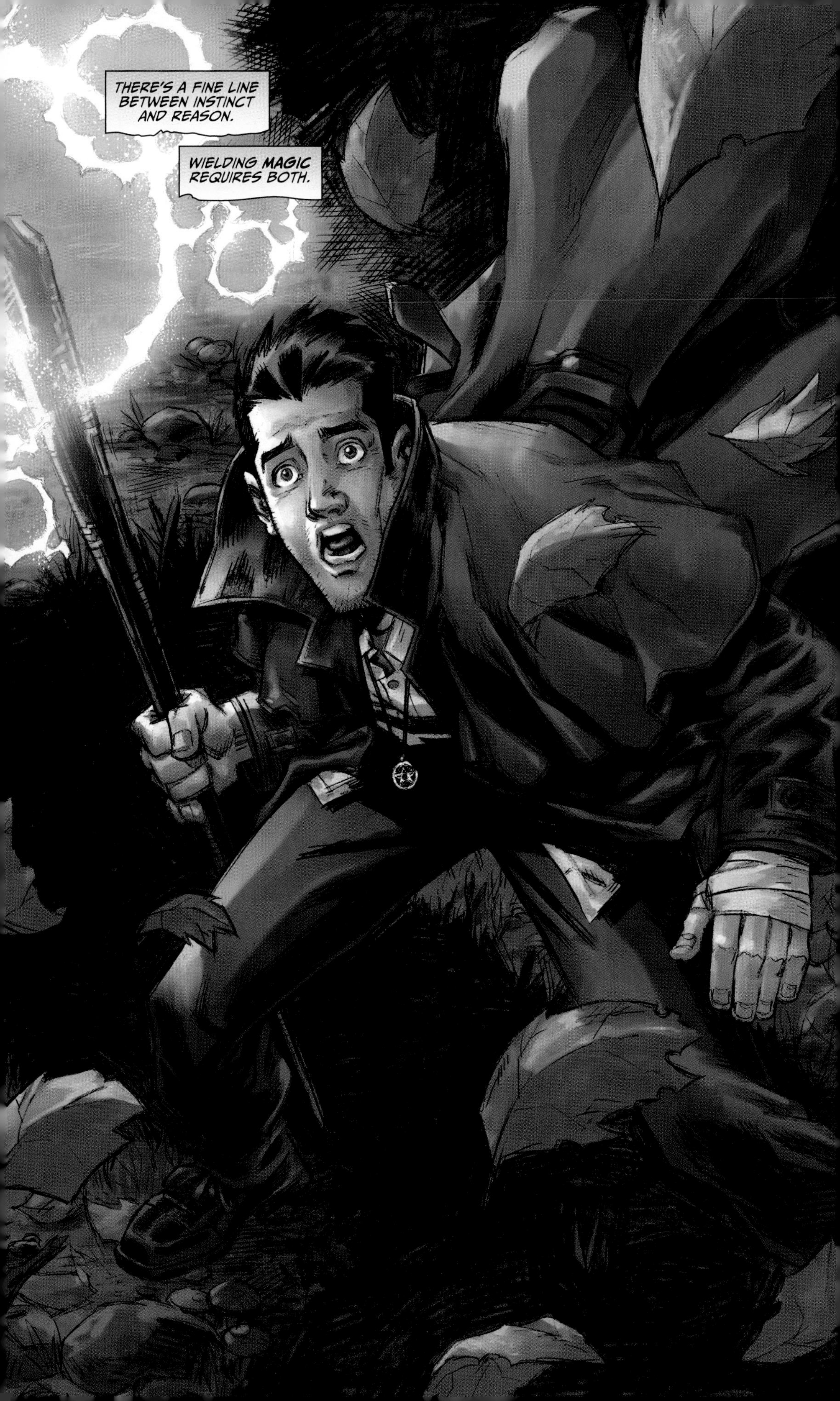
THERE'S A FINE LINE BETWEEN INSTINCT AND REASON.
WIELDING MAGIC REQUIRES BOTH.

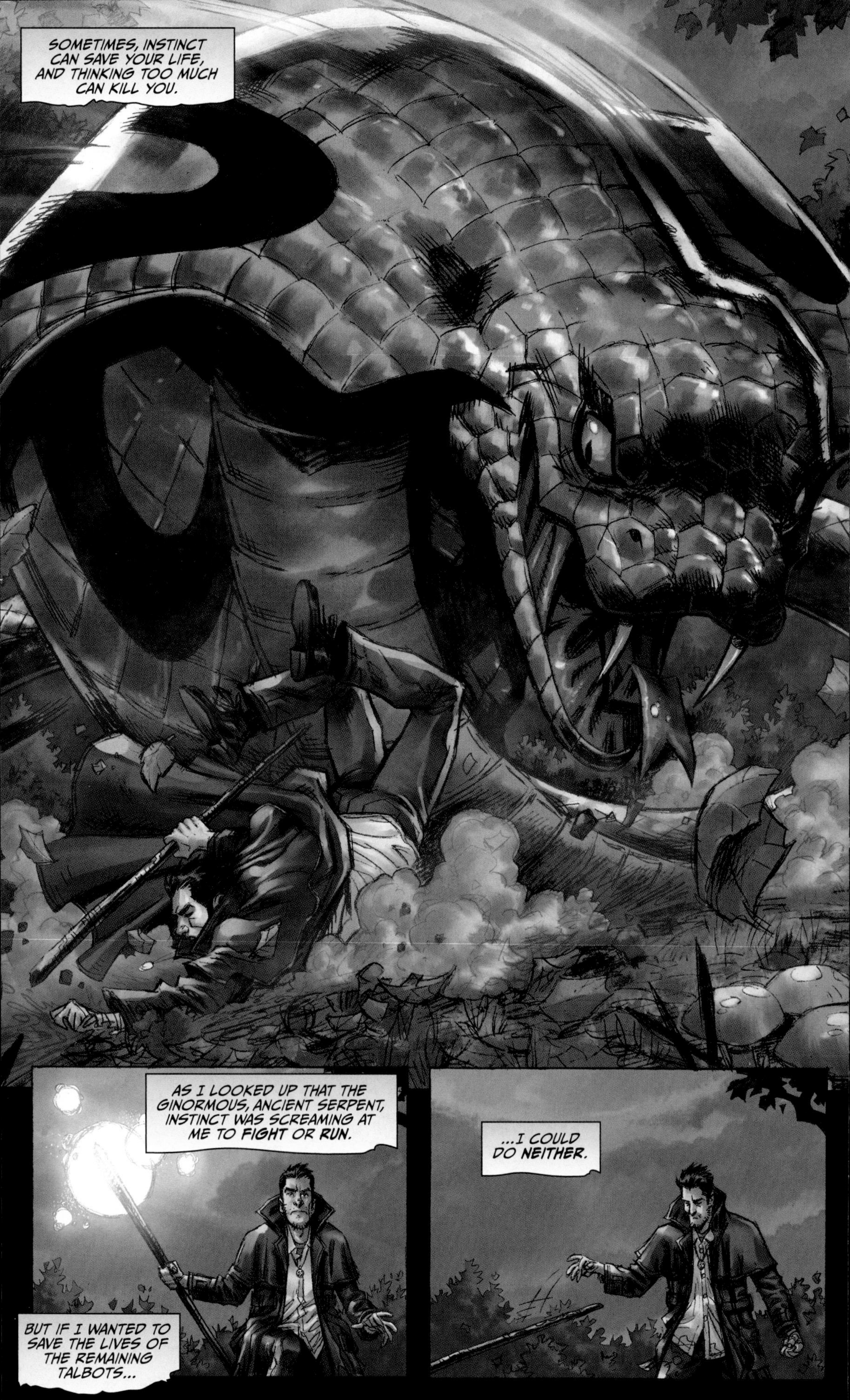
SOMETIMES, INSTINCT CAN SAVE YOUR LIFE, AND THINKING TOO MUCH CAN KILL YOU.
AS I LOOKED UP THAT THE GINORMOUS, ANCIENT SERPENT, INSTINCT WAS SCREAMING AT ME TO FIGHT OR RUN.
BUT IF I WANTED TO SAVE THE LIVES OF THE REMAINING TALBOTS...
...I COULD DO NEITHER.

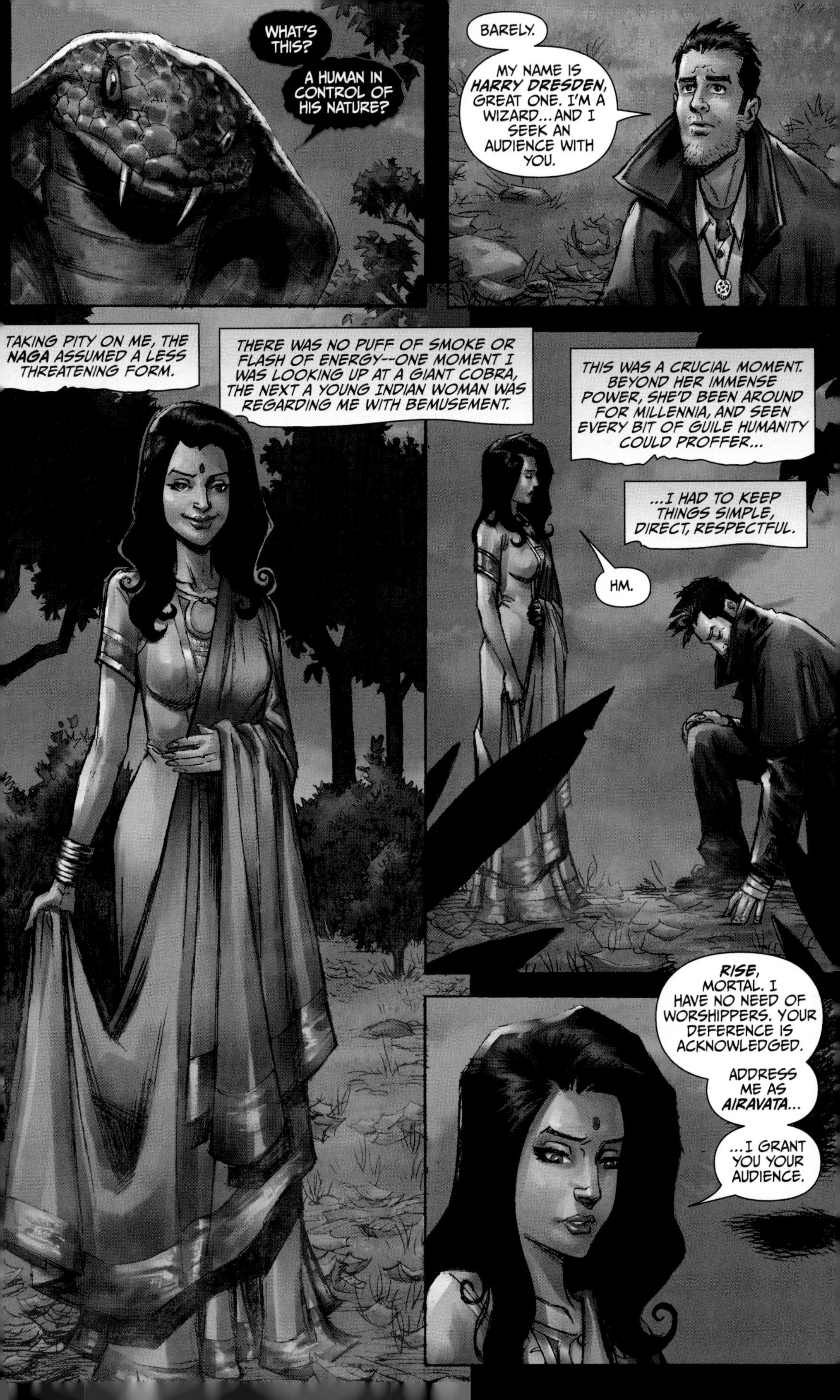
WHAT'S THIS?
A HUMAN IN CONTROL OF HIS NATURE?
BARELY.
MY NAME IS HARRY DRESDEN, GREAT ONE. I'M A WIZARD... AND I SEEK AN AUDIENCE WITH YOU.
TAKING PITY ON ME, THE NAGA ASSUMED A LESS THREATENING FORM.
THERE WAS NO PUFF OF SMOKE OR FLASH OF ENERGY--ONE MOMENT I WAS LOOKING UP AT A GIANT COBRA, THE NEXT A YOUNG INDIAN WOMAN WAS REGARDING ME WITH BEMUSEMENT.
THIS WAS A CRUCIAL MOMENT. BEYOND HER IMMENSE POWER, SHE'D BEEN AROUND FOR MILLENNIA, AND SEEN EVERY BIT OF GUILE HUMANITY COULD PROFFER...
...I HAD TO KEEP THINGS SIMPLE, DIRECT, RESPECTFUL.
HM.
RISE, MORTAL. I HAVE NO NEED OF WORSHIPPERS. YOUR DEFERENCE IS ACKNOWLEDGED.
ADDRESS ME AS AIRAVATA...
...I GRANT YOU YOUR AUDIENCE.

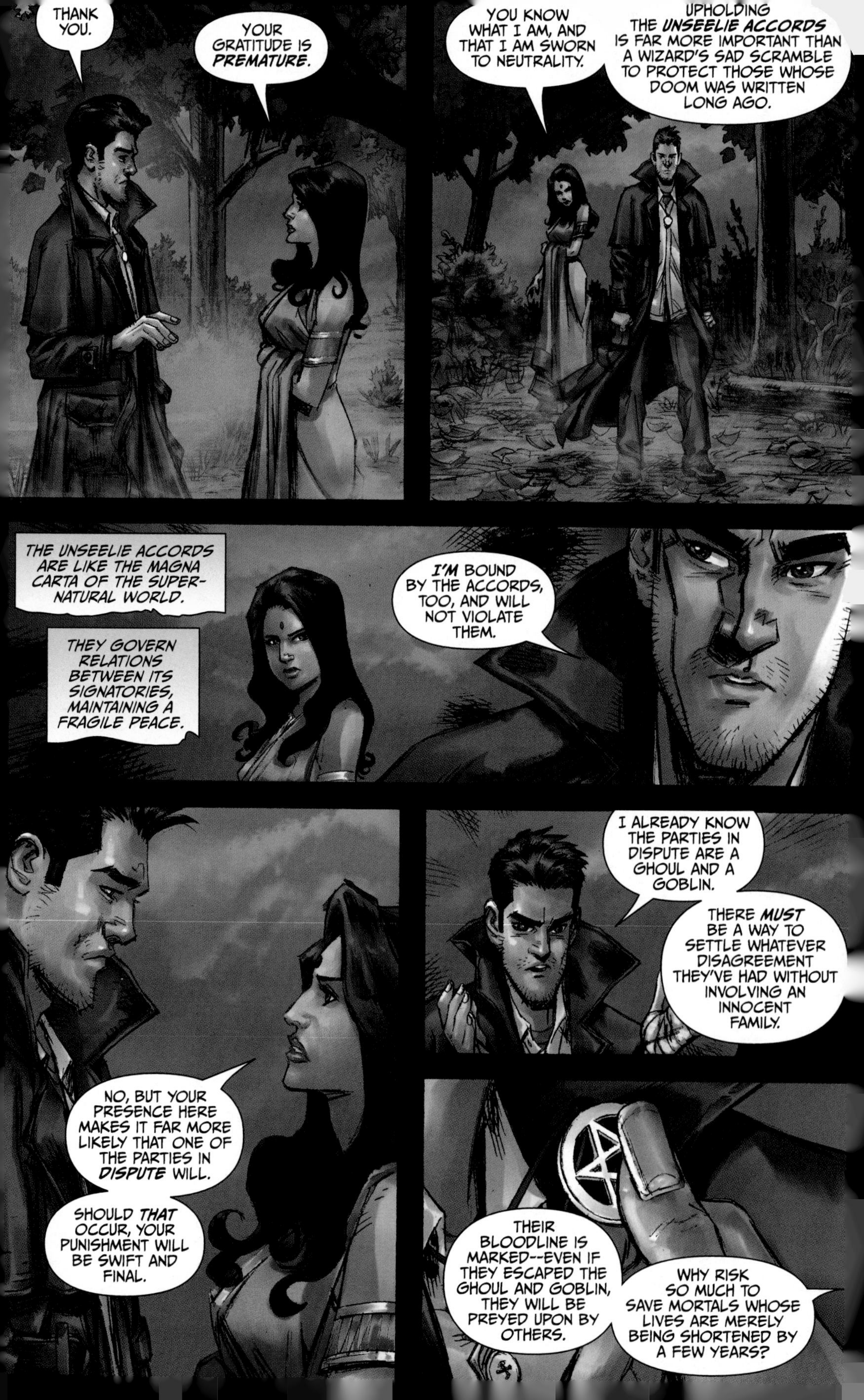
THANK YOU.
YOUR GRATITUDE IS *PREMATURE*.
YOU KNOW WHAT I AM, AND THAT I AM SWORN TO NEUTRALITY.
UPHOLDING THE *UNSEELIE ACCORDS* IS FAR MORE IMPORTANT THAN A WIZARD'S SAD SCRAMBLE TO PROTECT THOSE WHOSE DOOM WAS WRITTEN LONG AGO.
THE UNSEELIE ACCORDS ARE LIKE THE MAGNA CARTA OF THE SUPER-NATURAL WORLD.
THEY GOVERN RELATIONS BETWEEN ITS SIGNATORIES, MAINTAINING A FRAGILE PEACE.
I'M BOUND BY THE ACCORDS, TOO, AND WILL NOT VIOLATE THEM.
NO, BUT YOUR PRESENCE HERE MAKES IT FAR MORE LIKELY THAT ONE OF THE PARTIES IN *DISPUTE* WILL.
SHOULD *THAT* OCCUR, YOUR PUNISHMENT WILL BE SWIFT AND FINAL.
I ALREADY KNOW THE PARTIES IN DISPUTE ARE A GHOUL AND A GOBLIN.
THERE *MUST* BE A WAY TO SETTLE WHATEVER DISAGREEMENT THEY'VE HAD WITHOUT INVOLVING AN INNOCENT FAMILY.
THEIR BLOODLINE IS MARKED--EVEN IF THEY ESCAPED THE GHOUL AND GOBLIN, THEY WILL BE PREYED UPON BY OTHERS.
WHY RISK SO MUCH TO SAVE MORTALS WHOSE LIVES ARE MERELY BEING SHORTENED BY A FEW YEARS?

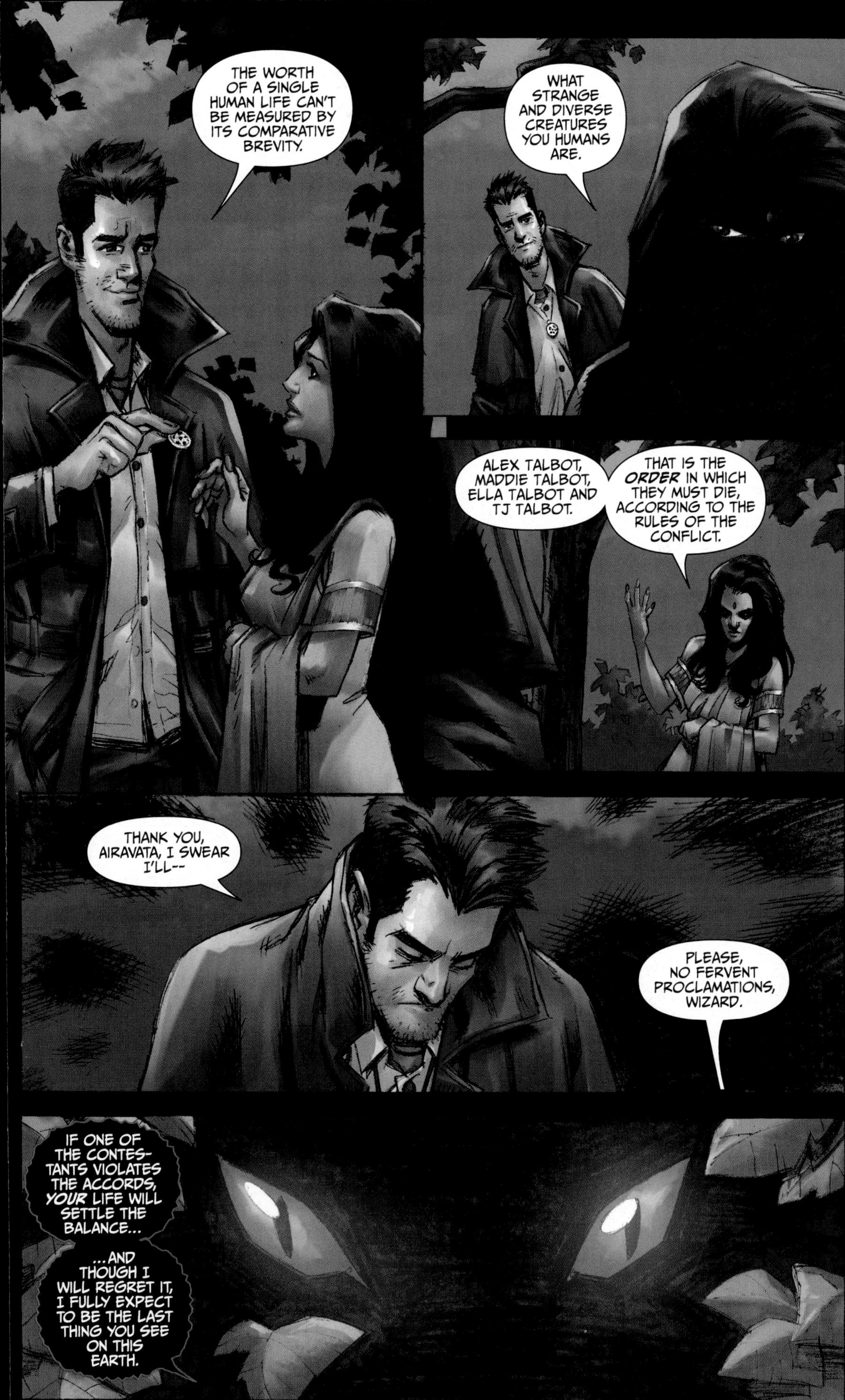
THE WORTH OF A SINGLE HUMAN LIFE CAN'T BE MEASURED BY ITS COMPARATIVE BREVITY.
WHAT STRANGE AND DIVERSE CREATURES YOU HUMANS ARE.
ALEX TALBOT, MADDIE TALBOT, ELLA TALBOT AND TJ TALBOT.
THAT IS THE *ORDER* IN WHICH THEY MUST DIE, ACCORDING TO THE RULES OF THE CONFLICT.
THANK YOU, AIRAVATA, I SWEAR I'LL--
PLEASE, NO FERVENT PROCLAMATIONS, WIZARD.
IF ONE OF THE CONTES-TANTS VIOLATES THE ACCORDS, *YOUR* LIFE WILL SETTLE THE BALANCE...
...AND THOUGH I WILL REGRET IT, I FULLY EXPECT TO BE THE LAST THING YOU SEE ON THIS EARTH.

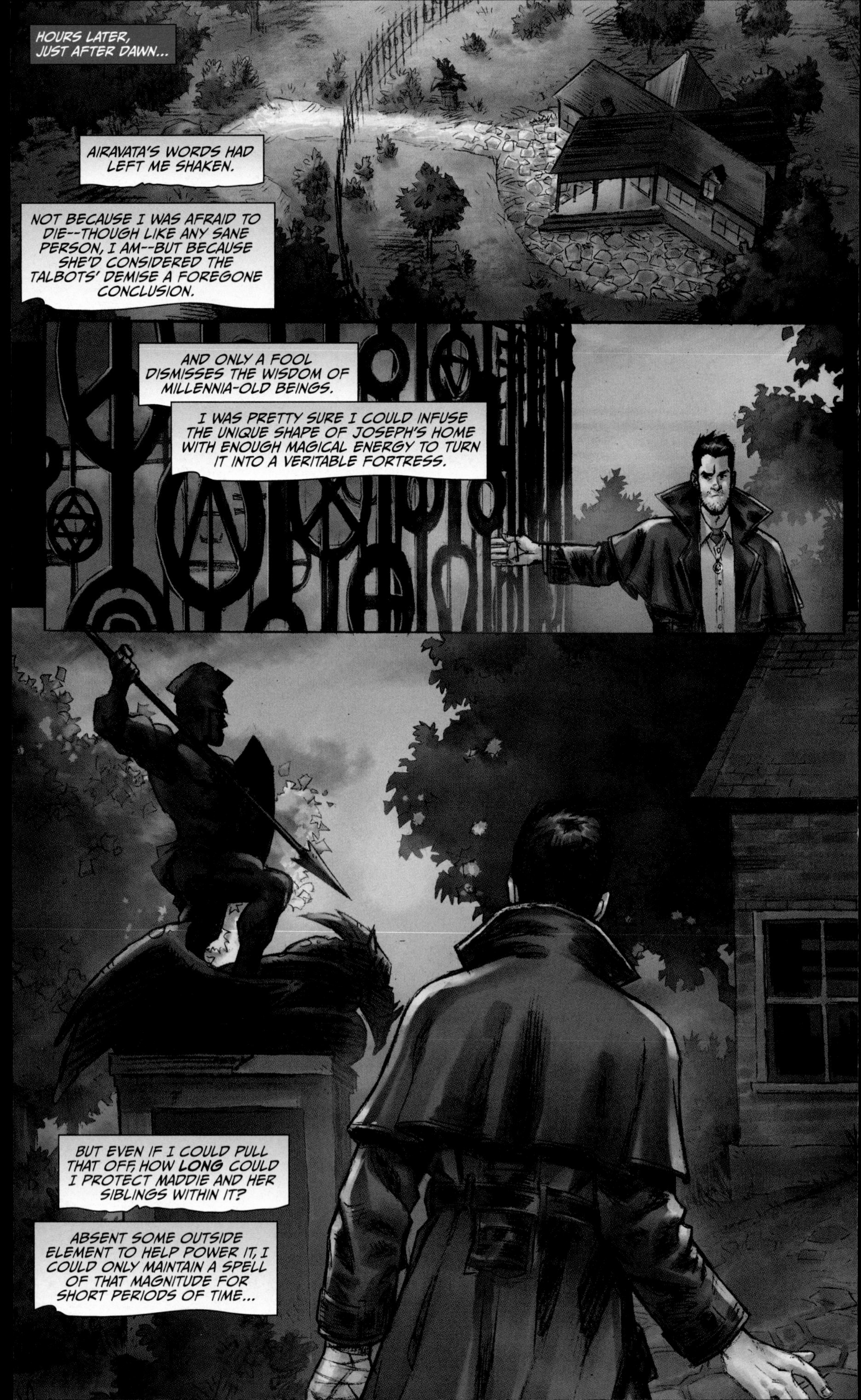
HOURS LATER, JUST AFTER DAWN...
AIRAVATA'S WORDS HAD LEFT ME SHAKEN.
NOT BECAUSE I WAS AFRAID TO DIE--THOUGH LIKE ANY SANE PERSON, I AM--BUT BECAUSE SHE'D CONSIDERED THE TALBOTS' DEMISE A FOREGONE CONCLUSION.
AND ONLY A FOOL DISMISSES THE WISDOM OF MILLENNIA-OLD BEINGS.
I WAS PRETTY SURE I COULD INFUSE THE UNIQUE SHAPE OF JOSEPH'S HOME WITH ENOUGH MAGICAL ENERGY TO TURN IT INTO A VERITABLE FORTRESS.
BUT EVEN IF I COULD PULL THAT OFF, HOW **LONG** COULD I PROTECT MADDIE AND HER SIBLINGS WITHIN IT?
ABSENT SOME OUTSIDE ELEMENT TO HELP POWER IT, I COULD ONLY MAINTAIN A SPELL OF THAT MAGNITUDE FOR SHORT PERIODS OF TIME...

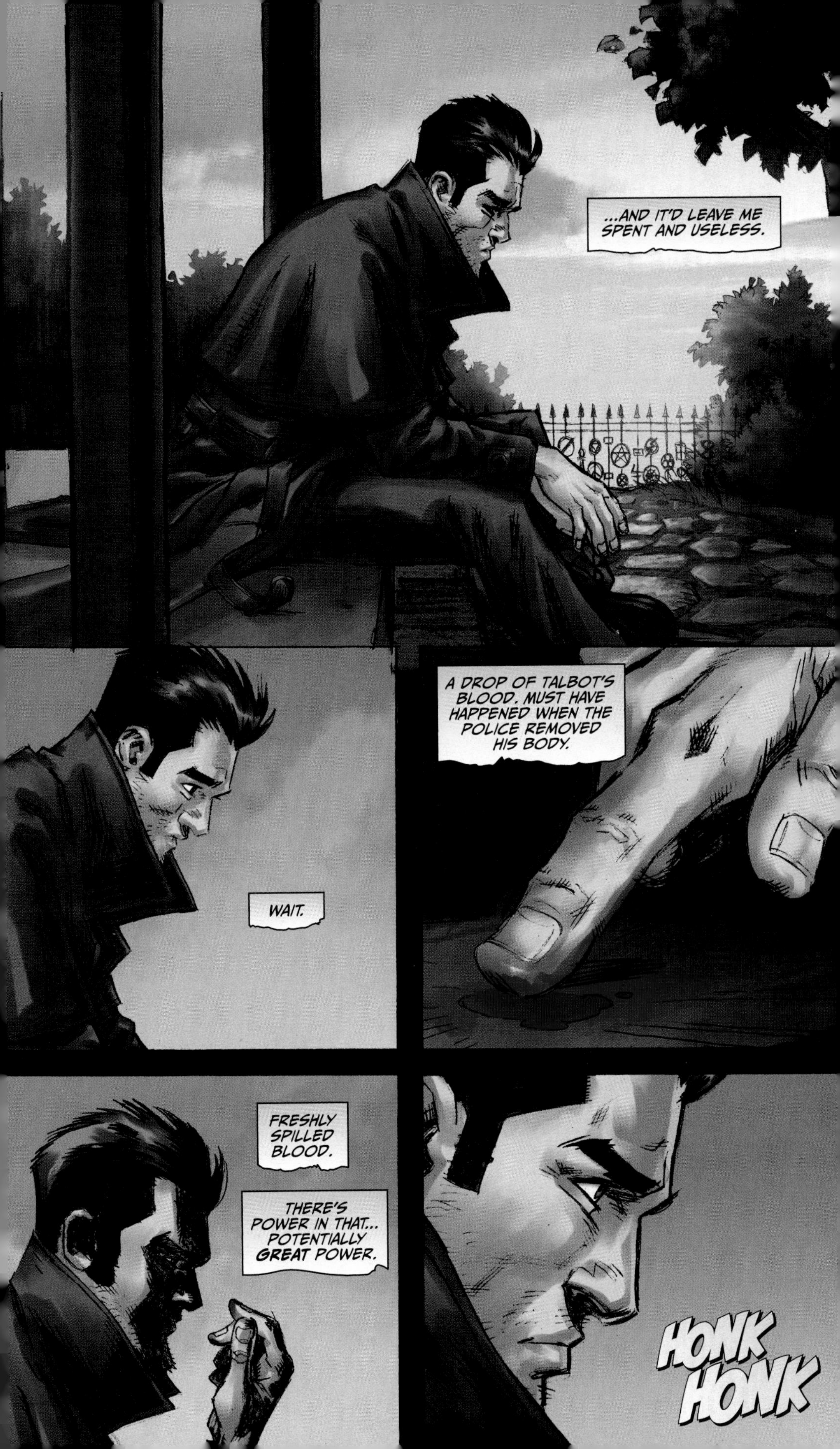
...AND IT'D LEAVE ME SPENT AND USELESS.
WAIT.
A DROP OF TALBOT'S BLOOD. MUST HAVE HAPPENED WHEN THE POLICE REMOVED HIS BODY.
FRESHLY SPILLED BLOOD.
THERE'S POWER IN THAT... POTENTIALLY GREAT POWER.
HONK HONK

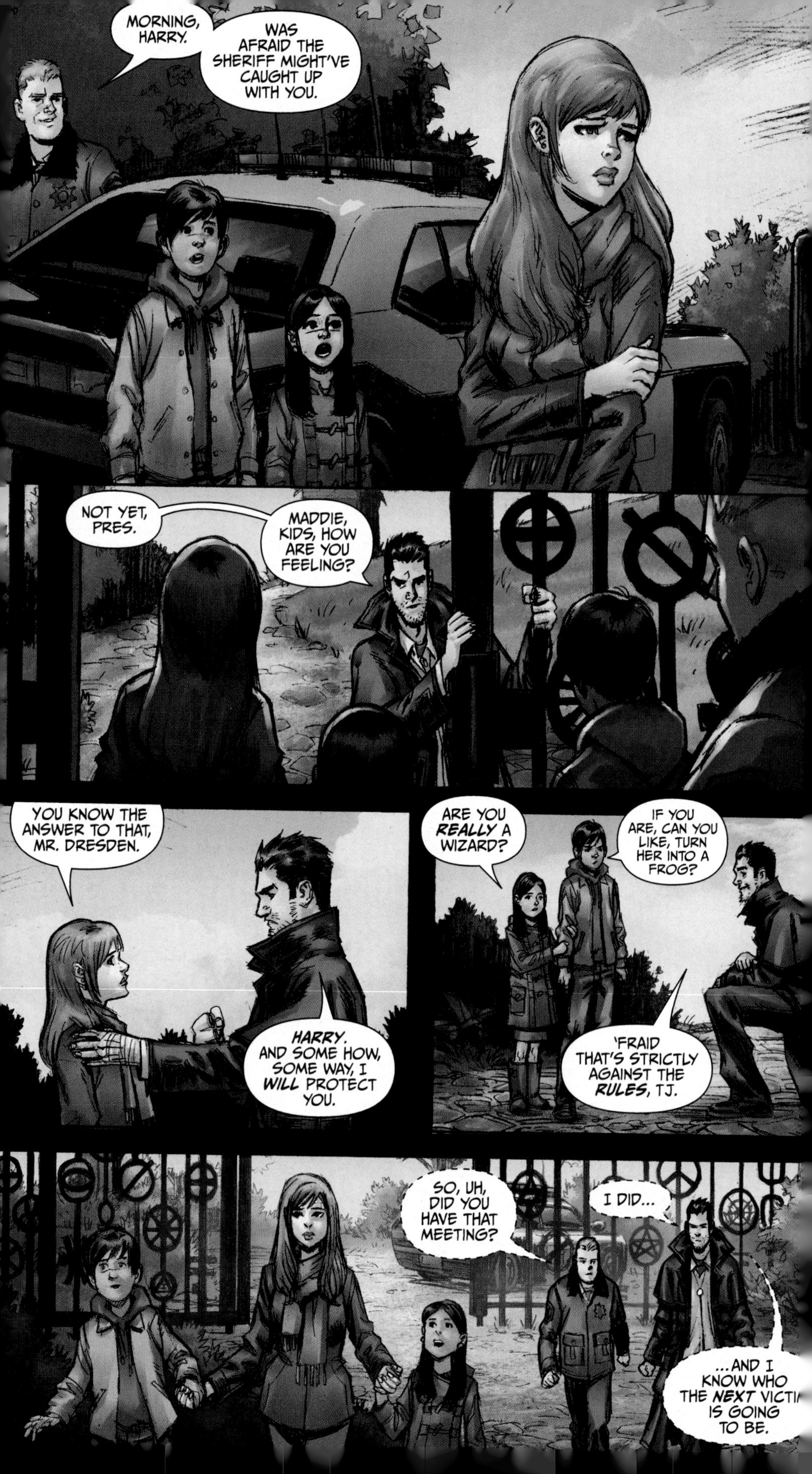
MORNING, HARRY.
WAS AFRAID THE SHERIFF MIGHT'VE CAUGHT UP WITH YOU.
NOT YET, PRES.
MADDIE, KIDS, HOW ARE YOU FEELING?
YOU KNOW THE ANSWER TO THAT, MR. DRESDEN.
HARRY. AND SOME HOW, SOME WAY, I WILL PROTECT YOU.
ARE YOU REALLY A WIZARD?
IF YOU ARE, CAN YOU LIKE, TURN HER INTO A FROG?
'FRAID THAT'S STRICTLY AGAINST THE RULES, TJ.
SO, UH, DID YOU HAVE THAT MEETING?
I DID...
...AND I KNOW WHO THE NEXT VICTI
IS GOING TO BE.

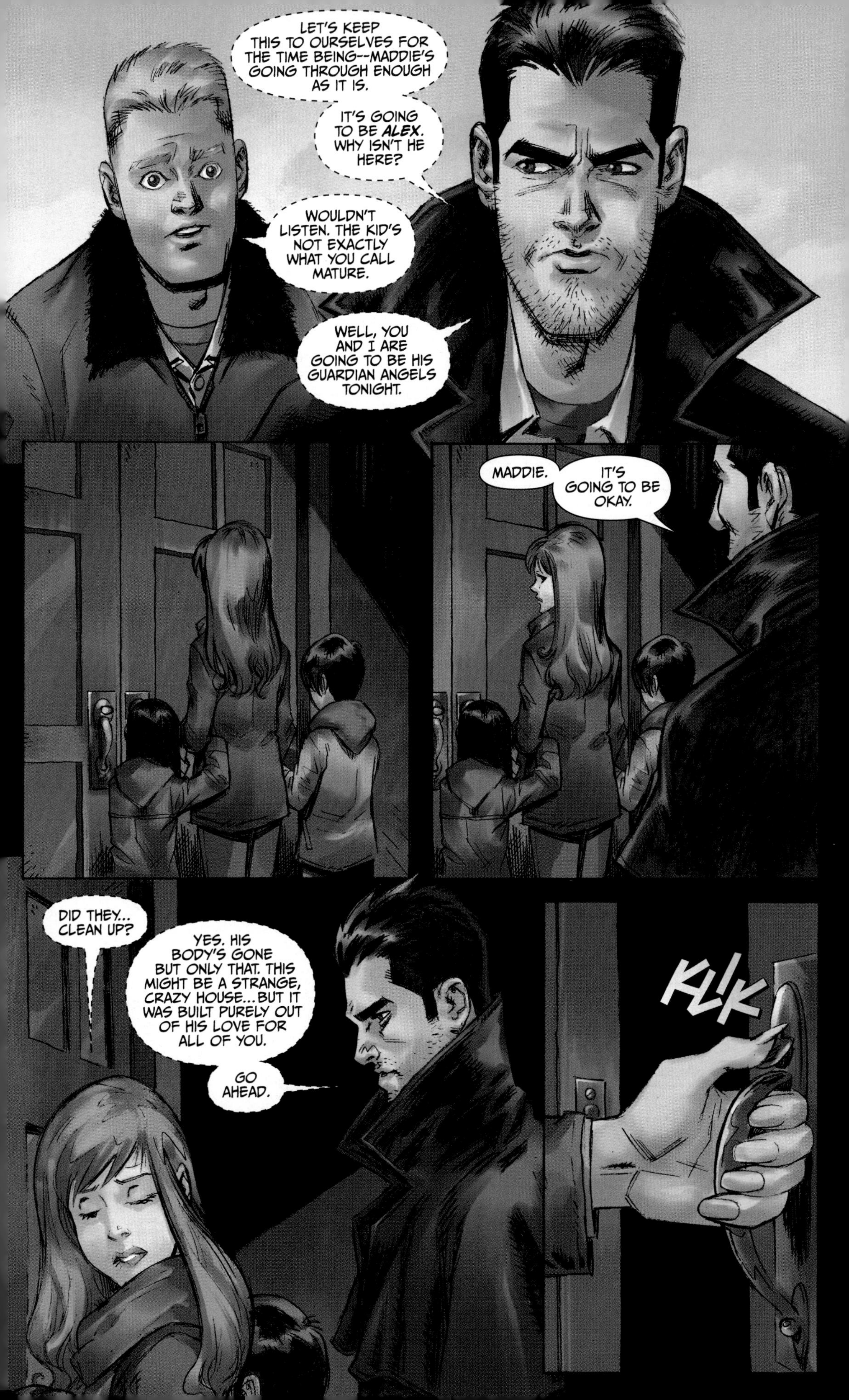
LET'S KEEP THIS TO OURSELVES FOR THE TIME BEING--MADDIE'S GOING THROUGH ENOUGH AS IT IS.
IT'S GOING TO BE ALEX. WHY ISN'T HE HERE?
WOULDN'T LISTEN. THE KID'S NOT EXACTLY WHAT YOU CALL MATURE.
WELL, YOU AND I ARE GOING TO BE HIS GUARDIAN ANGELS TONIGHT.
MADDIE.
IT'S GOING TO BE OKAY.
DID THEY... CLEAN UP?
YES. HIS BODY'S GONE BUT ONLY THAT. THIS MIGHT BE A STRANGE, CRAZY HOUSE...BUT IT WAS BUILT PURELY OUT OF HIS LOVE FOR ALL OF YOU.
GO AHEAD.
KLIK

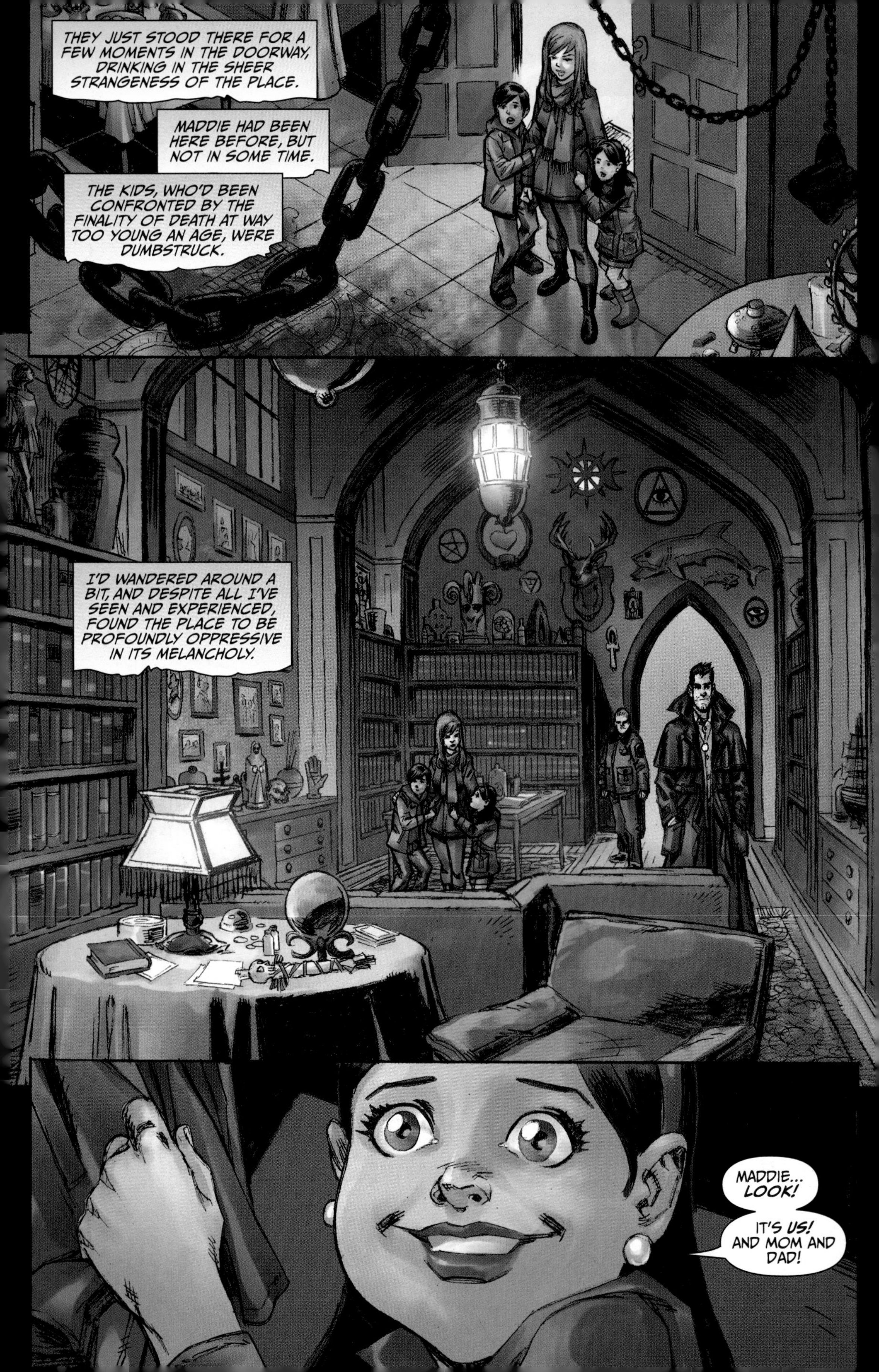
THEY JUST STOOD THERE FOR A FEW MOMENTS IN THE DOORWAY, DRINKING IN THE SHEER STRANGENESS OF THE PLACE.
MADDIE HAD BEEN HERE BEFORE, BUT NOT IN SOME TIME.
THE KIDS, WHO'D BEEN CONFRONTED BY THE FINALITY OF DEATH AT WAY TOO YOUNG AN AGE, WERE DUMBSTRUCK.
I'D WANDERED AROUND A BIT, AND DESPITE ALL I'VE SEEN AND EXPERIENCED, FOUND THE PLACE TO BE PROFOUNDLY OPPRESSIVE IN ITS MELANCHOLY.
MADDIE... LOOK!
IT'S US! AND MOM AND DAD!

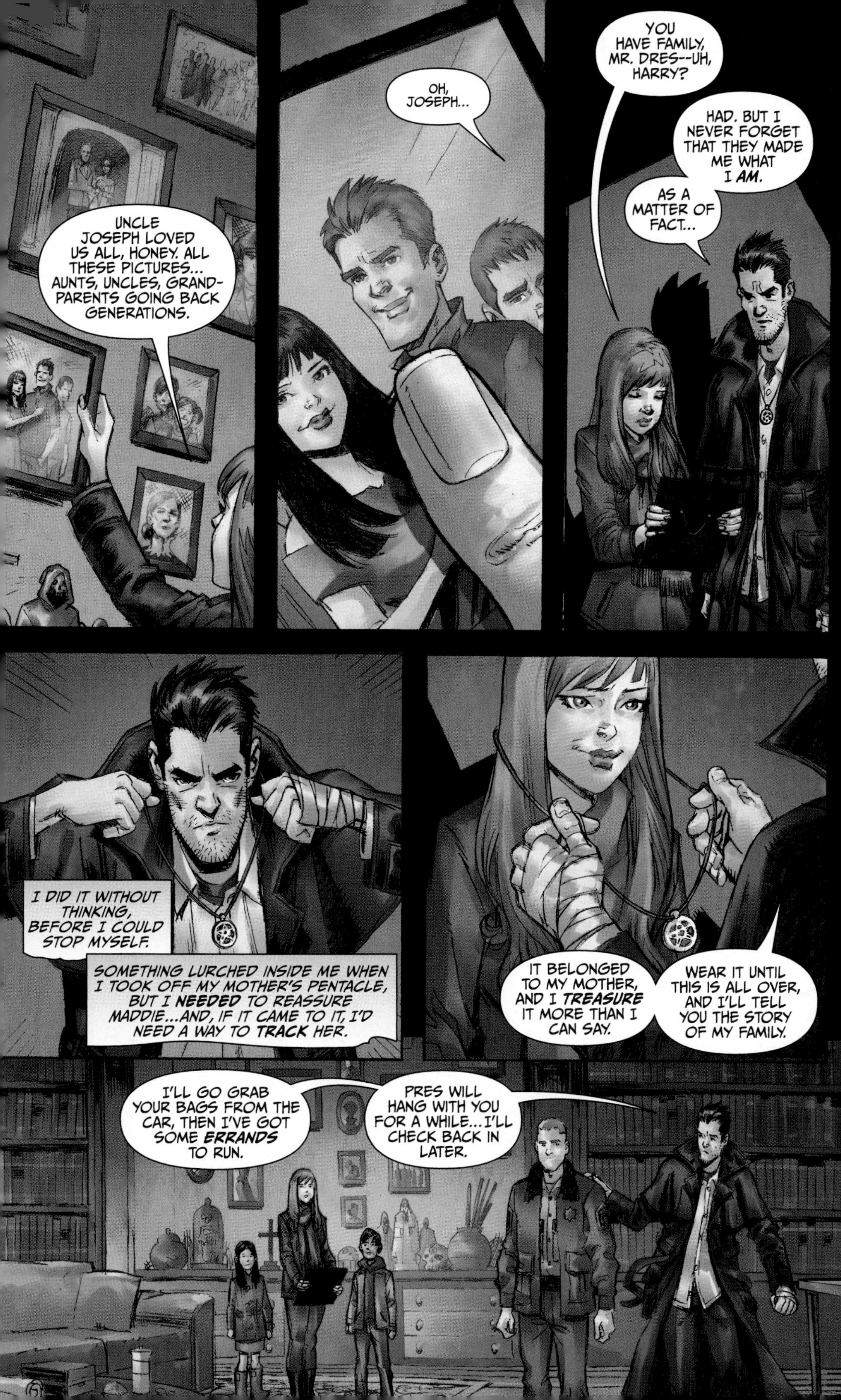
UNCLE JOSEPH LOVED US ALL, HONEY. ALL THESE PICTURES... AUNTS, UNCLES, GRAND-PARENTS GOING BACK GENERATIONS.
OH, JOSEPH...
YOU HAVE FAMILY, MR. DRES--UH, HARRY?
HAD. BUT I NEVER FORGET THAT THEY MADE ME WHAT I AM.
AS A MATTER OF FACT...
I DID IT WITHOUT THINKING, BEFORE I COULD STOP MYSELF.
SOMETHING LURCHED INSIDE ME WHEN I TOOK OFF MY MOTHER'S PENTACLE, BUT I NEEDED TO REASSURE MADDIE...AND, IF IT CAME TO IT, I'D NEED A WAY TO TRACK HER.
IT BELONGED TO MY MOTHER, AND I TREASURE IT MORE THAN I CAN SAY.
WEAR IT UNTIL THIS IS ALL OVER, AND I'LL TELL YOU THE STORY OF MY FAMILY.
I'LL GO GRAB YOUR BAGS FROM THE CAR, THEN I'VE GOT SOME ERRANDS TO RUN.
PRES WILL HANG WITH YOU FOR A WHILE...I'LL CHECK BACK IN LATER.

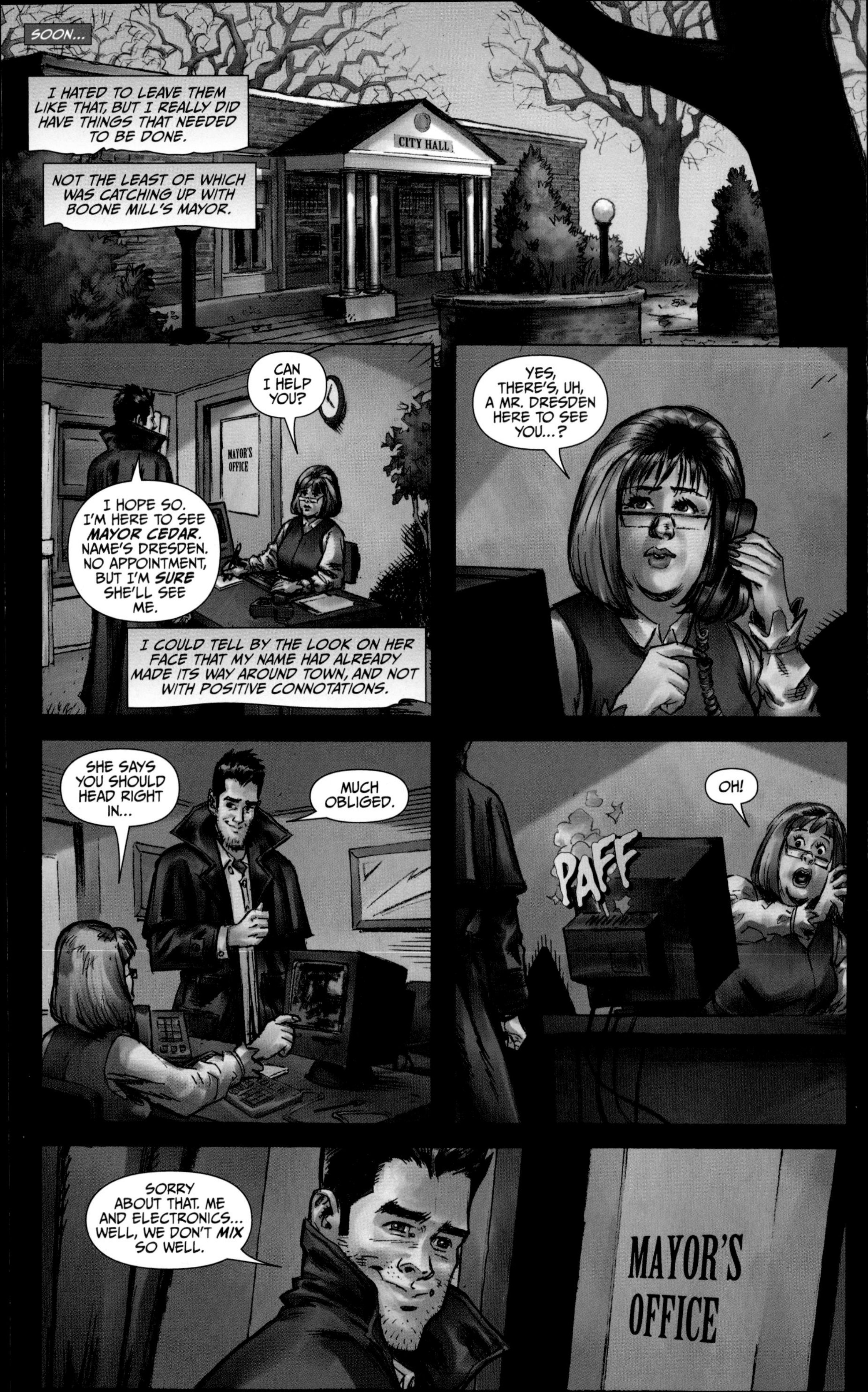
SOON...
I HATED TO LEAVE THEM LIKE THAT, BUT I REALLY DID HAVE THINGS THAT NEEDED TO BE DONE.
NOT THE LEAST OF WHICH WAS CATCHING UP WITH BOONE MILL'S MAYOR.
CITY HALL
CAN I HELP YOU?
MAYOR'S OFFICE
I HOPE SO. I'M HERE TO SEE MAYOR CEDAR. NAME'S DRESDEN. NO APPOINTMENT, BUT I'M SURE SHE'LL SEE ME.
I COULD TELL BY THE LOOK ON HER FACE THAT MY NAME HAD ALREADY MADE ITS WAY AROUND TOWN, AND NOT WITH POSITIVE CONNOTATIONS.
YES, THERE'S, UH, A MR. DRESDEN HERE TO SEE YOU...?
SHE SAYS YOU SHOULD HEAD RIGHT IN...
MUCH OBLIGED.
PAFF
OH!
SORRY ABOUT THAT. ME AND ELECTRONICS... WELL, WE DON'T MIX SO WELL.
MAYOR'S OFFICE

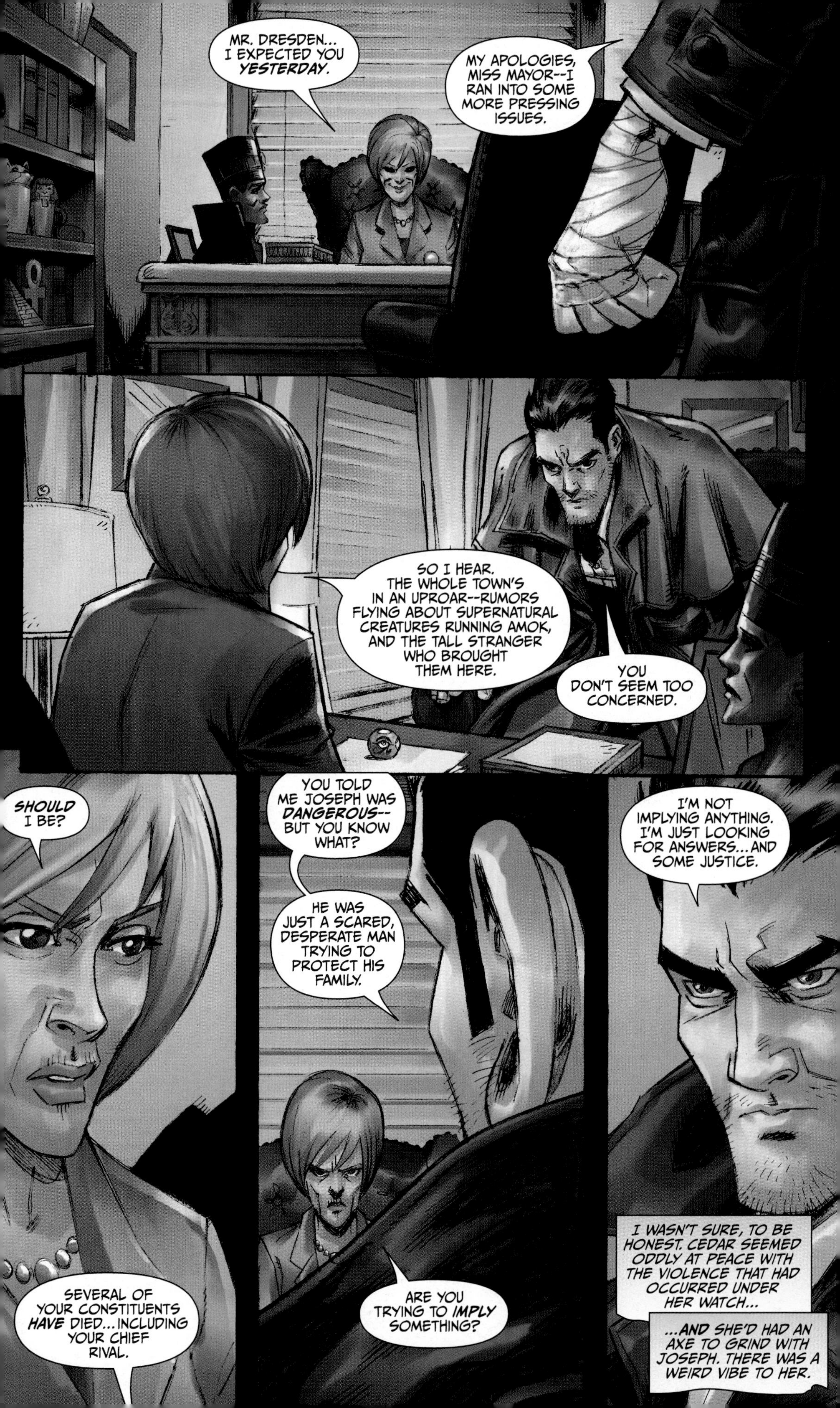
MR. DRESDEN... I EXPECTED YOU *YESTERDAY.*
MY APOLOGIES, MISS MAYOR--I RAN INTO SOME MORE PRESSING ISSUES.
SO I HEAR. THE WHOLE TOWN'S IN AN UPROAR--RUMORS FLYING ABOUT SUPERNATURAL CREATURES RUNNING AMOK, AND THE TALL STRANGER WHO BROUGHT THEM HERE.
YOU DON'T SEEM TOO CONCERNED.
SHOULD I BE?
SEVERAL OF YOUR CONSTITUENTS *HAVE* DIED...INCLUDING YOUR CHIEF RIVAL.
YOU TOLD ME JOSEPH WAS *DANGEROUS*-- BUT YOU KNOW WHAT?
HE WAS JUST A SCARED, DESPERATE MAN TRYING TO PROTECT HIS FAMILY.
ARE YOU TRYING TO *IMPLY* SOMETHING?
I'M NOT IMPLYING ANYTHING. I'M JUST LOOKING FOR ANSWERS...AND SOME JUSTICE.
I WASN'T SURE, TO BE HONEST. CEDAR SEEMED ODDLY AT PEACE WITH THE VIOLENCE THAT HAD OCCURRED UNDER HER WATCH...
...AND SHE'D HAD AN AXE TO GRIND WITH JOSEPH. THERE WAS A WEIRD VIBE TO HER.

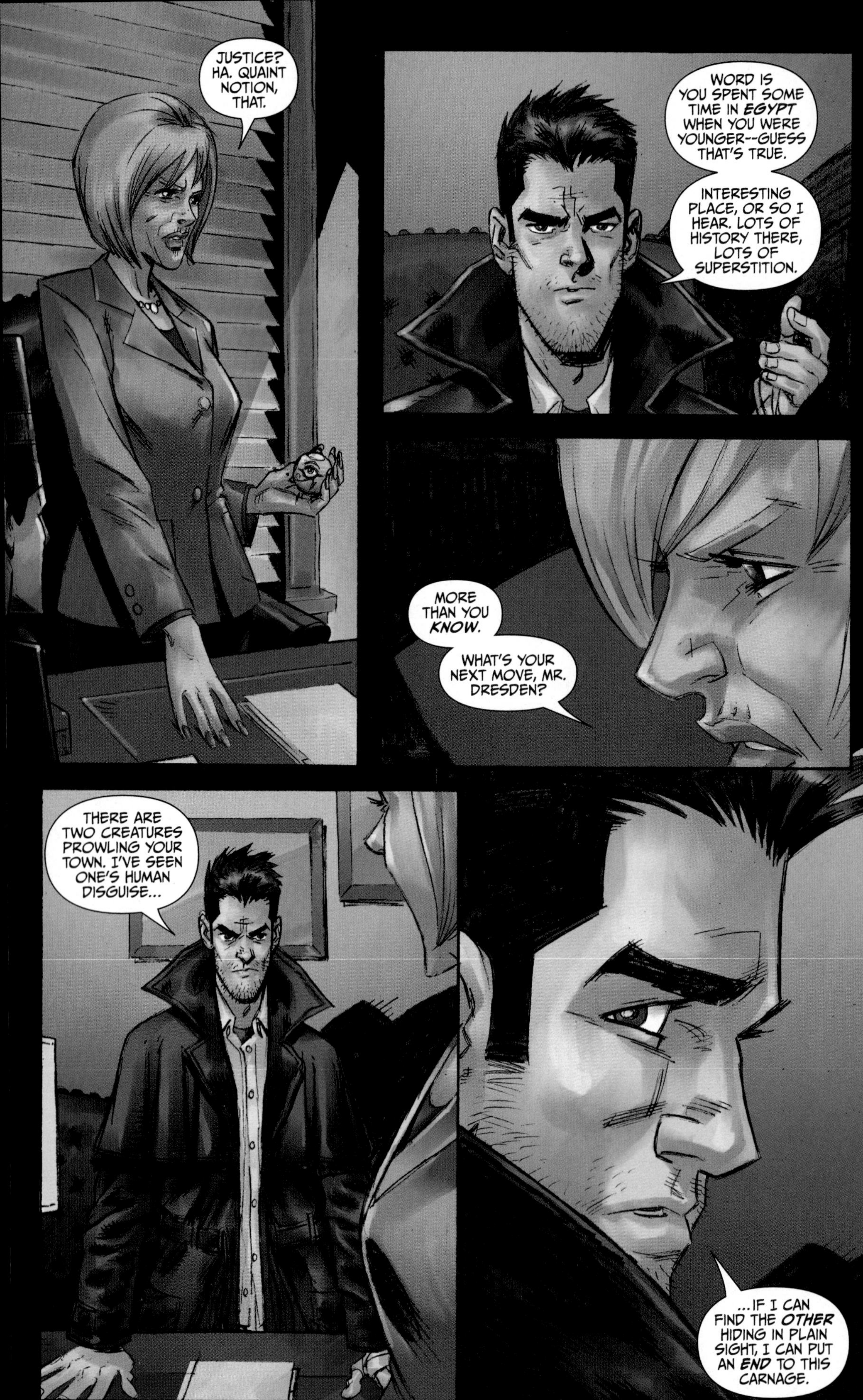
JUSTICE? HA. QUAINT NOTION, THAT.
WORD IS YOU SPENT SOME TIME IN *EGYPT* WHEN YOU WERE YOUNGER--GUESS THAT'S TRUE.
INTERESTING PLACE, OR SO I HEAR. LOTS OF HISTORY THERE, LOTS OF SUPERSTITION.
MORE THAN YOU ***KNOW***.
WHAT'S YOUR NEXT MOVE, MR. DRESDEN?
THERE ARE TWO CREATURES PROWLING YOUR TOWN. I'VE SEEN ONE'S HUMAN DISGUISE...
...IF I CAN FIND THE ***OTHER*** HIDING IN PLAIN SIGHT, I CAN PUT AN ***END*** TO THIS CARNAGE.

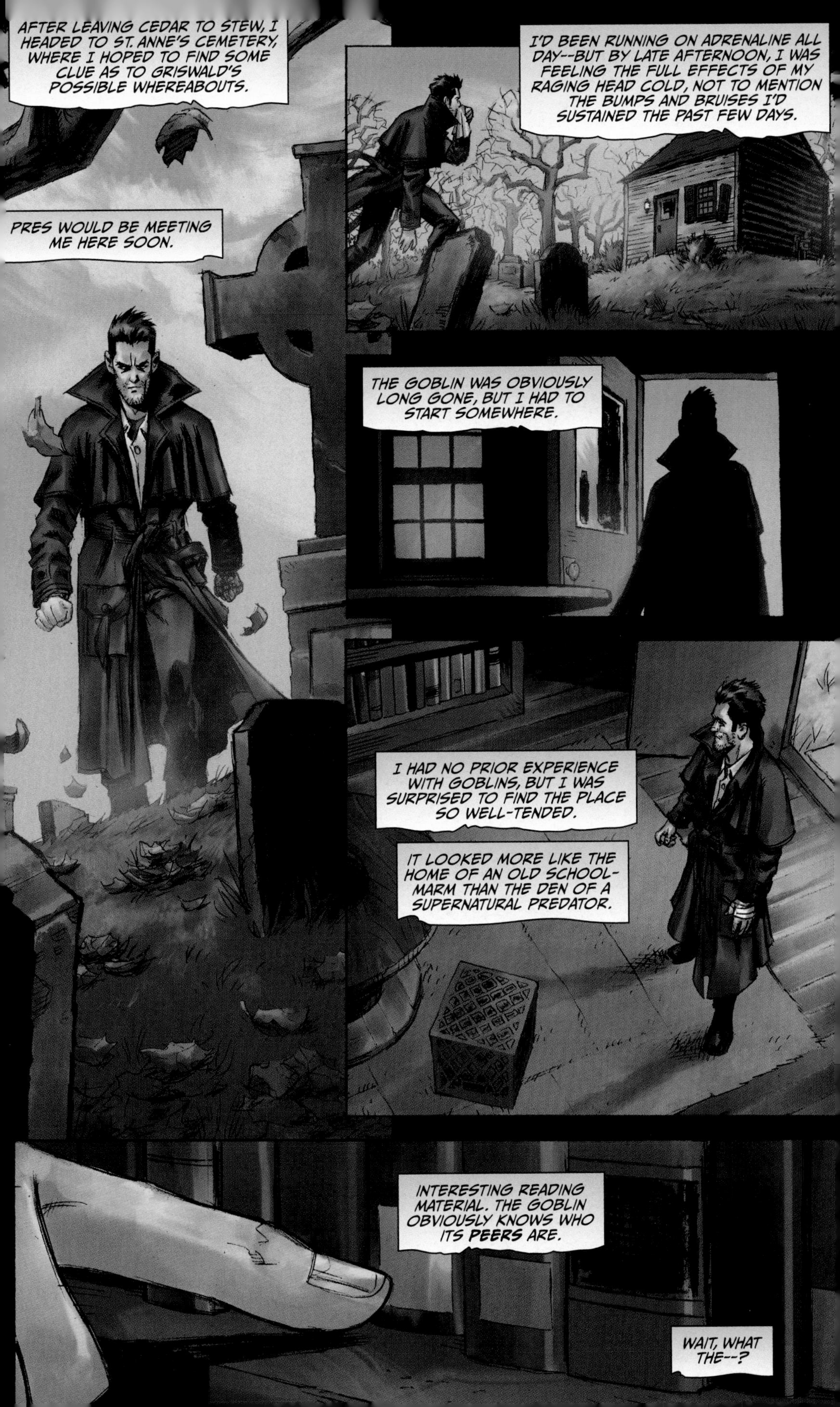
AFTER LEAVING CEDAR TO STEW, I HEADED TO ST. ANNE'S CEMETERY, WHERE I HOPED TO FIND SOME CLUE AS TO GRISWALD'S POSSIBLE WHEREABOUTS.
PRES WOULD BE MEETING ME HERE SOON.
I'D BEEN RUNNING ON ADRENALINE ALL DAY--BUT BY LATE AFTERNOON, I WAS FEELING THE FULL EFFECTS OF MY RAGING HEAD COLD, NOT TO MENTION THE BUMPS AND BRUISES I'D SUSTAINED THE PAST FEW DAYS.
THE GOBLIN WAS OBVIOUSLY LONG GONE, BUT I HAD TO START SOMEWHERE.
I HAD NO PRIOR EXPERIENCE WITH GOBLINS, BUT I WAS SURPRISED TO FIND THE PLACE SO WELL-TENDED.
IT LOOKED MORE LIKE THE HOME OF AN OLD SCHOOL-MARM THAN THE DEN OF A SUPERNATURAL PREDATOR.
INTERESTING READING MATERIAL. THE GOBLIN OBVIOUSLY KNOWS WHO ITS **PEERS** ARE.
WAIT, WHAT THE--?

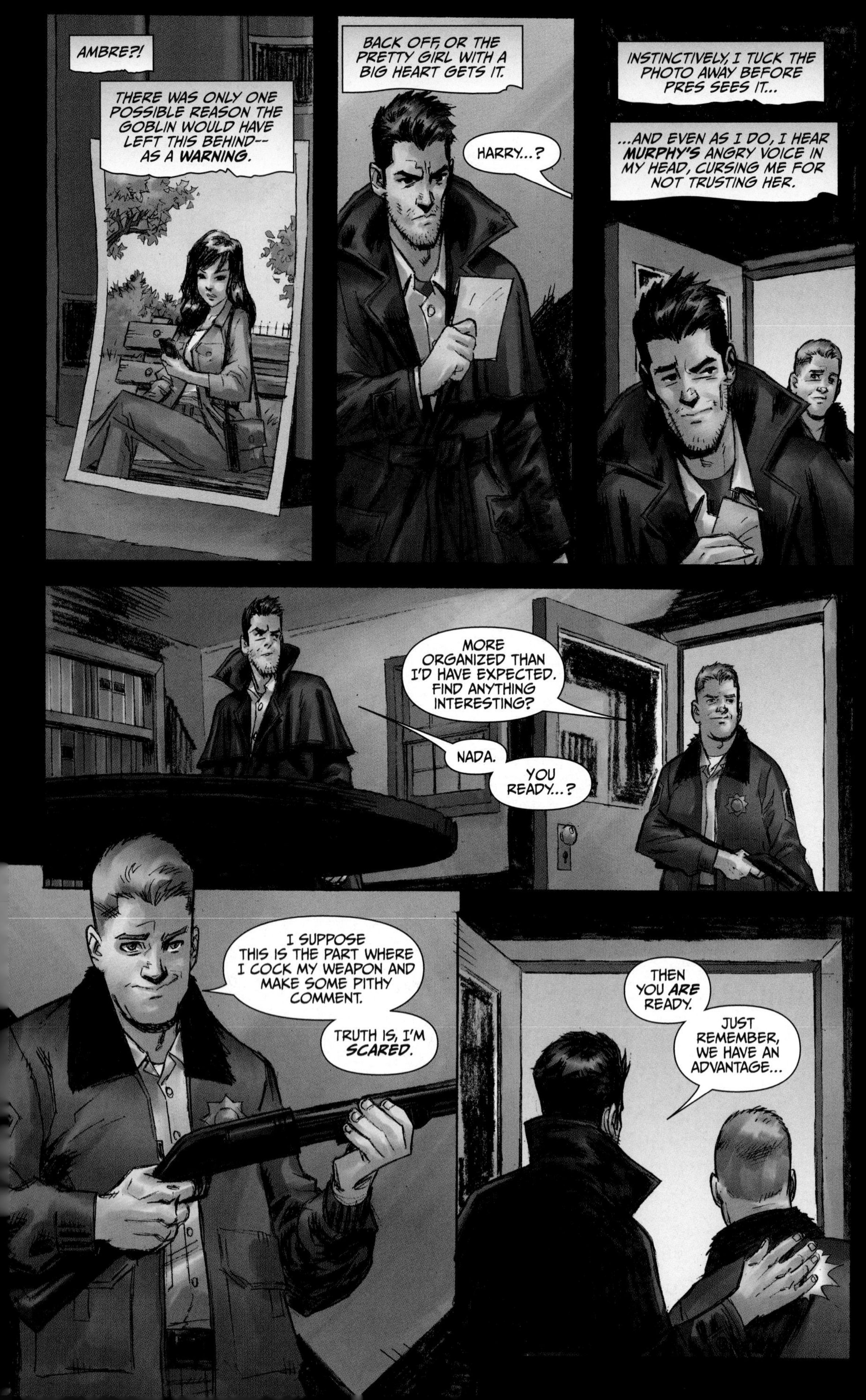
AMBRE?!
THERE WAS ONLY ONE POSSIBLE REASON THE GOBLIN WOULD HAVE LEFT THIS BEHIND-- AS A WARNING.
BACK OFF, OR THE PRETTY GIRL WITH A BIG HEART GETS IT.
HARRY...?
INSTINCTIVELY, I TUCK THE PHOTO AWAY BEFORE PRES SEES IT...
...AND EVEN AS I DO, I HEAR MURPHY'S ANGRY VOICE IN MY HEAD, CURSING ME FOR NOT TRUSTING HER.
MORE ORGANIZED THAN I'D HAVE EXPECTED. FIND ANYTHING INTERESTING?
NADA.
YOU READY...?
I SUPPOSE THIS IS THE PART WHERE I COCK MY WEAPON AND MAKE SOME PITHY COMMENT.
TRUTH IS, I'M SCARED.
THEN YOU ARE READY.
JUST REMEMBER, WE HAVE AN ADVANTAGE...

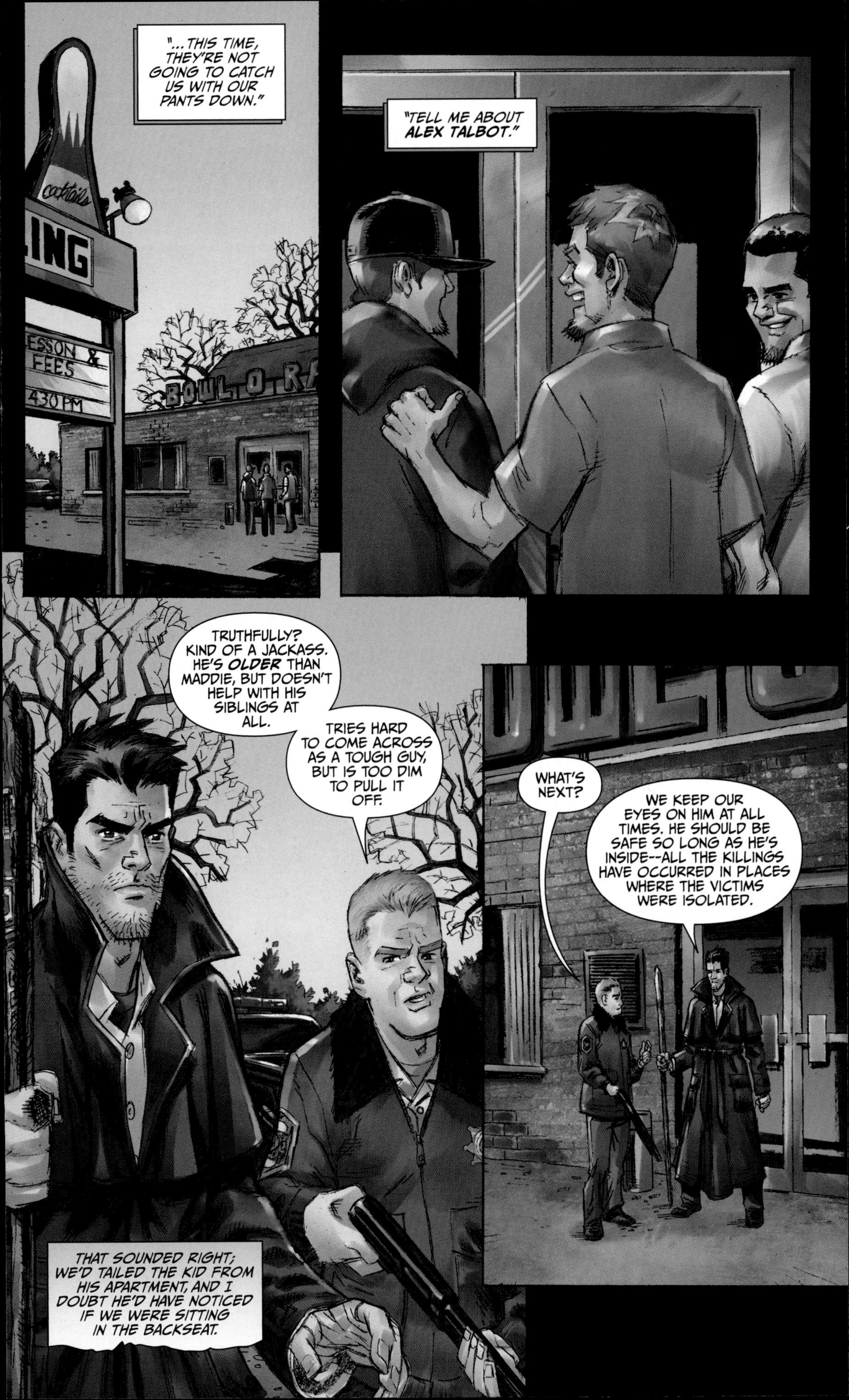
"...THIS TIME, THEY'RE NOT GOING TO CATCH US WITH OUR PANTS DOWN."
cocktails
LING
ESSON &
FEES
430 PM
BOWL O RA
"TELL ME ABOUT ALEX TALBOT."
TRUTHFULLY? KIND OF A JACKASS. HE'S OLDER THAN MADDIE, BUT DOESN'T HELP WITH HIS SIBLINGS AT ALL.
TRIES HARD TO COME ACROSS AS A TOUGH GUY, BUT IS TOO DIM TO PULL IT OFF.
THAT SOUNDED RIGHT; WE'D TAILED THE KID FROM HIS APARTMENT, AND I DOUBT HE'D HAVE NOTICED IF WE WERE SITTING IN THE BACKSEAT.
WHAT'S NEXT?
WE KEEP OUR EYES ON HIM AT ALL TIMES. HE SHOULD BE SAFE SO LONG AS HE'S INSIDE--ALL THE KILLINGS HAVE OCCURRED IN PLACES WHERE THE VICTIMS WERE ISOLATED.

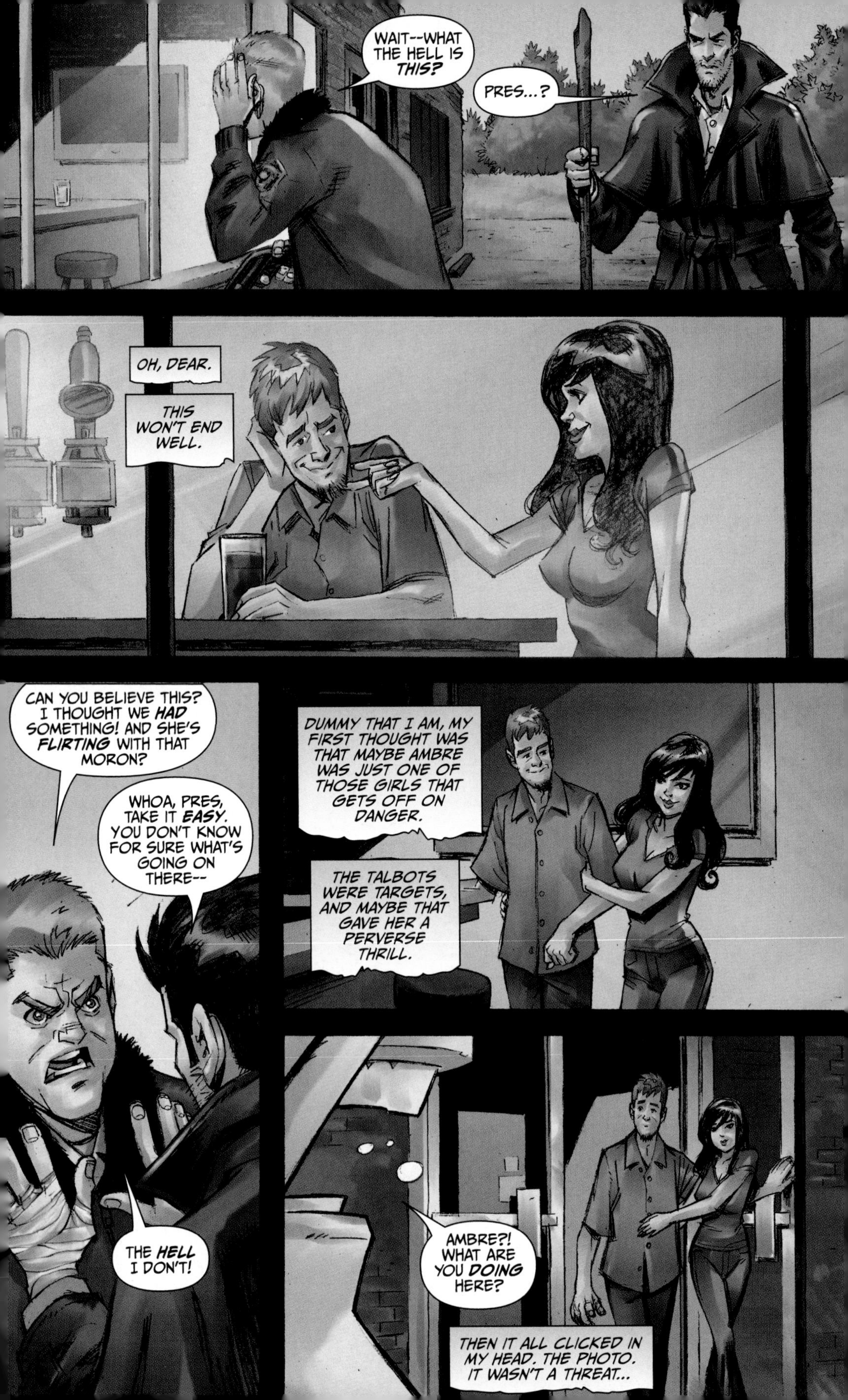
WAIT--WHAT THE HELL IS THIS?
PRES...?
OH, DEAR.
THIS WON'T END WELL.
CAN YOU BELIEVE THIS? I THOUGHT WE HAD SOMETHING! AND SHE'S FLIRTING WITH THAT MORON?
WHOA, PRES, TAKE IT EASY. YOU DON'T KNOW FOR SURE WHAT'S GOING ON THERE--
THE HELL I DON'T!
DUMMY THAT I AM, MY FIRST THOUGHT WAS THAT MAYBE AMBRE WAS JUST ONE OF THOSE GIRLS THAT GETS OFF ON DANGER.
THE TALBOTS WERE TARGETS, AND MAYBE THAT GAVE HER A PERVERSE THRILL.
AMBRE?! WHAT ARE YOU DOING HERE?
THEN IT ALL CLICKED IN MY HEAD. THE PHOTO. IT WASN'T A THREAT...

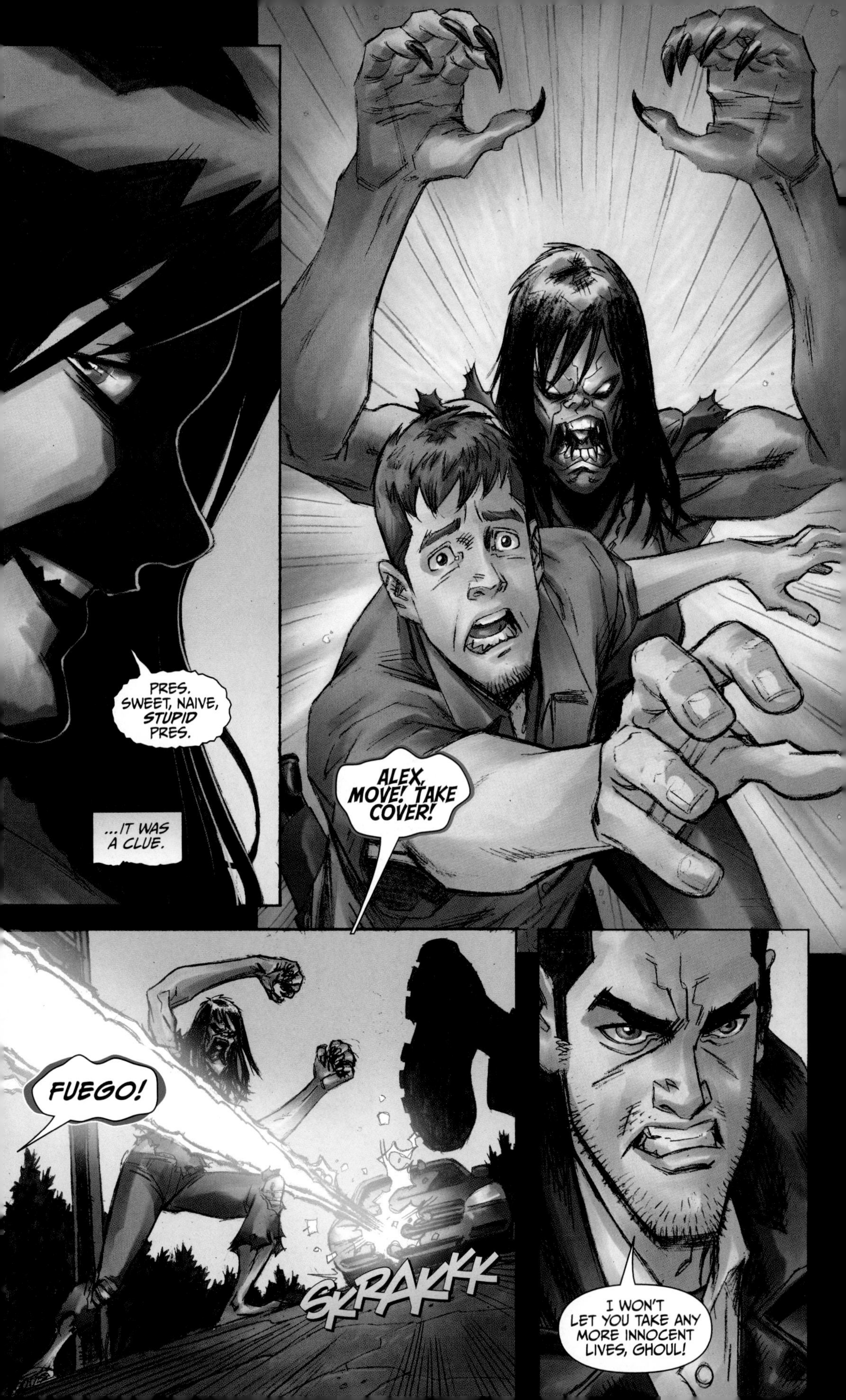
PRES. SWEET, NAIVE, STUPID PRES.
...IT WAS A CLUE.
ALEX, MOVE! TAKE COVER!
FUEGO!
SKRAKKK
I WON'T LET YOU TAKE ANY MORE INNOCENT LIVES, GHOUL!

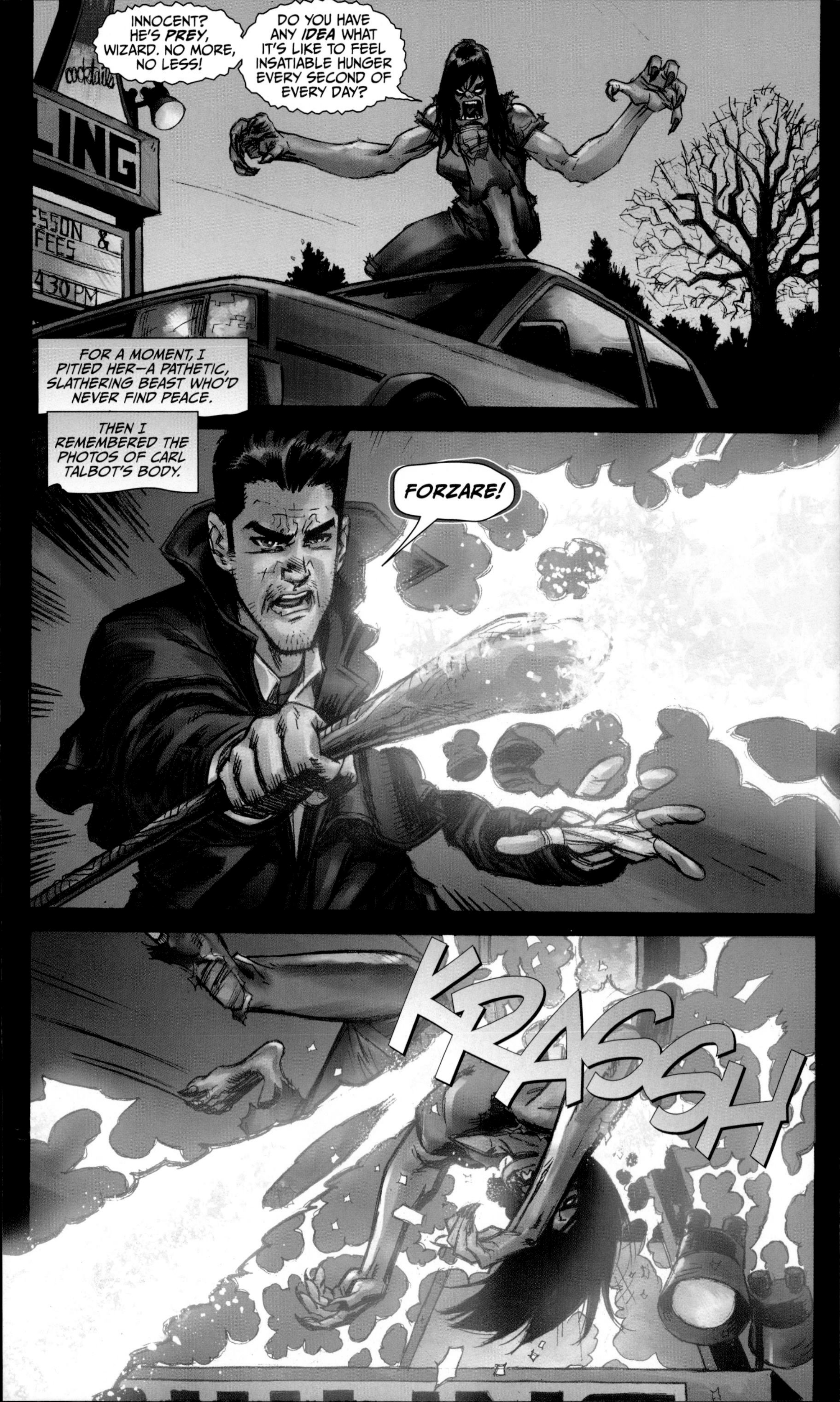

LING
INNOCENT? HE'S PREY, WIZARD. NO MORE, NO LESS!
DO YOU HAVE ANY IDEA WHAT IT'S LIKE TO FEEL INSATIABLE HUNGER EVERY SECOND OF EVERY DAY?
FOR A MOMENT, I PITIED HER—A PATHETIC, SLATHERING BEAST WHO'D NEVER FIND PEACE.
THEN I REMEMBERED THE PHOTOS OF CARL TALBOT'S BODY.
FORZARE!
KRASSH

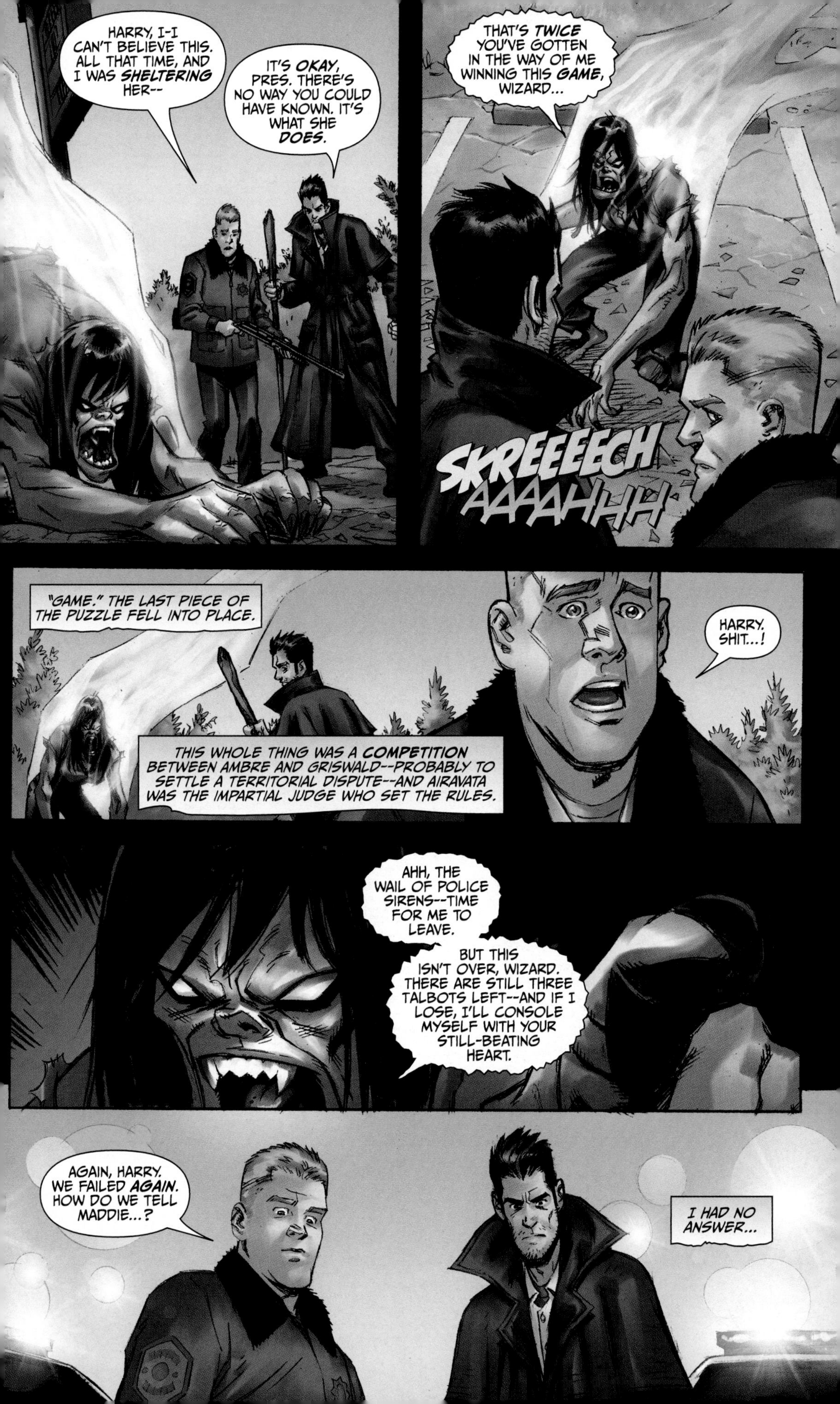

HARRY, I-I CAN'T BELIEVE THIS. ALL THAT TIME, AND I WAS SHELTERING HER--
IT'S OKAY, PRES. THERE'S NO WAY YOU COULD HAVE KNOWN. IT'S WHAT SHE DOES.
THAT'S TWICE YOU'VE GOTTEN IN THE WAY OF ME WINNING THIS GAME, WIZARD...
SKREEEEECH
AAAAHHH
"GAME." THE LAST PIECE OF THE PUZZLE FELL INTO PLACE.
HARRY. SHIT...!
THIS WHOLE THING WAS A COMPETITION BETWEEN AMBRE AND GRISWALD--PROBABLY TO SETTLE A TERRITORIAL DISPUTE--AND AIRAVATA WAS THE IMPARTIAL JUDGE WHO SET THE RULES.
AHH, THE WAIL OF POLICE SIRENS--TIME FOR ME TO LEAVE.
BUT THIS ISN'T OVER, WIZARD. THERE ARE STILL THREE TALBOTS LEFT--AND IF I LOSE, I'LL CONSOLE MYSELF WITH YOUR STILL-BEATING HEART.
AGAIN, HARRY. WE FAILED AGAIN. HOW DO WE TELL MADDIE...?
I HAD NO ANSWER...

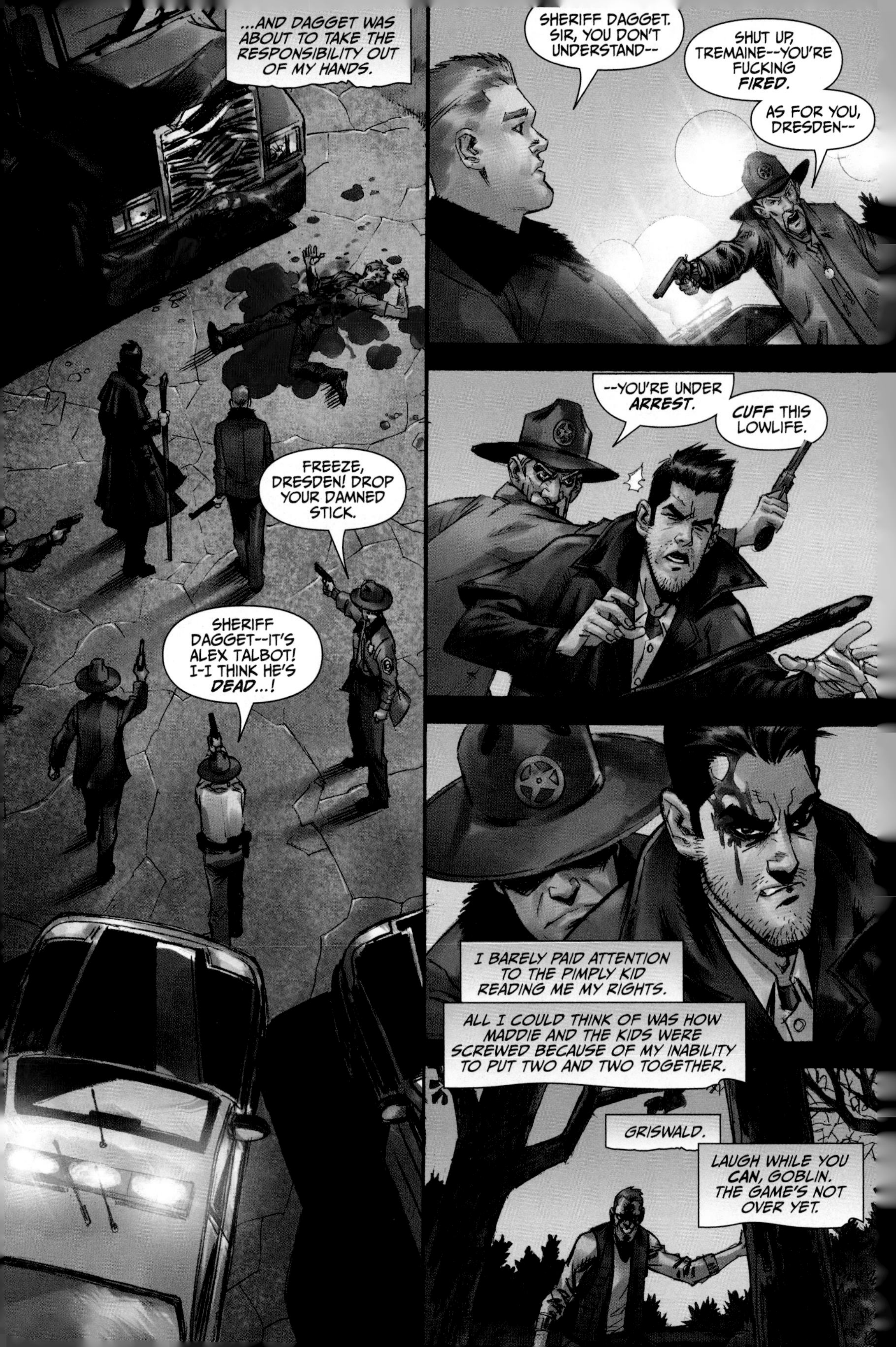
...AND DAGGET WAS ABOUT TO TAKE THE RESPONSIBILITY OUT OF MY HANDS.
FREEZE, DRESDEN! DROP YOUR DAMNED STICK.
SHERIFF DAGGET--IT'S ALEX TALBOT! I-I THINK HE'S DEAD...!
SHERIFF DAGGET. SIR, YOU DON'T UNDERSTAND--
SHUT UP, TREMAINE--YOU'RE FUCKING FIRED.
AS FOR YOU, DRESDEN--
--YOU'RE UNDER ARREST.
CUFF THIS LOWLIFE.
I BARELY PAID ATTENTION TO THE PIMPLY KID READING ME MY RIGHTS.
ALL I COULD THINK OF WAS HOW MADDIE AND THE KIDS WERE SCREWED BECAUSE OF MY INABILITY TO PUT TWO AND TWO TOGETHER.
GRISWALD.
LAUGH WHILE YOU CAN, GOBLIN. THE GAME'S NOT OVER YET.

ISSUE FIVE COVER BY
ARDIAN SYAF

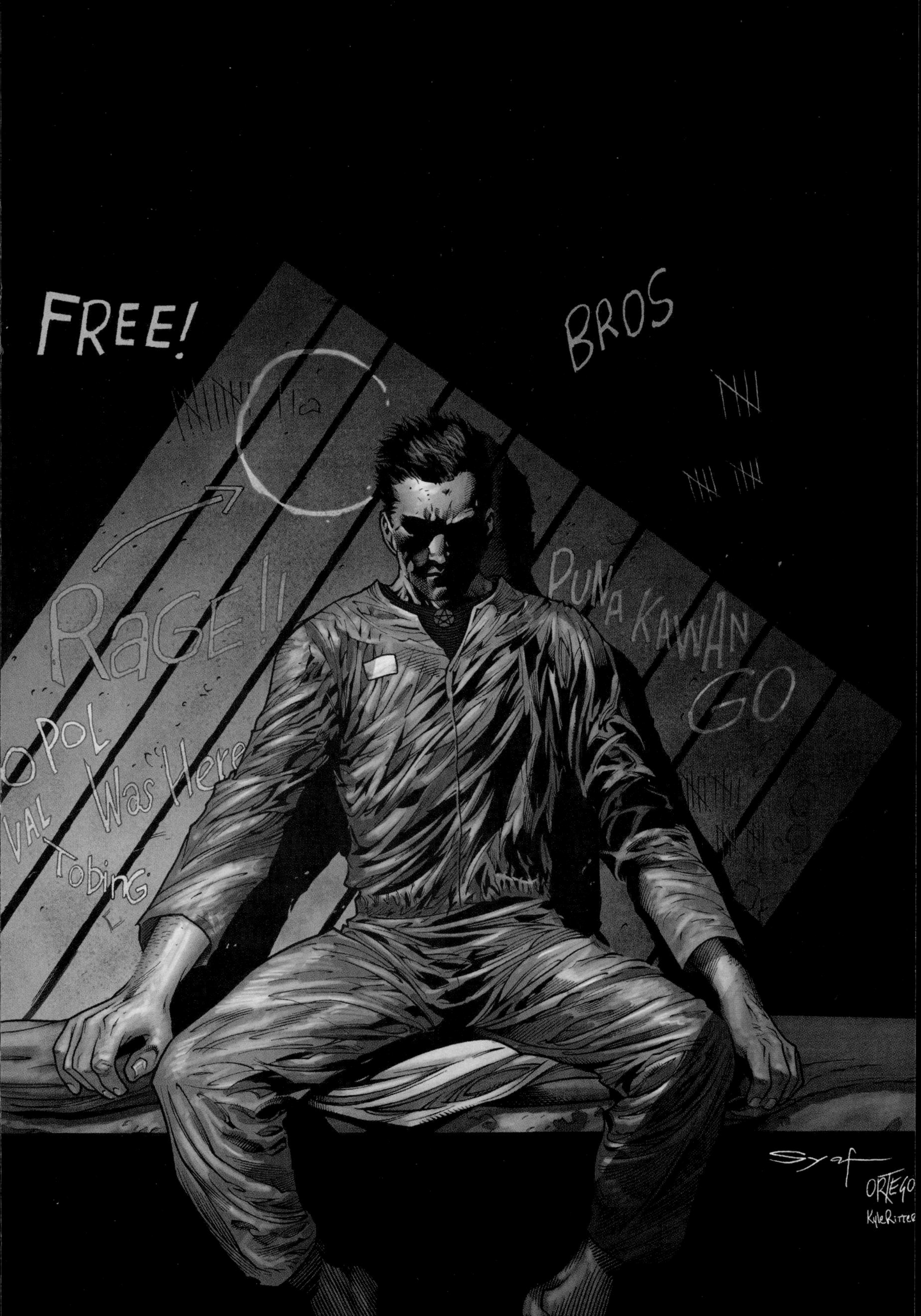
FREE!
BROS
RAGE!!
OPOL
VAL
Was Here
Tobing
PUNA KAWAN
GO
Syaf
ORTEGO
KyleRitter

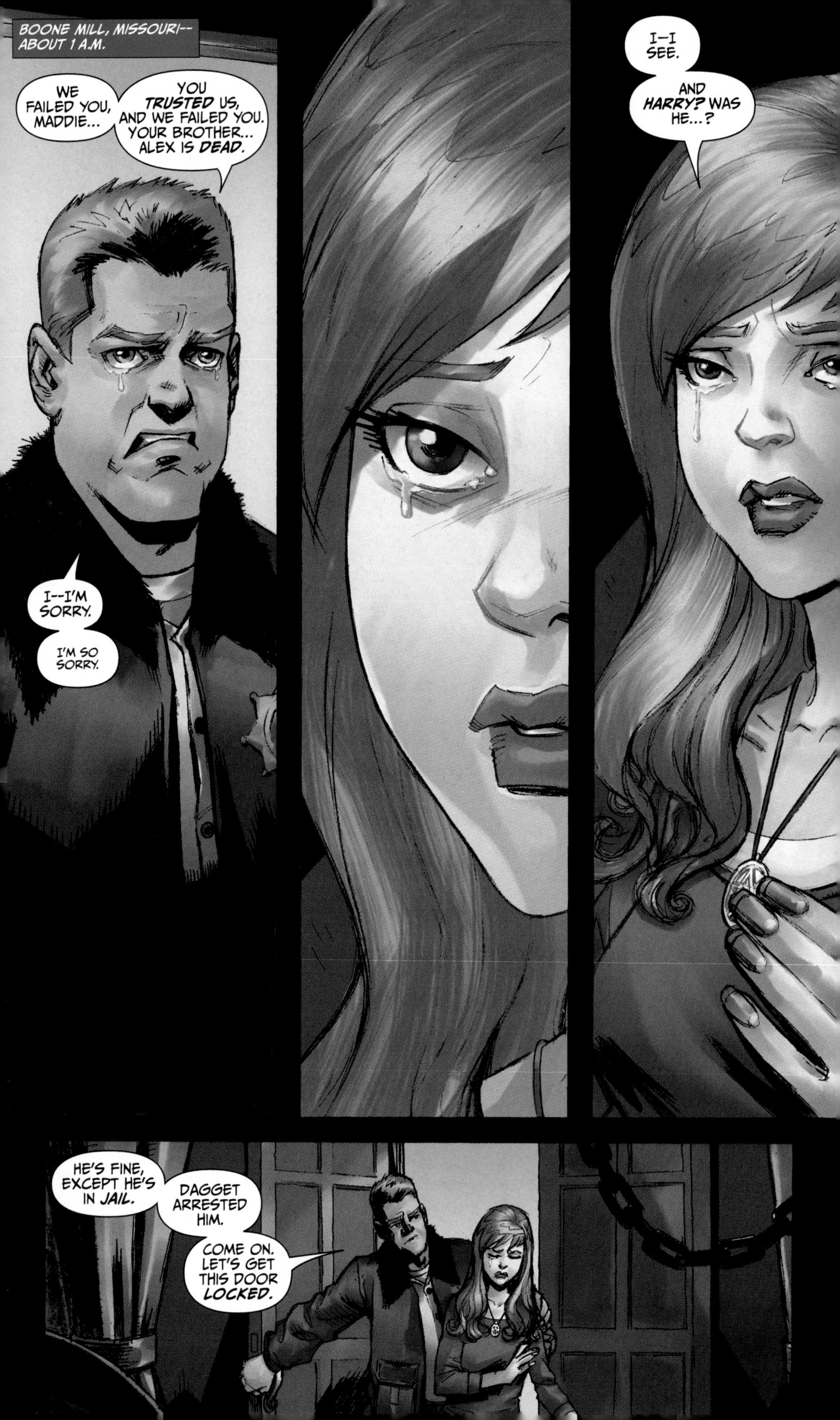
BOONE MILL, MISSOURI--
ABOUT 1 A.M.
WE FAILED YOU, MADDIE...
YOU TRUSTED US, AND WE FAILED YOU. YOUR BROTHER... ALEX IS DEAD.
I--I'M SORRY.
I'M SO SORRY.
I—I SEE.
AND HARRY? WAS HE...?
HE'S FINE, EXCEPT HE'S IN JAIL.
DAGGET ARRESTED HIM.
COME ON. LET'S GET THIS DOOR LOCKED.

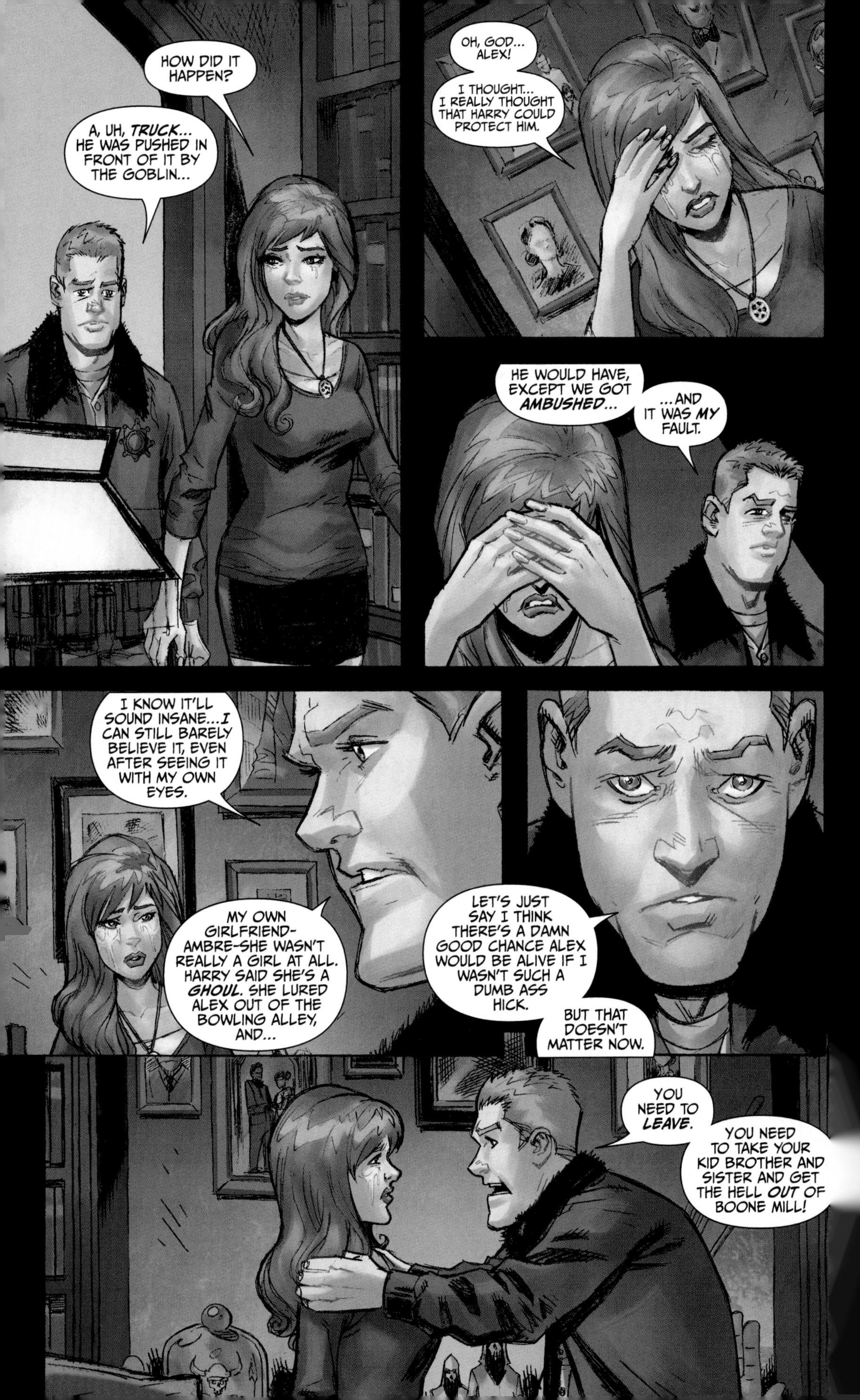
HOW DID IT HAPPEN?
A, UH, TRUCK... HE WAS PUSHED IN FRONT OF IT BY THE GOBLIN...
OH, GOD... ALEX!
I THOUGHT... I REALLY THOUGHT THAT HARRY COULD PROTECT HIM.
HE WOULD HAVE, EXCEPT WE GOT AMBUSHED...
...AND IT WAS MY FAULT.
I KNOW IT'LL SOUND INSANE... I CAN STILL BARELY BELIEVE IT, EVEN AFTER SEEING IT WITH MY OWN EYES.
MY OWN GIRLFRIEND-AMBRE-SHE WASN'T REALLY A GIRL AT ALL. HARRY SAID SHE'S A GHOUL. SHE LURED ALEX OUT OF THE BOWLING ALLEY, AND...
LET'S JUST SAY I THINK THERE'S A DAMN GOOD CHANCE ALEX WOULD BE ALIVE IF I WASN'T SUCH A DUMB ASS HICK.
BUT THAT DOESN'T MATTER NOW.
YOU NEED TO LEAVE.
YOU NEED TO TAKE YOUR KID BROTHER AND SISTER AND GET THE HELL OUT OF BOONE MILL!

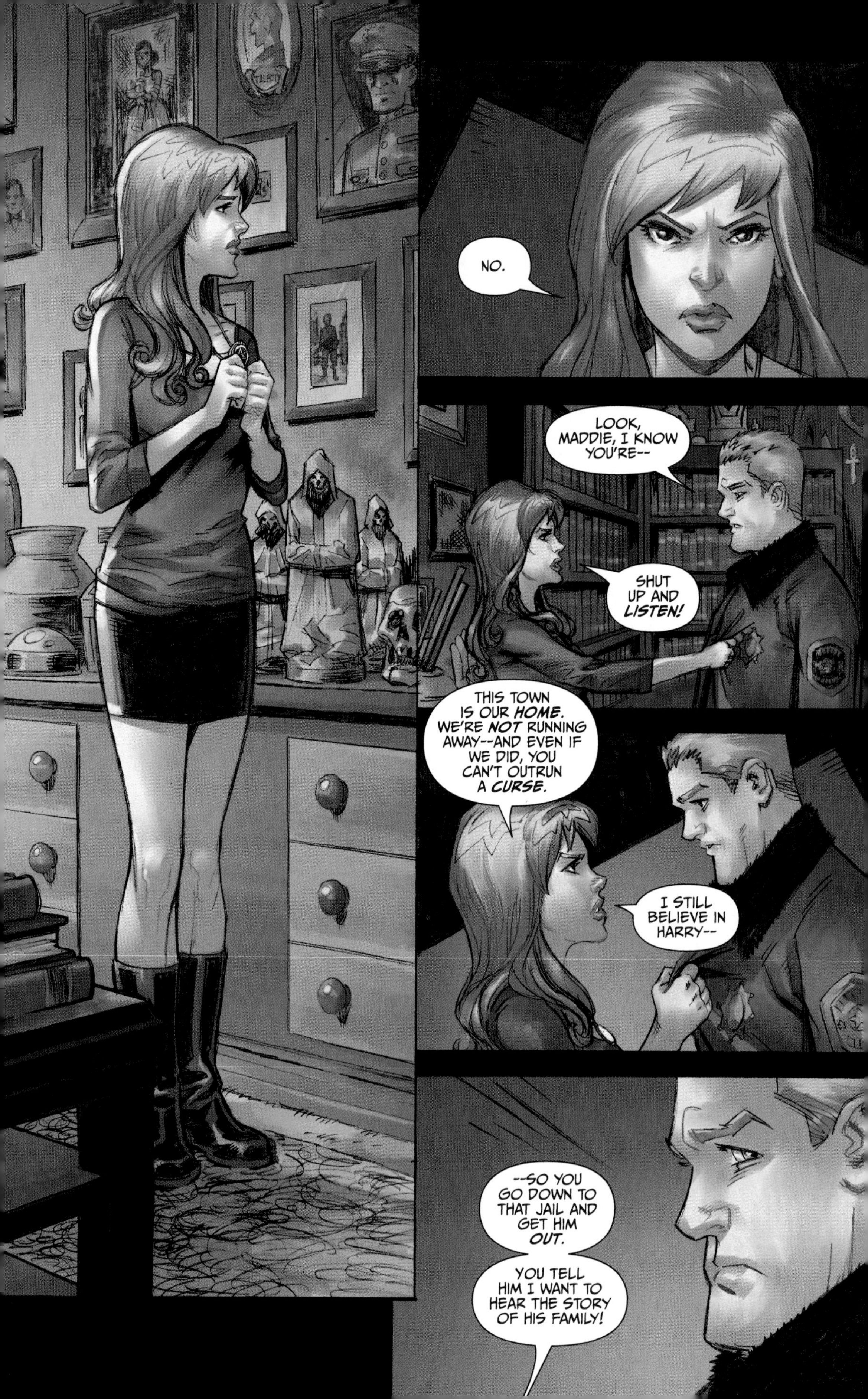
NO.
LOOK, MADDIE, I KNOW YOU'RE--
SHUT UP AND ***LISTEN!***
THIS TOWN IS OUR ***HOME***. WE'RE ***NOT*** RUNNING AWAY--AND EVEN IF WE DID, YOU CAN'T OUTRUN A ***CURSE***.
I STILL BELIEVE IN HARRY--
--SO YOU GO DOWN TO THAT JAIL AND GET HIM ***OUT***.
YOU TELL HIM I WANT TO HEAR THE STORY OF HIS FAMILY!

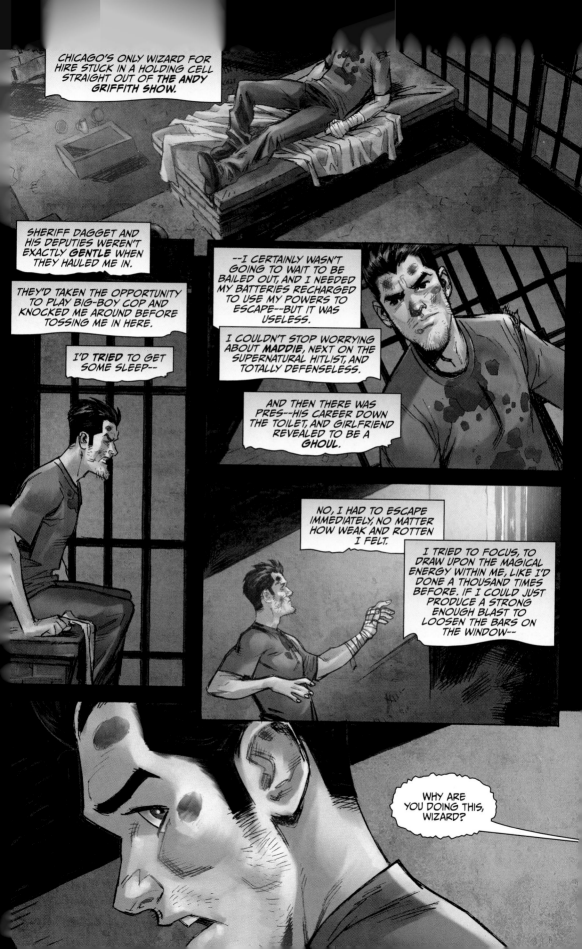

CHICAGO'S ONLY WIZARD FOR HIRE STUCK IN A HOLDING CELL STRAIGHT OUT OF *THE ANDY GRIFFITH SHOW.*

SHERIFF DAGGET AND HIS DEPUTIES WEREN'T EXACTLY *GENTLE* WHEN THEY HAULED ME IN.

THEY'D TAKEN THE OPPORTUNITY TO PLAY BIG-BOY COP AND KNOCKED ME AROUND BEFORE TOSSING ME IN HERE.

I'D TRIED TO GET SOME SLEEP--

--I CERTAINLY WASN'T GOING TO WAIT TO BE BAILED OUT, AND I NEEDED MY BATTERIES RECHARGED TO USE MY POWERS TO ESCAPE--BUT IT WAS USELESS.

I COULDN'T STOP WORRYING ABOUT MADDIE, NEXT ON THE SUPERNATURAL HITLIST, AND TOTALLY DEFENSELESS.

AND THEN THERE WAS PRES--HIS CAREER DOWN THE TOILET, AND GIRLFRIEND REVEALED TO BE A GHOUL.

NO, I HAD TO ESCAPE IMMEDIATELY, NO MATTER HOW WEAK AND ROTTEN I FELT.

I TRIED TO FOCUS, TO DRAW UPON THE MAGICAL ENERGY WITHIN ME, LIKE I'D DONE A THOUSAND TIMES BEFORE. IF I COULD JUST PRODUCE A STRONG ENOUGH BLAST TO LOOSEN THE BARS ON THE WINDOW--

WHY ARE YOU DOING THIS, WIZARD?

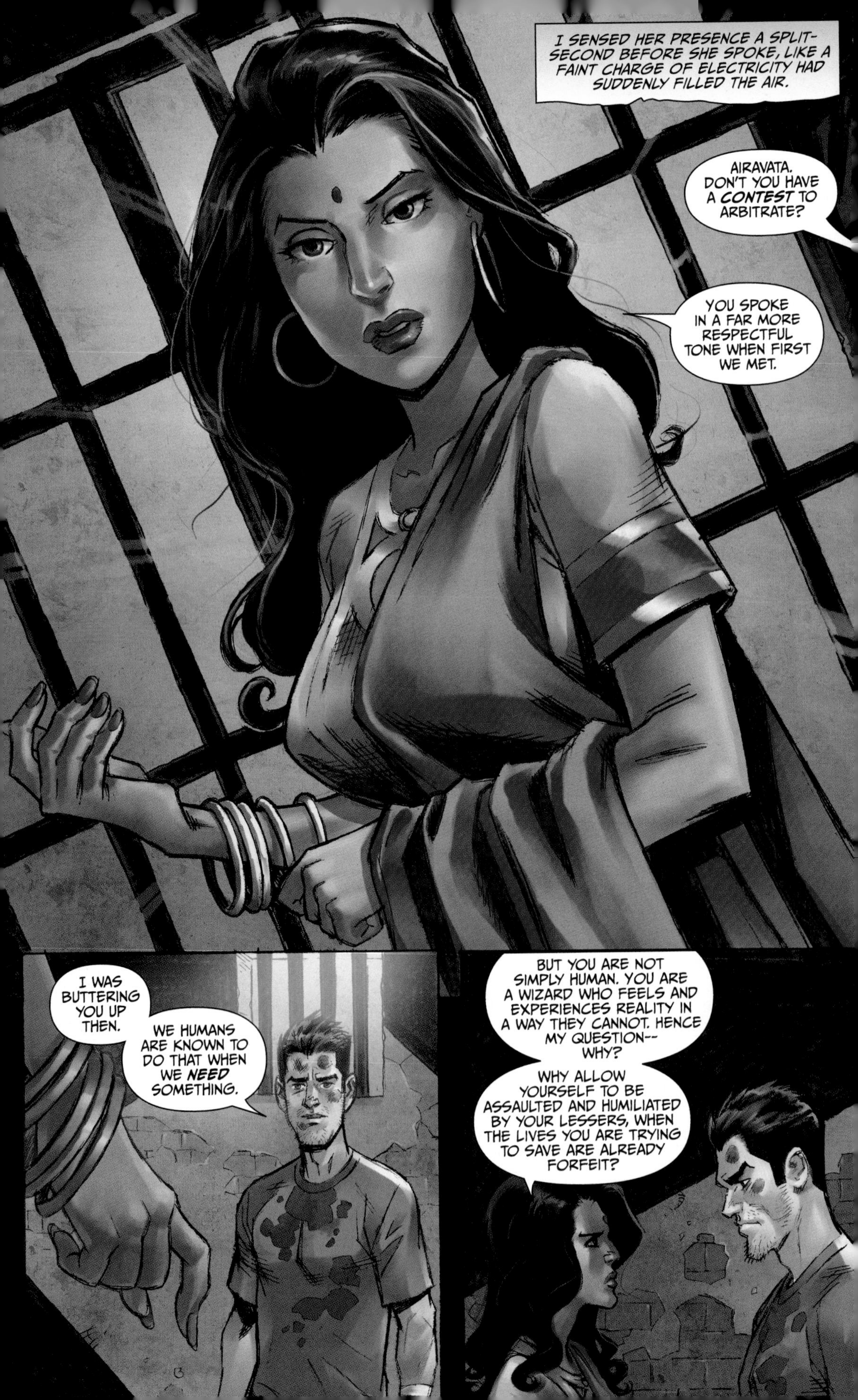
I SENSED HER PRESENCE A SPLIT-SECOND BEFORE SHE SPOKE, LIKE A FAINT CHARGE OF ELECTRICITY HAD SUDDENLY FILLED THE AIR.
AIRAVATA. DON'T YOU HAVE A CONTEST TO ARBITRATE?
YOU SPOKE IN A FAR MORE RESPECTFUL TONE WHEN FIRST WE MET.
I WAS BUTTERING YOU UP THEN.
WE HUMANS ARE KNOWN TO DO THAT WHEN WE NEED SOMETHING.
BUT YOU ARE NOT SIMPLY HUMAN. YOU ARE A WIZARD WHO FEELS AND EXPERIENCES REALITY IN A WAY THEY CANNOT. HENCE MY QUESTION-- WHY?
WHY ALLOW YOURSELF TO BE ASSAULTED AND HUMILIATED BY YOUR LESSERS, WHEN THE LIVES YOU ARE TRYING TO SAVE ARE ALREADY FORFEIT?

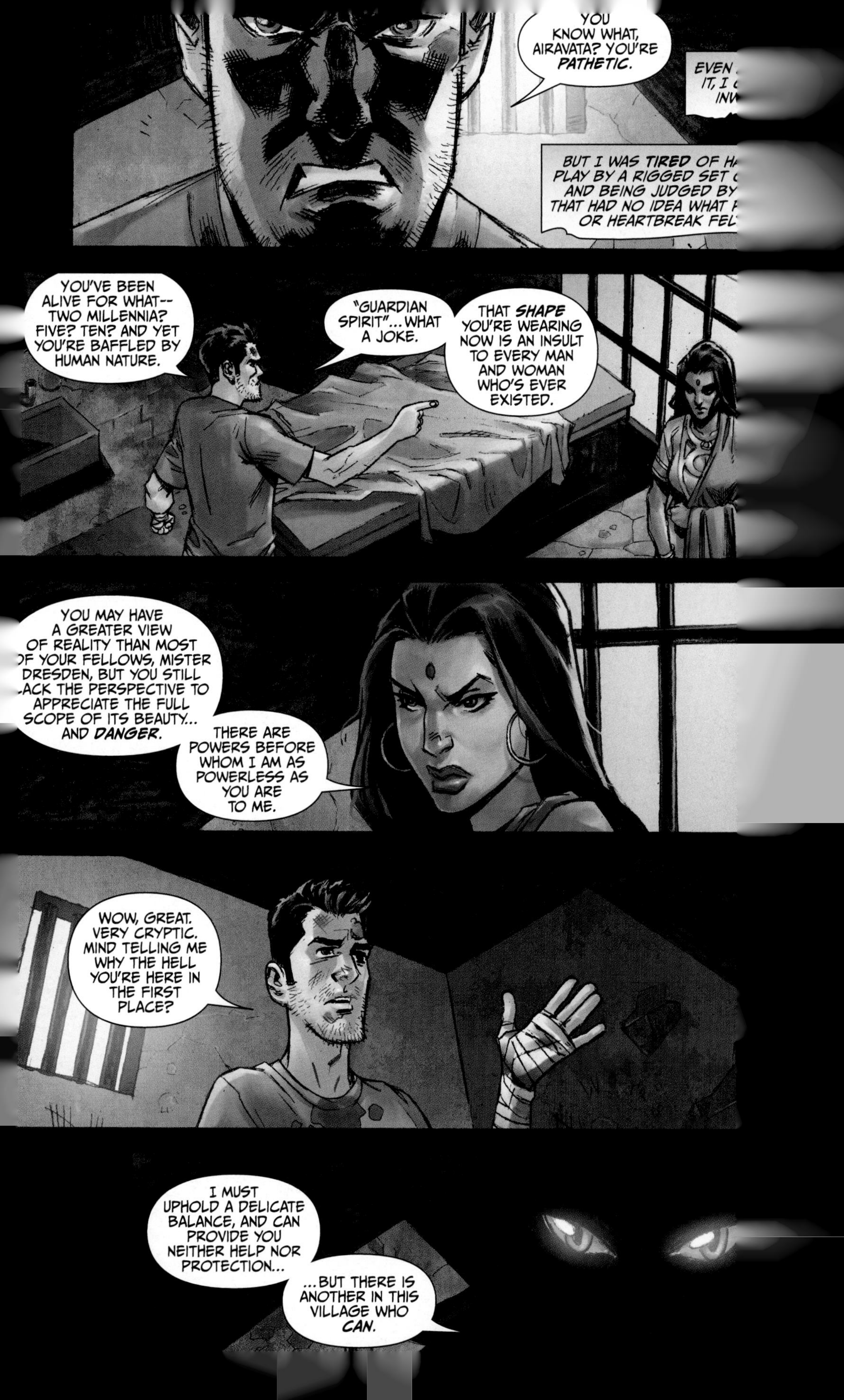

YOU KNOW WHAT, AIRAVATA? YOU'RE PATHETIC.
YOU'VE BEEN ALIVE FOR WHAT-- TWO MILLENNIA? FIVE? TEN? AND YET YOU'RE BAFFLED BY HUMAN NATURE.
"GUARDIAN SPIRIT"... WHAT A JOKE.
THAT SHAPE YOU'RE WEARING NOW IS AN INSULT TO EVERY MAN AND WOMAN WHO'S EVER EXISTED.
YOU MAY HAVE A GREATER VIEW OF REALITY THAN MOST OF YOUR FELLOWS, MISTER DRESDEN, BUT YOU STILL LACK THE PERSPECTIVE TO APPRECIATE THE FULL SCOPE OF ITS BEAUTY... AND DANGER.
THERE ARE POWERS BEFORE WHOM I AM AS POWERLESS AS YOU ARE TO ME.
WOW, GREAT. VERY CRYPTIC. MIND TELLING ME WHY THE HELL YOU'RE HERE IN THE FIRST PLACE?
I MUST UPHOLD A DELICATE BALANCE, AND CAN PROVIDE YOU NEITHER HELP NOR PROTECTION...
...BUT THERE IS ANOTHER IN THIS VILLAGE WHO CAN.

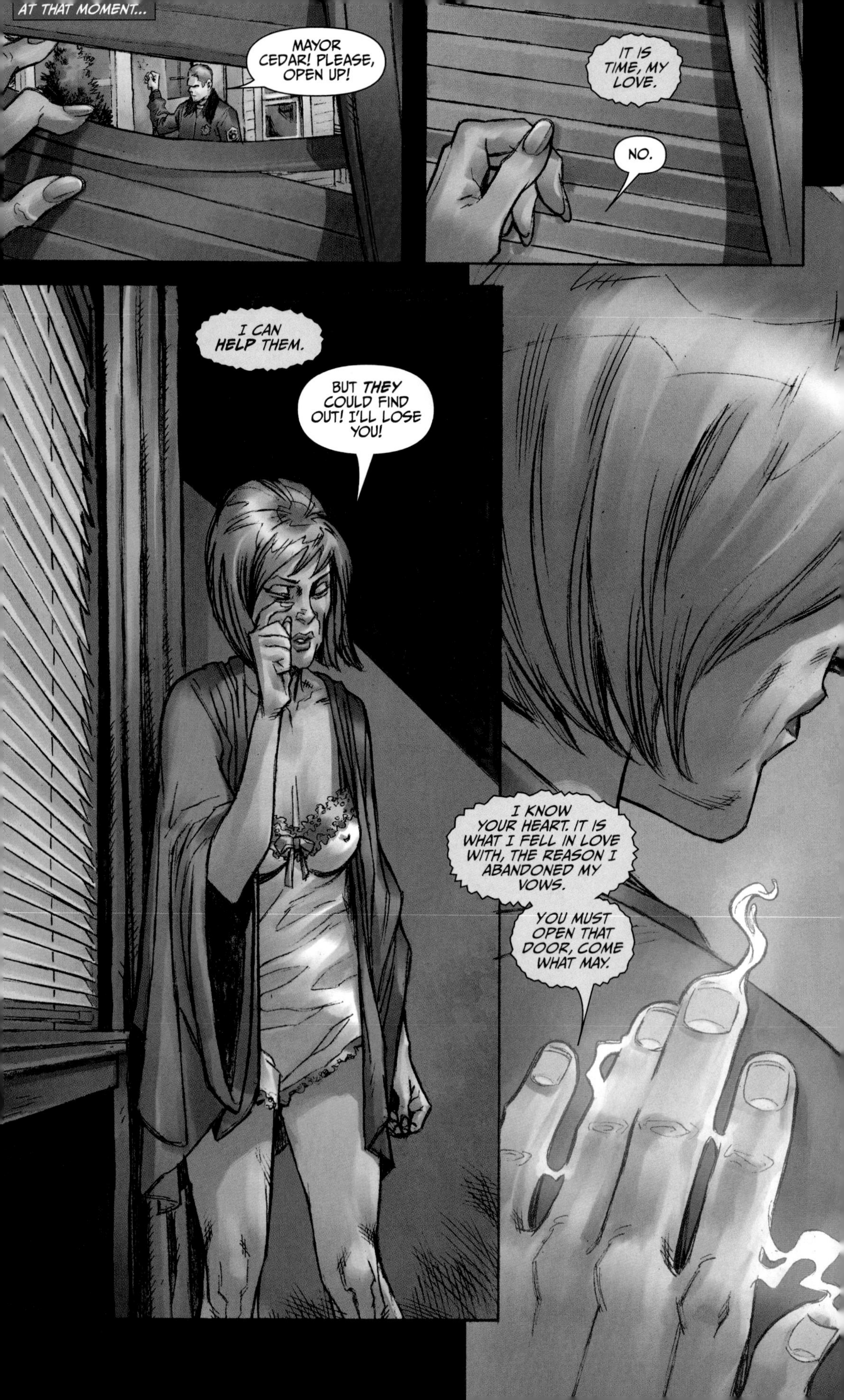
AT THAT MOMENT...
MAYOR CEDAR! PLEASE, OPEN UP!
IT IS TIME, MY LOVE.
NO.
I CAN HELP THEM.
BUT THEY COULD FIND OUT! I'LL LOSE YOU!
I KNOW YOUR HEART. IT IS WHAT I FELL IN LOVE WITH, THE REASON I ABANDONED MY VOWS.
YOU MUST OPEN THAT DOOR, COME WHAT MAY.

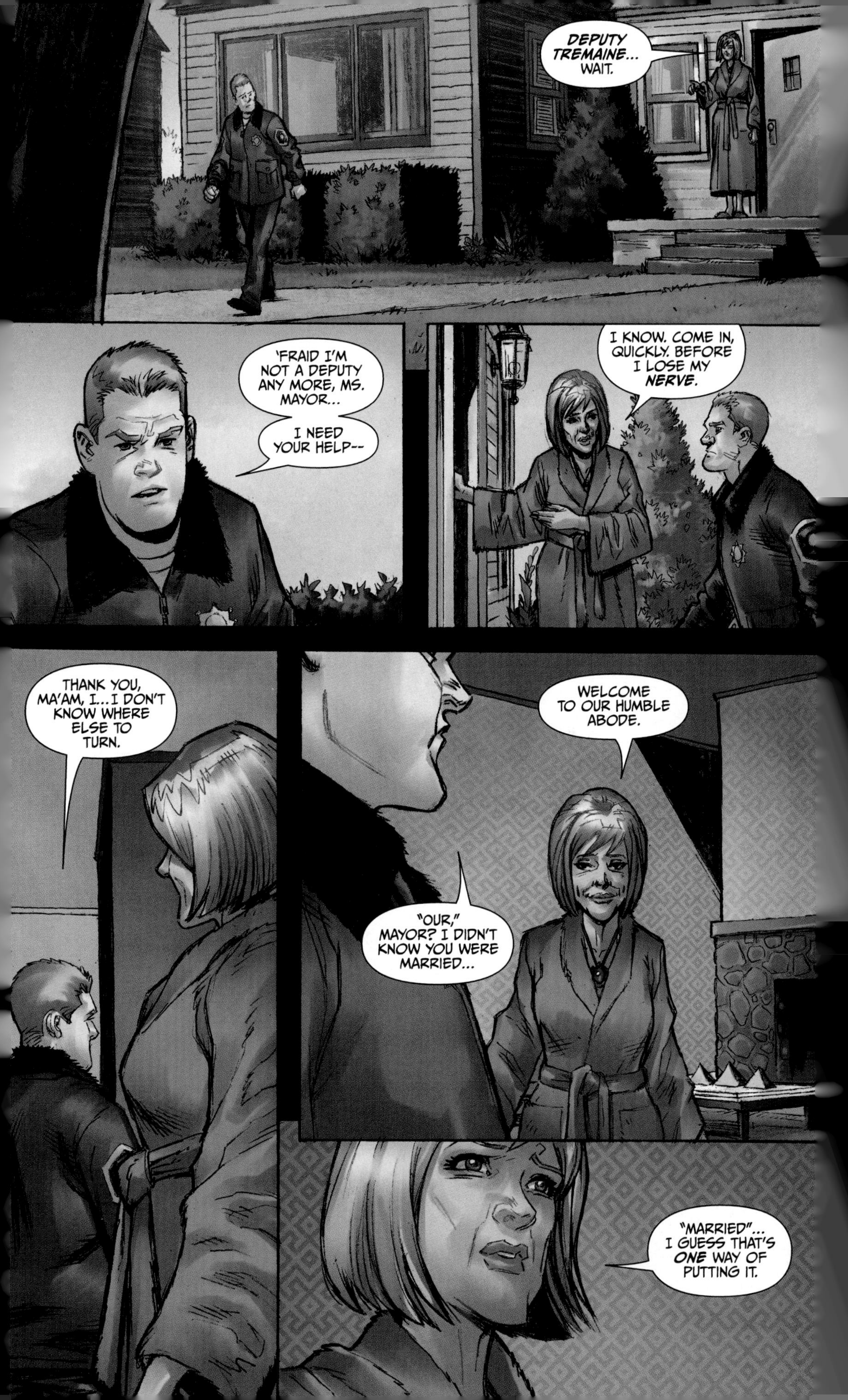
DEPUTY TREMAINE... WAIT.
'FRAID I'M NOT A DEPUTY ANY MORE, MS. MAYOR...
I NEED YOUR HELP--
I KNOW. COME IN, QUICKLY. BEFORE I LOSE MY NERVE.
THANK YOU, MA'AM, I...I DON'T KNOW WHERE ELSE TO TURN.
WELCOME TO OUR HUMBLE ABODE.
"OUR," MAYOR? I DIDN'T KNOW YOU WERE MARRIED...
"MARRIED"... I GUESS THAT'S ONE WAY OF PUTTING IT.

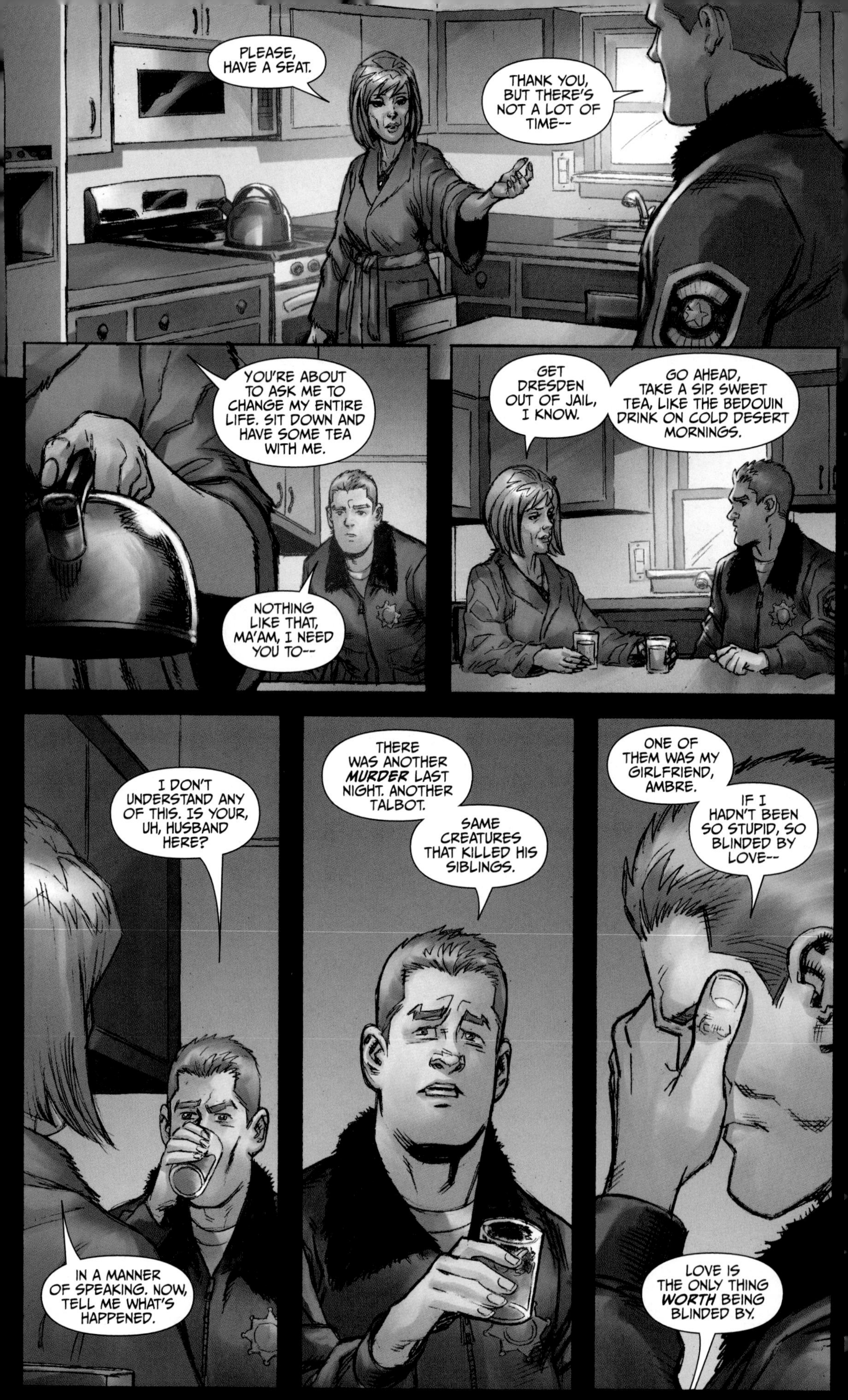
PLEASE, HAVE A SEAT.
THANK YOU, BUT THERE'S NOT A LOT OF TIME--
YOU'RE ABOUT TO ASK ME TO CHANGE MY ENTIRE LIFE. SIT DOWN AND HAVE SOME TEA WITH ME.
NOTHING LIKE THAT, MA'AM, I NEED YOU TO--
GET DRESDEN OUT OF JAIL, I KNOW.
GO AHEAD, TAKE A SIP. SWEET TEA, LIKE THE BEDOUIN DRINK ON COLD DESERT MORNINGS.
I DON'T UNDERSTAND ANY OF THIS. IS YOUR, UH, HUSBAND HERE?
IN A MANNER OF SPEAKING. NOW, TELL ME WHAT'S HAPPENED.
THERE WAS ANOTHER *MURDER* LAST NIGHT. ANOTHER TALBOT.
SAME CREATURES THAT KILLED HIS SIBLINGS.
ONE OF THEM WAS MY GIRLFRIEND, AMBRE.
IF I HADN'T BEEN SO STUPID, SO BLINDED BY LOVE--
LOVE IS THE ONLY THING *WORTH* BEING BLINDED BY.

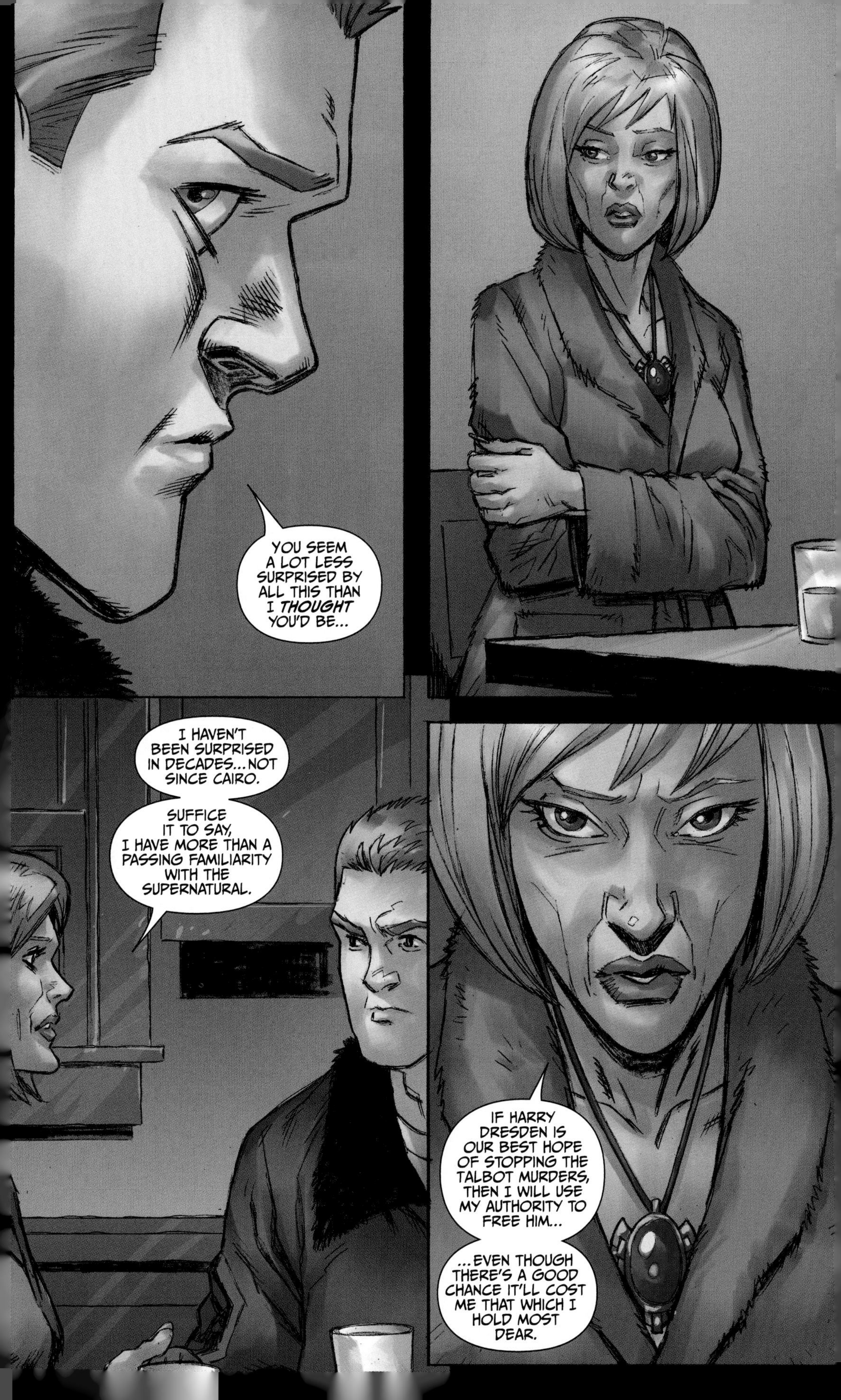
YOU SEEM A LOT LESS SURPRISED BY ALL THIS THAN I *THOUGHT* YOU'D BE...
I HAVEN'T BEEN SURPRISED IN DECADES...NOT SINCE CAIRO.
SUFFICE IT TO SAY, I HAVE MORE THAN A PASSING FAMILIARITY WITH THE SUPERNATURAL.
IF HARRY DRESDEN IS OUR BEST HOPE OF STOPPING THE TALBOT MURDERS, THEN I WILL USE MY AUTHORITY TO FREE HIM...
...EVEN THOUGH THERE'S A GOOD CHANCE IT'LL COST ME THAT WHICH I HOLD MOST DEAR.

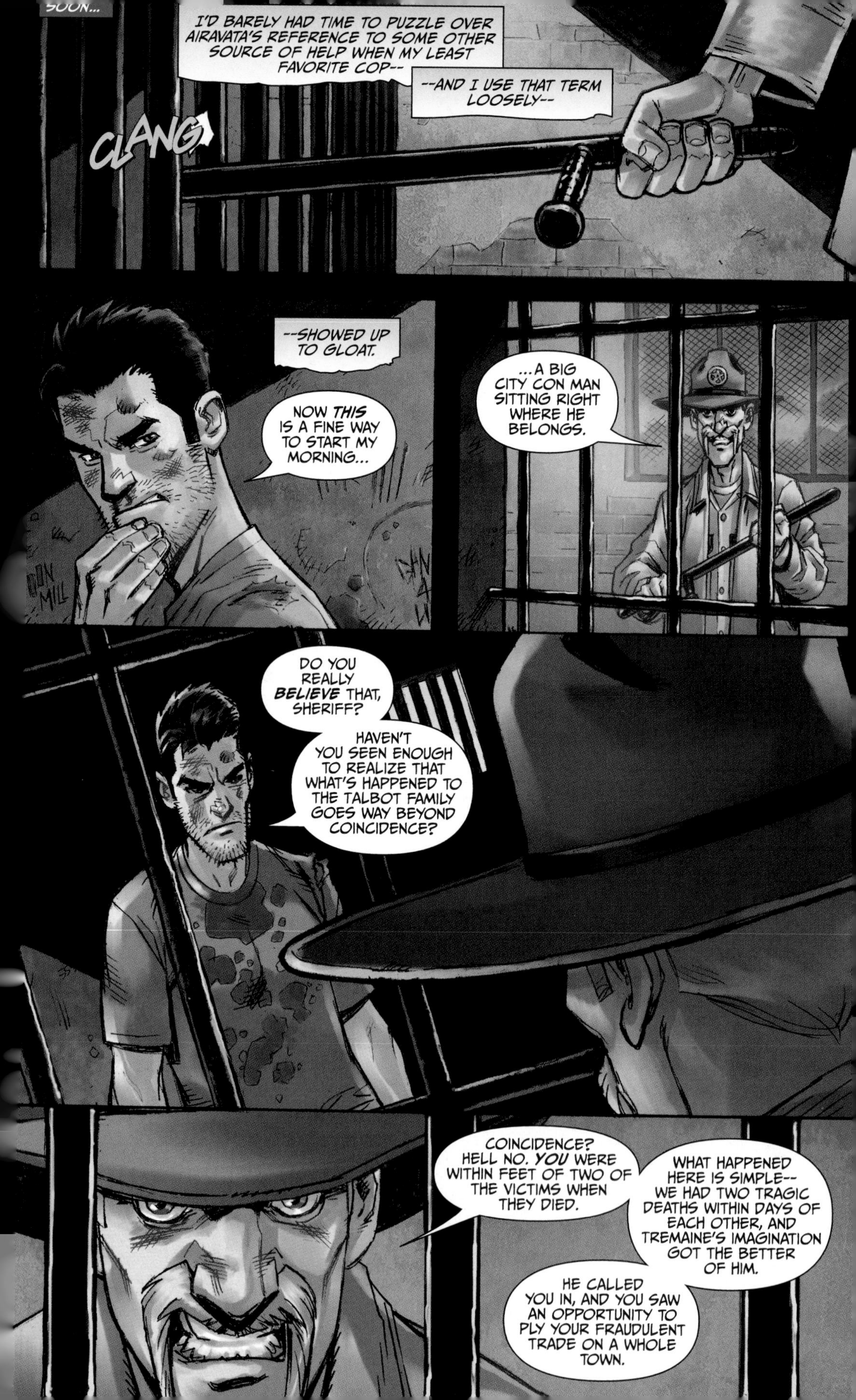
SOON...
I'D BARELY HAD TIME TO PUZZLE OVER AIRAVATA'S REFERENCE TO SOME OTHER SOURCE OF HELP WHEN MY LEAST FAVORITE COP--
--AND I USE THAT TERM LOOSELY--
CLANG
--SHOWED UP TO GLOAT.
NOW THIS IS A FINE WAY TO START MY MORNING...
...A BIG CITY CON MAN SITTING RIGHT WHERE HE BELONGS.
DO YOU REALLY BELIEVE THAT, SHERIFF?
HAVEN'T YOU SEEN ENOUGH TO REALIZE THAT WHAT'S HAPPENED TO THE TALBOT FAMILY GOES WAY BEYOND COINCIDENCE?
COINCIDENCE? HELL NO. YOU WERE WITHIN FEET OF TWO OF THE VICTIMS WHEN THEY DIED.
WHAT HAPPENED HERE IS SIMPLE-- WE HAD TWO TRAGIC DEATHS WITHIN DAYS OF EACH OTHER, AND TREMAINE'S IMAGINATION GOT THE BETTER OF HIM.
HE CALLED YOU IN, AND YOU SAW AN OPPORTUNITY TO PLY YOUR FRAUDULENT TRADE ON A WHOLE TOWN.

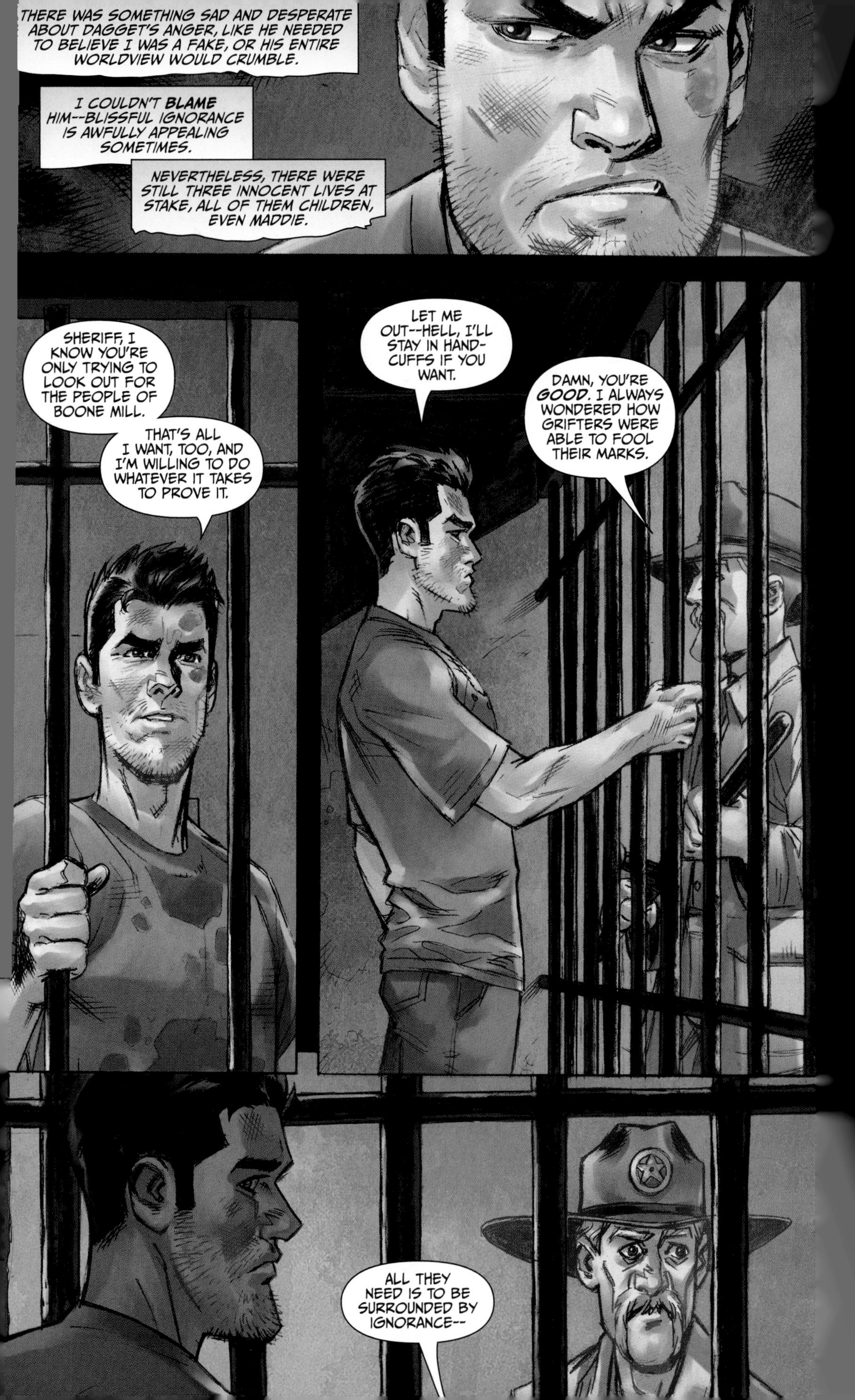
THERE WAS SOMETHING SAD AND DESPERATE ABOUT DAGGET'S ANGER, LIKE HE NEEDED TO BELIEVE I WAS A FAKE, OR HIS ENTIRE WORLDVIEW WOULD CRUMBLE.
I COULDN'T **BLAME** HIM--BLISSFUL IGNORANCE IS AWFULLY APPEALING SOMETIMES.
NEVERTHELESS, THERE WERE STILL THREE INNOCENT LIVES AT STAKE, ALL OF THEM CHILDREN, EVEN MADDIE.
SHERIFF, I KNOW YOU'RE ONLY TRYING TO LOOK OUT FOR THE PEOPLE OF BOONE MILL.
THAT'S ALL I WANT, TOO, AND I'M WILLING TO DO WHATEVER IT TAKES TO PROVE IT.
LET ME OUT--HELL, I'LL STAY IN HAND-CUFFS IF YOU WANT.
DAMN, YOU'RE **GOOD**. I ALWAYS WONDERED HOW GRIFTERS WERE ABLE TO FOOL THEIR MARKS.
ALL THEY NEED IS TO BE SURROUNDED BY IGNORANCE--

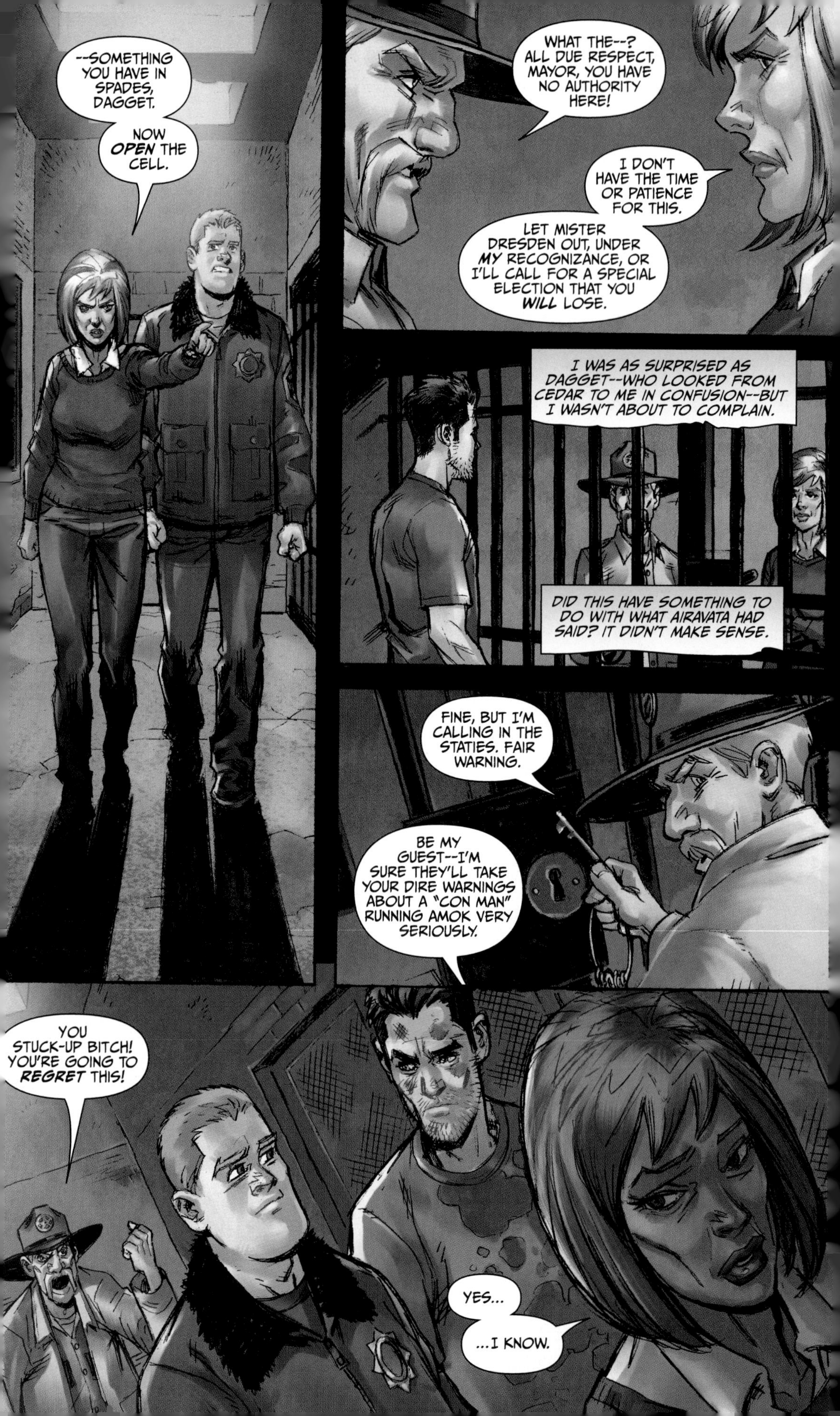
--SOMETHING YOU HAVE IN SPADES, DAGGET.
NOW OPEN THE CELL.
WHAT THE--? ALL DUE RESPECT, MAYOR, YOU HAVE NO AUTHORITY HERE!
I DON'T HAVE THE TIME OR PATIENCE FOR THIS.
LET MISTER DRESDEN OUT, UNDER MY RECOGNIZANCE, OR I'LL CALL FOR A SPECIAL ELECTION THAT YOU WILL LOSE.
I WAS AS SURPRISED AS DAGGET--WHO LOOKED FROM CEDAR TO ME IN CONFUSION--BUT I WASN'T ABOUT TO COMPLAIN.
DID THIS HAVE SOMETHING TO DO WITH WHAT AIRAVATA HAD SAID? IT DIDN'T MAKE SENSE.
FINE, BUT I'M CALLING IN THE STATIES. FAIR WARNING.
BE MY GUEST--I'M SURE THEY'LL TAKE YOUR DIRE WARNINGS ABOUT A "CON MAN" RUNNING AMOK VERY SERIOUSLY.
YOU STUCK-UP BITCH! YOU'RE GOING TO REGRET THIS!
YES...
...I KNOW.

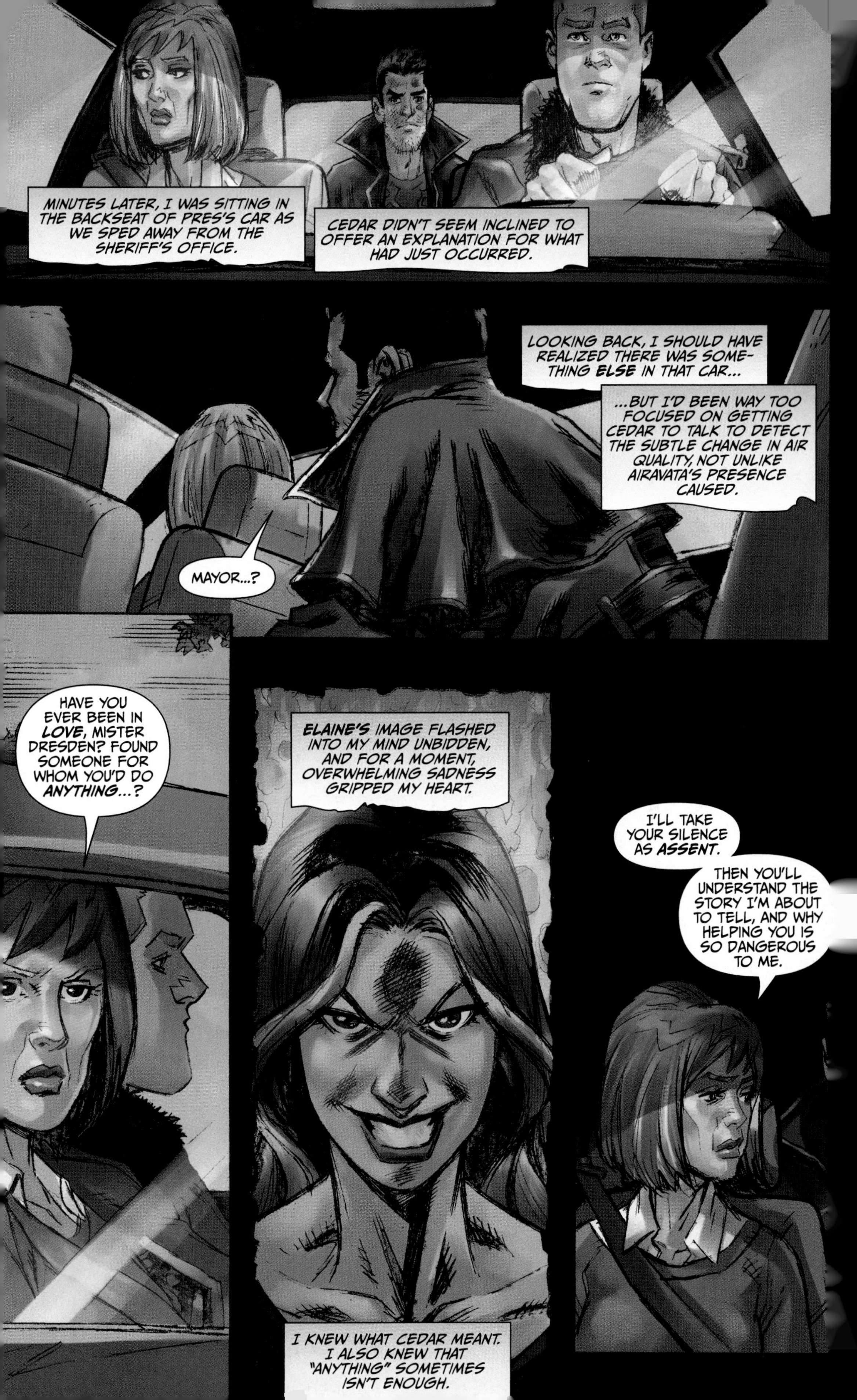
MINUTES LATER, I WAS SITTING IN THE BACKSEAT OF PRES'S CAR AS WE SPED AWAY FROM THE SHERIFF'S OFFICE.
CEDAR DIDN'T SEEM INCLINED TO OFFER AN EXPLANATION FOR WHAT HAD JUST OCCURRED.
LOOKING BACK, I SHOULD HAVE REALIZED THERE WAS SOMETHING ELSE IN THAT CAR...
...BUT I'D BEEN WAY TOO FOCUSED ON GETTING CEDAR TO TALK TO DETECT THE SUBTLE CHANGE IN AIR QUALITY, NOT UNLIKE AIRAVATA'S PRESENCE CAUSED.
MAYOR...?
HAVE YOU EVER BEEN IN LOVE, MISTER DRESDEN? FOUND SOMEONE FOR WHOM YOU'D DO ANYTHING...?
ELAINE'S IMAGE FLASHED INTO MY MIND UNBIDDEN, AND FOR A MOMENT, OVERWHELMING SADNESS GRIPPED MY HEART.
I'LL TAKE YOUR SILENCE AS ASSENT.
THEN YOU'LL UNDERSTAND THE STORY I'M ABOUT TO TELL, AND WHY HELPING YOU IS SO DANGEROUS TO ME.
I KNEW WHAT CEDAR MEANT. I ALSO KNEW THAT "ANYTHING" SOMETIMES ISN'T ENOUGH.

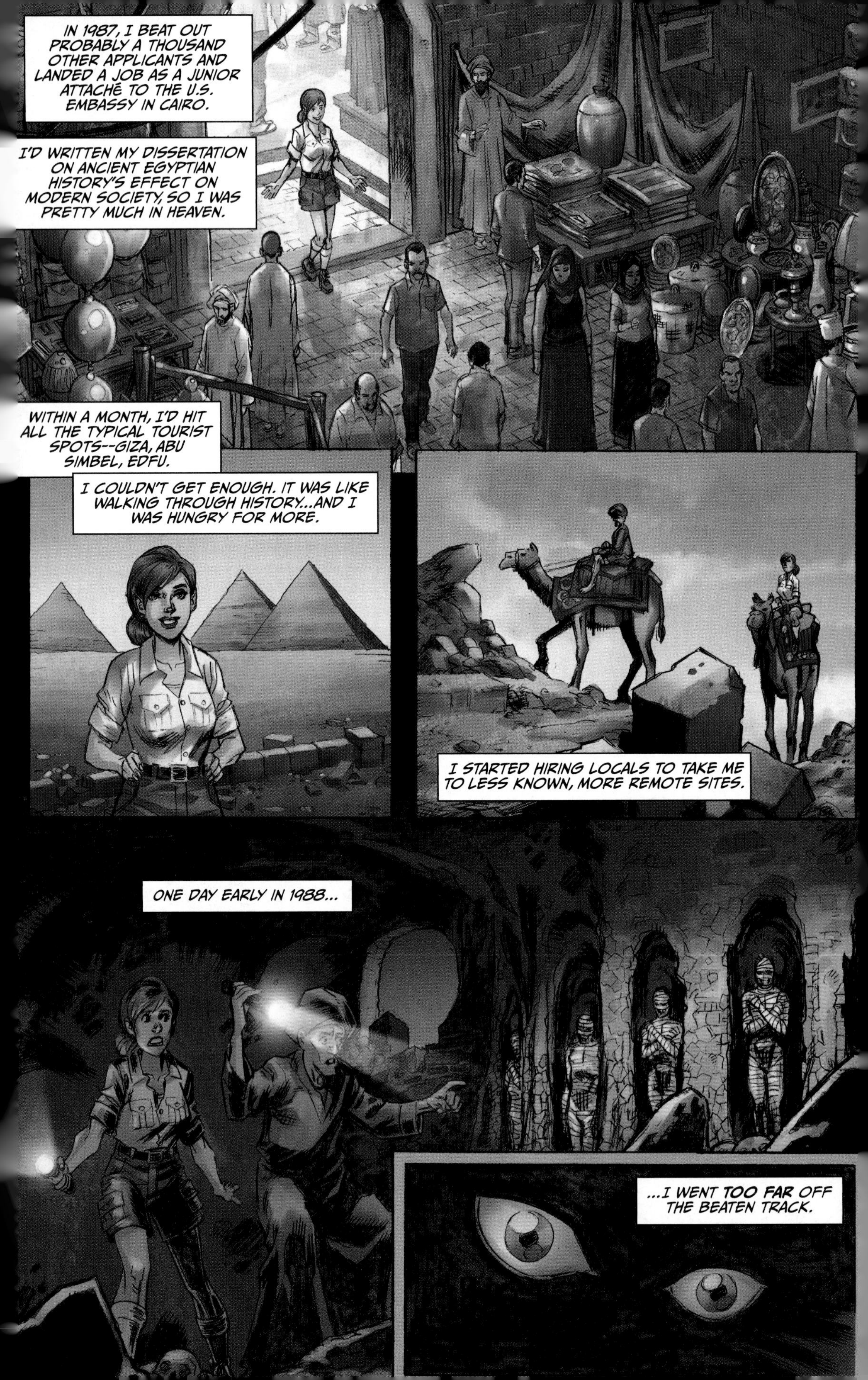
IN 1987, I BEAT OUT PROBABLY A THOUSAND OTHER APPLICANTS AND LANDED A JOB AS A JUNIOR ATTACHÉ TO THE U.S. EMBASSY IN CAIRO.
I'D WRITTEN MY DISSERTATION ON ANCIENT EGYPTIAN HISTORY'S EFFECT ON MODERN SOCIETY, SO I WAS PRETTY MUCH IN HEAVEN.
WITHIN A MONTH, I'D HIT ALL THE TYPICAL TOURIST SPOTS--GIZA, ABU SIMBEL, EDFU.
I COULDN'T GET ENOUGH. IT WAS LIKE WALKING THROUGH HISTORY...AND I WAS HUNGRY FOR MORE.
I STARTED HIRING LOCALS TO TAKE ME TO LESS KNOWN, MORE REMOTE SITES.
ONE DAY EARLY IN 1988...
...I WENT TOO FAR OFF THE BEATEN TRACK.

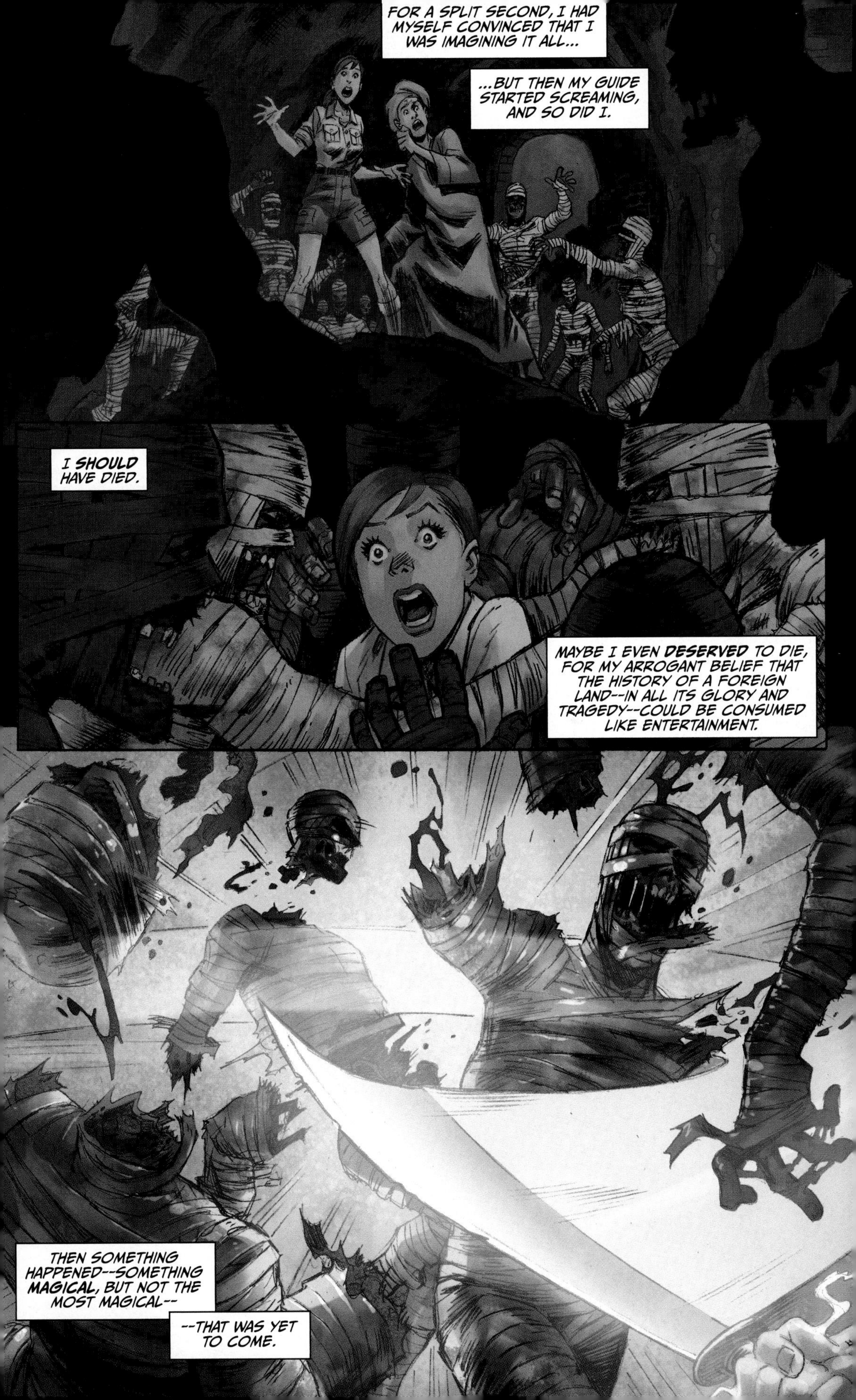
FOR A SPLIT SECOND, I HAD MYSELF CONVINCED THAT I WAS IMAGINING IT ALL...
...BUT THEN MY GUIDE STARTED SCREAMING, AND SO DID I.
I SHOULD HAVE DIED.
MAYBE I EVEN DESERVED TO DIE, FOR MY ARROGANT BELIEF THAT THE HISTORY OF A FOREIGN LAND--IN ALL ITS GLORY AND TRAGEDY--COULD BE CONSUMED LIKE ENTERTAINMENT.
THEN SOMETHING HAPPENED--SOMETHING MAGICAL, BUT NOT THE MOST MAGICAL--
--THAT WAS YET TO COME.

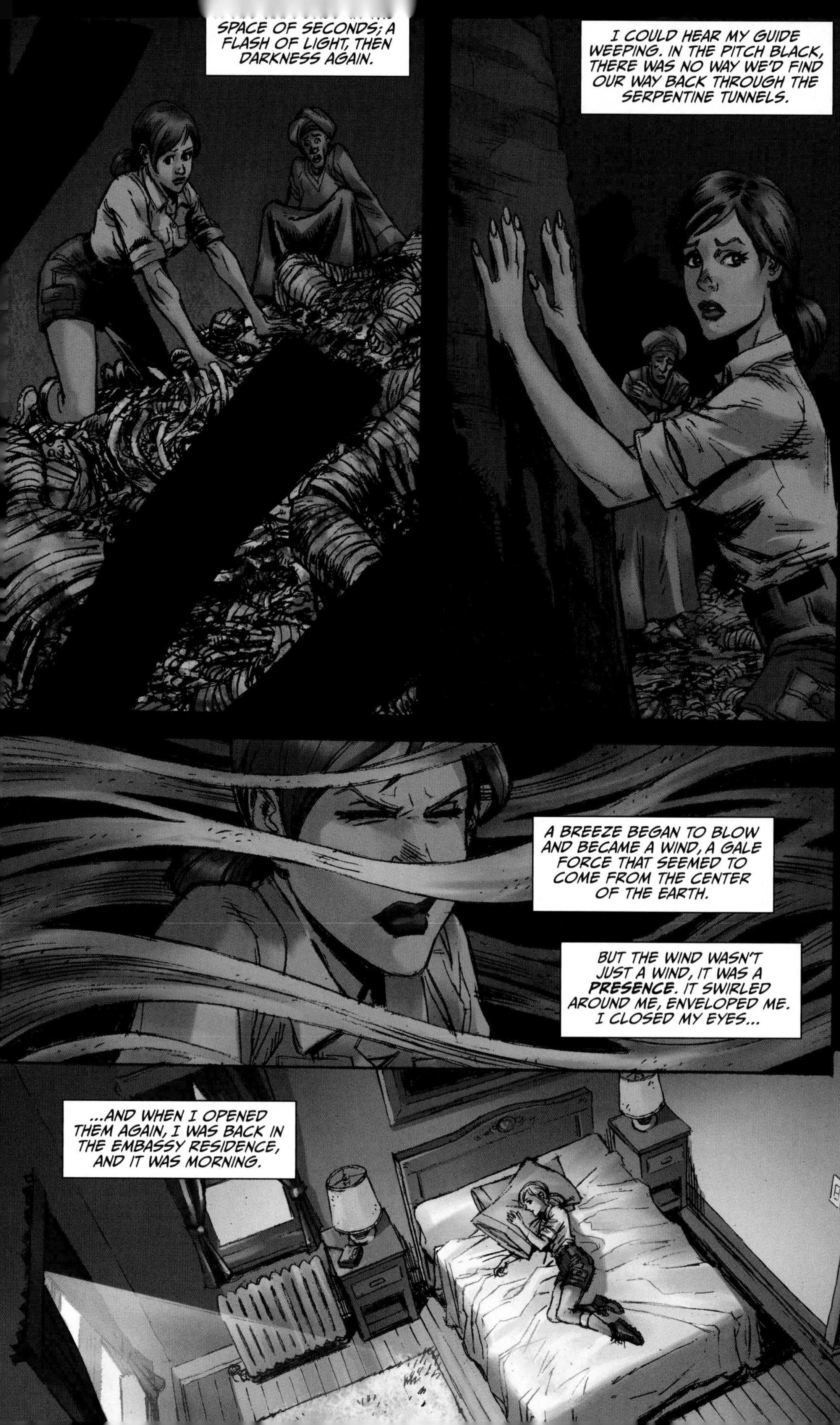
SPACE OF SECONDS; A FLASH OF LIGHT, THEN DARKNESS AGAIN.
I COULD HEAR MY GUIDE WEEPING. IN THE PITCH BLACK, THERE WAS NO WAY WE'D FIND OUR WAY BACK THROUGH THE SERPENTINE TUNNELS.
A BREEZE BEGAN TO BLOW AND BECAME A WIND, A GALE FORCE THAT SEEMED TO COME FROM THE CENTER OF THE EARTH.
BUT THE WIND WASN'T JUST A WIND, IT WAS A **PRESENCE**. IT SWIRLED AROUND ME, ENVELOPED ME. I CLOSED MY EYES...
...AND WHEN I OPENED THEM AGAIN, I WAS BACK IN THE EMBASSY RESIDENCE, AND IT WAS MORNING.

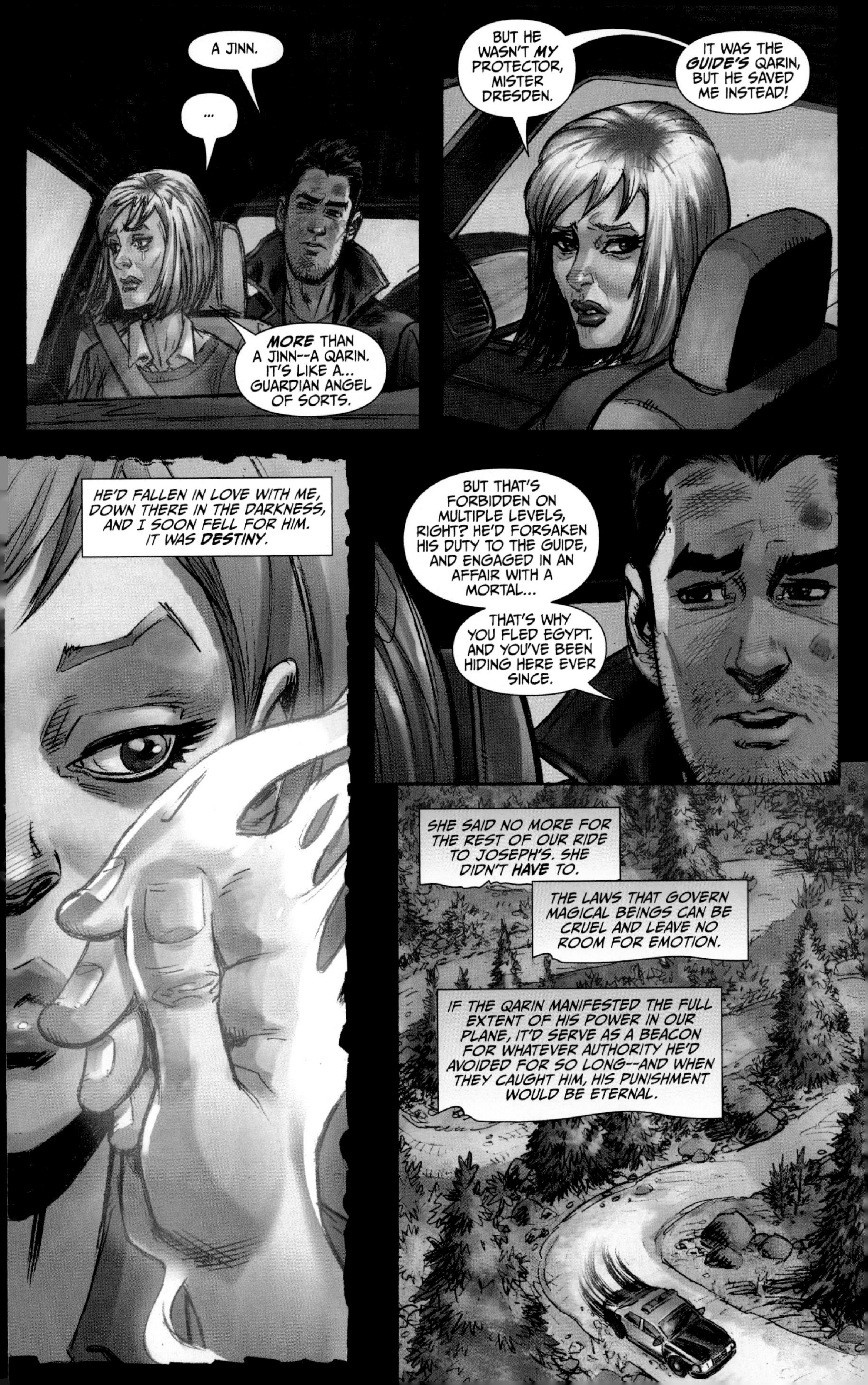
A JINN.
...
MORE THAN A JINN--A QARIN. IT'S LIKE A... GUARDIAN ANGEL OF SORTS.
BUT HE WASN'T MY PROTECTOR, MISTER DRESDEN.
IT WAS THE GUIDE'S QARIN, BUT HE SAVED ME INSTEAD!
HE'D FALLEN IN LOVE WITH ME, DOWN THERE IN THE DARKNESS, AND I SOON FELL FOR HIM. IT WAS DESTINY.
BUT THAT'S FORBIDDEN ON MULTIPLE LEVELS, RIGHT? HE'D FORSAKEN HIS DUTY TO THE GUIDE, AND ENGAGED IN AN AFFAIR WITH A MORTAL...
THAT'S WHY YOU FLED EGYPT. AND YOU'VE BEEN HIDING HERE EVER SINCE.
SHE SAID NO MORE FOR THE REST OF OUR RIDE TO JOSEPH'S. SHE DIDN'T HAVE TO.
THE LAWS THAT GOVERN MAGICAL BEINGS CAN BE CRUEL AND LEAVE NO ROOM FOR EMOTION.
IF THE QARIN MANIFESTED THE FULL EXTENT OF HIS POWER IN OUR PLANE, IT'D SERVE AS A BEACON FOR WHATEVER AUTHORITY HE'D AVOIDED FOR SO LONG--AND WHEN THEY CAUGHT HIM, HIS PUNISHMENT WOULD BE ETERNAL.

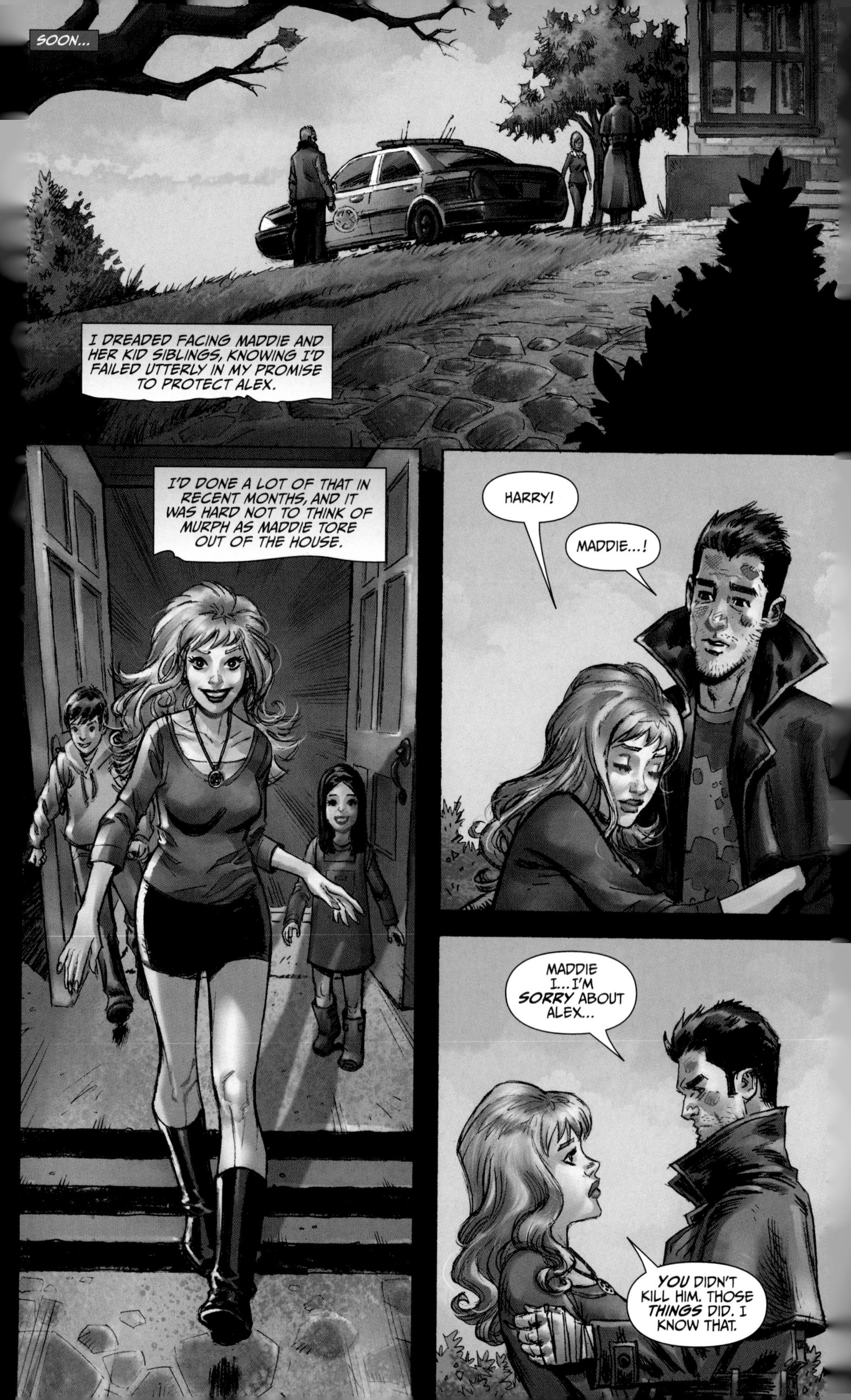
SOON...
I DREADED FACING MADDIE AND HER KID SIBLINGS, KNOWING I'D FAILED UTTERLY IN MY PROMISE TO PROTECT ALEX.
I'D DONE A LOT OF THAT IN RECENT MONTHS, AND IT WAS HARD NOT TO THINK OF MURPH AS MADDIE TORE OUT OF THE HOUSE.
HARRY!
MADDIE...!
MADDIE I...I'M SORRY ABOUT ALEX...
YOU DIDN'T KILL HIM. THOSE THINGS DID. I KNOW THAT.

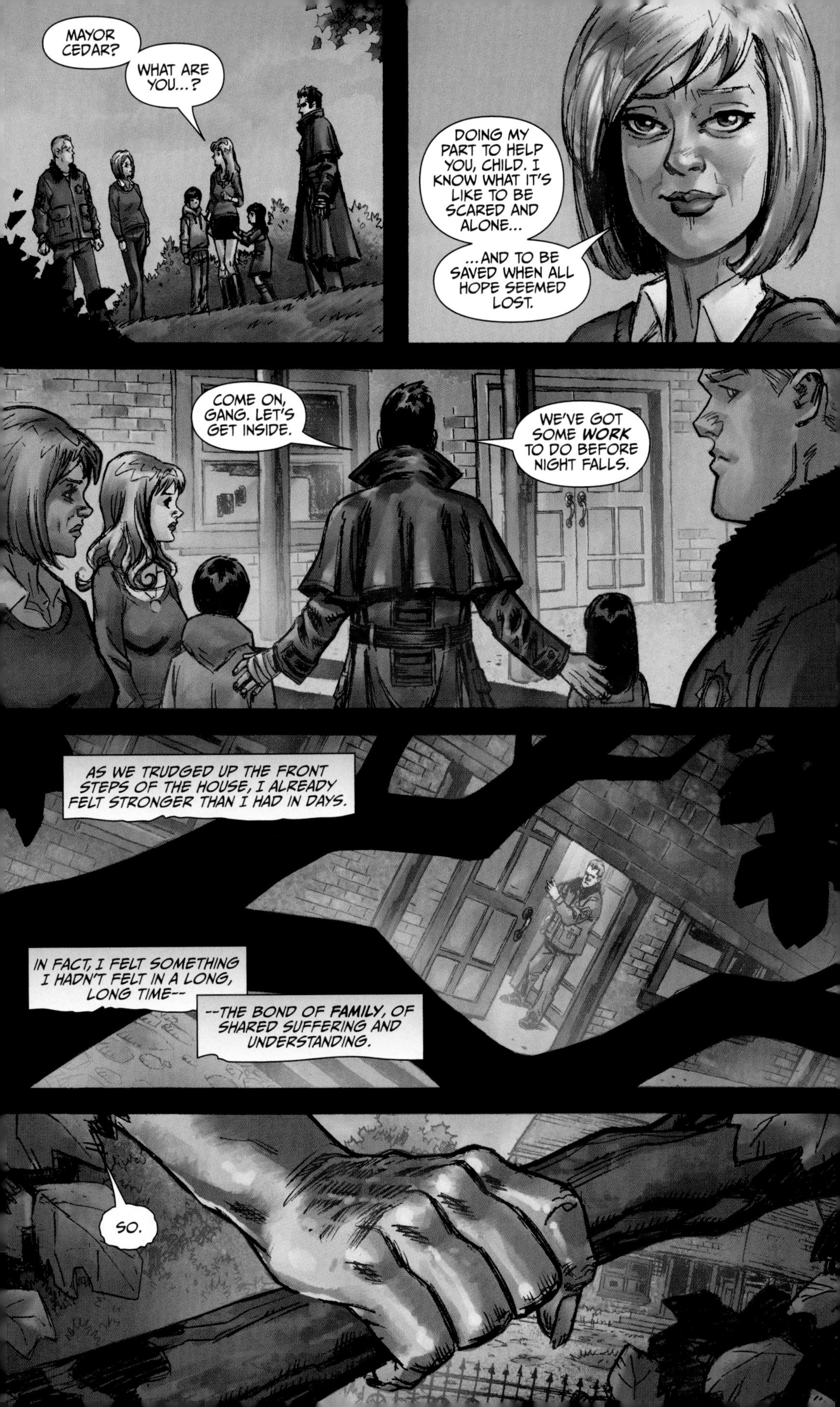

MAYOR CEDAR?
WHAT ARE YOU...?
DOING MY PART TO HELP YOU, CHILD. I KNOW WHAT IT'S LIKE TO BE SCARED AND ALONE...
...AND TO BE SAVED WHEN ALL HOPE SEEMED LOST.
COME ON, GANG. LET'S GET INSIDE.
WE'VE GOT SOME **WORK** TO DO BEFORE NIGHT FALLS.
AS WE TRUDGED UP THE FRONT STEPS OF THE HOUSE, I ALREADY FELT STRONGER THAN I HAD IN DAYS.
IN FACT, I FELT SOMETHING I HADN'T FELT IN A LONG, LONG TIME--
*--THE BOND OF **FAMILY**, OF SHARED SUFFERING AND UNDERSTANDING.*
SO.

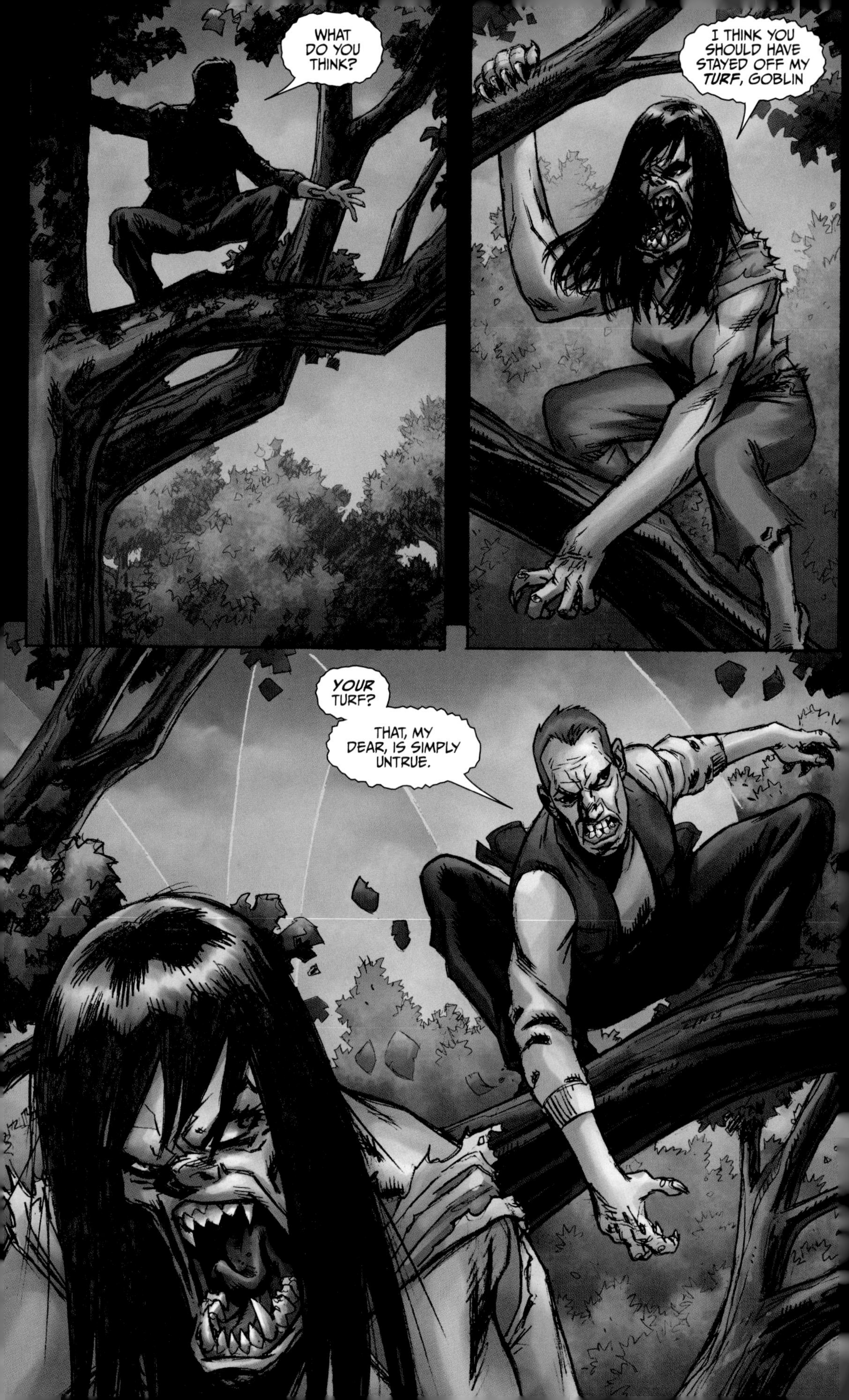
WHAT DO YOU THINK?
I THINK YOU SHOULD HAVE STAYED OFF MY *TURF*, GOBLIN
YOUR TURF?
THAT, MY DEAR, IS SIMPLY UNTRUE.

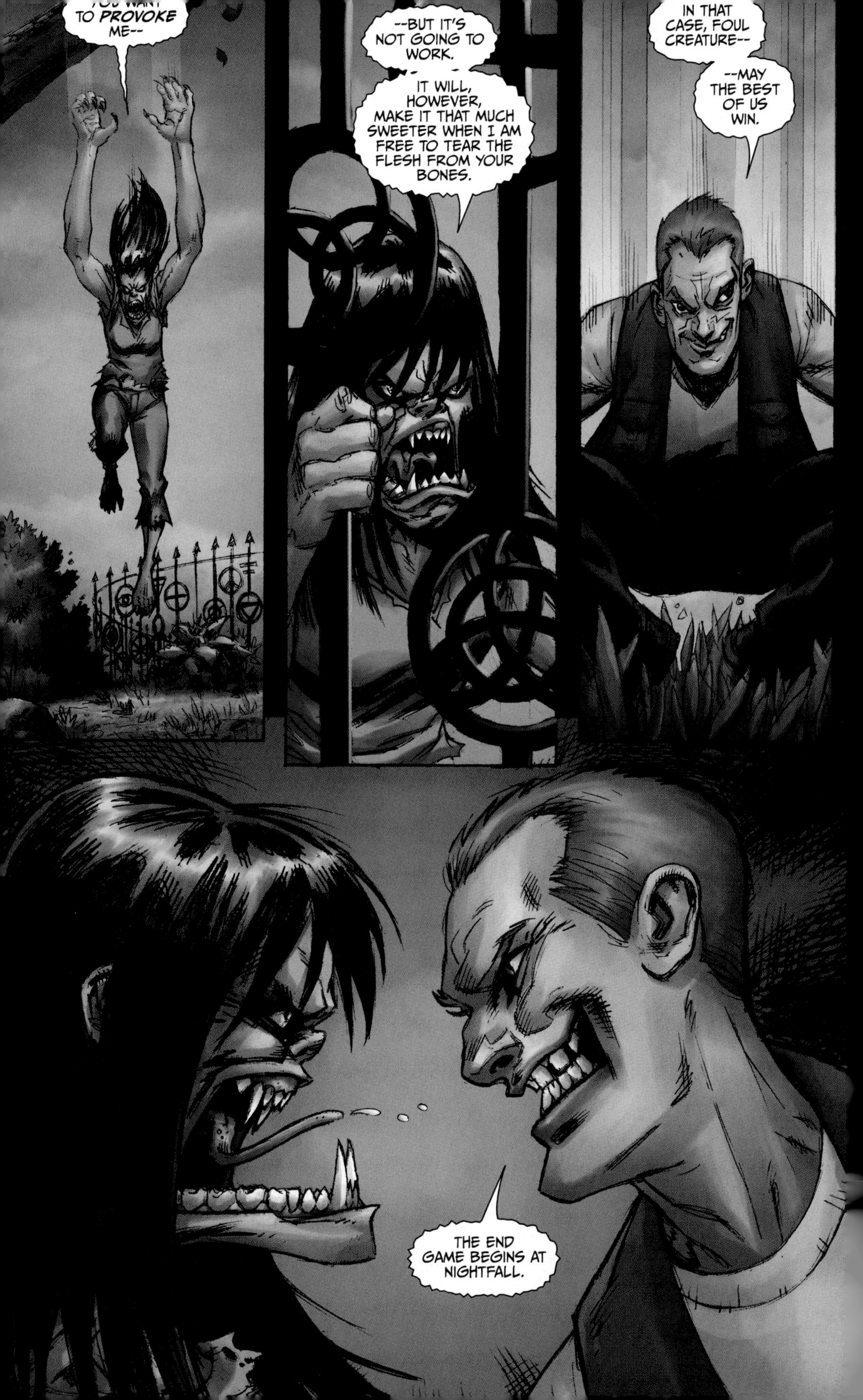
TO *PROVOKE* ME--
--BUT IT'S NOT GOING TO WORK.
IT WILL, HOWEVER, MAKE IT THAT MUCH SWEETER WHEN I AM FREE TO TEAR THE FLESH FROM YOUR BONES.
IN THAT CASE, FOUL CREATURE--
--MAY THE BEST OF US WIN.
THE END GAME BEGINS AT NIGHTFALL.

ISSUE SIX COVER BY
ARDIAN SYAF

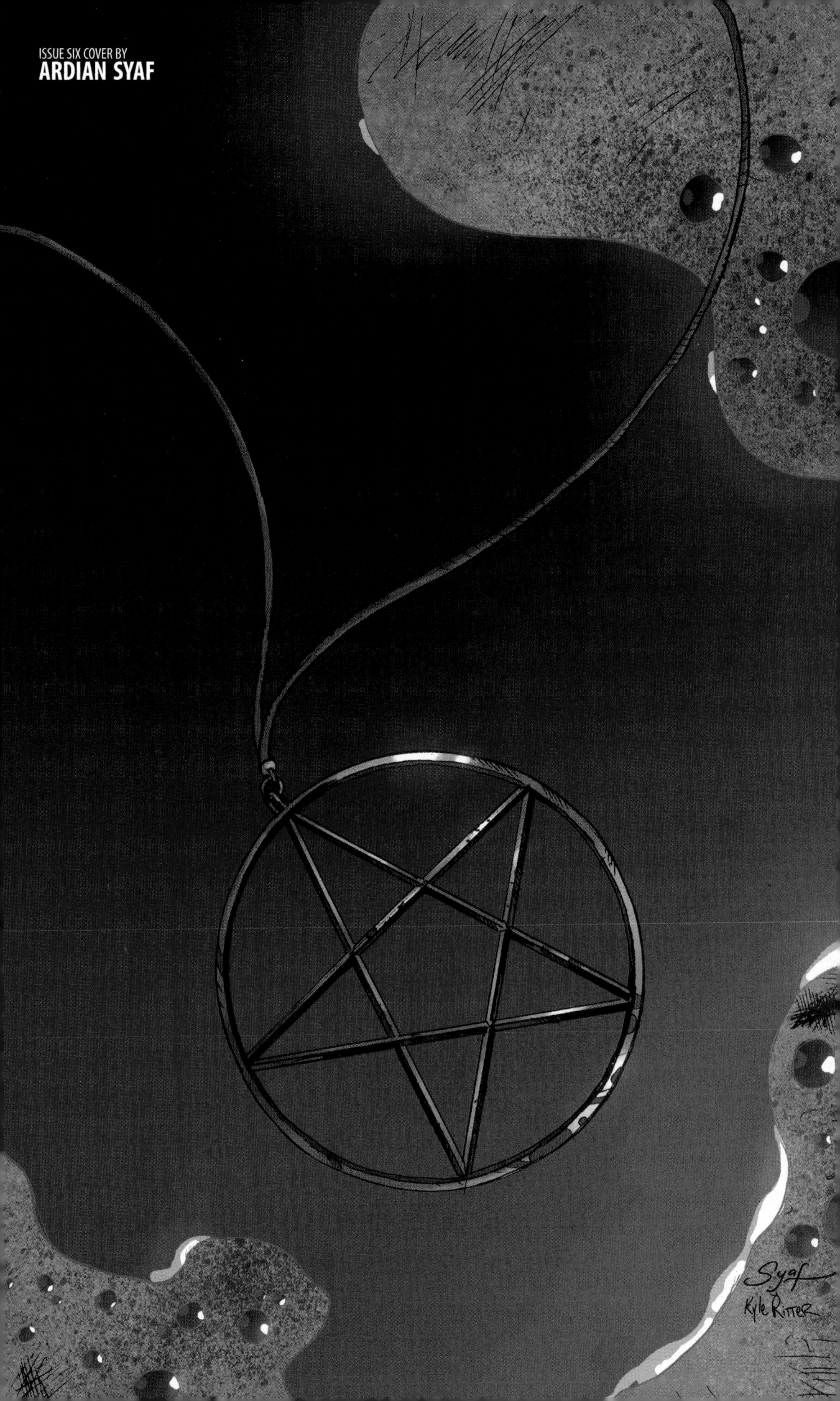
Syaf
Kyle Ritter

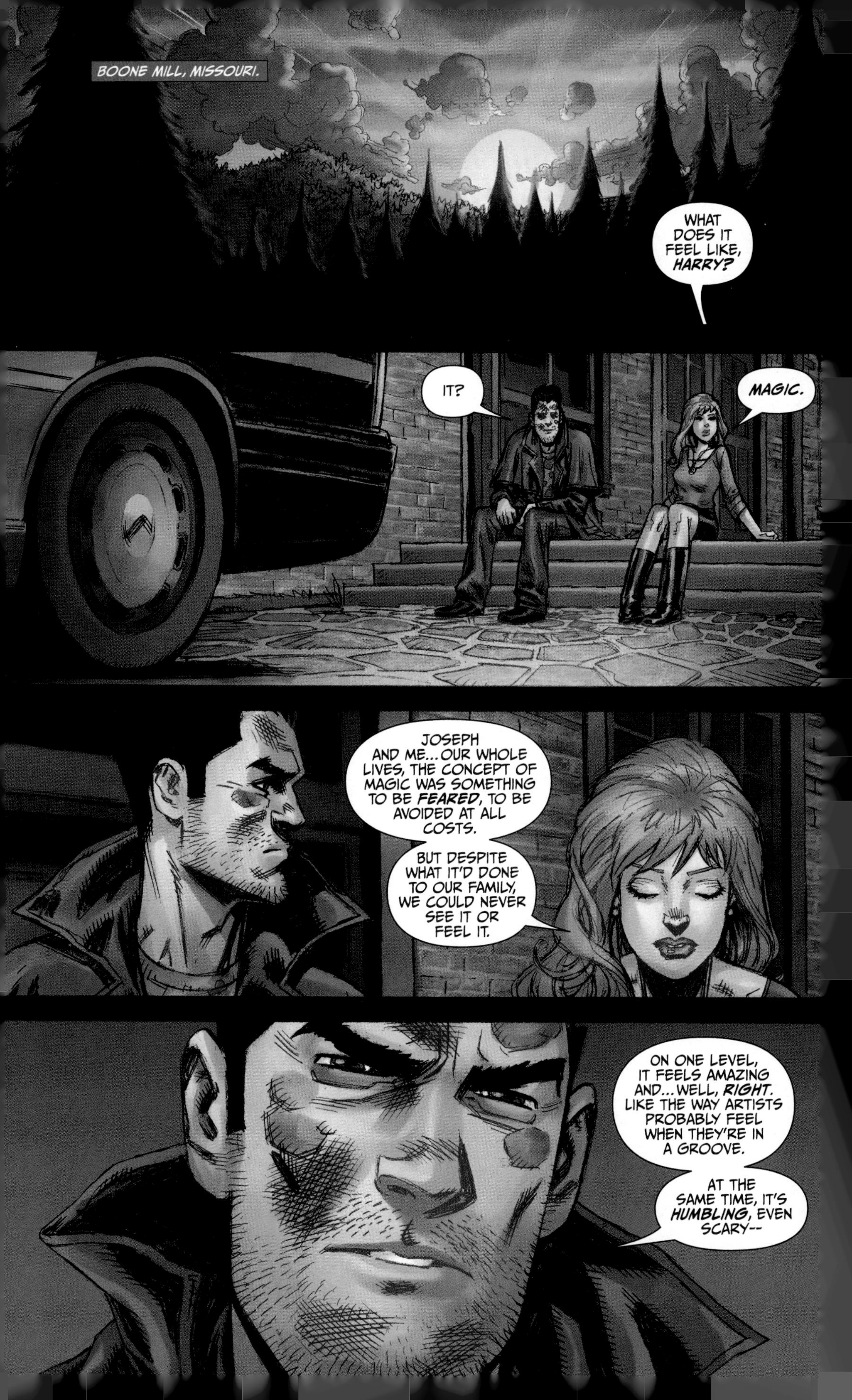
BOONE MILL, MISSOURI.
WHAT DOES IT FEEL LIKE, HARRY?
IT?
MAGIC.
JOSEPH AND ME...OUR WHOLE LIVES, THE CONCEPT OF MAGIC WAS SOMETHING TO BE FEARED, TO BE AVOIDED AT ALL COSTS.
BUT DESPITE WHAT IT'D DONE TO OUR FAMILY, WE COULD NEVER SEE IT OR FEEL IT.
ON ONE LEVEL, IT FEELS AMAZING AND...WELL, RIGHT. LIKE THE WAY ARTISTS PROBABLY FEEL WHEN THEY'RE IN A GROOVE.
AT THE SAME TIME, IT'S HUMBLING, EVEN SCARY--

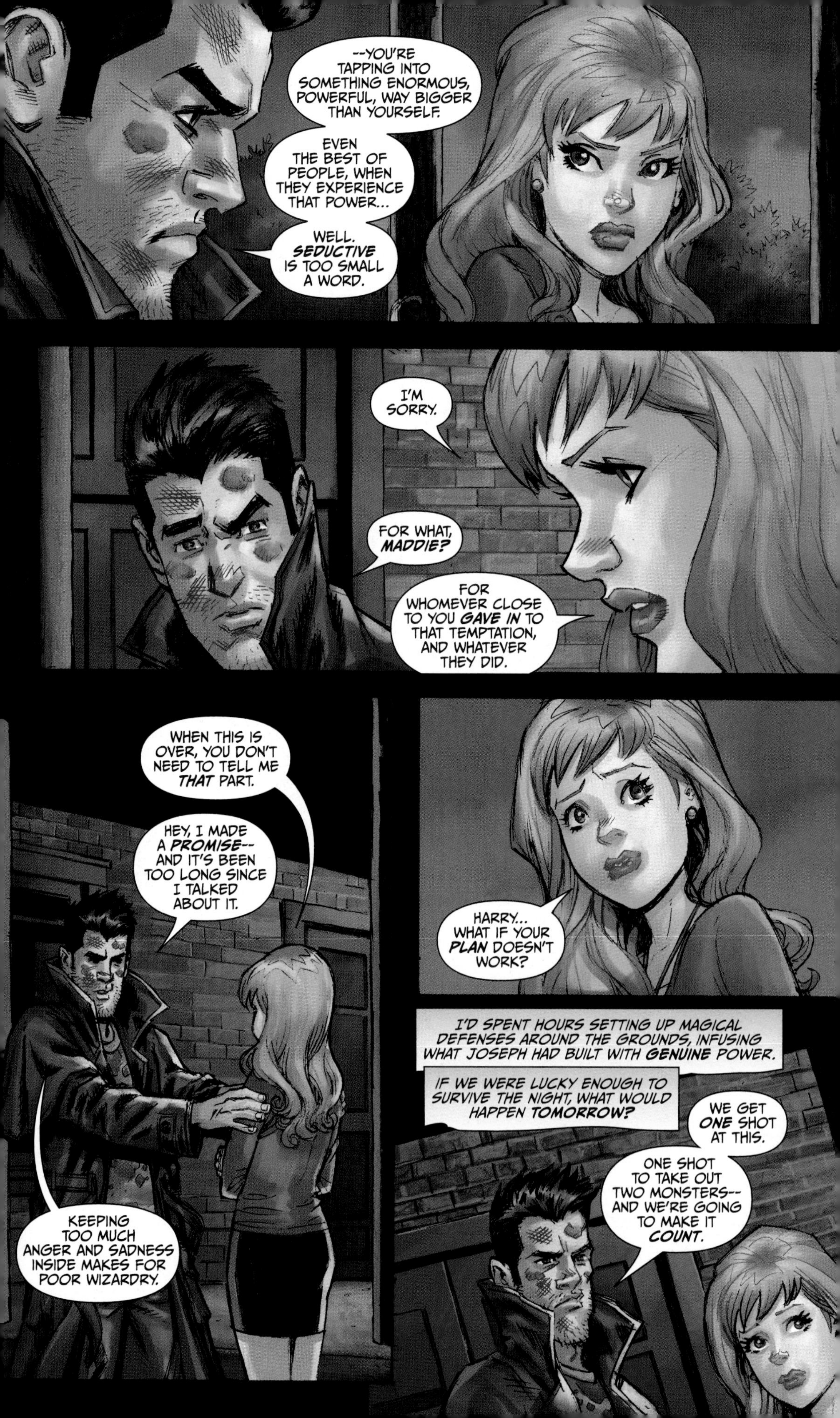
--YOU'RE TAPPING INTO SOMETHING ENORMOUS, POWERFUL, WAY BIGGER THAN YOURSELF.
EVEN THE BEST OF PEOPLE, WHEN THEY EXPERIENCE THAT POWER...
WELL. **SEDUCTIVE** IS TOO SMALL A WORD.
I'M SORRY.
FOR WHAT, **MADDIE?**
FOR WHOMEVER CLOSE TO YOU **GAVE IN** TO THAT TEMPTATION, AND WHATEVER THEY DID.
WHEN THIS IS OVER, YOU DON'T NEED TO TELL ME **THAT** PART.
HEY, I MADE A **PROMISE**-- AND IT'S BEEN TOO LONG SINCE I TALKED ABOUT IT.
KEEPING TOO MUCH ANGER AND SADNESS INSIDE MAKES FOR POOR WIZARDRY.
HARRY... WHAT IF YOUR **PLAN** DOESN'T WORK?
*I'D SPENT HOURS SETTING UP MAGICAL DEFENSES AROUND THE GROUNDS, INFUSING WHAT JOSEPH HAD BUILT WITH **GENUINE** POWER.*
*IF WE WERE LUCKY ENOUGH TO SURVIVE THE NIGHT, WHAT WOULD HAPPEN **TOMORROW?***
WE GET **ONE** SHOT AT THIS.
ONE SHOT TO TAKE OUT TWO MONSTERS-- AND WE'RE GOING TO MAKE IT **COUNT**.

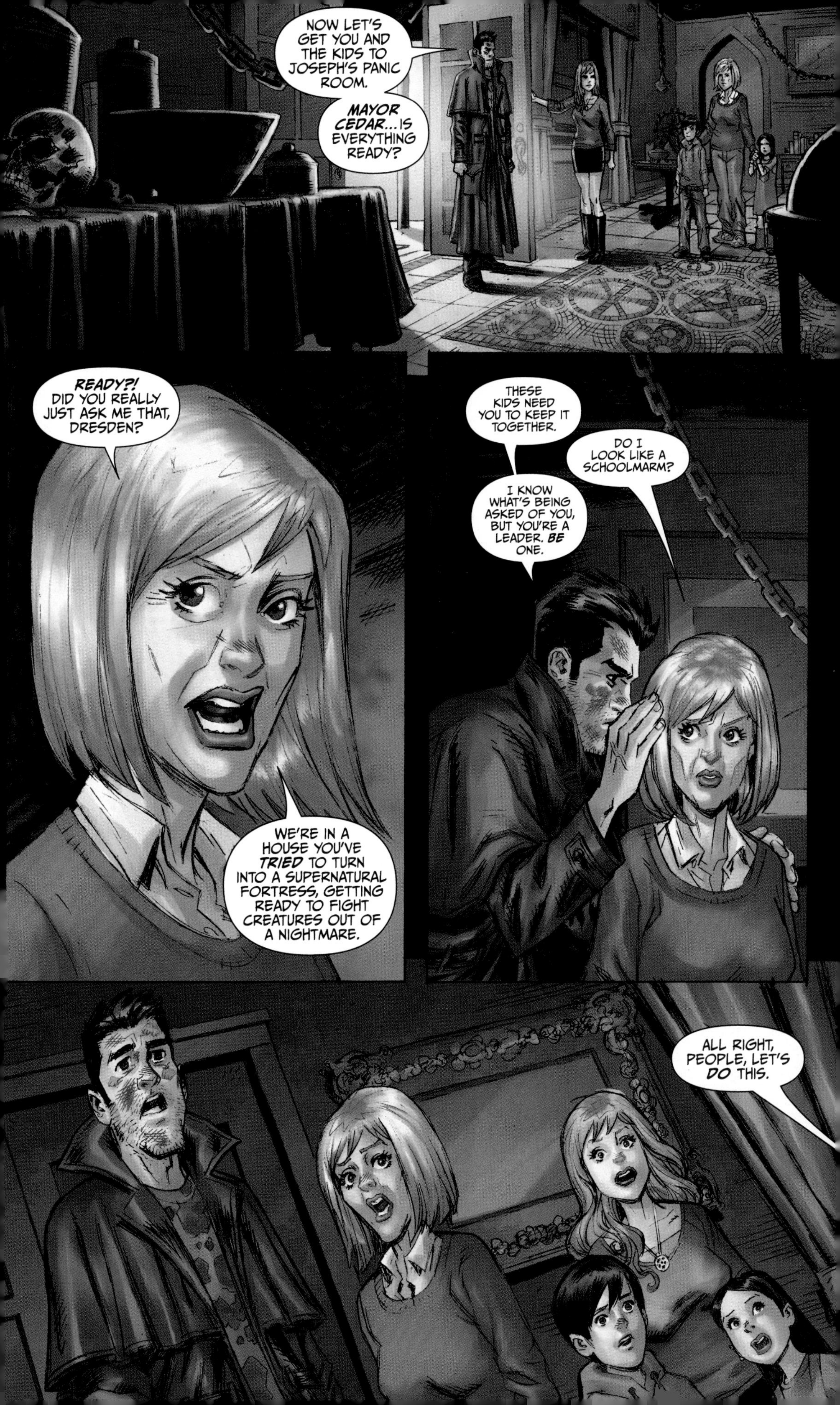
NOW LET'S GET YOU AND THE KIDS TO JOSEPH'S PANIC ROOM.
MAYOR CEDAR... IS EVERYTHING READY?
READY?! DID YOU REALLY JUST ASK ME THAT, DRESDEN?
WE'RE IN A HOUSE YOU'VE TRIED TO TURN INTO A SUPERNATURAL FORTRESS, GETTING READY TO FIGHT CREATURES OUT OF A NIGHTMARE.
THESE KIDS NEED YOU TO KEEP IT TOGETHER.
I KNOW WHAT'S BEING ASKED OF YOU, BUT YOU'RE A LEADER. BE ONE.
DO I LOOK LIKE A SCHOOLMARM?
ALL RIGHT, PEOPLE, LET'S DO THIS.

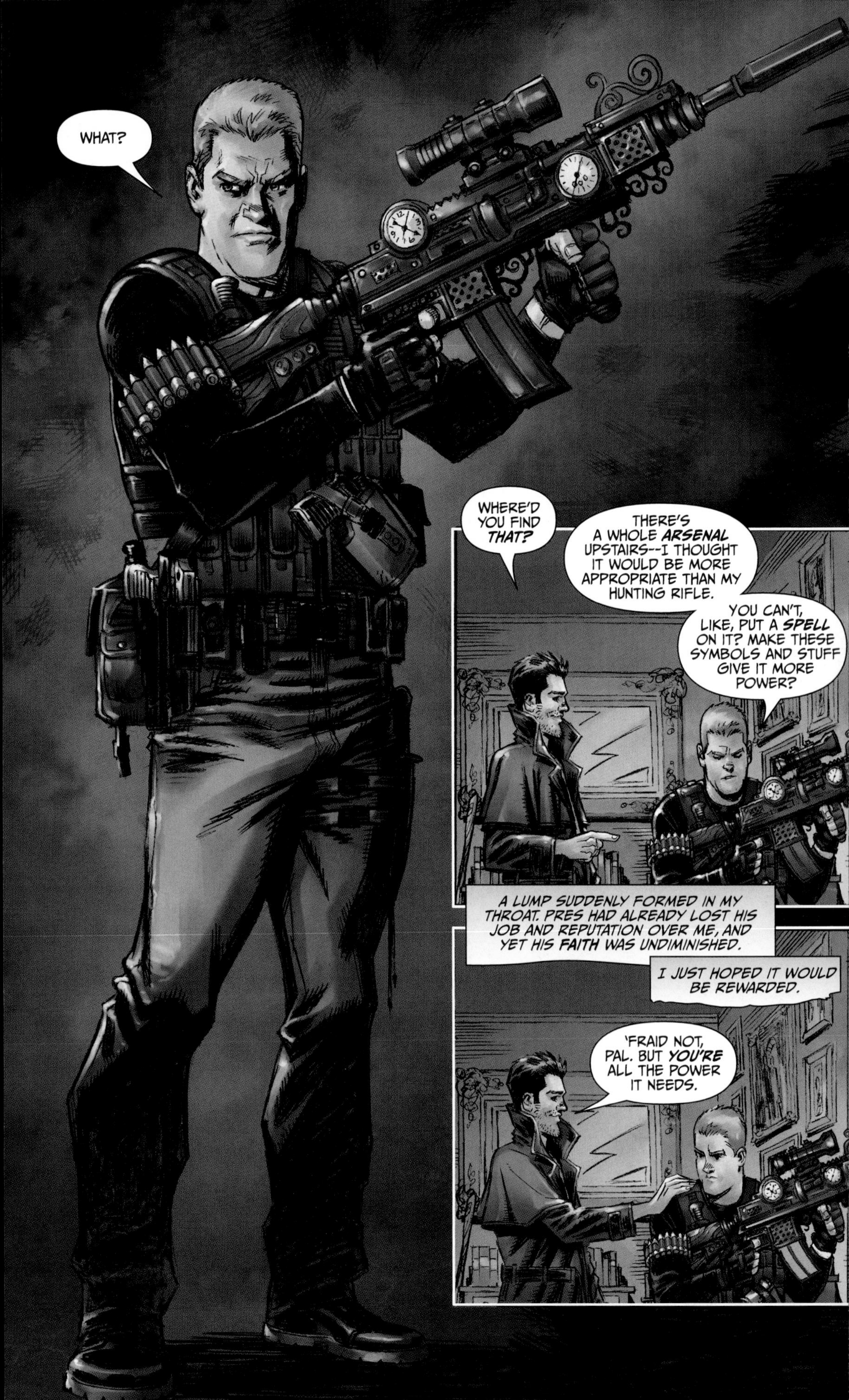
WHAT?
WHERE'D YOU FIND *THAT?*
THERE'S A WHOLE ***ARSENAL*** UPSTAIRS--I THOUGHT IT WOULD BE MORE APPROPRIATE THAN MY HUNTING RIFLE.
YOU CAN'T, LIKE, PUT A ***SPELL*** ON IT? MAKE THESE SYMBOLS AND STUFF GIVE IT MORE POWER?
*A LUMP SUDDENLY FORMED IN MY THROAT. PRES HAD ALREADY LOST HIS JOB AND REPUTATION OVER ME, AND YET HIS **FAITH** WAS UNDIMINISHED.*
I JUST HOPED IT WOULD BE REWARDED.
'FRAID NOT, PAL. BUT ***YOU'RE*** ALL THE POWER IT NEEDS.

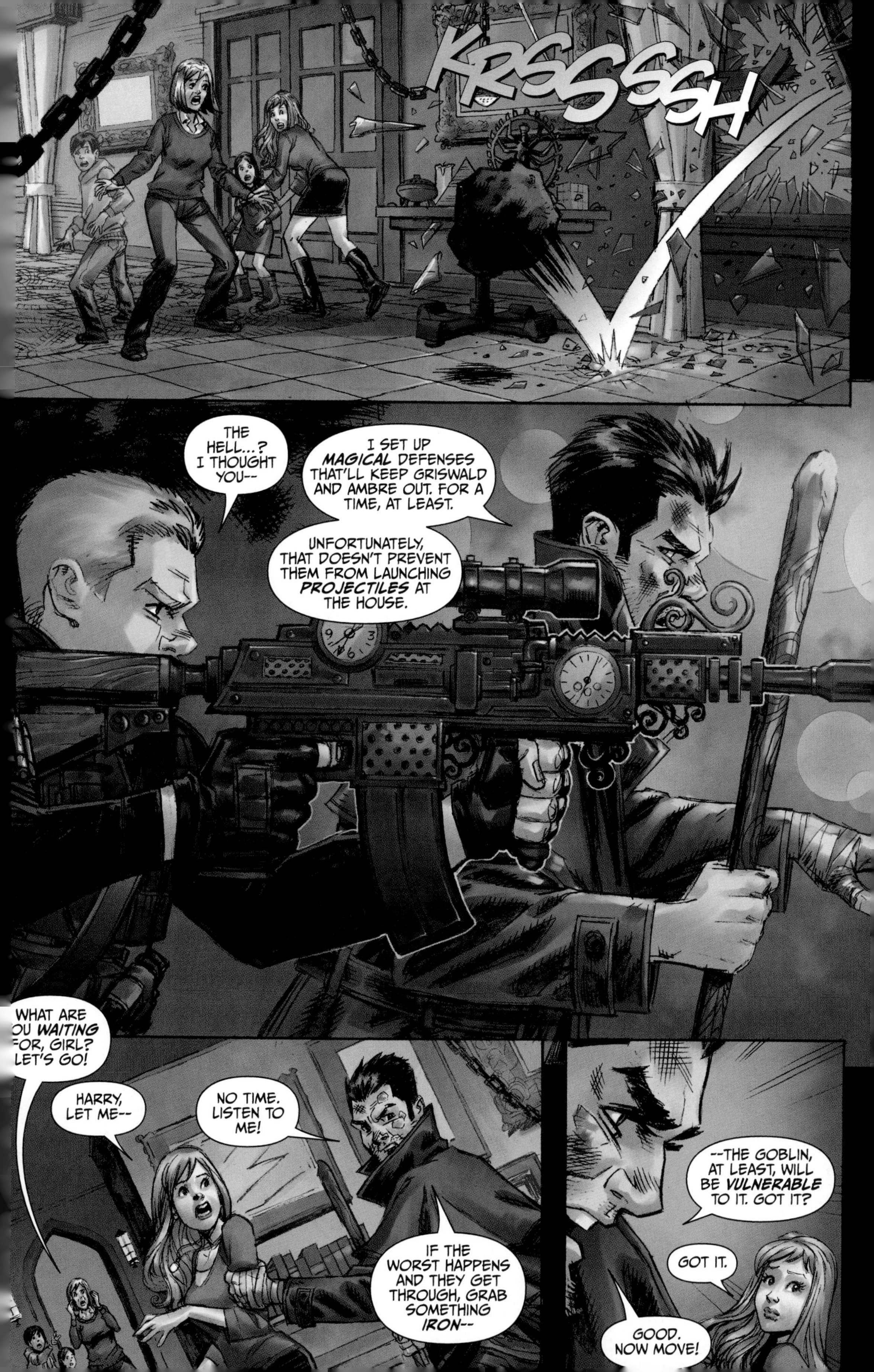
KRSSSSH
THE HELL...? I THOUGHT YOU--
I SET UP MAGICAL DEFENSES THAT'LL KEEP GRISWALD AND AMBRE OUT. FOR A TIME, AT LEAST.
UNFORTUNATELY, THAT DOESN'T PREVENT THEM FROM LAUNCHING PROJECTILES AT THE HOUSE.
WHAT ARE OU WAITING FOR, GIRL? LET'S GO!
HARRY, LET ME--
NO TIME. LISTEN TO ME!
IF THE WORST HAPPENS AND THEY GET THROUGH, GRAB SOMETHING IRON--
--THE GOBLIN, AT LEAST, WILL BE VULNERABLE TO IT. GOT IT?
GOT IT.
GOOD. NOW MOVE!

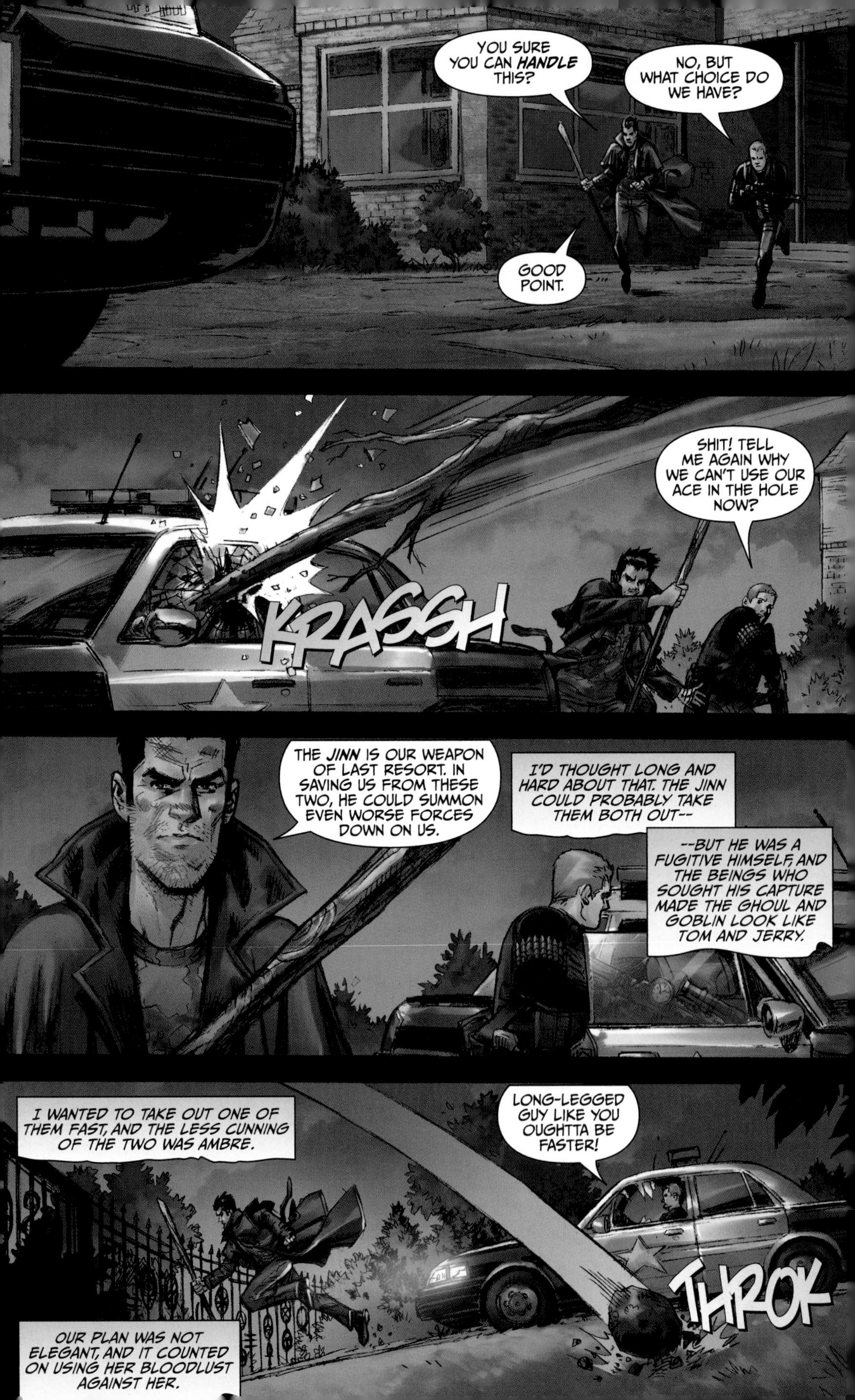
YOU SURE YOU CAN HANDLE THIS?
NO, BUT WHAT CHOICE DO WE HAVE?
GOOD POINT.
KRASSH
SHIT! TELL ME AGAIN WHY WE CAN'T USE OUR ACE IN THE HOLE NOW?
THE JINN IS OUR WEAPON OF LAST RESORT. IN SAVING US FROM THESE TWO, HE COULD SUMMON EVEN WORSE FORCES DOWN ON US.
I'D THOUGHT LONG AND HARD ABOUT THAT. THE JINN COULD PROBABLY TAKE THEM BOTH OUT--
--BUT HE WAS A FUGITIVE HIMSELF, AND THE BEINGS WHO SOUGHT HIS CAPTURE MADE THE GHOUL AND GOBLIN LOOK LIKE TOM AND JERRY.
I WANTED TO TAKE OUT ONE OF THEM FAST, AND THE LESS CUNNING OF THE TWO WAS AMBRE.
LONG-LEGGED GUY LIKE YOU OUGHTTA BE FASTER!
THROK
OUR PLAN WAS NOT ELEGANT, AND IT COUNTED ON USING HER BLOODLUST AGAINST HER.

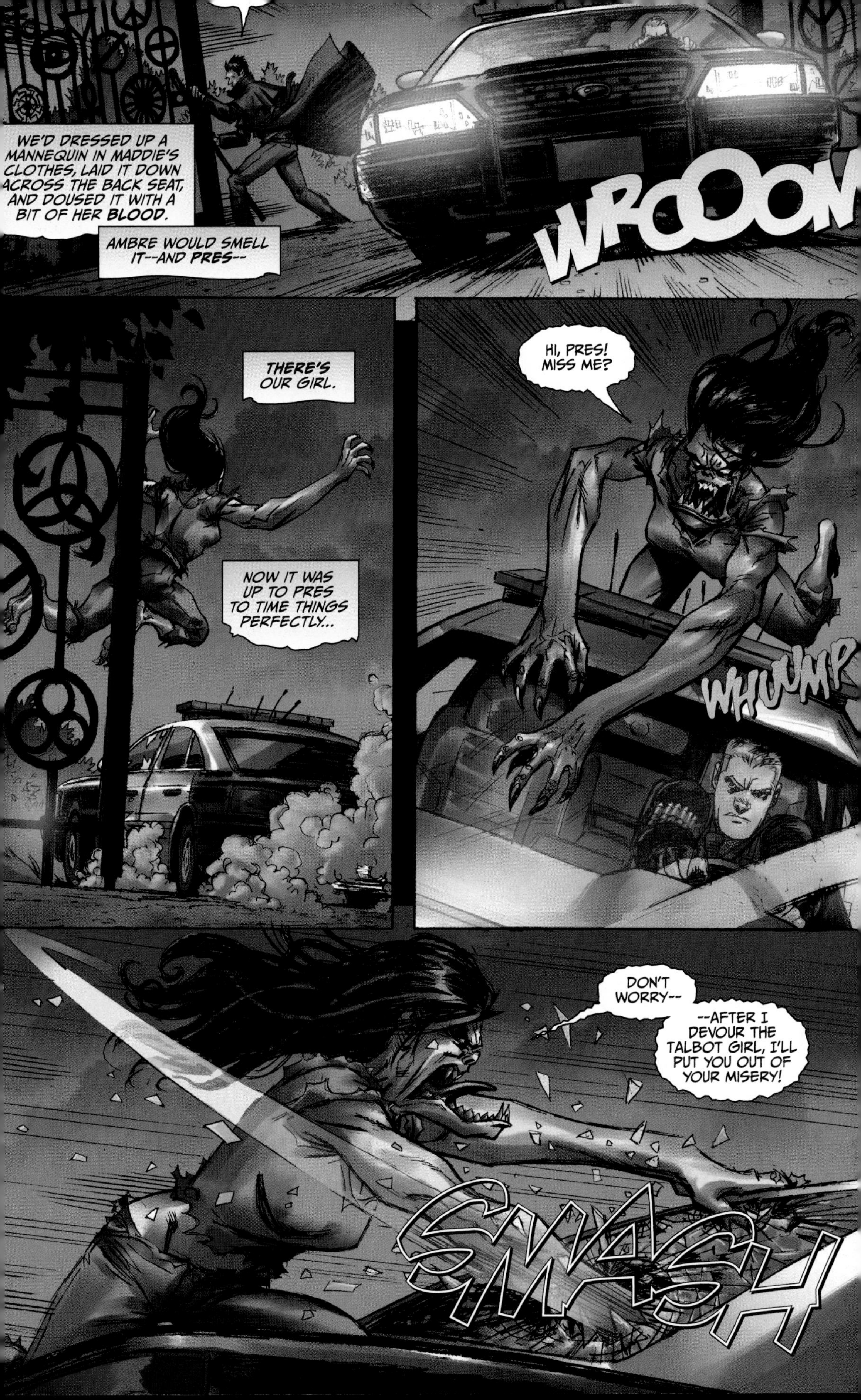
WE'D DRESSED UP A MANNEQUIN IN MADDIE'S CLOTHES, LAID IT DOWN ACROSS THE BACK SEAT, AND DOUSED IT WITH A BIT OF HER BLOOD.
AMBRE WOULD SMELL IT--AND PRES--
WROOOM
THERE'S OUR GIRL.
NOW IT WAS UP TO PRES TO TIME THINGS PERFECTLY...
HI, PRES! MISS ME?
WHUUMP
DON'T WORRY--
--AFTER I DEVOUR THE TALBOT GIRL, I'LL PUT YOU OUT OF YOUR MISERY!
SMASH

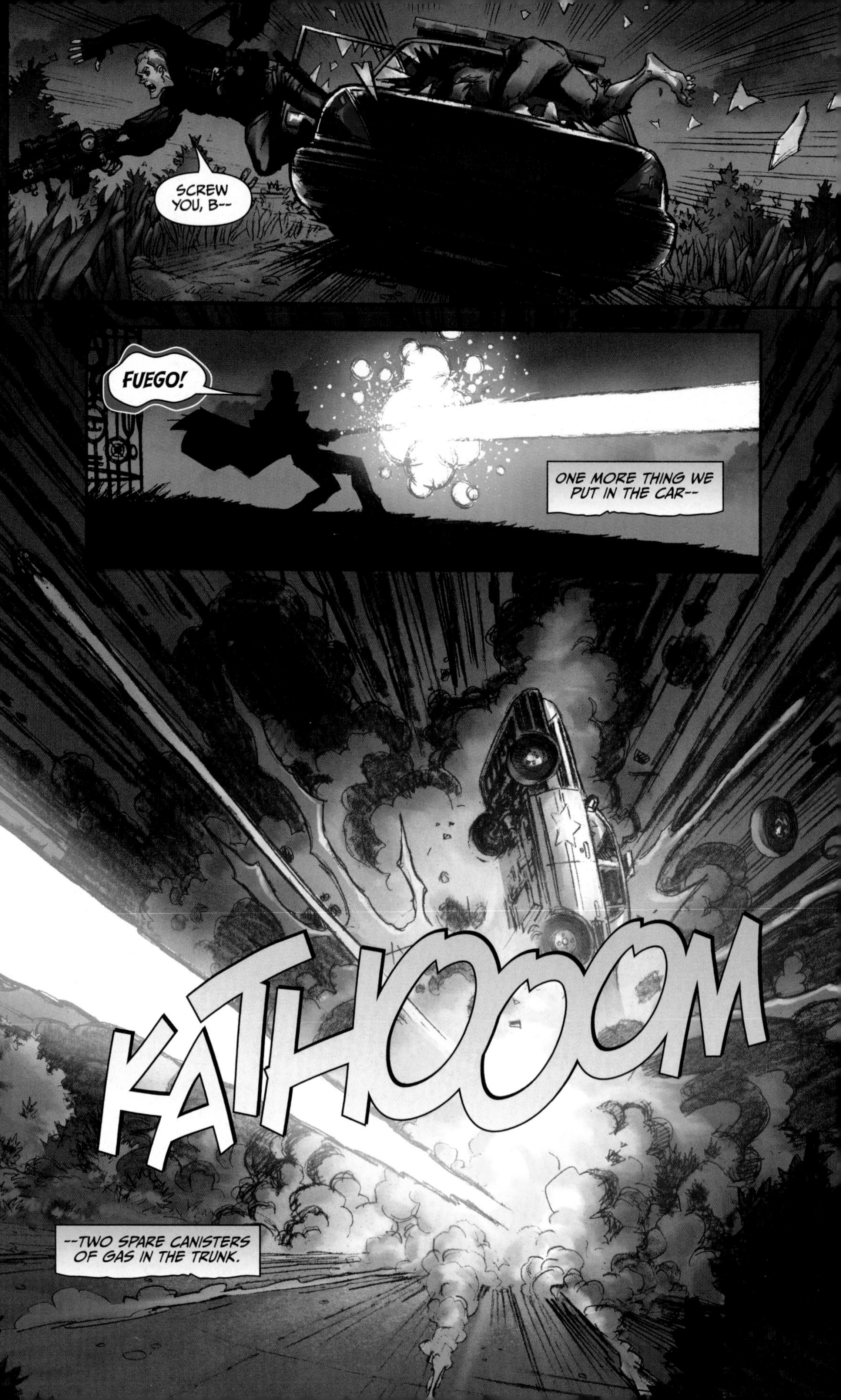
SCREW YOU, B--
FUEGO!
ONE MORE THING WE PUT IN THE CAR--
KATHOOOM
--TWO SPARE CANISTERS OF GAS IN THE TRUNK.

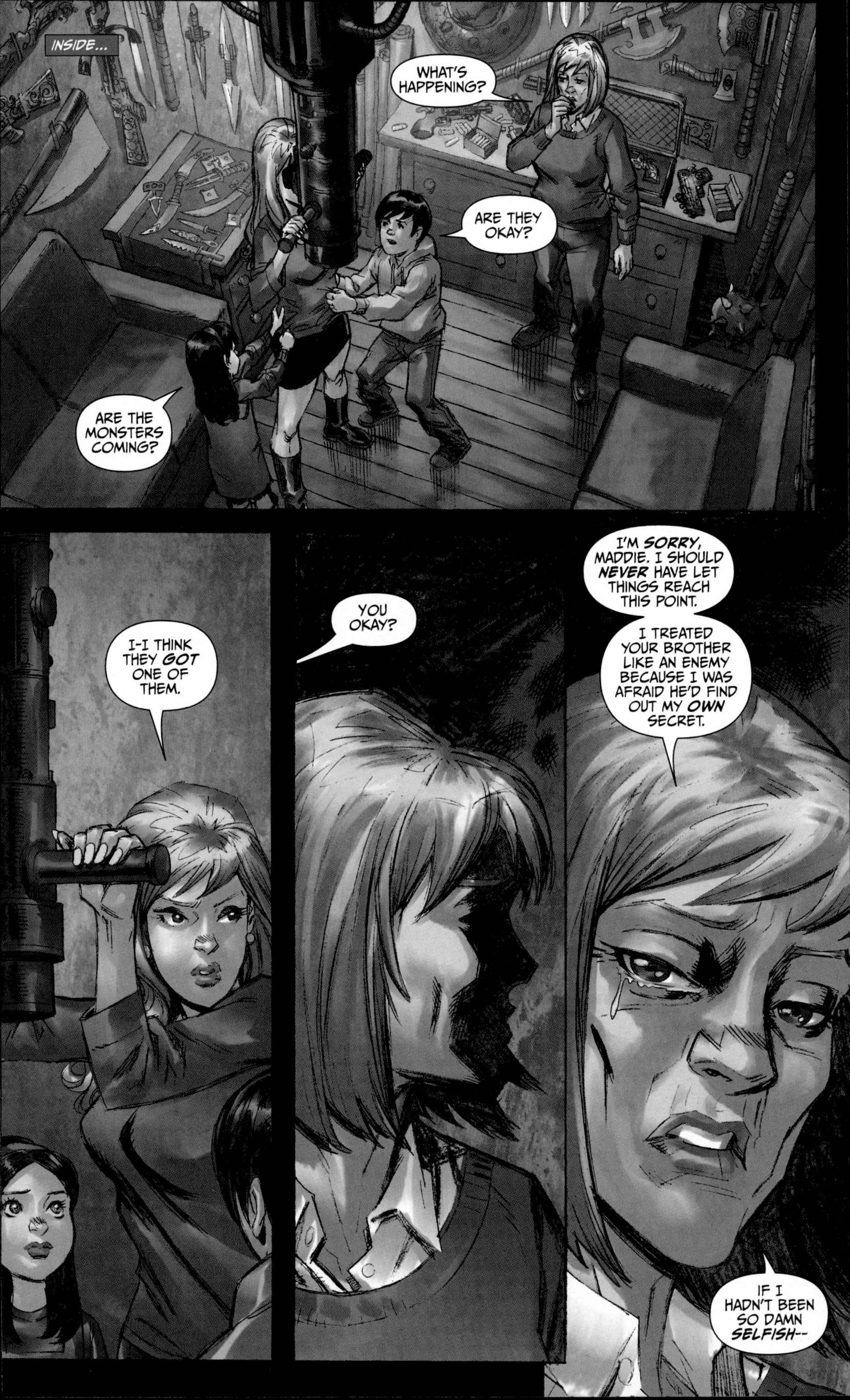
INSIDE...
WHAT'S HAPPENING?
ARE THEY OKAY?
ARE THE MONSTERS COMING?
I-I THINK THEY GOT ONE OF THEM.
YOU OKAY?
I'M SORRY, MADDIE. I SHOULD NEVER HAVE LET THINGS REACH THIS POINT.
I TREATED YOUR BROTHER LIKE AN ENEMY BECAUSE I WAS AFRAID HE'D FIND OUT MY OWN SECRET.
IF I HADN'T BEEN SO DAMN SELFISH--

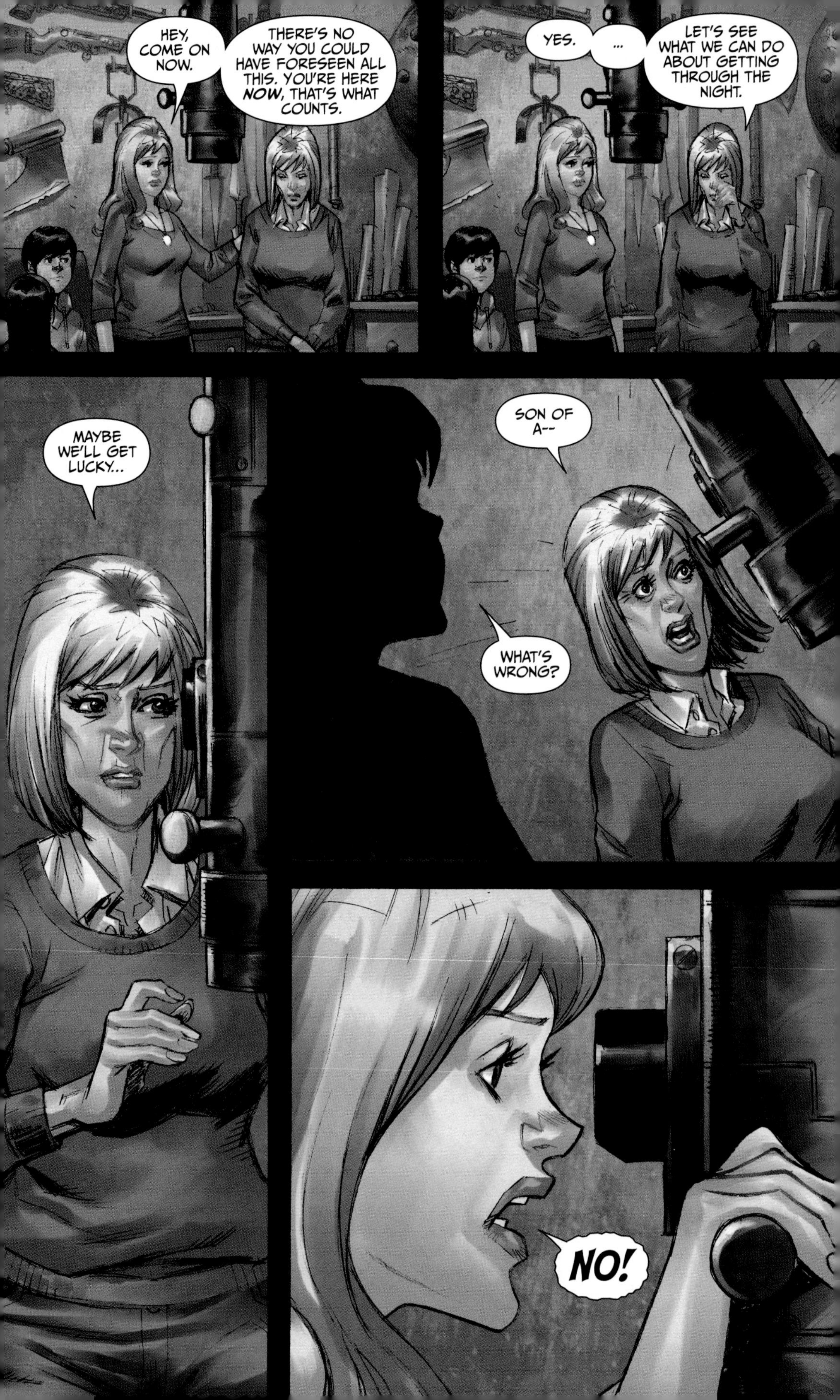
HEY, COME ON NOW.
THERE'S NO WAY YOU COULD HAVE FORESEEN ALL THIS. YOU'RE HERE *NOW*, THAT'S WHAT COUNTS.
YES.
...
LET'S SEE WHAT WE CAN DO ABOUT GETTING THROUGH THE NIGHT.
MAYBE WE'LL GET LUCKY...
SON OF A--
WHAT'S WRONG?
NO!

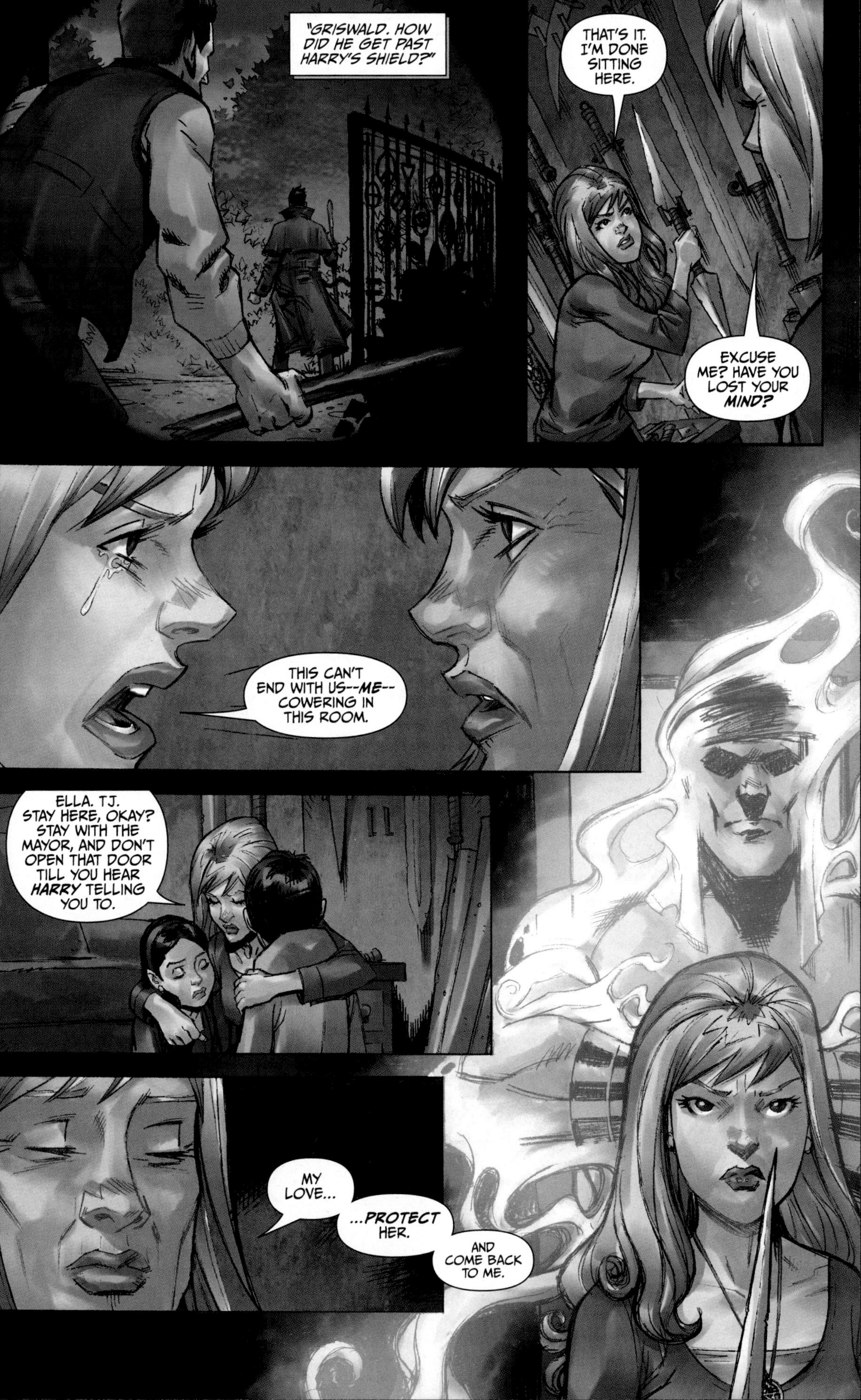
"GRISWALD. HOW DID HE GET PAST HARRY'S SHIELD?"
THAT'S IT. I'M DONE SITTING HERE.
EXCUSE ME? HAVE YOU LOST YOUR *MIND?*
THIS CAN'T END WITH US--*ME*--COWERING IN THIS ROOM.
ELLA. T.J. STAY HERE, OKAY? STAY WITH THE MAYOR, AND DON'T OPEN THAT DOOR TILL YOU HEAR *HARRY* TELLING YOU TO.
MY LOVE...
...*PROTECT* HER.
AND COME BACK TO ME.

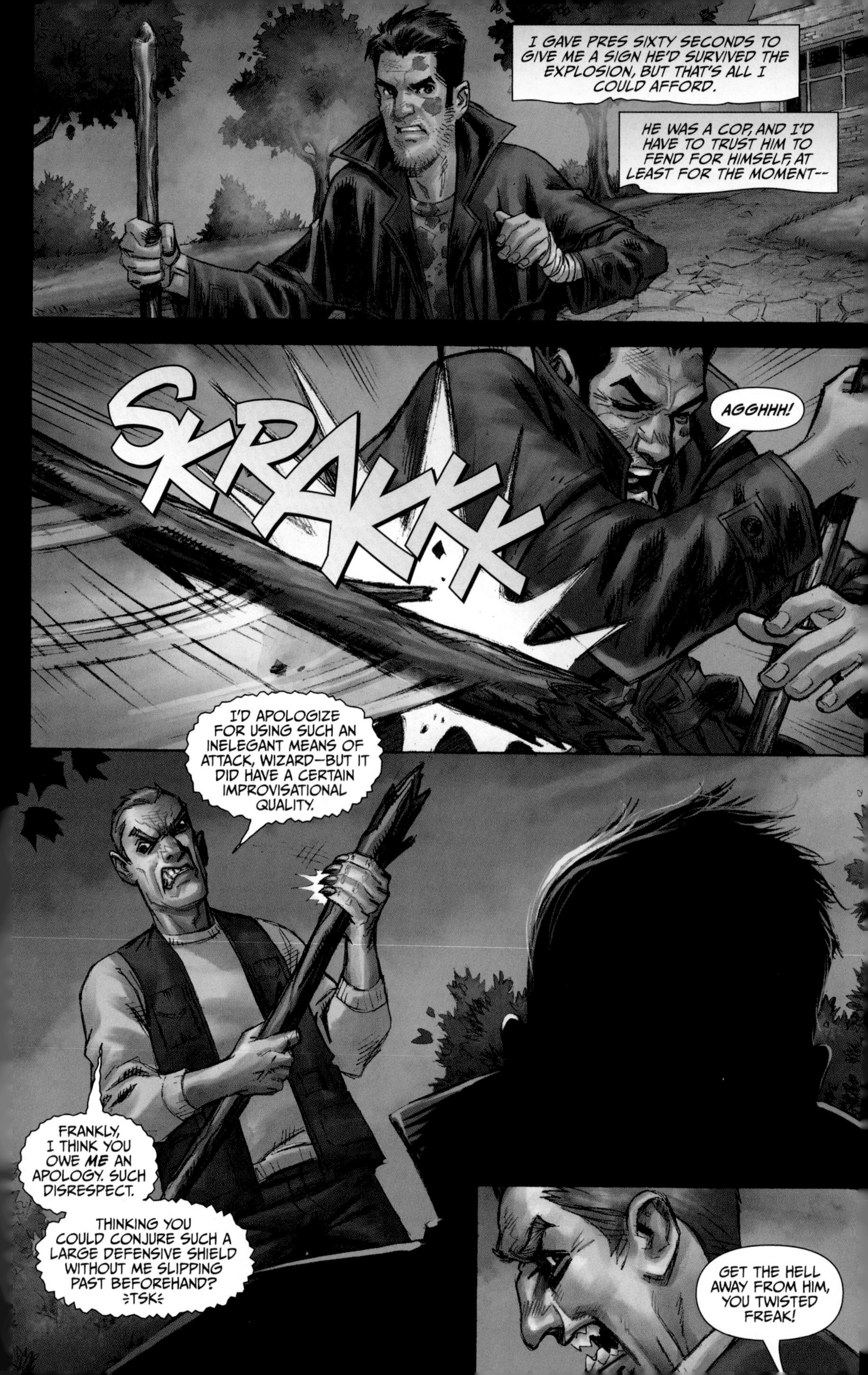

I GAVE PRES SIXTY SECONDS TO GIVE ME A SIGN HE'D SURVIVED THE EXPLOSION, BUT THAT'S ALL I COULD AFFORD.
HE WAS A COP, AND I'D HAVE TO TRUST HIM TO FEND FOR HIMSELF, AT LEAST FOR THE MOMENT--
SKRAKKK
AGGHHH!
I'D APOLOGIZE FOR USING SUCH AN INELEGANT MEANS OF ATTACK, WIZARD—BUT IT DID HAVE A CERTAIN IMPROVISATIONAL QUALITY.
FRANKLY, I THINK YOU OWE ME AN APOLOGY. SUCH DISRESPECT.
THINKING YOU COULD CONJURE SUCH A LARGE DEFENSIVE SHIELD WITHOUT ME SLIPPING PAST BEFOREHAND? TSK
GET THE HELL AWAY FROM HIM, YOU TWISTED FREAK!

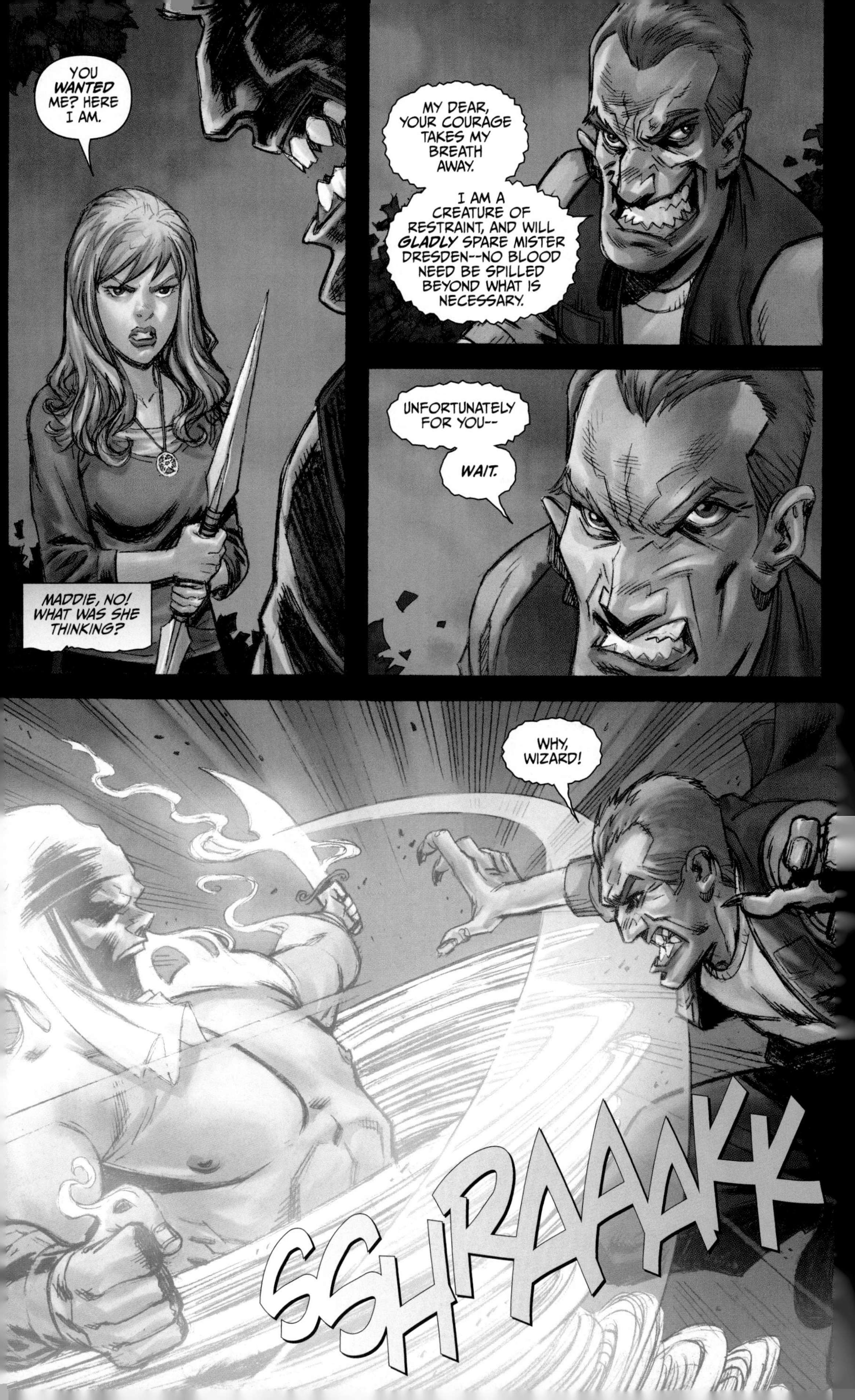
YOU WANTED ME? HERE I AM.
MADDIE, NO! WHAT WAS SHE THINKING?
MY DEAR, YOUR COURAGE TAKES MY BREATH AWAY.
I AM A CREATURE OF RESTRAINT, AND WILL GLADLY SPARE MISTER DRESDEN--NO BLOOD NEED BE SPILLED BEYOND WHAT IS NECESSARY.
UNFORTUNATELY FOR YOU--
WAIT.
WHY, WIZARD!
SSHRAAAKK

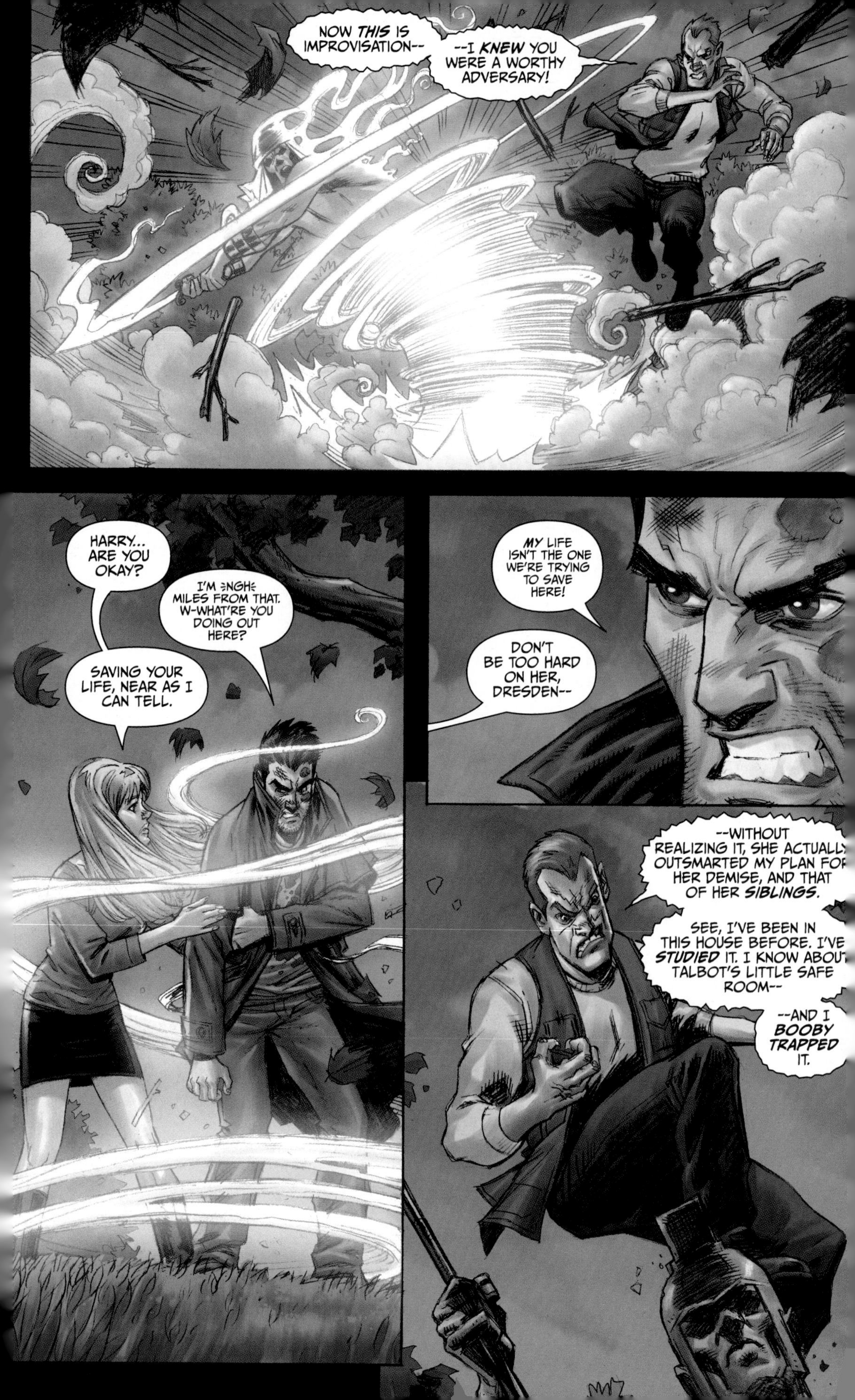
NOW *THIS* IS IMPROVISATION--
--I *KNEW* YOU WERE A WORTHY ADVERSARY!
HARRY... ARE YOU OKAY?
I'M =NGH= MILES FROM THAT. W-WHAT'RE YOU DOING OUT HERE?
SAVING YOUR LIFE, NEAR AS I CAN TELL.
MY LIFE ISN'T THE ONE WE'RE TRYING TO SAVE HERE!
DON'T BE TOO HARD ON HER, DRESDEN--
--WITHOUT REALIZING IT, SHE ACTUALLY OUTSMARTED MY PLAN FOR HER DEMISE, AND THAT OF HER *SIBLINGS*.
SEE, I'VE BEEN IN THIS HOUSE BEFORE. I'VE *STUDIED* IT. I KNOW ABOUT TALBOT'S LITTLE SAFE ROOM--
--AND I *BOOBY TRAPPED* IT.

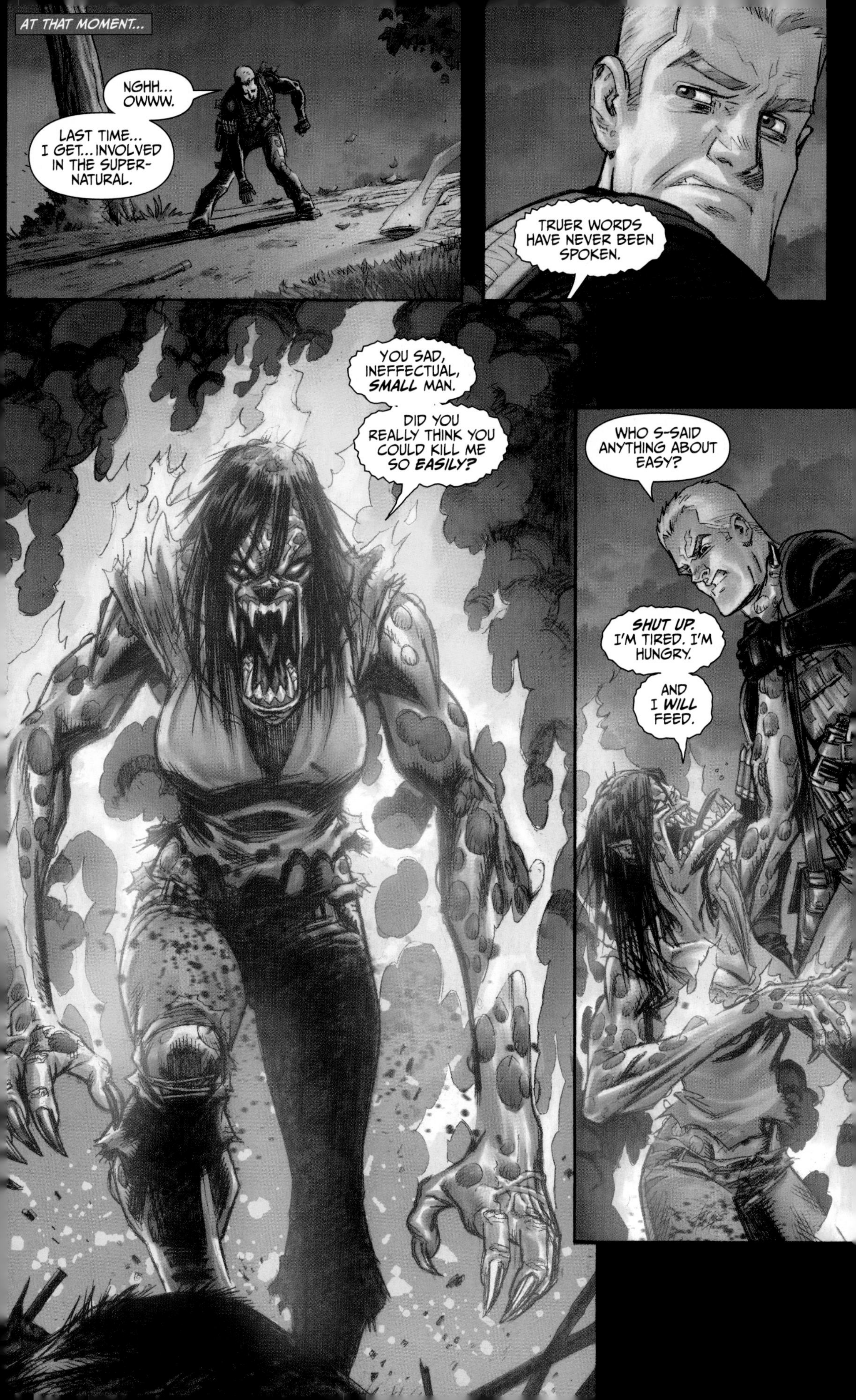
AT THAT MOMENT...
NGHH... OWWW.
LAST TIME... I GET...INVOLVED IN THE SUPER-NATURAL.
TRUER WORDS HAVE NEVER BEEN SPOKEN.
YOU SAD, INEFFECTUAL, SMALL MAN.
DID YOU REALLY THINK YOU COULD KILL ME SO EASILY?
WHO S-SAID ANYTHING ABOUT EASY?
SHUT UP. I'M TIRED. I'M HUNGRY.
AND I WILL FEED.

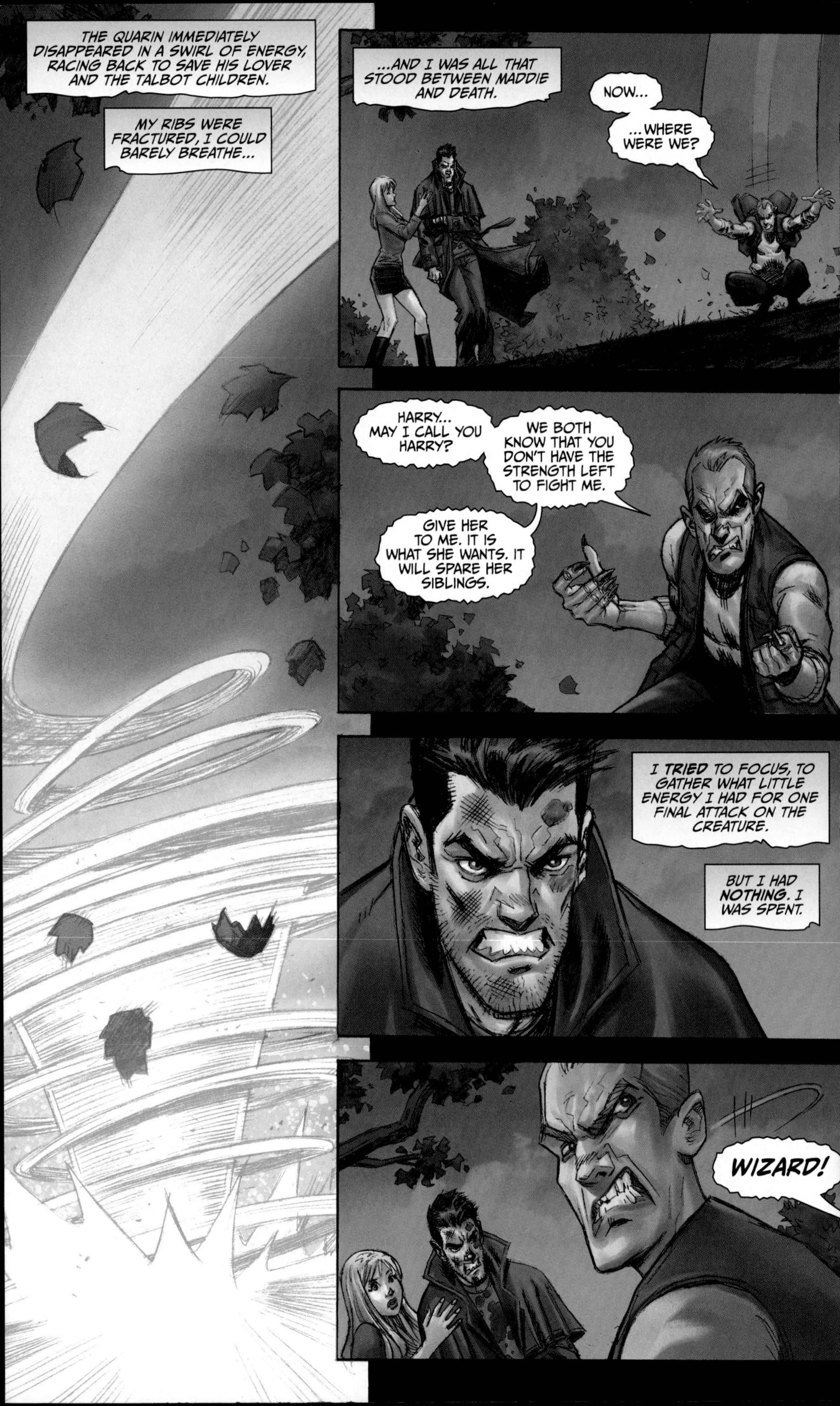
THE QUARIN IMMEDIATELY DISAPPEARED IN A SWIRL OF ENERGY, RACING BACK TO SAVE HIS LOVER AND THE TALBOT CHILDREN.
MY RIBS WERE FRACTURED, I COULD BARELY BREATHE...
...AND I WAS ALL THAT STOOD BETWEEN MADDIE AND DEATH.
NOW...
...WHERE WERE WE?
HARRY... MAY I CALL YOU HARRY?
WE BOTH KNOW THAT YOU DON'T HAVE THE STRENGTH LEFT TO FIGHT ME.
GIVE HER TO ME. IT IS WHAT SHE WANTS. IT WILL SPARE HER SIBLINGS.
I TRIED TO FOCUS, TO GATHER WHAT LITTLE ENERGY I HAD FOR ONE FINAL ATTACK ON THE CREATURE.
BUT I HAD NOTHING. I WAS SPENT.
WIZARD!

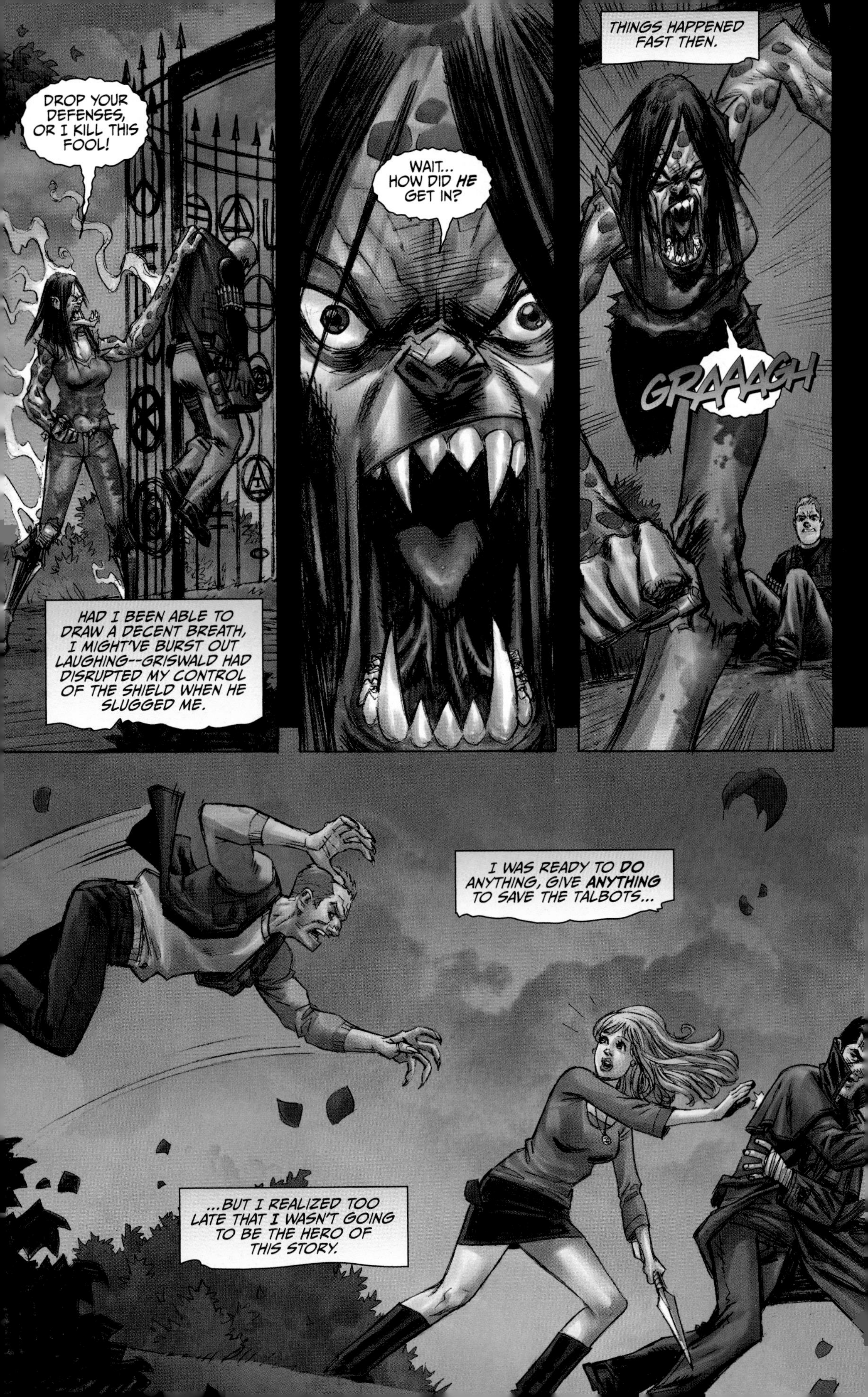

DROP YOUR DEFENSES, OR I KILL THIS FOOL!
HAD I BEEN ABLE TO DRAW A DECENT BREATH, I MIGHT'VE BURST OUT LAUGHING--GRISWALD HAD DISRUPTED MY CONTROL OF THE SHIELD WHEN HE SLUGGED ME.
WAIT... HOW DID HE GET IN?
THINGS HAPPENED FAST THEN.
GRAAAGH
I WAS READY TO DO ANYTHING, GIVE ANYTHING TO SAVE THE TALBOTS...
...BUT I REALIZED TOO LATE THAT I WASN'T GOING TO BE THE HERO OF THIS STORY.

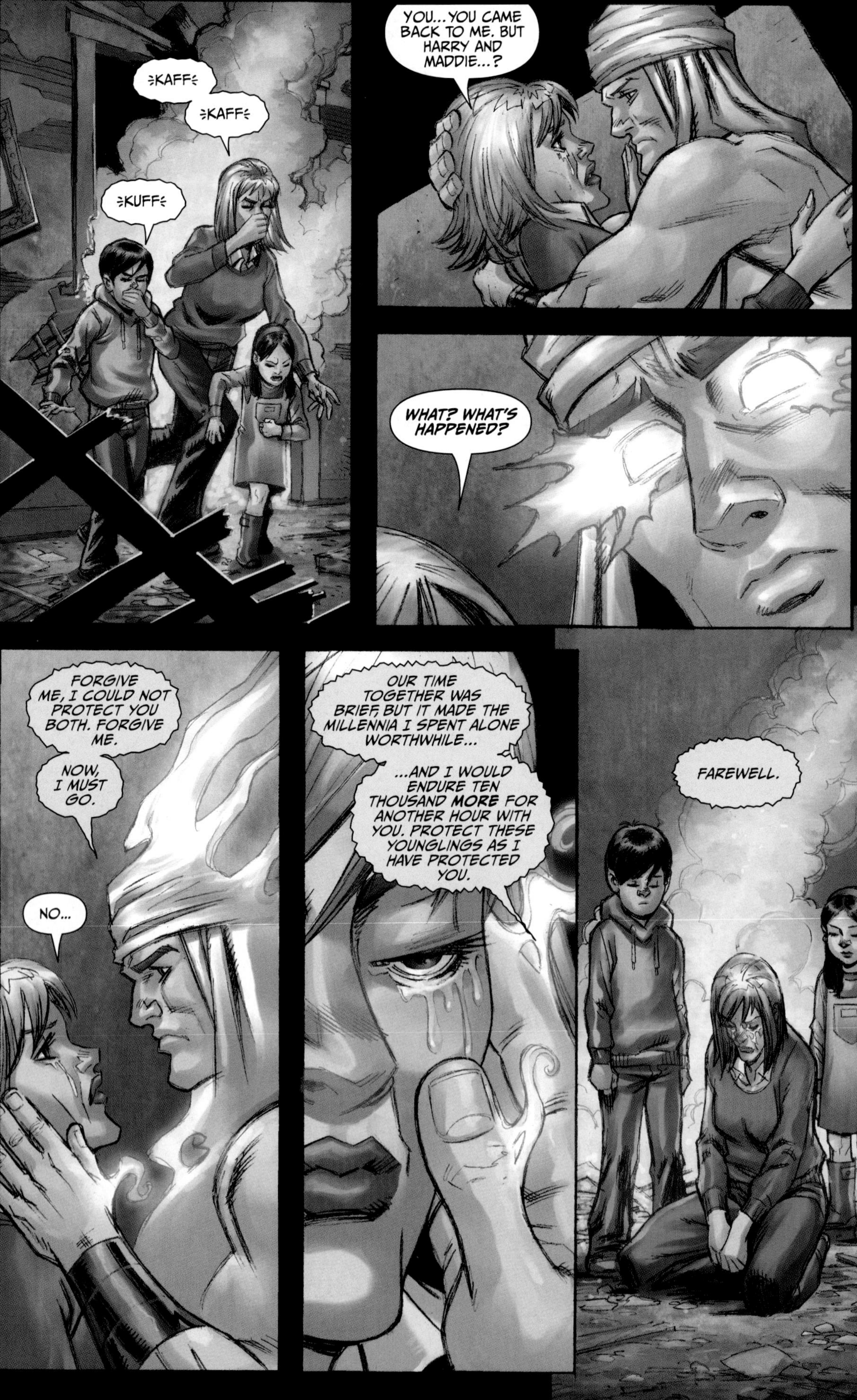
KAFF
KAFF
KUFF
YOU...YOU CAME BACK TO ME. BUT HARRY AND MADDIE...?
WHAT? WHAT'S HAPPENED?
FORGIVE ME, I COULD NOT PROTECT YOU BOTH. FORGIVE ME.
NOW, I MUST GO.
NO...
OUR TIME TOGETHER WAS BRIEF, BUT IT MADE THE MILLENNIA I SPENT ALONE WORTHWHILE...
...AND I WOULD ENDURE TEN THOUSAND MORE FOR ANOTHER HOUR WITH YOU. PROTECT THESE YOUNGLINGS AS I HAVE PROTECTED YOU.
FAREWELL.

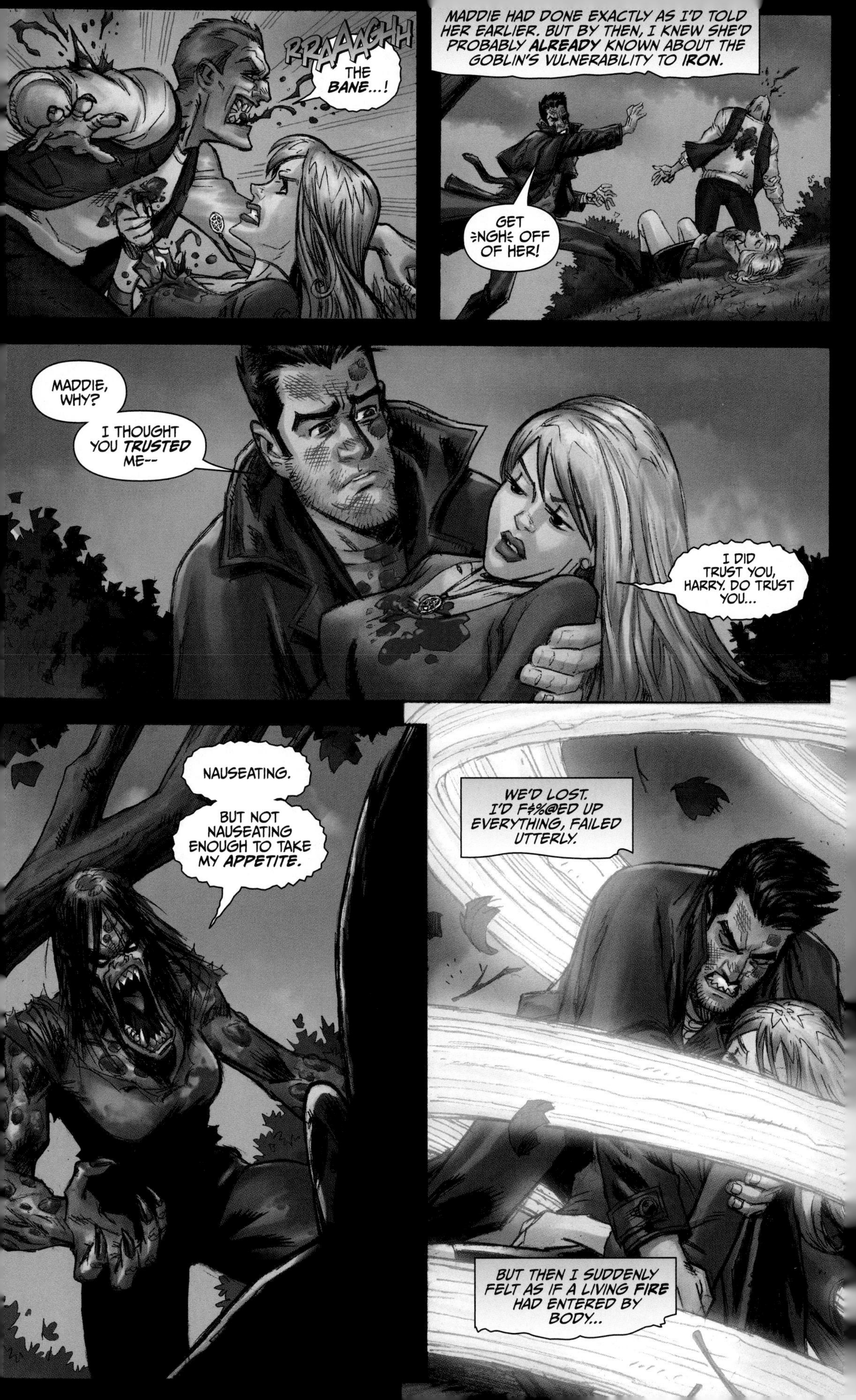
RRAAAGHH
THE BANE...!
MADDIE HAD DONE EXACTLY AS I'D TOLD HER EARLIER. BUT BY THEN, I KNEW SHE'D PROBABLY ALREADY KNOWN ABOUT THE GOBLIN'S VULNERABILITY TO IRON.
GET =NGH= OFF OF HER!
MADDIE, WHY?
I THOUGHT YOU TRUSTED ME--
I DID TRUST YOU, HARRY. DO TRUST YOU...
NAUSEATING.
BUT NOT NAUSEATING ENOUGH TO TAKE MY APPETITE.
WE'D LOST. I'D F$%@ED UP EVERYTHING, FAILED UTTERLY.
BUT THEN I SUDDENLY FELT AS IF A LIVING FIRE HAD ENTERED BY BODY...

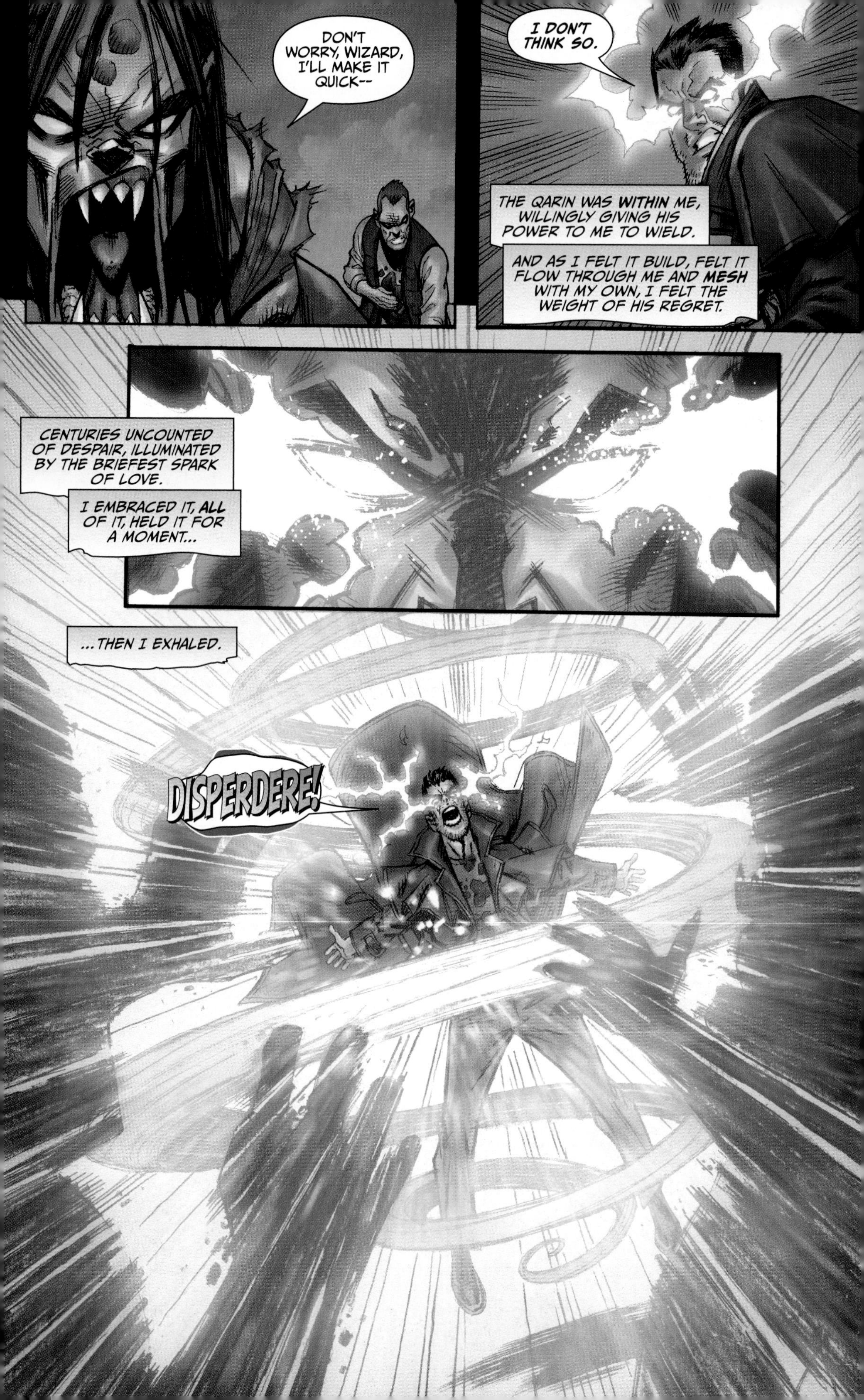
DON'T WORRY, WIZARD, I'LL MAKE IT QUICK--
I DON'T THINK SO.
THE QARIN WAS WITHIN ME, WILLINGLY GIVING HIS POWER TO ME TO WIELD.
AND AS I FELT IT BUILD, FELT IT FLOW THROUGH ME AND MESH WITH MY OWN, I FELT THE WEIGHT OF HIS REGRET.
CENTURIES UNCOUNTED OF DESPAIR, ILLUMINATED BY THE BRIEFEST SPARK OF LOVE.
I EMBRACED IT, ALL OF IT, HELD IT FOR A MOMENT...
...THEN I EXHALED.
DISPERDERE!

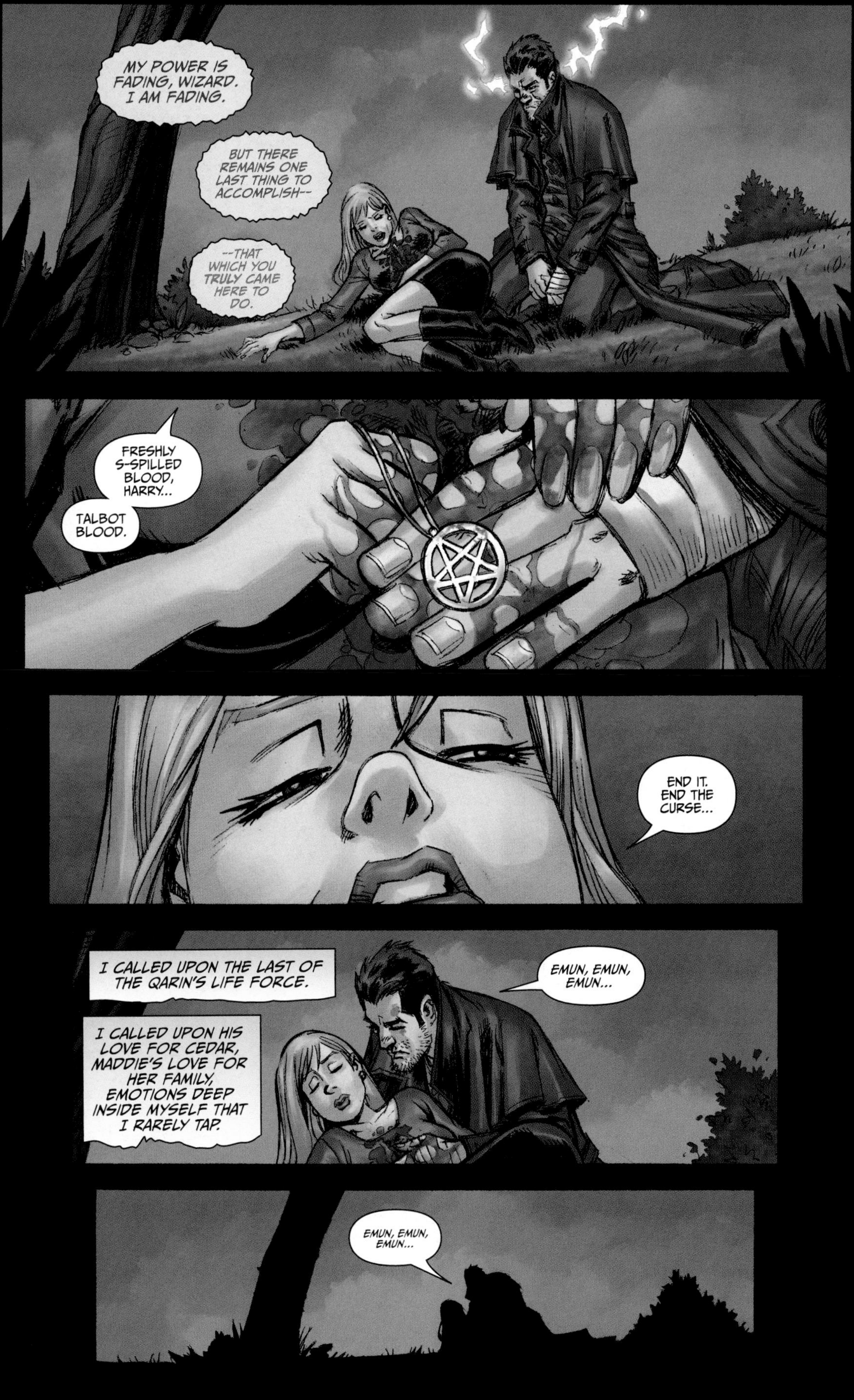
MY POWER IS FADING, WIZARD. I AM FADING.
BUT THERE REMAINS ONE LAST THING TO ACCOMPLISH--
--THAT WHICH YOU TRULY CAME HERE TO DO.
FRESHLY S-SPILLED BLOOD, HARRY...
TALBOT BLOOD.
END IT. END THE CURSE...
I CALLED UPON THE LAST OF THE QARIN'S LIFE FORCE.
EMUN, EMUN, EMUN...
I CALLED UPON HIS LOVE FOR CEDAR, MADDIE'S LOVE FOR HER FAMILY, EMOTIONS DEEP INSIDE MYSELF THAT I RARELY TAP.
EMUN, EMUN, EMUN...

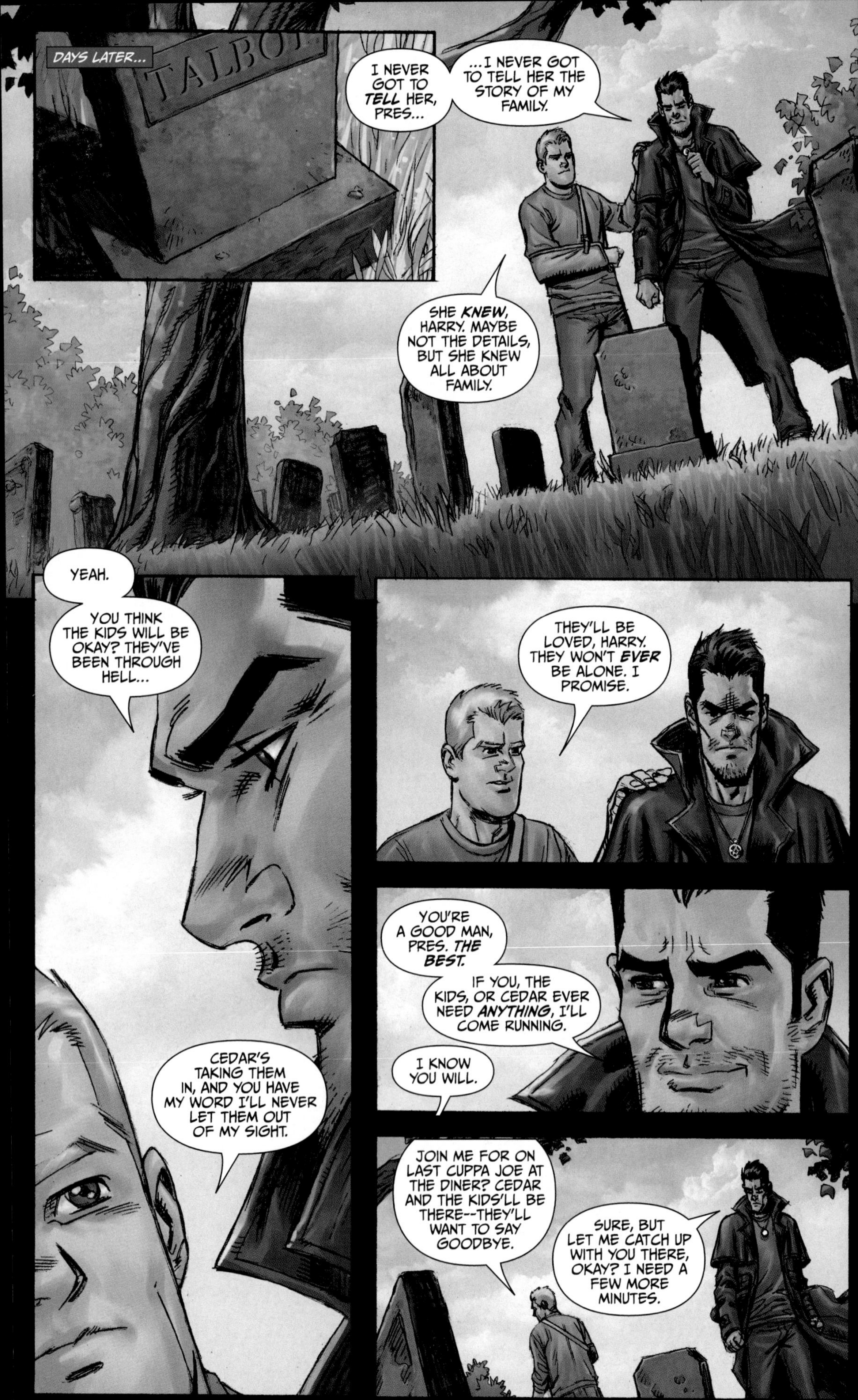
DAYS LATER...
TALBOT
I NEVER GOT TO TELL HER, PRES...
...I NEVER GOT TO TELL HER THE STORY OF MY FAMILY.
SHE KNEW, HARRY. MAYBE NOT THE DETAILS, BUT SHE KNEW ALL ABOUT FAMILY.
YEAH.
YOU THINK THE KIDS WILL BE OKAY? THEY'VE BEEN THROUGH HELL...
CEDAR'S TAKING THEM IN, AND YOU HAVE MY WORD I'LL NEVER LET THEM OUT OF MY SIGHT.
THEY'LL BE LOVED, HARRY. THEY WON'T EVER BE ALONE. I PROMISE.
YOU'RE A GOOD MAN, PRES. THE BEST.
IF YOU, THE KIDS, OR CEDAR EVER NEED ANYTHING, I'LL COME RUNNING.
I KNOW YOU WILL.
JOIN ME FOR ON LAST CUPPA JOE AT THE DINER? CEDAR AND THE KIDS'LL BE THERE--THEY'LL WANT TO SAY GOODBYE.
SURE, BUT LET ME CATCH UP WITH YOU THERE, OKAY? I NEED A FEW MORE MINUTES.

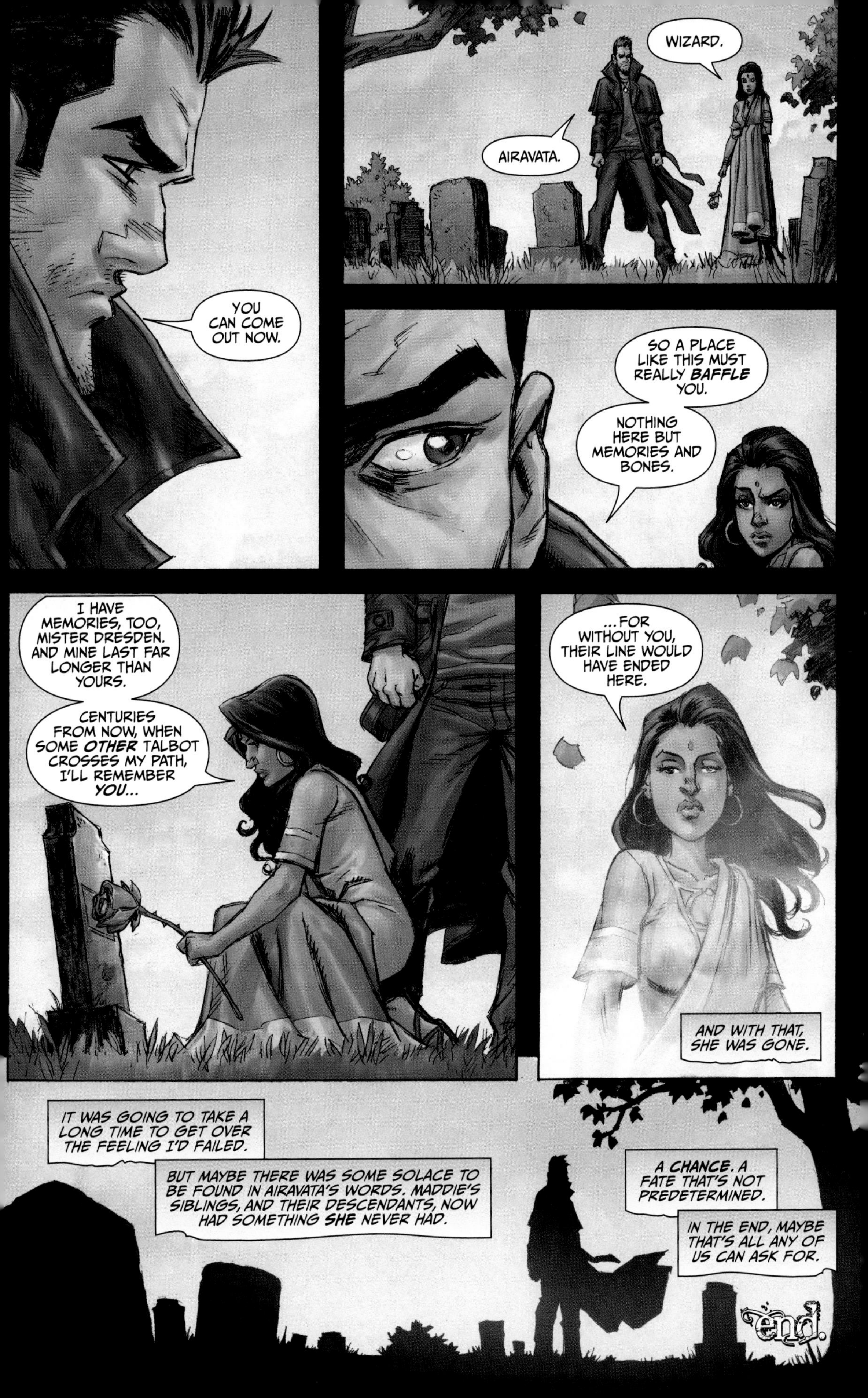

YOU CAN COME OUT NOW.
WIZARD.
AIRAVATA.
SO A PLACE LIKE THIS MUST REALLY **BAFFLE** YOU.
NOTHING HERE BUT MEMORIES AND BONES.
I HAVE MEMORIES, TOO, MISTER DRESDEN. AND MINE LAST FAR LONGER THAN YOURS.
CENTURIES FROM NOW, WHEN SOME **OTHER** TALBOT CROSSES MY PATH, I'LL REMEMBER **YOU**...
...FOR WITHOUT YOU, THEIR LINE WOULD HAVE ENDED HERE.
AND WITH THAT, SHE WAS GONE.
IT WAS GOING TO TAKE A LONG TIME TO GET OVER THE FEELING I'D FAILED.
BUT MAYBE THERE WAS SOME SOLACE TO BE FOUND IN AIRAVATA'S WORDS. MADDIE'S SIBLINGS, AND THEIR DESCENDANTS, NOW HAD SOMETHING **SHE** NEVER HAD.
A **CHANCE**. A FATE THAT'S NOT PREDETERMINED.
IN THE END, MAYBE THAT'S ALL ANY OF US CAN ASK FOR.
end.

BONUS MATERIALS

SUMMARY

When bizarre and gruesome deaths fall upon two of seven children of a country family, Harry Dresden and a small-town Sherriff's Deputy set out to protect the others. But can they succeed when they learn that two supernatural super-predators are holding a contest to see which one of them is the deadliest hunter?

CAST

Ambre Marie LaChaise is a *ghoul*—a flesh-eating supernatural predator who can look perfectly innocent and normal until the joy of the hunt is upon her. She's a perky brunette co-ed at Boone Mill's small private college on the outside—but on the inside, she's a gape-jawed, fanged, clawed escapee from a Japanese horror cartoon. She's dating Prescott Tremaine, in order to be sure she knows it should the mortals ever begin to take note of her predation. In her natural form, she is viciously quick and harder to kill than a New York cockroach.

Tormented by near-constant hunger, she isn't a mental powerhouse, but she has yards and yards of low cunning and the conscience of a great white shark.

Griswald is a *goblin*. In the Dresden Files universe, goblins are not cannon fodder. They are not Tolkien-esque. They bear no relation to the Dungeons and Dragons version of goblins. These guys are serial-killing Hannibal-Lecter ninjas with frickin' magic powers to help them cheat.

Though Griswald isn't large, he is stronger than your average NFL lineman, and could backflip in circles around Olympic gymnasts. He's several centuries old, and he's spent them all hunting and killing things that could hunt and kill him back.

Worse, he's smart. He knows exactly what he can do and has centuries of successful experience to draw upon when he plans. As one of the Fae, Griswald can be burned by the touch of iron or any iron-alloyed metal, and he has a demented but inflexible sense of honor. He, too, is able to appear human by means of illusion magic known as glamour, though he maintains no single specific identity. He is about five foot six, with unnaturally long arms and legs, a bit of a hunched posture, and subtly asymmetric features. He isn't necessarily evil—he's a predator, who sees his actions as something both necessary and justified and takes a craftsman's pride in his kills.

Prescott Tremaine is the only full-time Deputy Sherriff in town. Though he dates Ambre, he has no idea that she isn't human. He's a big, amiable blond kid, the kind of guy who was probably a star running back on his high school team, but who wasn't able to play college ball. He's a few pounds overweight—but he's smarter than his boss or the part-timers. He thinks there is something damned peculiar going on, and to such a degree that he seeks out Harry Dresden to take a look at the situation. He's a likeable guy, and as patient as a saint. Which he'll need to be, hanging around with Dresden.

Harry Dresden is a wizard PI who can never stop himself from lipping off and can't seem to get an even break. Nuff said.

Airavata is a *naga*, an ancient race of guardian serpents from the region of today's India and Tibet. She is the Emissary, effectively the judge in the contest that is going on between Griswald and Ambre. She does not at all care for what is happening, but she is bound to remain neutral in the affair, and ensure that the provisions of the Unseelie Accords are respected. She appears as a lovely Indian woman, though she can only be seen by mortal eyes when she wishes to appear to them. She can also take the form of a forty-foot king cobra.

The Talbots are a family cursed many generations ago to be subjected to the attention of wicked beings of the supernatural world. If there's a Talbot in town and a vampire gets peckish, you can bet that it will decide to snack on the Talbot bloodline. Invading werewolves? A Talbot is going to get bitten first.

Their curse is moderately famous in the supernatural world—and though not all members of the family truly believe in their curse, they've all heard the stories. If forewarned, they tend to be much more resourceful than your average victim.

The local branch of the Talbot family consists of seven members, five of them adults, two minors. Their parents came to an unfortunate demise during a river-rafting trip years ago, and the Talbot children have clung together ever since.

Sherriff Dagget is Boone Mill's Sherriff, re-elected every term for thirty years. A wiry little guy in his sixties, Dagget is the kind of law-officer who gets along by getting along. He rarely carries a gun and has probably been guilty of overlooking matters of justice in order to smooth ruffled feathers and maintain the peace. He's not a bad guy, but he's the sort who is very happy to brand things accidents rather than murders and is, in short, the worst kind of law officer imaginable when supernatural shenanigans are afoot.

BACKGROUND

In Boone Mill, a small town in rural Missouri, two supernatural stalker-killers have had an altercation over territorial hunting rights. Pursuant to the Unseelie Accords that regulate supernatural hostilities to personal disputes in order to prevent all-out wars, they have agreed to a duel—in this case, a contest of skill. Locally, there are seven children of the cursed family line of the Talbots, long subjected to supernatural terror. Whichever killer can claim the most victims, taken one by one, from eldest to youngest, will be declared the winner.

Two of the seven Talbot children, both adults, are already dead. The eldest brother, Carl Talbot, was thrown from a bridge into a thirty-foot gorge while he was out jogging. Ambre couldn't resist ripping a few steaks out of his legs and eating them, but the body was also fed upon by a pack of coyotes and other natural carnivores, thinly covering the damage. Griswald evened the score by taking the eldest sister, Sarah Patterson-Talbot, who was found sitting in her living room chair, dead, with her eyes open and her knitting in her lap. No cause of death could be determined, though Griswald in fact slipped an exotic paralytic poison into her tea and then strangled her quite gently with a silk cloth, and cleaned up all evidence of his presence neatly behind him.

SIMPLE SUMMARY

Start off with a teaser scene of the first two Talbots dying. One is thrown from the bridge and

devoured by a shadowy ghoul figure and wild creatures. One is just a still figure seen from several angles in shadow, and then revealed to be a corpse.

Pres shows up at Dresden's office to hire him for the job—find out what really happened to the Talbots. When they arrive in town, both Pres's boss and his girlfriend give Dresden grief.

They set off to watch over the Talbots at the double funeral. Ambre is already there, of course, and Dresden has a spell set to catch any supernatural types who approach under a veil of magic. He detects the gravedigger as a possible bad guy, and has a highly disruptive chase scene through the graveyard. Dresden gets a look at Griswald with his Sight, and the goblin exchanges some dialogue before leaving Dresden eating dust.

Dresden is on the outs with the eldest surviving Talbots after screwing up the funeral, and Dagget tries to run him out of town.

That works as well as it always does, and leaves Dresden lurking outside the eldest Talbot's home the next night, when Ambre shows up to kill him. Dresden slugs it out with the ghoul, but it's his first, and he isn't prepared for exactly how stupidly hard to kill they are. Ghouls can be /hideously/ mangled and still come out of it. Imagine a cockroach running away on two legs with its intestines hanging out after you partially step on it, and you get the idea. Dresden is wounded in the fight. Worse, while he was busy with Ambre, Griswald got through. Eldest Talbot (the jerk) falls down some stairs and through a plate glass window. Griswald is now up 2-1.

Dresden goes hunting for information, using Bob the Skull, who he has stored in the trunk of the Beetle. With Bob's help, Dresden calls up a local nature spirit to grill, and finds out about the presence of Airavata. Dresden hunts down Airavata—which really isn't difficult, given that she is a major supernatural power. She isn't pleased to be disturbed, and tries to warn Harry off the case.

The Talbots, as far as she is concerned, are doomed. She doesn't like it, but she doesn't have the moral authority to interfere, and if Dresden makes too much of a pest of himself, she'll squash him. Dresden does manage to wrest information out of her—specifically, the order the Talbots have to die in. He knows the next target.

Dresden goes to Pres and convinces him to help him stand watch over Talbot #4, a young man. They follow him out to the bar/bowling alley, and watch through the windows.

They get to see Ambre start flirting with the guy, which bums the hell out of Pres. Dresden attempts lamely to console him, as Ambre leaves with Talbot #4, but Pres storms off, furious, to confront them. Dresden has a lightbulb moment as he does, and rushes off to defend Pres and Talbot 4—and manages to save the Talbot just before Ambre guts him with her claws. Pres gets to see his girlfriend turn into a monster, and it's all the wounded Dresden can do to save Pres' life. Ambre escapes—and while Dresden has been busy saving Pres, Griswald nails Talbot #4, invisibly pushing the inebriated young man out in front of an oncoming truck.

Dagget arrests Dresden and puts him in jail for disturbing the peace, but his bail is paid by Talbot #5, who should be an eligible young woman. She's the smart one of the bunch, the one who remembers all the old stories about curses. She knows she's in danger, and she is the one caring for the youngest two Talbots, a boy and a girl, one about 15 the other 11. She helps care for Dresden's injuries, and Dresden forts up their home, establishing wards to defend the house using the house's powerful threshold to support the magic.

Ambre and Griswald come the next night—and Harry kicks the ever loving shit out of them both, on prepared ground, using steel/iron to defeat the ninja-esque Griswald and suckering Ambre with a decoy set of Talbot #5's clothing stuffed with cloth and stained with her blood. But before he can kill them, Airavata intervenes, if reluctantly—and causes a localized earthquake that brings the Talbot house down. She is completely out of Harry's weight class.

Harry and the Talbots go on the run, but the Blue Beetle just isn't a powerhouse of a getaway car. They barely make the highway before they're forced off it by Ambre, driving a stolen big rig, and the Beetle spins out into an abandoned truck stop. Harry leads the Talbots into a vacant Burger King and prepares to die defending them.

By this point, Harry should know exactly what's going on with the trial, and he can explain it to Talbot #5 along the way. She doesn't want Dresden to die, and she understands that Griswald

is ahead 3 to 1. She smacks Dresden on the head and walks out into the darkness alone, intending to sacrifice herself to save her brother and sister. But instead of Griswald, she finds Ambre waiting for her. Dresden staggers up out of being clonked on the noggin, which, let's face it, happens a LOT, so he's used to it. He takes it to Ambre as best he can, telling Talbot #5 to fight, to keep going, to never give up.

Talbot #5 gets away from Ambre, bleeding, thanks to Harry—but a look at her brother and sister make up her mind for her. She steps back into the shadows and closes her eyes. Griswald is waiting for her, little more than evil eyes and a shine of light on a knife. Ambre, meanwhile, has Harry on the ropes, and is about to gut him, when Talbot#5 Screams—and then falls abruptly silent. Airavata appears in thunder and smoke, and just happens to knock Ambre off of Dresden in doing so. She declares the duel over, with Griswald the victor—and looks at Dresden as she announces that her duties are concluded: IE, greenlight to use lethal force.

Dresden WASTES Ambre in some suitably cataclysmic fashion. I'm thinking the stolen tractor-trailer being a fuel truck probably plays into it. Exhausted, wounded, still furious, he turns to confront Griswald—who finally faces him openly. Griswald doesn't want a fight with Dresden, and actually respects him. He agrees to leave the town and its inhabitants in peace for seven times seven years, if Dresden will consider their account balanced.

Dresden isn't happy with that outcome, but he's on the verge of collapse, and showing weakness would put an end to Griswald's act of contrition.

The wizard takes what he can get.

The two kids are safe.

The ghoul is gone. Griswald is out of the picture for a couple of generations. But as he gets the kids to safety, dropping them off before Dagget can arrest him again, Griswald watches the Beetle leave, an ugly smile on his face. He is, after all, immortal. Waiting just makes the hunt that much sweeter in the end.

FINIS.

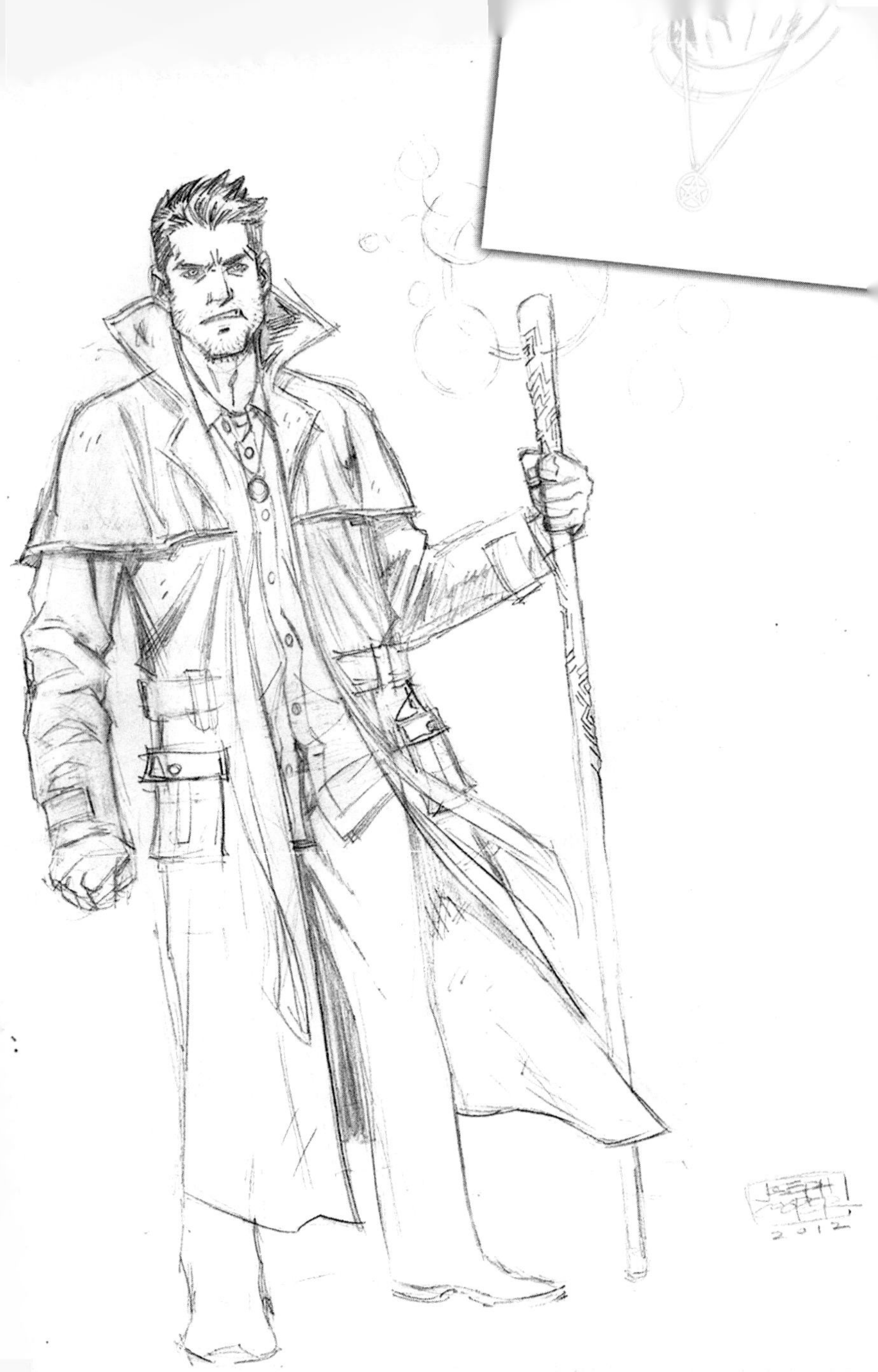
2012

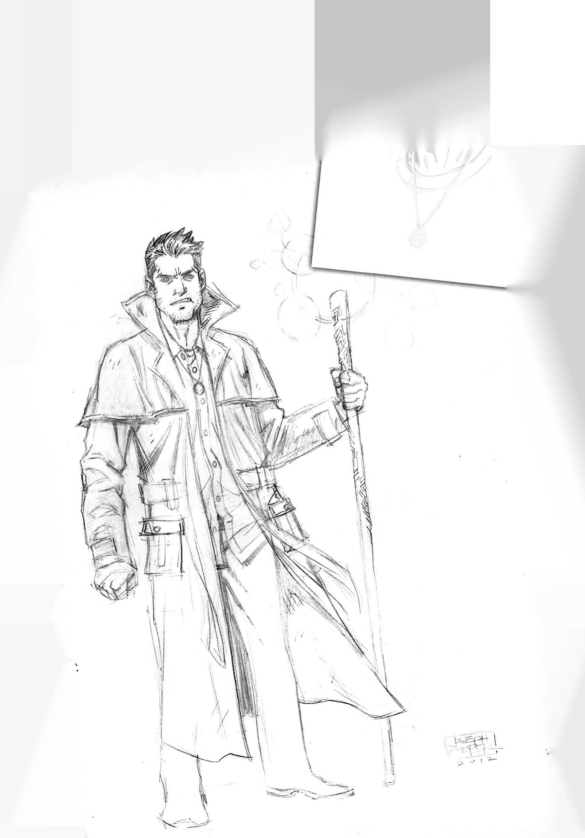

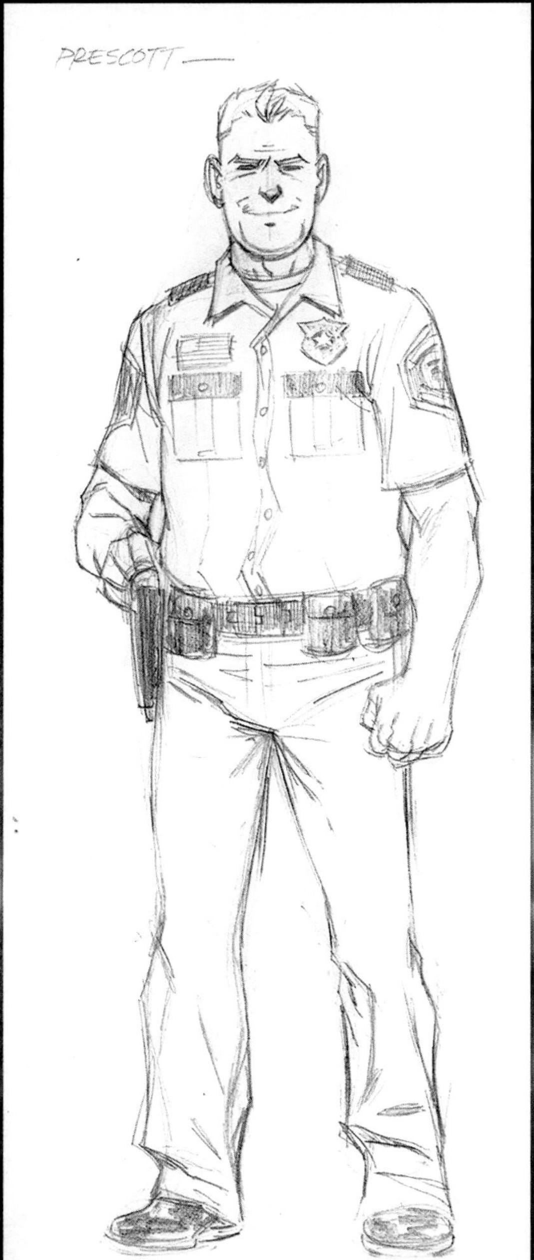
PRESCOTT

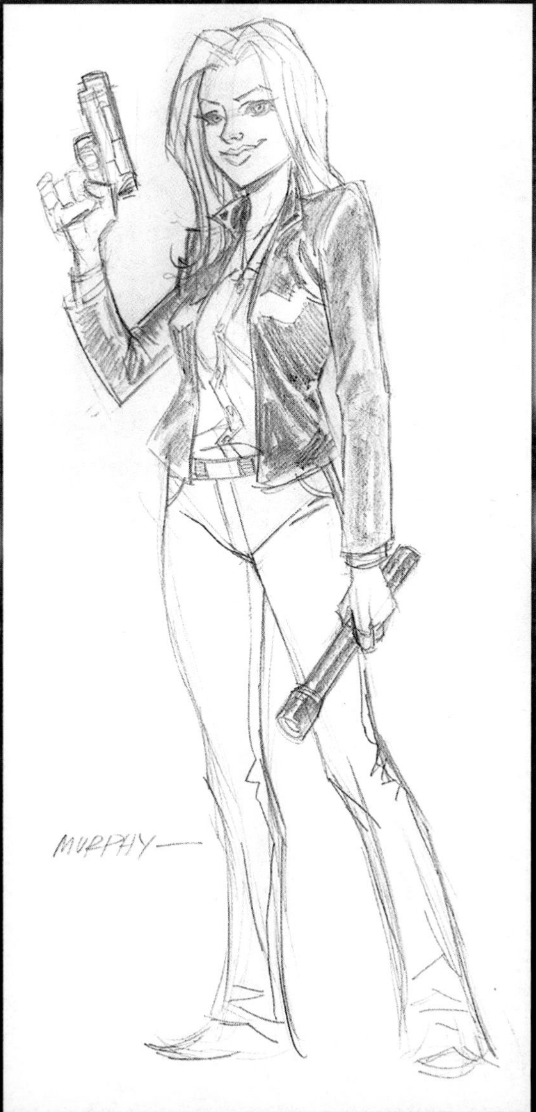
MURPHY

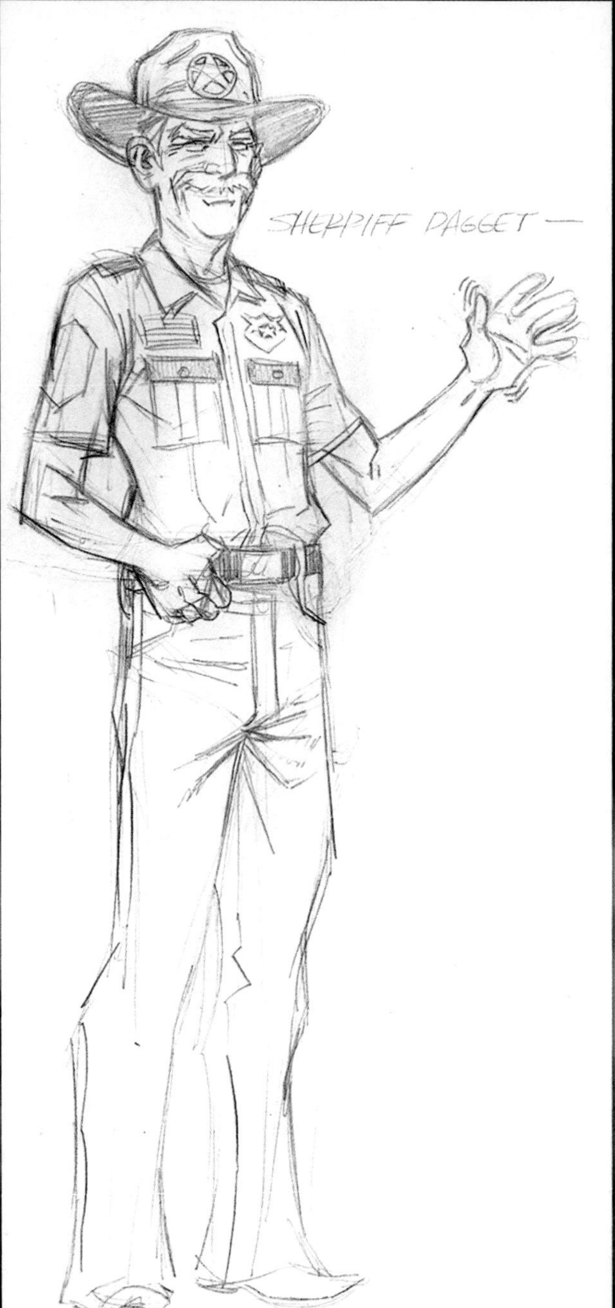
SHERRIFF DAGGET —

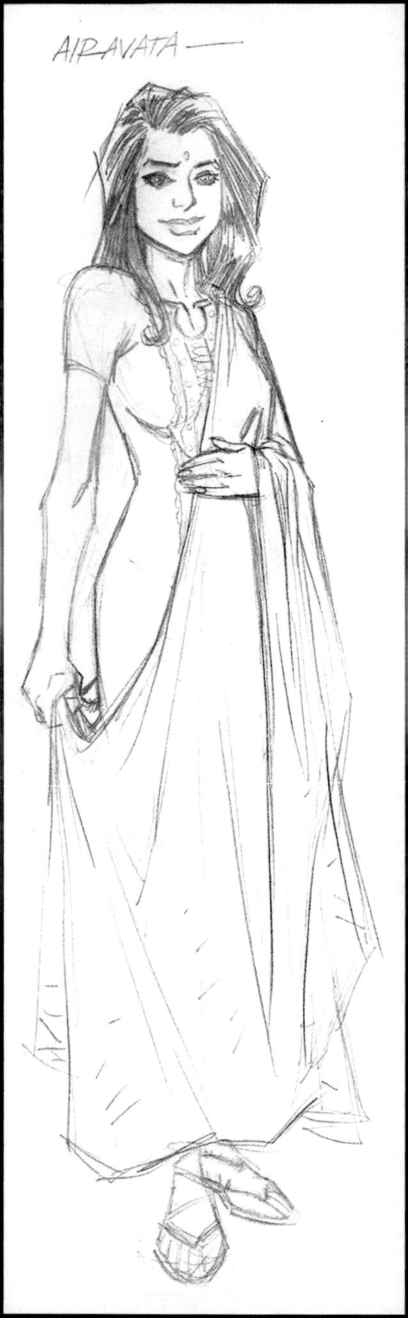
AIRAVATA —

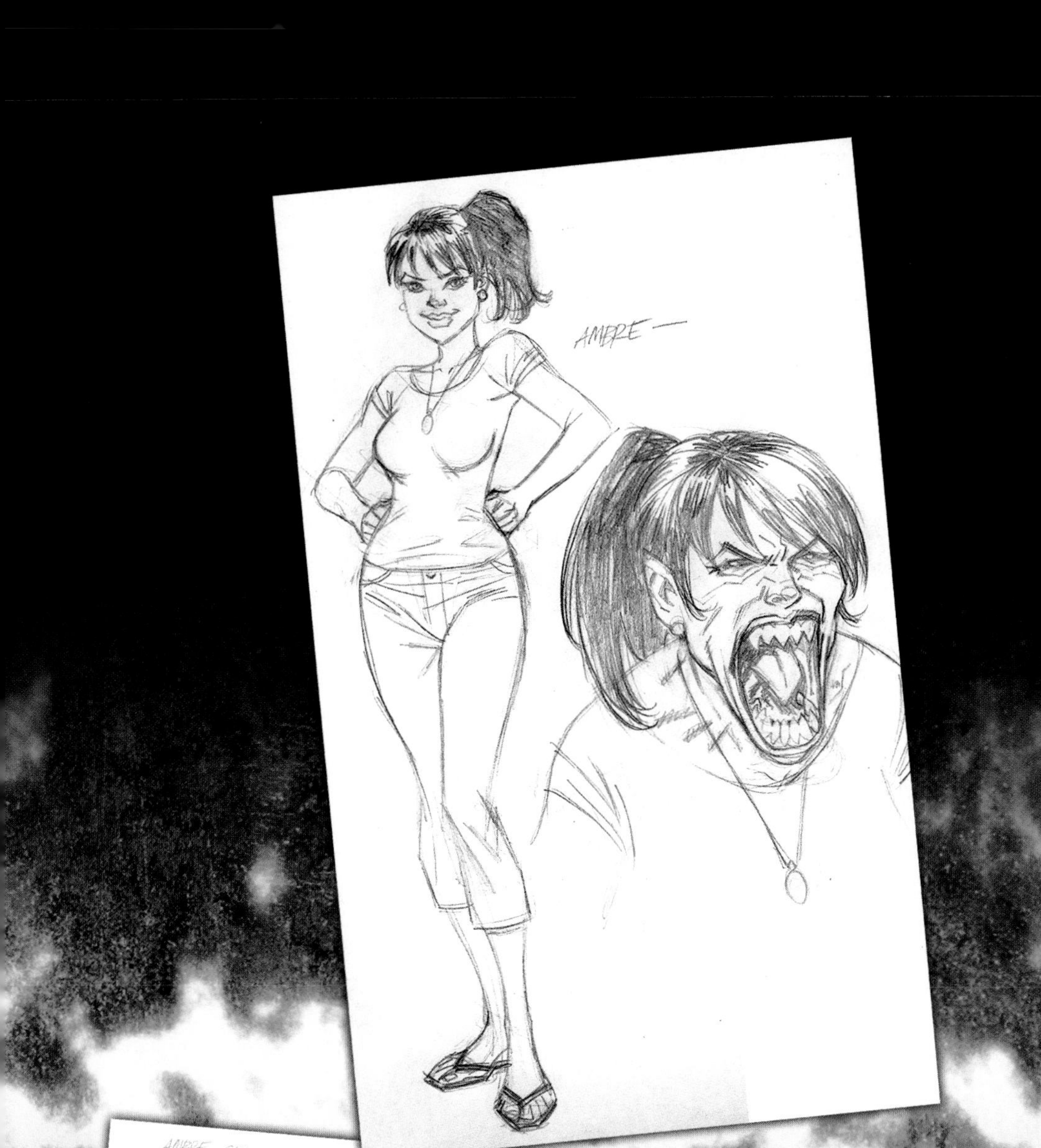
AMBRE —

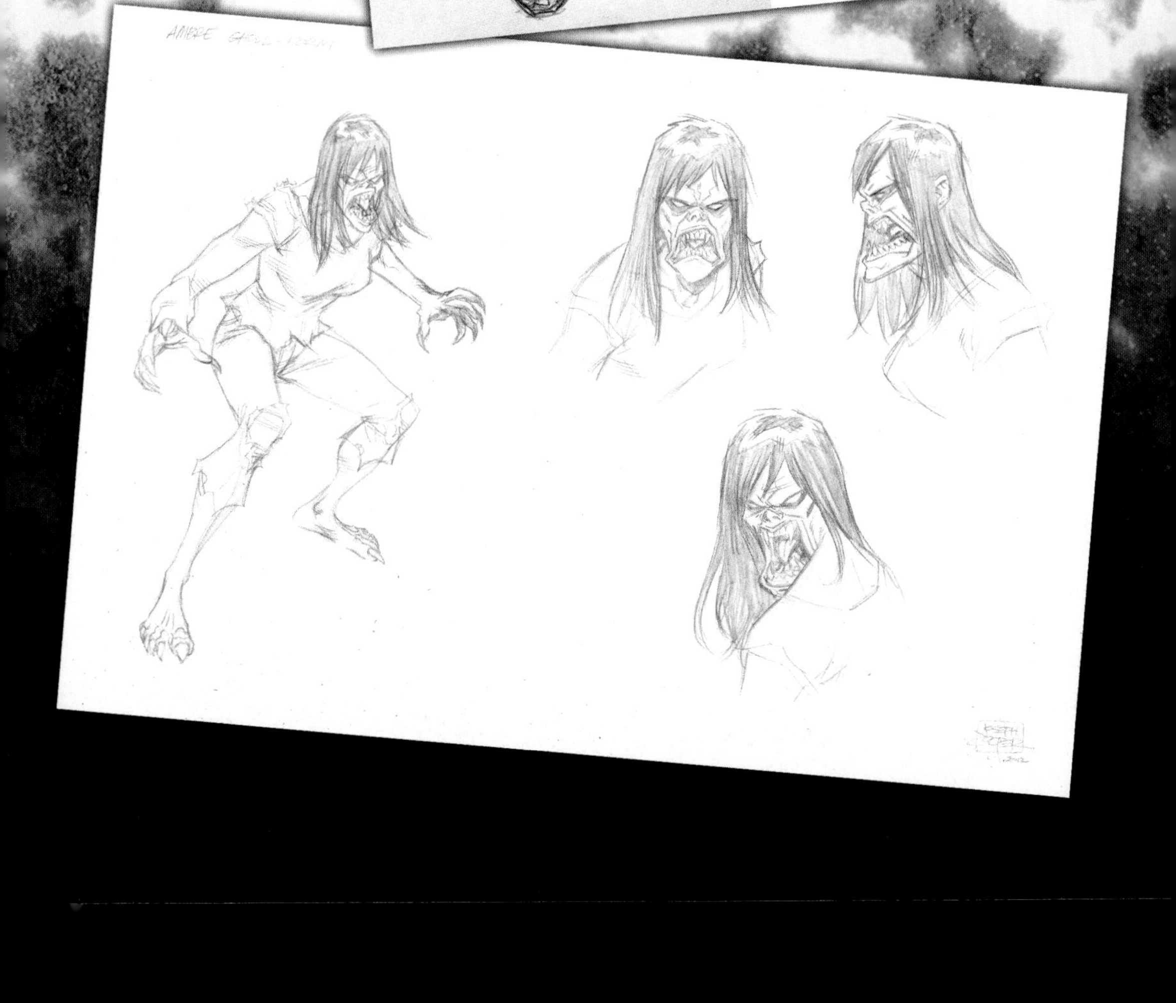
AMBRE

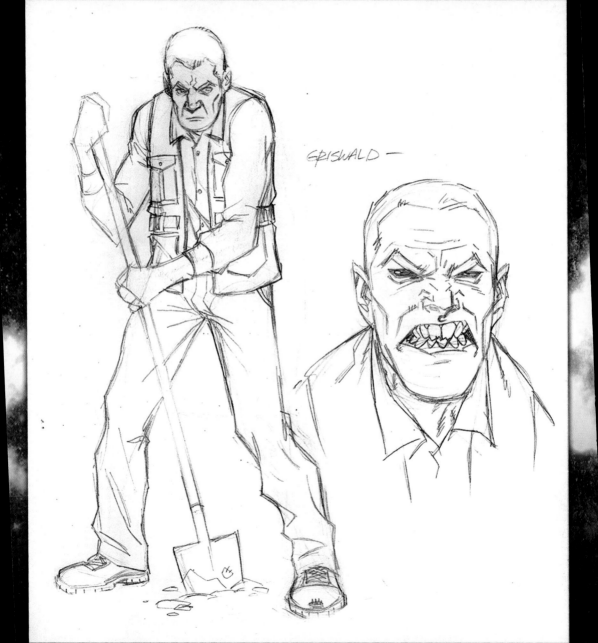

GRISWALD —

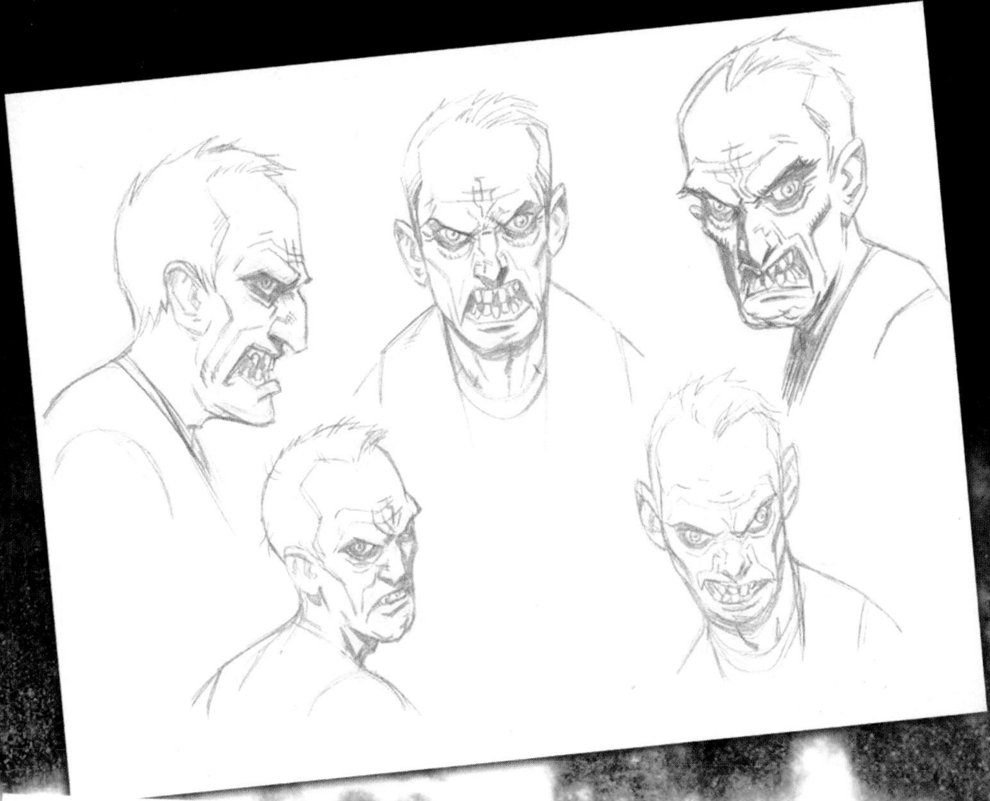

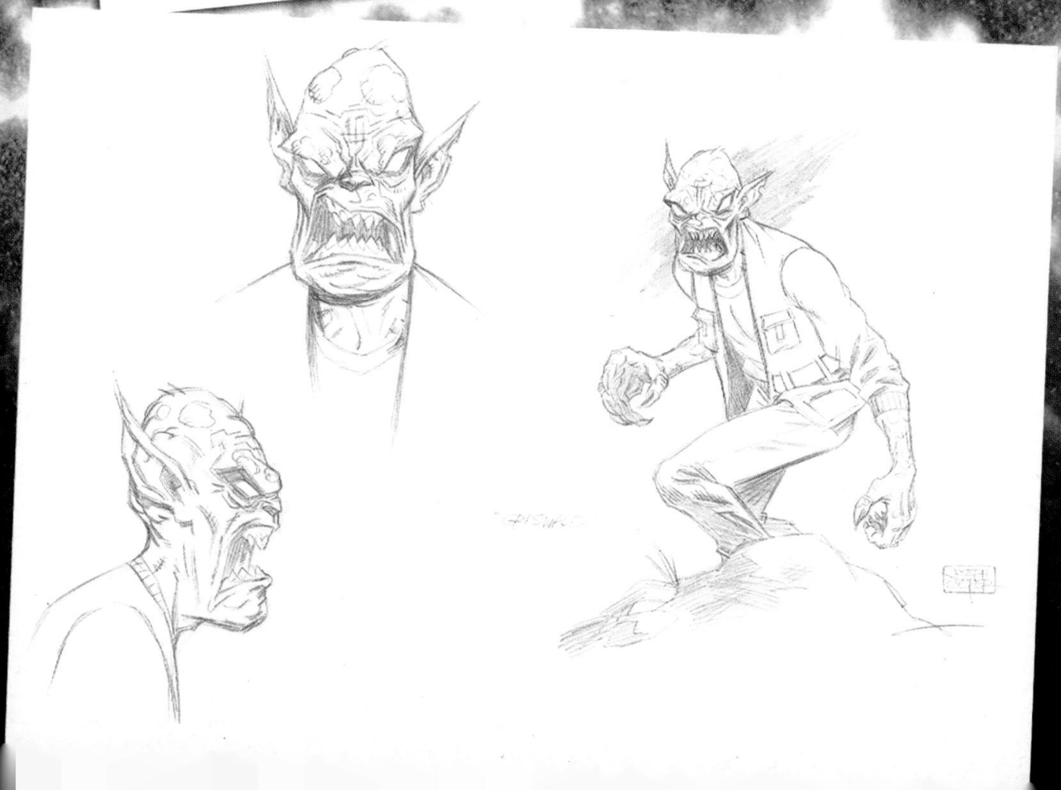

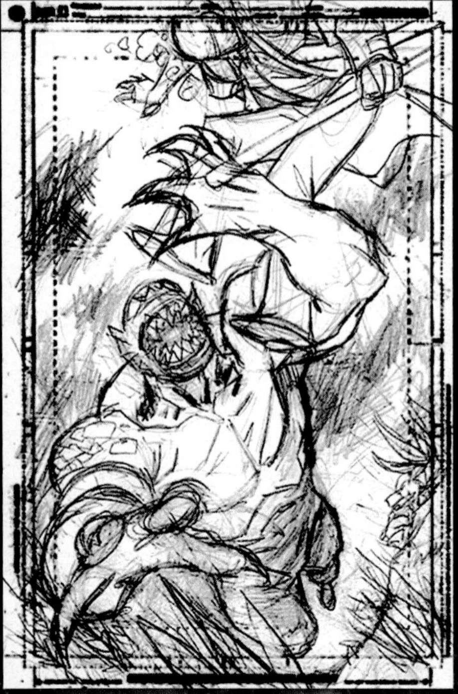

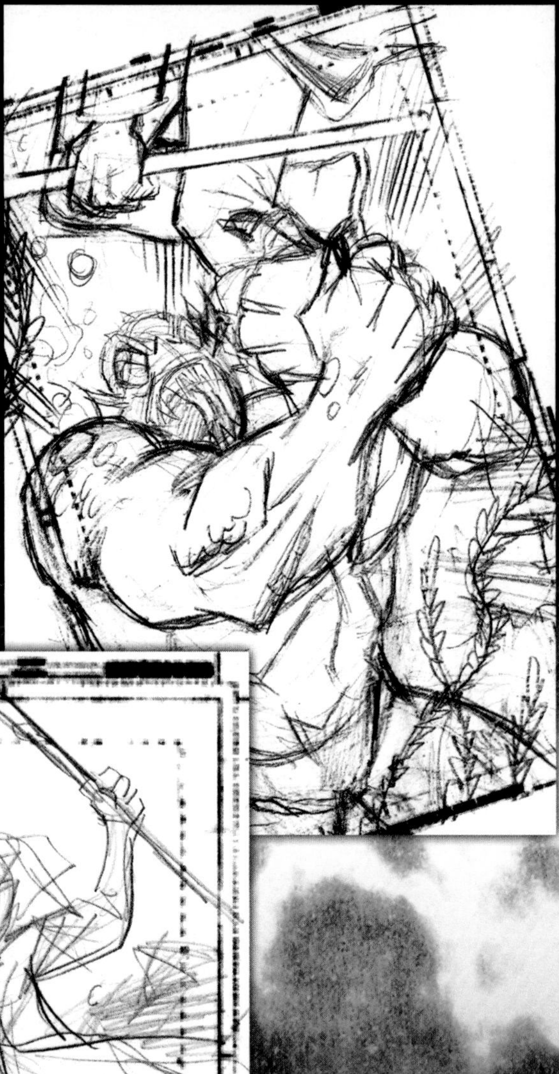

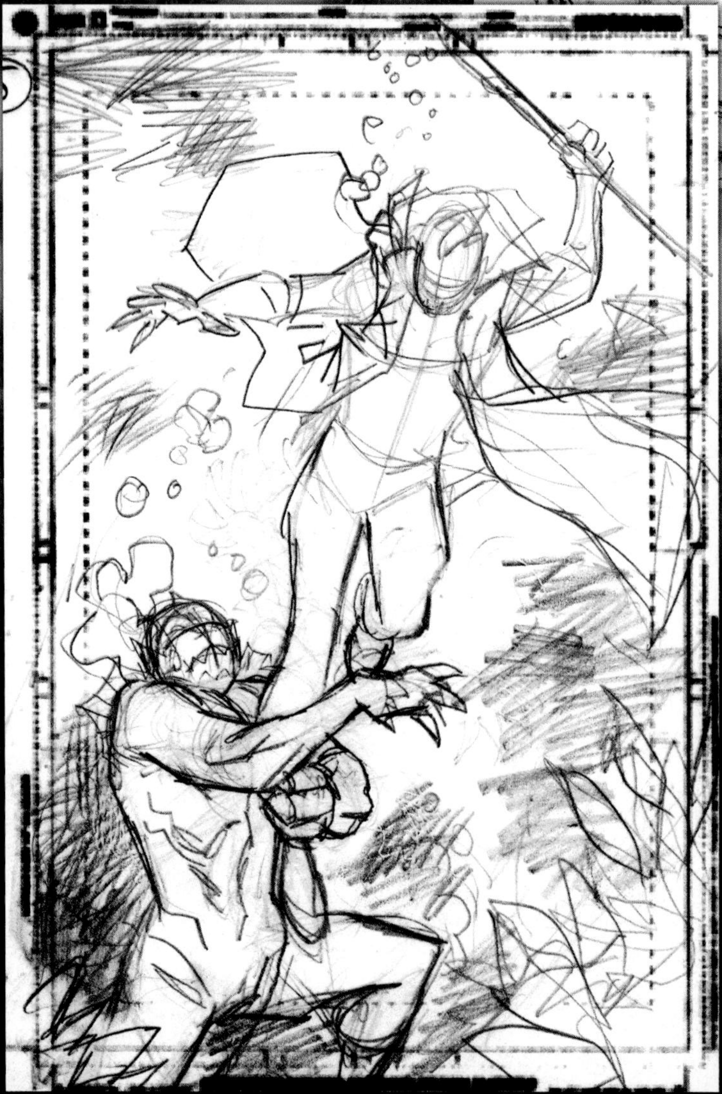

PENCILLER INKER PAGE# 5
TITLE DF: GHOUL, GOBLIN ISSUE # 1 MONTH INTERIORS

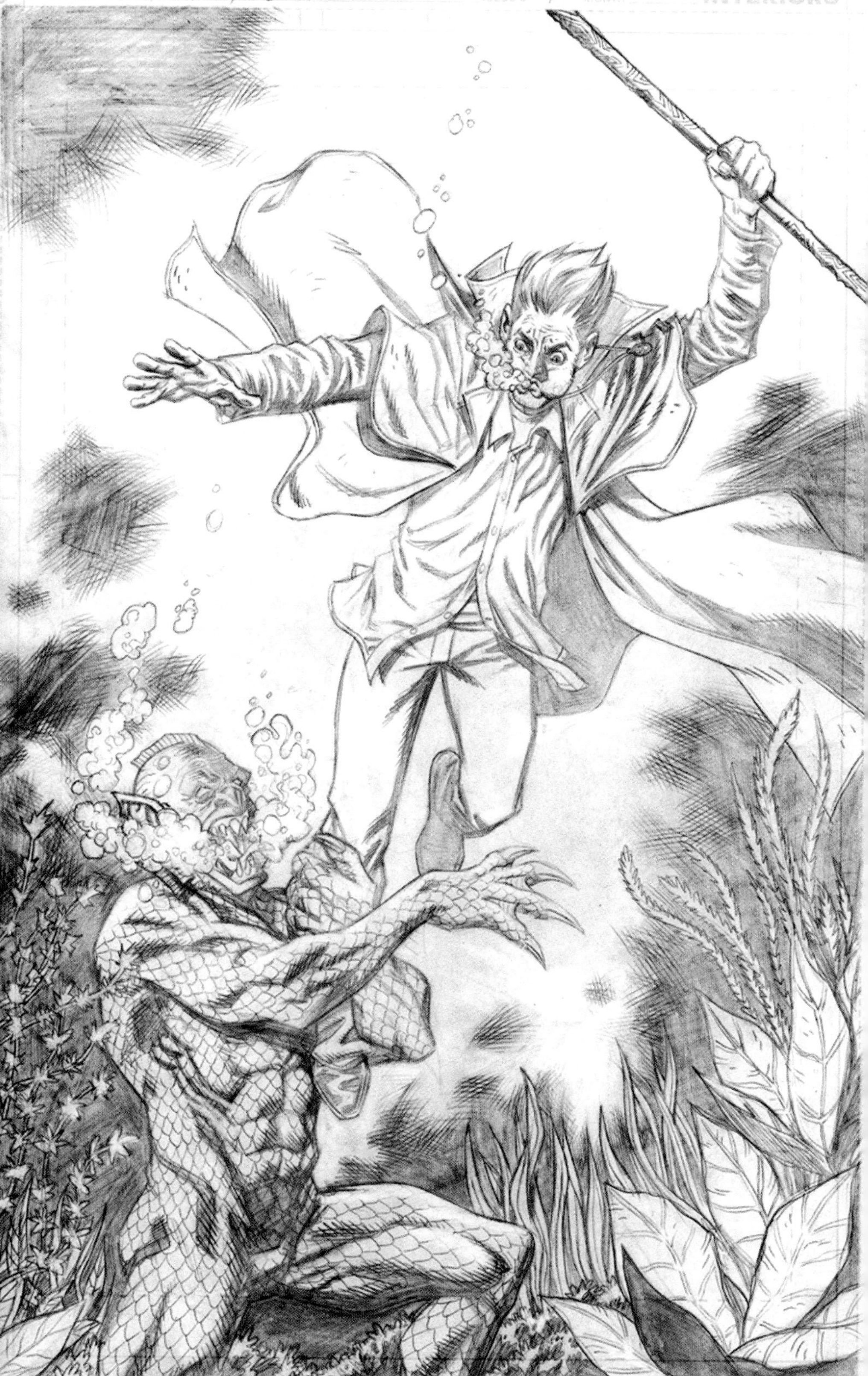

DOUBLE PAGE SPREAD: CUT AS SHOWN, ABUT PAGE EDGES, TAPE ON BACK, DO NOT OVERLAP

PAGE TWENTY

Panel One
Ambre begins to mock Harry...
> AMBRE: Don't worry, Wizard, I'll make it quick—

Panel Two
...until he looks up, and we can see that his eyes are glowing with the pink energy of the Jinn.
> HARRY: I DON'T THINK SO.
> HARRY/CAPTION: The Qarin was within me, willingly giving his power to me to wield.
> HARRY/CAPTION: And as I felt it build, felt it flow through me and mesh with my own, I felt the weight of his regret.

Panel Three
Close in on Harry as he takes on an almost Dark Phoenix type look, eyes glowing in fury.
> HARRY/CAPTION: Centuries uncounted of despair, illuminated by the briefest spark of love.
> HARRY/CAPTION: I embraced it, all of it, held it for a moment...

Panel Four
Biggest panel on the page: pull back to show Harry unleash a 360-degree wave of pink energy that reduces both Ambre and the still-prone Griswald to blackened ash.
> HARRY/CAPTION: ...then I exhaled.
> HARRY: *DISPERDERE!*

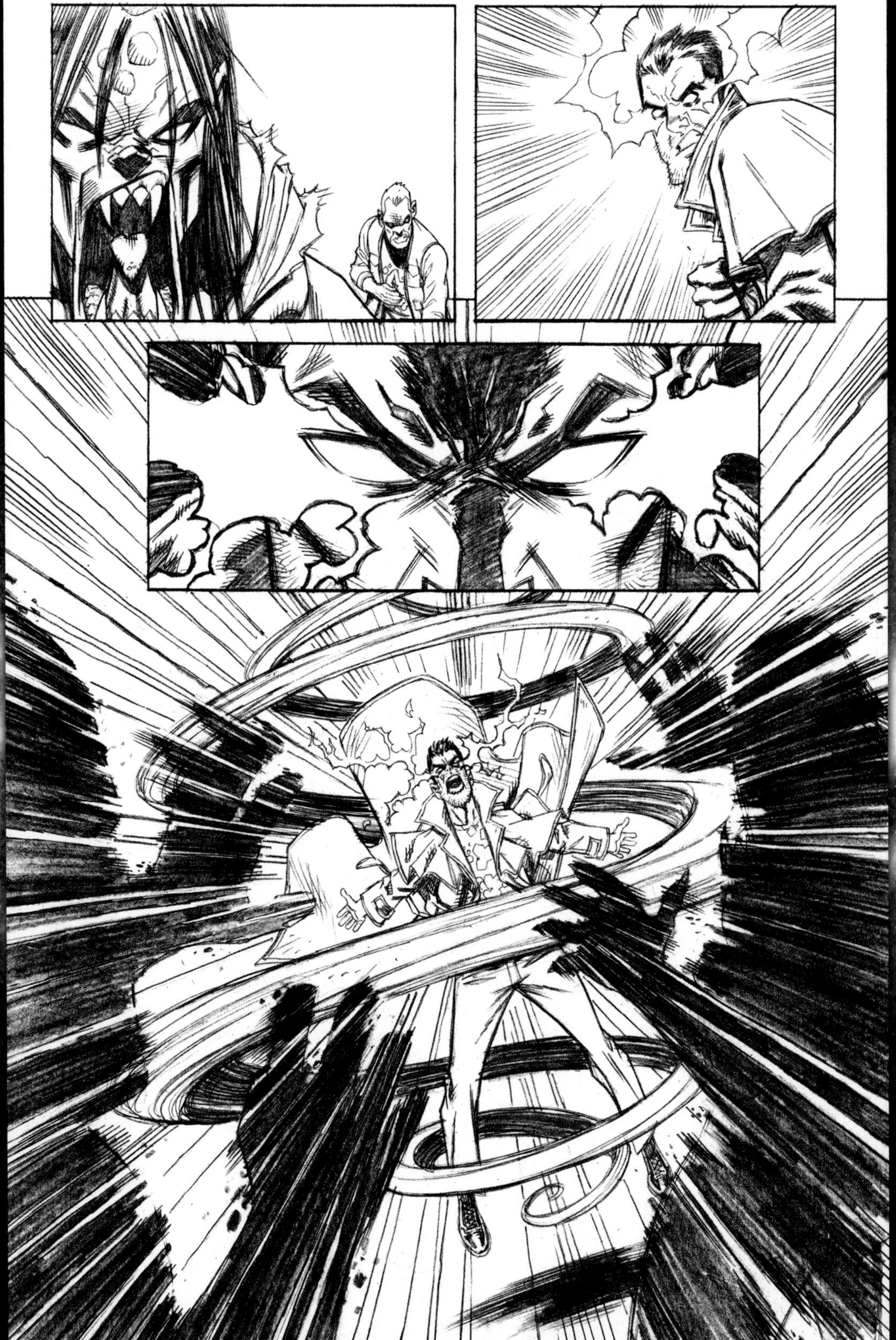

Panel One
Close in on a tombstone. Though it's cropped, we can tell the name "Talbot" is spelled out on it.
> CAPTION: Days later...
> HARRY (from off): I never got to tell her, Pres...

Panel Two
Pull back to show Harry and Pres standing at Maddie's graveside; Pres has one arm in a sling, but he's resting his other hand on Harry's shoulder, as if to console him. Harry's fingering his pentacle. The sun is shining; it's a beautiful day.
> HARRY: ...I never got to tell her the story of my family.
> PRESCOTT: She knew, Harry. Maybe not the details, but she knew all about family.

Panel Three
In profile, Harry continues to look down at Maddie's off panel gravestone; just beyond him, Pres is turned to face the camera.
> HARRY: Yeah.
> HARRY: You think the kids will be okay? They've been through hell...
> PRESCOTT: Cedar's taking them in, and you have my word I'll never let them out of my sight.

Panel Four
Close in on the two men; Pres grips Harry's shoulder again.
> PRESCOTT: They'll be loved, Harry. They won't ever be alone. I promise.

Panel Five
Harry turns to face Pres (who can be off panel here), a small, sad smile on his face.
> HARRY: You're a good man, Pres. The best.
> HARRY: If you, the kids, or Cedar ever need anything, I'll come running.
> PRESCOTT (from off): I know you will.

Panel Six
Pres begins to move away from the gravesite, while Harry remains.
> PRESCOTT: Join me for on last cuppa joe at the diner? Cedar and the kids'll be there—they'll want to say goodbye.
> HARRY: Sure, but let me catch up with you there, okay? I need a few more minutes.

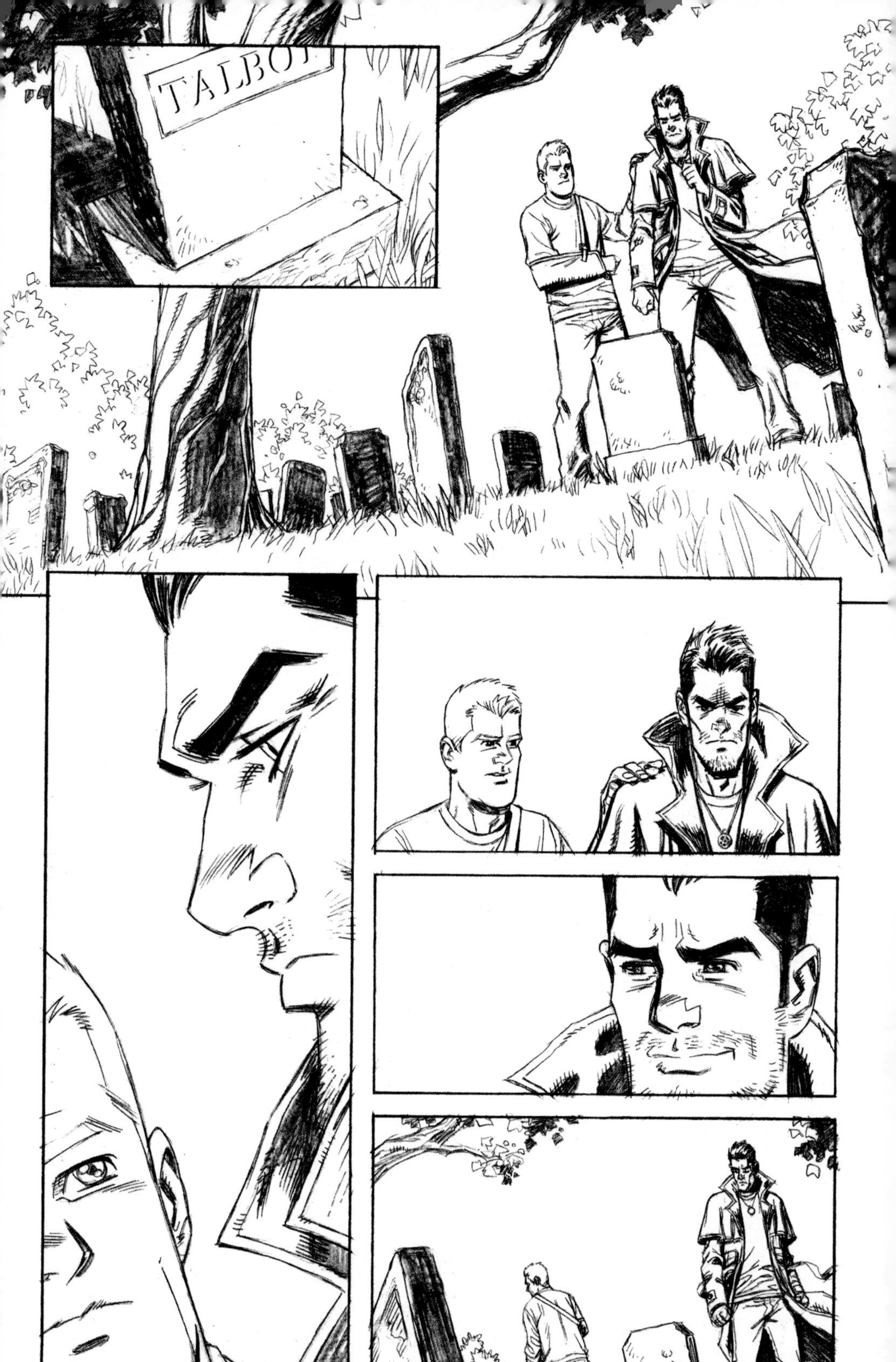
TALBOT

The DRESDEN FILES®

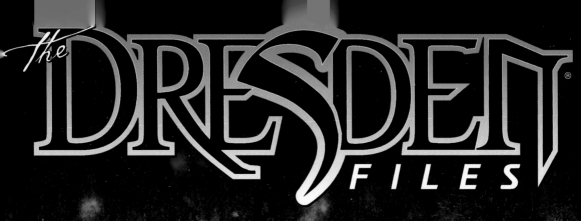

GHOUL GOBLIN